The Regions
of Germany

NORTH SEA

SWEDEN

LATVIA

BALTIC SEA

DENMARK

LITHUANIA

RUSSIA

Bremerhaven

Schleswig-Holstein

Mecklenburg-Western Pomerania

POLAND

Hamburg

Bremen

Lower Saxony

Berlin

NETHER-LANDS

Brandenburg

Saxony-Anhalt

BELGIUM

North Rhine-Westphalia

Hesse

Thüringia

Saxony

Rhineland-Palatinate

CZECH REPUBLIC

SLOVAKIA

LUXEMBOURG

Saarland

Baden-Württemberg

Bavaria

HUNGARY

FRANCE

AUSTRIA

ROMANIA

SWITZERLAND

SLOVENIA

CROATIA

ITALY

BOSNIA-HERZEGOVINA

YUGOSLAVIA

ADRIATIC SEA

LIGURIAN SEA

The Regions
of Germany

A Reference Guide
to History and Culture

Dieter K. Buse

GREENWOOD PRESS
Westport, Connecticut • London

Library of Congress Cataloging-in-Publication Data

Buse, Dieter K.
   The regions of Germany : a reference guide to history and culture / Dieter K. Buse.
     p. cm.
   Includes bibliographical references and index.
   ISBN 0-313-32400-X (alk. paper)
   1. Germany—States—Encyclopedias. 2. Germany—States—History—Encyclopedias.
3. Germany—Politics and government—1990—Encyclopedias. I. Title.
DD290.25.B87 2005
943′.003—dc22   2004028173

British Library Cataloguing in Publication Data is available.

Library of Congress Catalog Card Number: 2004028173
ISBN: 0-313-32400-X

First published in 2005

Greenwood Press, 88 Post Road West, Westport, CT 06881
An imprint of Greenwood Publishing Group, Inc.
www.greenwood.com

Printed in the United States of America

The paper used in this book complies with the
Permanent Paper Standard issued by the National
Information Standards Organization (Z39.48-1984).

10 9 8 7 6 5 4 3 2 1

The publisher has done its best to ensure that the instructions and/or recipes in this book are correct.
However, users should apply judgment and experience when preparing recipes, especially parents and
teachers working with young people. The publisher accepts no responsibility for the outcome of any
recipe included in this volume.

Contents

Preface

Germany is worth knowing. The country and its past are crucial to any attempt to understand the twentieth century. Its contributions, in terms of ideas, innovations, and to the movement of ideas and people, shaped the contemporary world. Yet, knowledge about this country has become highly specialized. A large gap has opened between the reading public and the intellectuals, who undertake detailed and important research. To bridge that gap, informed mediators are necessary. Encyclopedias and reference works can help, but they frequently offer only snippets and very general information organized without considering how the parts fit with the whole. This book seeks to fit between the specialized academic and the generalized reference works.

This book began in collaboration with my friend, Juergen C. Doerr. Cancer made him too ill to participate, but he offered some verbal guidance before he passed away in October 2002. The book is dedicated to the nearly 40 years of fruitful exchanges with him about modern German history. When we met at the University of Oregon in 1964, we did not know that we shared a heritage of families who had frequently migrated, his in Russia and eastern Germany, mine in eastern Germany, Poland, and Russia. Both families ended up in western Germany and then western Canada after World War II. Migrants often travel between two worlds, the heritage of their parents and that of their new land. In our exchanges and in teaching modern German history at small Canadian universities, we tried to transmit a thorough understanding of the German past in all its regional diversity. We tried to make that past relevant to the North American present. The contents of our research and teaching sought to provide a balanced appreciation of people's different homelands, such as the diverse regions of Germany. Hopefully we also conveyed our cosmopolitan values and intentions. At the beginning of the twenty-first century, though, the world is physically highly mobile, and the electronic movement of data spreads too much information and ideas quickly. More attention needs to be placed on one of the elements that can provide a source of stability for people's lives: the immediate region in which they live.

In the post–World War II era, through physically rebuilding the war-damaged country and through renewed appreciation of federalism, German regions received reinforcement. Since the world war and since the Reunification of the two German states in 1990, regional identity has been nurtured. The pattern of physically rebuilding the east, as well as reintroducing federalism to match the well-established western pattern, gave regions new significance.

The Germans have a long tradition of studies in *Landeskunde*. The word means regional studies combining geography, history, ethnography, and major attributes including customs and cuisine of an area. All such studies have to generalize and to choose a few examples to represent a larger mass of information. I take responsibility for the choices made in creating this work, realizing that different information could have created a different combination while still seeking the essence of each region. However, I believe that regions underpin part of the present outlook of German people and more should be known about them.

——————— ACKNOWLEDGMENTS ———————

This book is built on over 30 years of working with the history of Germany. Travels and research throughout the country have widened my understanding of regional differences and taught me an appreciation of its diversity. The local pride and identification with a rebuilt world has been frequently encountered. The stereotypes of Germans and Germany can best be broken by experiencing the diverse countryside, viewing and hearing the rich cultural heritage, eating regional specialties, drinking local beers and wines, encountering a variety of Germans in different social settings as they work and celebrate, and noting the different histories of its regions.

The author is indebted to many persons. Judith M. Buse, Lisa J. Buse, and Uta Doerr read all the text at various stages. Patty Fink and Gillian Kajganovich cheerfully searched for information. Critical, helpful, and positive comments came from: Gerhardt Siegmüller, John Abbot, Brian Ladd, Werner Künzel, Konrad Emshäuser, Carolyn Kay, Walter Mühlhausen, Sabine Bock, Susan Boettcher, David Imhoff, Andreas Kost, Michaela Veith, Edwin Dillmann, Thomas Adam, Siegfried Weichlein, Wilfried Welz, Leo Larivieré (maps), Mary Taylor (photos), and Antonio Peter.

Introduction: Why Germany's Regions Matter

Germany encompasses many regions. Whether one uses demographic, geographic, historical, or economic criteria, the country has always been made up of diverse parts.

Its population of 82 million people is among the richest in the world. Though it shares many industrial societies' problem of an aging population, the birth rate remains low but stable. More people live in the western, very urbanized part of the country. Migration west and southward from the eastern areas attached to the Federal Republic in 1990 through Reunification has slowed but not stopped. High rates of unemployment continue to plague the east, which is financially supported by tax transfers from the west. Approximately 10 percent of the population are not citizens, though some have lived in the country for decades. Few foreigners live in the former East.

Germany's pretty, very green countryside is varied, ranging from mountains in the south to coastal plains in the north. Predominantly, its rivers run toward the north-northwest, aside from the Danube, which flows northeast and then southeast. The remains of each European style of building and culture are evident everywhere: Prehistoric tools and objects fill museums, while Roman ruins, such as aqueducts and defense works, can be found in the Eifel area near one of the Roman empire's four capitals, Trier. The Rhine River in the west and the Thuringian hills in the east are dotted with medieval fortresses and castles, some renovated as youth hostels and exclusive hotels. Renaissance *Rathauses* (city halls) and baroque palaces illustrate the influence of Italian styles and artisans' skills from the sixteenth to eighteenth centuries. Romanesque, Gothic, and rococo churches attest to the French and Catholic influences. However, in the north, brick buildings meld more with Dutch and

Danish styles. A specialty of German regions is the variety and profusion of half-timbered structures. Half-timbered houses, city halls, barns, even castles reflect local styles of construction, and each region has its own patterns to show the wood timbers. Germany appears pretty because nearly everything is well kept, highly organized, and dressed with flowers. Perhaps a paradox development is under way as nearly all European countries have fostered awareness of regional differences for tourist purposes, so that regions claim to be different yet much is standardized.

Underneath the façade of similarity lie three distinct geographic regions: the coastal plains with slightly undulating countryside; the central rolling uplands, with some distinctive formations such as the Harz hills and Swabian Alb; and the highlands of the Alp Mountains. The rivers running north-northwest further divide these regions. In the west the Rhine starts in Switzerland and ends in the Netherlands. The Weser is a less-used transport system than the Rhine and the slightly larger Elbe but is tied to both by canals. While the Rhine valley bears scars from many conflicts with France, the Oder/Neisse rivers mark the much fought-over boundary with Poland. The Danube drains much of Bavaria and Württemberg and provided ties to southeast Europe.

Germans have experienced and experimented with many forms of political institutions: empires, varieties of nation-states (north German dynastic, Pan-German racist), and particularist entities (dukedoms, city-states, bishoprics). Since the Middle Ages, the locales in which Germans lived have frequently been more significant than larger political entities, such as the Holy Roman Empire of the German Nation. Those regional realities need to be recaptured for the present. Since World War II, regional identification attained new importance as the Allied victors wanted to destroy and to limit the centralism associated with Prussia and Nazism. The reunification of the two major German states—the Federal Republic (FRG) and the Democratic Republic (GDR)—in 1990 has confirmed the consequences of division from 1945 to 1989 and the importance of federalism in postwar Germany.

Regions in Germany, as elsewhere, need to be understood historically.[1] Most regions developed due to geographic barriers or simply size constraints. Only in the nineteenth century did railways, roads, and canals tie various places together and reshape many regions. For example, Germany's main political regions today comprise smaller subregions with which many people still identify and to which they ascribe special traits. The present state of Hesse, for instance, comprises river valleys (Rhine, Lahn, Main) and rolling uplands. The latter are subdivided into the Taunus, Vogelsberg, and Rhön highlands and the Odenwald (in the southeast). The river valleys offer great variety from moors to highly productive agricultural lands, including vineyards on the steep banks of the Rhine. Because of climate, soils, and settlement patterns, historical-geographic units developed, which became anchored in people's consciousness as homeland (Heimat).

Though regions and federal states cannot be completely equated, the new Länder (states) of post-1945 Germany have become one of the main reference points in politics and daily life. Federalism has a long history in Germany's political and social life.[2] It provided post–World War II Germans with a structure that fit with traditions, even if many boundary changes were made, most by the occupying Allies, to create new states from 1945 to 1947. Hence, this reference will use the *Länder* and their continued importance for self-identification as the basic regional units. In each state, legal systems, education, and other institutions force people to relate to the regional political structures. Therefore, regional identities are reconstructed, some new ones are created, and some old ones are reinforced. In addition to being the places where Germans have found or still seek a new homeland, the regions have served as places with which to identify because of the difficulties of identifying with the post-Nazi national past. In that context, the regions have helped to overcome a "shattered [national] past."[3] That concept was employed by a recent historical study to suggest no master narratives fit German historical experience in the twentieth century. Perhaps that perspective should be modified to acknowledge what has been achieved within the regions. The rebuilding of Germany after 1945 mostly occurred in the context of the decentralization imposed by the Allies. That approach found easy acceptance because of the previous particularistic, small-state, and federalist tradition of central Europe, with which regional leaders could readily identify and thereby avoid the immediate Nazi past.

Regions and small states have a long heritage in central Europe. Just before the French Revolution, some 300 small states and hundreds of tiny bishoprics or city-states defined the German-speaking lands politically. By the nineteenth century they did not fit well with the country's technological or economic capabilities. Napoleon's wars, occupations, and defeat led to a federation of 39 states, in which Austria and Prussia dominated. After a series of wars resulted in the formation of the Prussian-led Reich in 1871, it claimed the right to represent Germans, at the expense of Austria. Within the increasingly centralized Prussian-German state, though, the regions continued to be significant until the Nazi regime unilaterally reorganized the Reich, partly along party district *(Gau)* lines from 1933 to 1937.

Within the three main geographic regions, a large number of historical subregions exist, bounded by rivers or changes in the height of terrain. These reflect geographic but also traditional historical units. Sometimes they are easily identifiable by features such as woods, for instance, the Black Forest, sometimes by craggy mountains, such as the Saxon Alps. Many people identify with these older subregions, for example, the Eifel between Belgium/France and Germany, the Ruhr valley, the Taunus north of Frankfurt, the Thuringian hills, or the Mecklenburg coast. The political provinces, used as regions for this book, provide larger patterns of organization and identification. Some would argue that this type of recent political identification is new and only came once secularization undercut religious ties and the nation-state failed to clarify ethnic loyalties.

Economically, Germany, too, has been a country of regions. Statistically, it may be the world's third-largest economy, but diversity marks its pattern of development. A few major regions led German industrialization: the Rhine/Ruhr, Saxony, Silesia, Berlin, and Stuttgart. The port cities of Bremen and Hamburg prospered as trading centers, especially in the late-nineteenth century. Berlin and Munich had the advantages of being administrative centers. Those cities became cultural centers, similar to the court residences and regional capitals such as Weimar, Dresden, Leipzig, or Hanover. After World War II, the previous areas of heavy industry, such as the Ruhr or Saxony, have only in part made the transition to service and knowledge economies. Based on export of automobiles and high-technology engineering, Germany remains the economic locomotive of Europe, even if it pulls more slowly at times. In the postwar divided country, the southwest, especially Baden-Württemberg and Bavaria, advanced to high-tech production as well as making the transition to service industries. Ironically, a study of the economy of Germany in the 1930s (reprinted repeatedly during the Nazi era) emphasized regions that overlap with many of the present provincial boundaries. For instance, North Rhine-Westphalia and Lower Saxony were seen as natural economic units. However, few today would argue that some special relationship exists between race, region, and economic development, as such studies did.

Culturally, German regions have additional strong differences. Those differences are reflected in the literature and art produced, especially before the twentieth century. Even the cuisine varied, so examples from both culture and cuisines will be provided here. People become what they eat, and with globalization Germany has become as big a pizza and burger consumer as many other places. However, traditional foods and specialties associated with each region continue to be popular and mark part of the identity of each region. The popularity of the new foods, such as Turkish *döner kebab* in Berlin and *pommes frites* (french fries) with curry sausages in the Ruhr, help to continue regional differences, as do the traditional specialties. As elsewhere in the world, this sometimes leads to regional homogenization and stereotyping and occasionally to overemphasizing differences.

Visitors and tourists experience Germany regionally. For instance, at present, two geographically and culturally very different "German" places draw visitors. In 2002, the top tourist destination was Cologne's magnificent Gothic cathedral *(Kölner Dom)*, with 6 million visitors. But, Munich's beer-swilling *Oktoberfest* achieved some 5.9 million visitors. Some nature parks drew many, especially now that the unspoiled eastern landscape is becoming well known. The Pomeranian Bodden Landscape Nature Reserve on Germany's starkly rugged Baltic seacoast drew 2.5 million visitors, and eastern Germany's Saxon Swiss National Park, a rugged mountainous terrain, lured 2.2 million outdoor enthusiasts. Among cultural sites, 3 million visitors came to the main medieval street in the town of Rüdesheim (a UNESCO world heritage site). The glass-domed *Reichstag* building in Berlin attracted 2.7 million people. Carnival parades in Cologne and Düsseldorf drew about 1.5 million and 1.25 million spectators, respectively, while Berlin's previously annual gay event, the Love Parade, attracted an estimated 750,000 revelers. Some visitors may have been at all the sites and events, but most likely foreigners visited only one or two areas. The traditional tourist spots, namely southern villages and Rhine castles, reinforced by cold war divisions until 1990, now have competition from Berlin's architecture and UNESCO heritage sites of the east, especially the unspoiled Baltic seacoast. The foreign image of Germany and Germans is being altered.

Identity, whether tied to a nation or a region, relates to the way people see themselves as well as how others see them. In Germany, legends grew about the lighthearted

Rhinelanders, the somber Bremer, the jovial Bavarians, the caustic Berliners, and the stubborn Westphalians. Yet, like all stereotypes, they do not capture the diversity of the people. Nor do such approaches help one understand the way people see their own region. A survey at the beginning of 2003 tried to find out what Germans thought about *Heimat*—a word with broad and deep connotations commonly translated as "homeland" or "home." The concept has been used to foster nationalist fervor as well as to spread local loyalty, emotional sentiments, and understanding about one's own city or place. In 2002, the social research institute, Emnid, reporting in *Reader's Digest Deutschland*, found that some 94 percent of Germans have a concept of *Heimat*. "For 32 percent of these, it is the place 'where I live now,' while for 14% it is Germany as a whole." Another 13 percent equate *Heimat* with family, 12 percent with their birthplace, 11 percent with "a certain region or landscape," another 11 percent with "where I feel at ease," and an equal number with the idea of "home in general" (*The Week in Germany*, May 30, 2003, Internet publication of the German Information Office). This finding is probably not dissimilar from what might be found in other countries, since employment moves people and modern transport allows quick spatial shifts. However, it does underscore the regional attachments of Germans.

One stereotype about Germans is the idea that beer and sausage were the main German foods. Ironically, outside of France, no country has attained more high ratings for its restaurant fare than Germany, due to gourmet delicacy hunters *(Feinschmecker)* and refined gluttons *(Schlemmer)*. Certainly, Germany does have fine sausages, which vary from region to region (white in Munich, brat in Thuringia, thin and crusty in Nuremberg). Most remarkable is the quality and variety of bread, from little rolls *(Brötchen)* to light ryes, from three-grain to heavy pumpernickel. Local varieties and specialties compete with some that have become nationalized and homogenized. The same applies to beer and wine. The local brew is drunk from *Fass* (barrel), near the brewery, or in the producer's cellar.

This book hopes to show that German regions matter in terms of identity and in overcoming the shattered national past. If one could total the sums spent on rebuilding postwar and post-Reunification Germany, one would understand better the extent of investment in restoring material and personal dignity. The physical and spiritual rebuilding has taken place in the regions and confirmed regional variety. Its material results hint at the identification with and strong pride in the restored physical *Heimats*. In 2004, for example, a Hamburg pride movement *(Elblove)* sold thousands of T-shirts and posters lauding the seaport as a special place and is being imitated in other areas. Germans in all regions have and continue to acknowledge their problematic past, especially relating to the Holocaust. But they also seek a positive identity in the past and present regions with their rebuilt diversity.

Supposedly Germany has become a postnational society. Patriotism seeks to support the democratic constitution, not to aim at some ethnic and linguistic purity, and especially not at an imposed unity and external aggression. Nationalism as an attitude of superiority has been replaced by identification with Europe and peaceful, civilized behavior. Yet, strong vestiges of the former nation remain, especially within the federated regions. Within the regions some cultural artifacts are identified as specifically German, representing traditional German values. Traditional customs, dress, and foods often are presented in such a fashion at the regional level to sell some local product. Among cosmopolitan intellectuals, Europe-oriented politicians, and global business people, much irony and sarcasm dominate in reference to earlier worship of such identifiers. In sum, mostly European and regional identification has displaced nationalist sentiments.

This new Germany, slowly created since World War II, especially since the 1960s, with another stage since Reunification in 1990, is a regionally diverse place. Yet, its antinationalistic outlook should not be confused with loss of national identity. Like other peoples, Germans function within the legal structures of their nation-state, and they exist like the rest of us within a national economic framework defining social norms. Those norms have been especially progressive until recent reversals, ironically introduced under Social Democratic leadership, though much advocated by all political parties. A consensus about which norms to "reform" has been lacking. Those norms included a balance of state intervention and subsidies mixed with regulated private enterprise. Lengthy holidays, adequate pensions, and high rates of social support for the unemployed and disadvantaged were hallmarks of the complex welfare system. Postwar integration of refugees, later of foreign workers, and in the 1990s of asylum seekers, demonstrated an increasingly liberal society with only occasional fallbacks to ethnic, discriminatory outbreaks. At first, after Reunification in 1990, the eastern regions showed less of that liberality, but at present the antiforeigner xenophobia seems almost gone.

The elements of what contemporaries since the 1970s termed "model Germany" included emphasis upon education, high technology—especially in the main export industry of automobiles—quality products, and a federated system of government. That "model Germany" continues to exist, but it has been challenged by ideologies seeking to dismantle the welfare state. Insecurities brought by global markets—frequently a cover for the strongest states to impose their rules and their monopolies—and terrorism have panicked some politicians. Some have tried to rewrite the terms of federalism. The role of the nation in the new context is not yet clear, but it is evident that national identity continues even if nationalism has been buried. For instance, the new citizenship law of 1999 changed the fundamental designation of nationality. A person becomes German by residing in Germany, not just by having a German parent. The role and nature of the regions as components of that identity within the German national framework remain an open issue, but the present regional states seem firmly embedded in law and identity.

One way to perceive the importance of regions is to look at one suburb in Berlin, Charlottenburg. Within a four-block area, it is possible to visit a Russian, an Italian, a Japanese, and a Persian bookstore, all operated by people from those countries. In the same area, a Georgian restaurant competes with Italian, Portuguese, Japanese, Greek, and traditional German cuisine. As might be expected, none of those choices can be found at the opposite corner of the country, in rural Bavaria. If one goes there from Berlin, mountains replace sandy flatlands and green uplands have colorful villages dominated by Catholic churches. Obergammergau passion plays about Jesus' crucifixion underscore the difference between a secular, cosmopolitan world-class city such as Berlin and the professed piety and ritualized processions of provincial life. This urban/provincial difference could just as likely be found in other countries or even if one used Munich, the Bavarian capital, instead of Berlin. But some aspects and activities go beyond the stereotype to patterns of regional behavior. During 2003 in Berlin, the mayor could take a lead role in the Love Parade—the main festival of gays and lesbians, claimed to comprise over 10 percent of the cosmopolitan capital's population. The main leader of Bavaria, meanwhile, seems hardly changed from 1988, when he helped others lay to rest the local political hero, Franz Josef Strauss. In that parade an honor guard in gray-green costumes and feathered hats of traditional Bavarian dress accompanied the coffin. The contrast in the two public events could provide work for ethnographers seeking to discover the essence of each group of people and the influence of regional differences. Or perhaps such examples illustrate that Germans—by finding such activities and dress normal—are confronting long-existing diversity in a more liberal fashion.

Such different public roles as have been taken by political leaders may relate to the role of religion in the different parts of the country. In Bavaria, when asked their religious affiliation, 65 percent state Catholic, 24 percent state Protestant, and only 10 percent say none. By contrast, West Berlin respondents report as 11 percent Catholic, 53 percent Protestant, and 31 percent none. East Berliners, by contrast, admit to 2 percent Catholic, 17 percent Protestant, and 80 percent none. Indeed, the old Federal Republic had 42 percent Catholic and 42 percent Protestant compared to 12 percent none, while the eastern states had on average 4 percent Catholic, 27 percent Protestant, and 66 percent none. This is the continuation of a late nineteenth-century trend toward secularization that fostered a northeast/southwest regional divide.

Across the country in the farthest northeastern corner of Mecklenburg-Western Pomerania is the small city of Anklam. There, in a rougher-looking place than its counterparts in the west, one finds acknowledgment and appreciation of a former national hero. A local museum is dedicated to Germany's pioneer in flight, Otto Lilienthal. At Easter, one might find a large influx of Berliners on hiking holidays, accompanied by Easter "water." The pope has not blessed such "water"—which is really an alcoholic drink—and the term is a secular play on Catholic beliefs. But with more than half the working-age population of Anklam unemployed, no foreign language bookstore and no passion plays are in evidence. The mayor is distraught about the difficulties of mastering the economic and social situation of a city that starkly underlines the east/west economic divide and regional differences in levels of prosperity.

Westward in the small East Frisian town of Otterndorf (nearly in the Netherlands), one finds that provincial places need not have limited horizons. A well-organized gallery of very modern, mostly abstract, art is exhibited in the converted city warehouse. Local pride and a relaxed attitude are in evidence, even though an old world of half-timbered houses is encountering a global art market.

These few examples illustrate that place makes a difference and that regions matter in Germany, as elsewhere. Discovering and knowing all aspects is impossible, but those claiming to understand the country should go beyond Bavarian fairy-tale castles to the small villages or city suburbs and listen to the locals speak in dialect about their beliefs, desires, and achievements. In Berlin, they should wander away from the imaginative architecture of the Jewish Museum and go to the German-Russian museum in the former Soviet command center. There, the experiences of World War II on both sides are well presented, and the state of the buildings in the area better represents daily existence for Berliners than do the showcases of the city center. Or perhaps a mostly unknown museum dedicated to the Founding Era (1871–1890) in the Berlin suburb of Mahlsdorf would be an appropriate experience of a regional niche. There one can learn about a transvestite who built up his museum in a dilapidated manor house during the Communist era. There, too, on occasion, organ-grinder concerts present the local folk and city songs of Berlin, which the tourists and the opera fans huddled in the city's middle rarely encounter. Similarly, *Frühschoppen* (early drinks) in a Düsseldorf pub or *Kölsch* beer drinking in Cologne jazz halls where customers are seated together wherever space exists at long tables are other options—such activities will inform about German patterns of consumption and sociability, including the famed conviviality *(Gemütlichkeit)*. Some observers might contend that in Germany similar patterns of leisure activities such as hiking, cooking, and sports—despite the minute regional distinctions—have homogenized and made commerce out of mythical differences. Yet, a crucial element should be noted in traversing German lands.

In such rambling, mostly one should note what has been rebuilt, restored, and preserved. The restoration of Germany after war, but also preservation against natural decay, means that for many, *Heimat* (homeland) remains a special and a seemingly traditional place. The constant rebuilding or improvement of the physical environment, and even the movements that advocate leaving the environment alone, has had the consequence of focusing people on their region. They have found an identity, and the states foster it through publicly financed offices for political education within their regions. Here, Germans have been able to reestablish themselves after the traumas of the twentieth century destroyed a former identity grounded in nationalism or falsely stylized by dictatorship.

Sixteen years after the end of the Berlin Wall and Reunification, eastern and western Germany remain different. The present political boundaries fail to capture some important facts. The west has gained more than 2.7 million people, while only 1.7 million have shifted eastward since Reunification. That pattern, though slowed, continues. Unemployment in the east averages 18.5 percent, whereas it is at 8.4 percent in the west. The population in the east is aging, and young skilled people are leaving. Though a similar rail and road infrastructure has been built in the east as in the west, and though some industries have made the adjustment to a more global market, much of the huge transfers of monies eastward went into the hands of western consultants and firms. The integration of eastern Germany and eastern Germans will take a long time. Whether the political regions will be a sufficient basis for raising the east to western standards without destroying people's dignity and social norms (such as the successful medical clinics) has yet to be clarified. However, in each of the new states, building regional identity is an active and energetically fostered project. Who would have thought in 1989 that, in the early twenty-first century, histories of Brandenburg, of Mecklenburg–Western-Pomerania, of Saxony, of Saxony-Anhalt, and of Thuringia would be pouring off the presses. The question is justified, since those states had ceased to exist in 1952, though elements of regional awareness evidently remained. But, then, 16 years ago a huge wall, a long and heavily guarded frontier, and a now nonexistent country still made Germany into two very distinct places. Who could have imagined that the physical wall would disappear so quickly, and who would have guessed that the mental walls would remain so long? Despite the difficulties of unification and integration, one country with many regions emerged.

This book is a contribution to what one author claimed about postwar German identities but none has shown. She asserted: "a story is told about a common past, certain values and features are emphasized and sung from on high, common rituals and symbols serve to forge a visible community, common institutions and experience shape similarities of behavior, expression and outlook. . . . Regions certainly proved to be a prime basis of identity for many Germans in the Federal Republic."[4] Since the great horrors of Nazism, Germany has been physically and spiritually reconstructed. Part of that reconstruction, even recivilizing, came through re-creation and identification with historically remolded regions. The results of that remolding need to be noted and summarized.

The present *Länder* serve as the organizational base in this book and the topics include:

Special Aspects: stereotypes, climate, dialect, claimed identity, greetings, humor

Regional Traits: basic demographics, location and size, flag, coat of arms

Geographic Features: soils, rivers or lakes, uplands, special consequences

History: prehistory; major events, with focus on 1850 to 2000, posing the question whether some special identity emerges from regional history

Economy: pattern of development, present situation, types of work, and meaning

Main Cities: Capital, size, historical formation, industries, and significant features, especially the restored cultural heritage

Attractions: tourists' sites and inhabitants' markers of identity such as prehistory artifacts, ruins, castles, palaces, churches, cloisters, half-timbered buildings, open-air museums, hiking paths, museums, and galleries

Customs: festivals, special celebrations, dress *(Trachten)*, folklore

Cultural Attributes and Contributions:

    Visual Arts: painting, sculpture, architecture, film

    Literature: about and created in region, famous writers

    Music: types, festivals but including folk songs

Civics and Remembrance: regional history, political education, and memorial sites

Cuisine: local favorite and traditional recipes

The photographs seek to illustrate the regional diversity and with what Germans can and do identify: landscapes, cities, cultural creations, monuments and their rebuilt places, or *Heimats.*

NOTES

1. The most comprehensive account remains Robert E. Dickinson, *Germany: A General and Regional Geography* (London: Methuen, 1953), especially Parts V and VI. The attempts to revise historical borders during the Weimar era are well presented in his book *The Regions of Germany* (London: Kegan Paul, 1945), viii, in which he speaks of "Eleven major natural provinces with two smaller city states. . . ."

2. See Maiken Umbach, ed., *German Federalism: Past, Present, Future* (Basingstoke: Palgrave, 2002), especially the introduction.

3. Konrad H. Jarausch and Michael Geyer, *Shattered Past: Reconstructing German Histories* (Princeton, NJ: Princeton University Press, 2003).

4. Mary Fulbrook, *German National Identity after the Holocaust* (Cambridge, England: Arnold, 1999), 199–200.

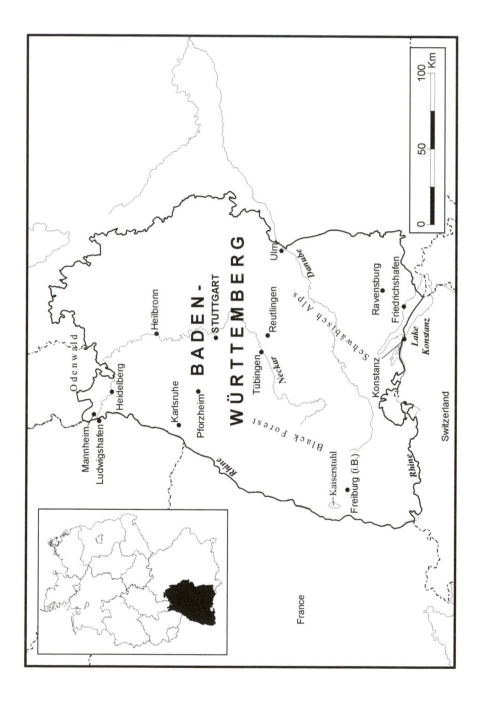

Chapter 1

𝕭𝕒𝕯𝕖𝕟-𝖂ü𝖗𝖙𝖙𝖊𝖒𝖇𝖊𝖗𝖌

SPECIAL ASPECTS

The local dialect, which adds "l" endings to words and a questioning "gel?" to sentences, is widespread (and adopted by migrants to the area). Local wine remains the favored drink, and Romanesque architectural gems abound. The villages, bedecked in season with flowers and carved designs on many of the half-timbered houses, have a rustic yet well-kept look. This region is known as part of Romantic Germany, where people are friendly and engaging. The old customs survive well: May Day, *Fasnet* (a carnival in the southwest from pagan pre-Lent celebrations), and *Fasching* (a carnival in the north and southeast with balls and processions). But the special costumes *(Trachten)* appear in only a few villages at festive holidays. By contrast, the larger cities, having been heavily bombed during World War II, are glass-and-concrete modern with state-of-the-art industries and services. At present, the combination of rustic countryside and high-tech cities is the pride of the region, which advertises itself as "paradise" due to economic success combined with many cultural opportunities, which allows an excellent lifestyle.

REGIONAL TRAITS

Though united during the eighteenth century, this region combines two separate political entities. The west and north, mostly drained by the Rhine and Neckar rivers, comprises Baden. The east and southeast, mainly drained by the Danube River, comprises Württemberg. Baden is mostly Catholic while Württemberg is predominantly Protestant. Many jokes and stories highlight the differences between the two states, which united in 1952. One Baden pun suggests there are Badeners

Figure 1.1
Farm village with onion-domed church in Black Forest, Baden-Württemberg.

Source © Press and Information Office, Germany.

and Unsymbadencrs or, literally, those from Baden and those who are not congenial—from Württemberg. A reverse version explains the complete decline of a *Schwabe*, the colloquial term by which Württembergers are known: first serving in the lowest ranks of the military, then becoming a radical, next marrying a Catholic, and finally dying in Baden.

The third largest and third most populated state of Germany covers nearly 36,000 square kilometers. It borders France in the west, Switzerland in the south, and Austria in the southeast. Bavaria is to the east, Hesse to the north, and Saarland to the northwest. Among its population of 10.6 million, many are second-generation migrants from eastern German states and some 1.3 million are foreigners, mostly from southern Europe. The region is known for its automobile and electronic industries and idyllic rural countryside, pockmarked by medieval and early modern architectural treasures.

The flag is simple: black on top and yellow below. The coat of arms has a buck and a griffin holding a shield. At the top of the shield are small representations of historical entities. The main body has three black lions on a gold background.

GEOGRAPHIC FEATURES

The Rhine River along the western border with France and Rhineland-Palatinate, the Neckar River in the north, and the Danube River in the southeast provide large valleys and lowlands. Between the river valleys high steep uplands remained separate territories until linked by roads and communication systems in the nineteenth and twentieth centuries. The middle "mountains" of the southern part of the Odenwald, Stromberg, and a stretch of Swabian hills separate many small and agriculturally productive valleys. The Black Forest is the best known of these uplands, rising to 1,500 meters east of the Rhine River. Pine and oak forests line extensive hiking paths in a long, narrow rectangle from Karlsruhe and Pforzheim in the north to the Swiss border in the south. Since the 1970s, browning and dieback of trees, assumed to be the result of industrial pollution, has affected the forest. A few of the uplands are mere high protrusions, such as the Kaiserstuhl, covered with vineyards, orchards, and specialty produce crops. The Schwäbisch Alb upland, south of Stuttgart, is less high than the Black Forest, but it is the source of both the Danube and Neckar rivers. Those rivers and their tributaries contribute to the rolling, idyllic countryside of pretty villages tucked into little valleys. The Bodensee, the largest lake in Germany at 14 kilometers by 80 kilometers (10 miles by 50 miles), separates Swabia from Switzerland. The Rhine flows out its western end. Baden-Württemberg is more an economic and political entity than a geographic one.

The 11 traditional subregions, some derived from previous dynastic or other political entities, remain points of identification for the population. Many emerged before trains and automobiles broke the isolation of regions defined by how far a person could walk or ride in a few days: Kurpfalz (Palatinate); Badische Kernlande (Baden Core); Ortenau; Breisgau und Markgräflerland; Grenzland am Hochrhein (Borderland on the Upper Rhine); Württembergische Kernlande (Württemberg Core); Altwürttemberg (Old Württemberg); Hohenlohe; Ostwürttemberg (East Württemberg); Oberschwaben (Upper Swabia); and Hohenzollern. Except historically and in providing local variants of dialects, festivals, and costumes, their differences continue to decline. However, state efforts encourage this multiplicity of identification, and the state acknowledges the communal strength that exists in the diversity of the subregions.

MAIN CITIES

Stuttgart, Mannheim, Heidelberg, Heilbronn, Karlsruhe, Pforzheim, Freiburg im Breisgau, Ulm. Aside from Stuttgart, nearly all range from approximately 100,000 to 300,000 people and thus retain a humane size and compact quality. Most of these cities have special traits revealing their historic pasts, especially as princely residences.

CAPITAL

Stuttgart (population 600,000) reflects its princely past in gardens and palaces that provide relaxation oases from the predominant glass and concrete structures. The latter, such as the angular state gallery *(Staatsgallerie)*, with an impressive collection (from Rembrandt to Manet, from Schlemmer to Picasso), replaced the bombed buildings and rubble of World War II. However, some fine older buildings, such as the main ducal palace *(Neues Schloss)*, with its extensive park in the center of the city, provide a pleasant contrast. The industrial suburbs run into the city of Esslingen, once Stuttgart's industrial rival due to its machine building. Esslinger's old center, *Altstadt*, is a contrast to modern Stuttgart.

Aside from the concrete and glass architecture of the rebuilt city, Stuttgart's modernism is especially identified with Gottlieb Daimler, Carl Benz' competitor in creating the automobile during the 1880s. Presently, the auto giant Daimler-Chrysler remains part of the city's electronics and automobile research and industrial center. However, service industries increasingly predominate, including administrative offices and a major prison. University and technical colleges reinforce the state's emphasis on research.

As the capital, Stuttgart city has extensive parks, gardens, and an International Bach Academy, as well as a top-ranked ballet. The city has the main state and city art galleries as well as the regional museum in the old palace. The Linden Museum offers ethnology from around the world, while the Mercedes-Benz Museum, the Porsche Museum, and the Swabian Beer Museum emphasize regional contributions and specialties.

As a result of a prince's dream, **Mannheim** (population 325,000, of which 63,000 are foreigners) was laid out in a checkerboard pattern as an administrative and pleasure city. The central streets have no names; identification is by letter and number within a grid. In 1720 it became the residence city for a Palatinate ruler who left war-ravaged Heidelberg some 15 kilometers to the southeast. Although its gardens and parks still reflect its origins, the present city is important as a port for oil and chemicals, a research center with a university, and a cultural center, especially its National Theater. The latter offers a predominantly classical repertoire, with plays by Friedrich Schiller. The art gallery, the Reiss-Engelhorn Museum (extensive ethnographic and local artifacts), a pop art academy, and a film festival provide a diversity of cultural choices. The university is housed mainly in the largest baroque palace of Germany. Foreigners comprise 20 percent of the population though some are Turks and Italians born in Germany. Nearby Schwetzingen is known for its pretty (in pink) baroque palace and for asparagus. The garden is extensive and combines a rambling French area and a very structured English section. Mozart played in the ornate palace theater, which presently is home to a summer music festival culminating in Mozart celebrations.

Freiburg im Breisgau (population 210,000, with 15 percent foreigners) is known for its forest and hill setting in the southern Black Forest. Despite its growth, it remains charming with its city towers and walls into which colorful houses have been built. The *Martinstor*, or main gate to the old city, and the cathedral are marvels in stone, the former painted and the latter a beautiful natural red. Many buildings constructed of red sandstone such as the city hall and the merchant's guild, have intricate carvings. Especially noteworthy are the tiny canals, cascading down the sides of most streets, which help keep the old city clean and fresh. One restaurant, the Golden Bear, which dates from the twelfth century, claims to be the oldest in Germany. Freiburg's cathedral certainly has the oldest open-roofed church tower, and its museum tapestries go back to the tenth century. Some depict women riding men, symbolically controlling and making fools of them.

The old city is surrounded by a newer one of glass and concrete in which the service and research industries predominate. Solar technology, communications, and biotechnology are among the areas in which industry and university research overlap.

Heilbronn (population 120,000) is on the Neckar River and is the administrative center of Franconia. At the end of the nineteenth century it developed into the second largest industrial, machine-building city of the state of Württemberg. Automobiles, food processing, and electronics remain strong elements of the economy, which is aided by the city's location as a crossroads. Due to extensive bomb damage in World War II, a rebuilt city emerged, though an astronomical clock on the city hall and churches from the fifteenth to eighteenth centuries offer ties to the past. The well-organized city museum and theater probably do not draw as many outsiders as the wines, especially during the week-long *Weindorf* (wine village) festival. Hundreds of local samples are offered in little booths. Broom-pubs *(Besenwirtschaften)*, so-called because small wine producers hang a broom above a doorway and sell fairly cheap fare of varying quality, are a local tradition.

Pforzheim (population 115,000) is the jewelry export center of Germany. During the eighteenth century, the watch and jewel industries began as a way to train and occupy orphans. Now about 10 percent of the workforce is active in gold smithing and jewelry making. The *Reuchlinhaus* has a large collection of locally produced jewelry on display, and the technical museum offers demonstrations of jewelry making. The city, heavily damaged by bombing, has rebuilt some of its late medieval churches. It is the northern starting point of three major Black Forest hiking paths *(Westweg, Ostweg, Mittelweg)*.

Old Heidelberg (population 140,000) is known for its university (founded in 1386), its castle ruins above the city, and varied city streets. Ironically, most of the buildings are relatively new since fire and warfare destroyed much of the medieval city in the eighteenth century. A few buildings, such as the Hotel Haus zum Ritter, provide evidence, via delightful stone carvings in the region's red sandstone, of the earlier town façades. Germany's oldest university, and among its most reputable, is spread about in a mix of old and new buildings, some abutting treed squares. The famous student pubs, with heavy wooden paneling, still remind one of generations of dueling fraternities. The composite image remains pretty: a charming central, relaxed *Altstadt* (old city) with medieval castle ruins towering above it, all set in lush, green hills.

A Philosopher's Walk winds through the hills on the north side of the Neckar, crossed by a notable stone bridge. In the old city numerous Protestant and Catholic churches represent the dominant styles of the seventeenth to nineteenth centuries. The Palatinate Museum contains local artifacts as well as an important archeological collection. Most shops and restaurants sport detailed ironwork signs identifying their artisan origins or type of business. A large eighteenth-century palace with extensive gardens is worth a trip to Schwetzingen, also known for its asparagus in springtime.

Karlsruhe (population 270,000) is Germany's judicial center, home to the Federal Court (highest appeals) and the Federal Constitutional Court (relating to principles and rights). It is also home to major research centers. Known for its fanlike layout, the compartments *(Fächer)* illustrate city planning of a court residence at its founding

Figure 1.2
Heidelberg with castle ruins, Baden-Württemberg.

Source Courtesy of the author.

in 1715. With no defensive walls and open to the countryside, it emphasized peace and pleasure. In 1967 Karlsruhe attained the designation of "city in the green," partly due to its easy access to the Black Forest. As a former ducal capital it has palaces *(Residenz)* but is also one of the Rhine's busiest industrial ports.

Having been the capital of Baden, Karlsruhe sports theaters, an opera, a strong music tradition, and special museums, for example, the city museum and the museum for literature of the Upper Rhine. The Baden state theater, plus many small companies, complement the music college and art galleries. One of the ducal princes was buried in a wooden pyramid structure in the main market. Rebuilt in stone during 1825, the commemoration marker has become a symbol for the city.

Ulm (population 114,000) on the Danube contains the highest church tower (161.5 meters, or 500 feet) in Germany and the world. A historic center, once home to fishing and leather-working families, Ulm rebuilt many tiny streets and little bridges after World War II. As an old imperial city it has many memorable buildings, including a decorated city hall. Outside the center are cloisters. Wiblingen, in ornate baroque, is among the most noteworthy. A number of fortresses such as Wilhelmsburg perch above the city. An important museum is devoted to the history of bread, including the communal bake oven and a full-scale model of a bakery from 1900. The museum holds more than 14,000 objects relating to bread, from pans to wooden molds.

Some smaller cities contain notable edifices. **Reutlingen** (population 107,000), in the Schwäbische Alb, has many half-timbered buildings including a city gate similar to Freiburg's. Picturesque **Tübingen** (population 75,000) is the site of another famous university, with 30,000 students who dominate the city. Half-timbered houses and winding streets remind one of an earlier era of artisans and regional commerce. **Schwäbish Hall** has very many remarkable half-timbered houses, carefully restored to preserve a unified cityscape and an unshattered part of the past. Some see this as the picture-perfect town with stately façades on its marketplace, once the center of a large salt trade. One could add Ravensburg (city of towers and gates), Konstanz on the Bodensee, or Lake Constance and Friedrichshafen ("Town of Zeppelin"), since all have major tourist attractions.

HISTORY

In 1945 the states of Baden, Württemberg-Hohenzollern, and Württemberg were occupied as separate political units by the American and then French military. By plebiscite they were united in 1952 into Baden-Württemberg. The region, however, has a much longer and more colorful history than the successful political unit created to make Germany's third largest state.

For the variety of Germanic tribes—Pfalzer, Franks, Badener, Schwabians, and Alemannen—to become one entity took a long time and is perhaps an incomplete process. In succession, many civilizations and people have lived in the valleys and forests. Many of the prehistory finds have been assembled and put on display in the state Archeological Museum at Konstanz. One area, around the Federsee in Upper Swabia has been preserved as a nature and archeological park. The Celts left many artifacts, especially tools and small cult figures. At Hochdorf, a rich gravesite with a wagon, loaded with the items to accompany a ruler into the other world, is a centerpiece to the Celtic Museum. East of the Rhine Valley, the Romans built limes, or long fortifications of wood and stone, to separate their military colonies from the tribes they could not control. Some have been reconstructed near Grab, while a Roman villa has been unearthed at Oberndorf-Bochingen.

In the medieval era the dukedom of the Swabians began to consolidate some territories that other powers such as the Habsburgs sought to annex. By 1488, the Swabian federation brought together as one political entity a number of earldoms, cloisters, and free cities. However, the Reformation brought new divisions as Württemberg mostly became Protestant while the majority of Baden remained Catholic. Typical of the princely patchwork of territories, the Protestant Hohenzollerns controlled small areas around their namesake castle, Hohenzollern, before they became rulers of Brandenburg-Prussia. Twenty-five "free" cities comprised another aspect of the patchwork. In 1771 the two main territories were temporarily united under one ruler.

Under Napoleonic dominance from 1802 to 1810, the separated states of Baden and Württemberg were enlarged as many small territories were added to them. The independent cities and church properties disappeared as separate political entities. Württemberg gained the most from French control since it supplied soldiers due to its poverty and dense population. Demographic changes and population growth also pushed emigration to America and Russia. Württemberg even attained elevation to a kingdom but one with censorship and heavy-handed controls.

At the Vienna congress of 1815, both states were able to retain their territorial gains but, as separate states, stayed somewhat distrustful of each other's expansionist intentions. For instance, during the Revolution of 1848, when Baden remained a liberal and radical holdout, Württemberg troops helped the Prussian military put down the democratic uprising. Lacking land and suffering competition from English industrial products, many peasants and artisans migrated abroad, especially after the 1830s. Within the federation of German states, both entities favored decentralized power and sought to avoid the dominance of either Prussia or Austria. In 1866 they favored Austria in the war with Prussia, but until the war with France in 1870 they successfully avoided having to take sides.

In the union of German states under reactionary Prussian dominance in 1871, both these south German territories were seen as liberal because, early in the nineteenth century, they had ended serfdom and developed constitutions. As late-nineteenth-century industrialization and urbanization changed the social landscape, a strong labor movement emerged in the cities. Just before World War I the southwestern states even accepted Social Democratic state ministers within limited, parliamentary governments. Both states maintained their independent identity under a duke and king, respectively, until the revolutions of 1918, when all the dynasties were swept away and republics formed. A bloodless revolution created a democratic constitution with universal suffrage and extended social rights and welfare.

In the Weimar Republic, the two states maintained their territorial base even if their beer taxes, separate military, and railways were brought under central national control after 1919. Social Democrats and liberals cooperated but could not agree on the extent of state control and welfare, especially during the depression of 1929. In 1933 both states lost their independence, as they were "coordinated" into the Nazi system and the parliamentary system dissolved. The local Nazi district leaders dominated and had few difficulties controlling a passive populace after repressing the left-wing parties and eliminating all political and dissenting groups by mid-1933. During World War II the larger cities, such as Stuttgart and Mannheim, were heavily bombed, but Polish and Soviet slave laborers kept the agricultural base of the economy functioning. Though forced laborers also worked in industry, the area had no major concentration camps, though it had many subcamps with inhumane working conditions.

The American occupation soon encouraged the reestablishment of parliamentary government. At first the liberal Free Democratic Party (FDP) under Reinhold Maier ruled in coalition with the conservative Christian Democratic Union (CDU), the Social Democratic Party (SPD), and the party of the refugees. After some complicated coalition shifts, his ministry was replaced by the CDU in 1953. The SPD usually came second in total election votes, especially in the industrial cities. Under Kurt Kiesinger, the CDU began a long hold on power, being succeeded by Hans Filbinger and Lothar Spaeth. The Greens made inroads during the 1980s. In the 1990s the

Social Democrats and Greens began to challenge the CDU, but the small FDP and a new right-wing group helped split the vote and the CDU remained in power. In 1992 Erwin Teufel created a "great coalition" of the CDU and SPD. In 1996 he organized a coalition with the liberals, which has been governing ever since. It defended itself in the elections of 2001 on the platform of a successful economic record.

The identity fostered by the state in its advertising of itself as a paradise seeks to combine a rural, picturesque homeliness with being relaxed in a modern but highly productive fashion. Some authorities claim that Calvinism continues to influence the northwest, the Palatinate area. Old Württemberg is still thought to be rigidly Protestant in its serious attitude toward diligence in work, while Baden is where life is enjoyed. Whether the reality matches this image is questionable, though the region has maintained many traditions, and integrated diverse groups, while succeeding in a global marketplace.

ECONOMY

Though appearing rural, industry has been important to this region since the late nineteenth century. With few resources and limited energy sources, people have been the main wealth. From sewing machines to zeppelins, from automobiles to computers, Baden-Württemberg has had specialized industrial output and produced many innovative entrepreneurs for hundreds of years. The Black Forest cuckoo clocks involved intricate carving and gears that developed mechanical skills applicable in many ways. Some of those were transferred to the machinery and automotive industries. Electronics firms such as SAP and IBM have joined Daimler-Chrysler, Bosch, and Porsche in locating their headquarters here. Baden-Württemberg has the highest per capita investment in research infrastructure in Europe. Its biotechnology sector is large and its data transmission system up-to-date. Its nine universities, 39 technical colleges, and some 130 research centers attest to the state's support for research. Heidelberg's university, founded in 1386 is the oldest, while Karlsruhe has Germany's first technical college. A high level of education, a solid work mentality, and many small firms have contributed to economic success. In addition to automobiles, machine building and electronics, textiles, wood, and plastics do well. Boss (clothing); Salamander (shoes); Triumph, Steiff (teddy bears); Uhu (glue); and WMF (fine metals) are among the many trademarks from the region. High-quality specialties have kept the loyalty of customers in wines, asparagus, cherries (distilled), sauerkraut, hops, and strong cheese.

The region has had some important economic theorists but mostly innovative entrepreneurs. Friedrich List, who advocated railways and high tariffs to encourage economic development in the 1840s in order to unite Germany, came from this area. In Esslingen, an industrial city emerged by the late nineteenth century devoted to producing machinery, especially locomotives. Near Stuttgart, Carl Benz began to create the modern automobile, while Robert Bosch developed electronic parts such as spark plugs for motors. Though Albert Einstein came from Ulm, he mostly worked in Switzerland and Berlin before emigrating due to the Nazi regime. At

Friedrichshafen Count Ferdinand Zepplin built huge airships, which his successor, Hugo Erckner, made popular around the world until the *Hindenburg* burned up during its landing at New York in 1936. By then, Ferdinand Porsche had created the prototype of the Volkswagen as well as his own special racing vehicles in Stuttgart. During the 1920s to 1950s, Ernst Heinkel built a variety of commercial airplanes, jets, and military planes. In 1932 Claudius Dornier founded his airplane and flying boat factory at Friedrichshafen, which continued after World War II and is at present involved in space research. The historical association with innovation continues in present-day research efforts. One local author asserted that the lack of resources required a special inventiveness to succeed economically.

An important aspect of entrepreneurial life has been the use of family and firm monies to create foundations, which started in the late nineteenth century. Whether for charitable or research purposes, individuals such as Robert Bosch dedicated profits toward scientific research, educational institutions, and cultural development. Zeppelin and the brothers Mahle also established foundations to aid the dispossessed. Gustav Werner's version, in the Foundation Bruderhaus, operated with funds from machine and paper factories and sought to aid the disabled after 1981. The press primarily serves the region, but Stuttgart is also a radio and television production center. The region leads Germany in the publication of specialty journals as well as academic book publishing.

Pockets of high technology relating to automobiles and trucks continue to fuel the economy, but the service sector has become a driving element. Though agriculture may employ few people, growing grain, hops, and especially grapes remains not only important to the economy but also to the regional rustic, rural identity. The latter relates to tourism, one of the region's major industries.

ATTRACTIONS

A very pretty, rolling countryside offers endless hiking, which can be combined with the viewing of castles, palaces, cathedrals, and bridges. Brooks and streams cascade through red sandstone toward the scenic Neckar, Rhine, or Donau rivers. In the south, Germany's largest lake, the Bodensee, is shared with Switzerland. As in most parts of the country, the styles of the half-timbered houses are different in each historical subregion, sometimes with patterns being quite different within tiny areas. Especially noteworthy are those in Konstanz, with mottoes carved into the horizontal timbers. Some have been dismantled and reassembled in open-air museums *(Freilichtmuseum)* to remind visitors of an agricultural, simpler, and perhaps happier past than the troubled twentieth century, which is acknowledged with many memorials to the Holocaust. The clock museum at Furtwangen demonstrates the development, by thousands of examples, of the Black Forest cuckoo clocks.

Late medieval or Renaissance castles, mostly restored or rebuilt in the nineteenth and twentieth centuries, such as Vellberg, Weikersheim, or Horneck, overlook valleys their knightly inhabitants once protected as well as exploited. Some were completely created during the nineteenth-century fascination with medieval ideals, such as Lichtenstein built by the Württemberg dukes in the Swabian Alb. By the eighteenth century, palaces became more commonplace as residences of the local rulers or rich estate owners. Freudenthal near Gnaden or Favorite in Rastatt, both in the baroque style, are two examples. Rastatt has elaborate gardens both at the palace (Schloss) and in the town. The ornate, overly decorated baroque interiors became common in churches of Catholic southern Germany by the early eighteenth century. The pearl of the Upper Swabian version of this style is the abbey church in Zwiefalten.

The remains and restored medieval cloisters appear throughout much of the Obermünstertal south of Freiburg. One of the best preserved in the state is the Cistercian cloister at Maulbronn. It shows the economy of the medieval monks, their defense works as well as their churches. The Romanesque church has had Gothic additions including a covered well with half-timbering above the supporting arches and below the roof. The unity of the complex has earned it a UNESCO heritage site designation. Another special example, because it has hardly changed over the centuries, is at Ocksenhausen. This Benedictine cloister has a late Gothic church that only had a few baroque additions made in the eighteenth century.

The Black Forest uplands, with high meadows as well as heavy dark woods, remain as inviting as they are legendary in song and folklore. Acid rain, however, has eaten away at the tree cover since the 1970s. Tucked against the hillside are many farmhouses, which combine house and barn. These are the typical Black Forest houses, with one side of the roof sloping down more than the other to allow snow to slide down the south side while its accumulation on the north acts as insulation. Set against sloping meadows, these houses tucked against a hillside draw admiration.

The Neckar Valley, though it overlaps with other regions and has developed too many parking lots, is important to hikers. Heidelberg, Neckargemünd, Dilsberg, Neckarsteinach, and Heilbronn offer castles, half-timbered towns, and green vistas. Neckargemünd has castle ruins, but what attracts the viewers and wanderers is the market square with its colorful half-timbered houses at all angles to the narrow street and each other. A former wine dealer's villa in stone with turret serves as the city officials' office space. The streets full of half-timbered buildings draw the gaze of visitors, though persons from the Ruhr sometimes find it all too pretty and cute. Dilsberg sits atop a large hill and has much of its defensive walls intact. Entrance is through a fortified gate. Views over the river and countryside are best from the castle tower. Neckarsteinach has become a health resort, but its castle towers still peek through solid green. Again, strong beams combine with special patterns in the half-timbered houses, while a rounded Catholic chapel contrasts with the Gothic Protestant church. Neckerhausen is the stop for boating, kayaking, swimming, and canoeing enthusiasts. At Hirschhorn, defensive walls running up the hills, gated town, castle with tower, and Carmelite cloisters return the traveler to the essence of the Neckar Valley.

Many medieval castles and Romanesque churches also dot the towns of the south. A superb example is St. George in Oberzell on the island of Reichenau in the

Bodensee. Because of the simplicity of its exterior lines, interior wall paintings that are at least a thousand years old, and huge wooden beams, this tenth-century building has been declared a UNESCO heritage site. Another special site is the tower of St. Michael, dating from 1156, on the main market square of Schwäbisch Hall. The central building was reconstructed with pointed Gothic windows and arches during the fifteenth century. The Gothic style is best seen at Freiburg. The striking red-rock cathedral is similar in style to many across the Rhine River in France. It illustrates the international urban trends, which more than regional or national ones once influenced architectural patterns.

Sculpted gardens in this region exhibit a variety of styles from formal on the island of Reichenau to cascading tulip landscapes at Ludwigsburg. Schwetzingen, Stuttgart (Hohenheim, Killesberg Park, Wilhelma), and Weinheim all have formal, sometimes very elaborate and extensive, sculpted gardens.

A different type of museum is at Untertürkheim just outside of Stuttgart. It honors Gottlieb Daimler for his creation of the first automobile in 1886. Daimler had met the inventor of the internal combustion engine, Nikolaus Otto, near Cologne, but they could not work together. Instead, with his companion, Wilhelm Maybach, he experimented with four-cylinder motors to create his mobile buggy.

To experience this region, the carnival processions and sessions, called *Fasnet*, in any of the major cities during February are a prerequisite. Just wandering the countryside and little villages helps understand the *Heimat* (homeland) ties of Badeners and Swabians. However, the surface appearance of rural tranquility and romantic heritage is challenged by a very productive, highly educated, and research-oriented urban world.

CUSTOMS

Local costumes *(Trachten)* in the rural areas are mostly worn only on very festive occasions. During such local—mostly religious—holidays some women wear 14 large red puffballs on white hats (which makes the symbol of a cross from all directions). Others have tiny pearllike shiny balls alternating with red and green ones covering a round hat.

Carnival *(Fasnet and Fasching)* is a very popular peoples' holiday *(Volksfest)* and strongly upheld tradition. It is characterized by masks and devils' or fools' costumes. Planning the events, making costumes by hand, and composing elaborate speeches takes months. Dancing girls, marching bands, processions, plus ritualized but very humorously staged events reinforce the joviality of *Fasnet*. Each village, as well as the main centers, has its carnival club with elected kings and annual presidents. *Fasching* is a trademark of the region and exemplifies the populace's conviviality.

In addition to carnival, many traditional holidays such as Easter and May Day are celebrated with processions or dancing. Sharpshooting festivals become elaborate affairs with processions and "sittings," meaning staged banquets.

The region contains many spas, some of which date back to Roman times. "Taking the waters" for health reasons is widely practiced. Not only the wealthy now go to Baden-Baden with its casino and Badenweiler where the rich of the nineteenth century cavorted.

CULTURAL ATTRIBUTES
AND CONTRIBUTIONS

The region likes to be seen as a cultural entrepot with two state theaters, 150 theater festivals, and many literary prizes.

VISUAL ARTS

The Romanesque and Gothic cathedrals with intricate carvings, the cloisters and castles, and the half-timbered buildings may be the main artistic creations. But some painters have contributed to national and international styles. For example, Oscar Schlemmer became known in the 1920s for rounded figures with offsetting colors in the Bauhaus. Later, Willi Baumeister offered abstract combinations in his paintings that were not as harsh as those of his contemporaries. Crafts such as jewelry making remain a viable art form that emerged from a long tradition of gold- and silversmiths, especially at Pforzheim. Franz Gutmann a contemporary sculptor, uses wood, stone, and metal to create rural images in his *Heimat* of the Obermünstertal, to which he returned after achieving fame.

LITERATURE

Marbach houses the German Literature Archive with the papers of many of Germany's major writers. Two of the great Romantic poets, Ludwig Uhland and Justinus Kerner, composed here. Another, Eduard Mörike (1804–1875), wrote many poems extolling his Württemberg homeland. Friedrich Schiller (1759–1805), Georg Hegel (1770–1831), and Martin Heidegger (1889–1976) are among the internationally acclaimed authors and philosophers who worked here. Unlike Schiller's humanitarian cosmopolitanism, Heidegger identified with the region's soil and forests in a racist fashion. By contrast, Friedrich Hoelderlin (1770–1843) and others, such as Hermann Hesse (1877–1962), found a more simple and less ideological inspiration in the same landscape. In the nineteenth century the Swabians especially prided themselves in being a people of poets and writers. Many regional writers sought to spread their knowledge of local customs, especially carnival and dialects.

MUSIC

The region is known as the "orchestra paradise," with major ensembles in Stuttgart and Karlsruhe. Heidelberg offers a series of concerts as well as plays at its *Schlossfestspiele* in the castle. Freiburg has a two-week tent festival that combines jazz and contemporary music with classical. Many places have adopted a major musician, though the annual repertoire is much broader: Mozart at Schwetzingen, Bach in Stuttgart. A radio symphony also operates at the spa center Baden-Baden. Locals, especially at village festivals and during carnival, sing traditional folksongs about the forests and peasant life. They might even sing the Baden hymn about their home-land's hills and fine villages.

CIVICS AND REMEMBRANCE

The state office for political education offers well-illustrated publications about the history of the region. A dual tactic is usually followed: fostering democracy by offering materials, presentations, and seminars especially for teachers and students on parliament, political parties, and on being an informed, involved citizen. A second approach involves contrasting the positive past of the region with upholding the memory and acknowledging the negative past of the Nazi era. The head of the institution has asserted that political education is a necessity, not a luxury. A sample from the program offerings in 2003 includes: "genocide in German southwest Africa [100 years since repression of the local population by German troops]," "fifty years of the state constitution," "critical citizenship," and "globalization." Publications, generally offered free to students and teachers, include books on concentration camps and euthanasia institutions.

Partly due to the large number of refugees from former eastern German territo-ries at Pforzheim, a large collection of artifacts sought to show daily life as well as the problems of the former German Democratic Republic. By contrast, during the 1980s an attempt was made to adjust the way Karlsruhe remembered the Nazi era. The idea of honoring some Nazi high court judges incarcerated by the Soviets after 1945 was challenged by some of those judges' victims. They thereby corrected the cold war version of history, which forgot the Nazi crimes and focused on Soviet ones. At present, a more balanced version is offered.

Much emphasis in state political education has been placed on providing docu-mentation to citizens to help them to make informed decisions, but especially to encourage participation in debates and social endeavors. Confronting violence and right-wing extremism is combined with fostering patriotism to the regional and the federal constitution. Uncomfortable themes such as attacks on foreigners and the problematic past are not avoided. Two major principles—not overruling the views of others and discussing controversies from all angles—are part of the consensus approach to fostering democracy.

CUISINE

As the home of Black Forest Cake, one must start with that dessert. But other traditional foods also mark this region, especially the flour-based pasta *(Spaetzle)* and the little pasta pockets *(Maultaschen)* filled with various meats, including wild boar. Onion cake *(Zwiebelkuchen)* is found in many pubs during the autumn. Among the many tasty foods of this region, *Spaetzle* and *Maultaschen* probably reflect local cuisine best. Light and aromatic Baden red wines are drunk with such delicacies. They come in quarter-liter glasses *(Schoppen)* filled to the brim. *Weissherbst* is a highly prized rosé produced in very limited quantities in the southwest.

BLACK FOREST CAKE

Make two cakes, each with following ingredients:

6 eggs, separated	5 teaspoons kirsch
1/2 cup sugar	1/3 cup unsweetened cocoa powder
1 teaspoon vanilla extract	3/4 cup all-purpose flour

Preheat oven to 350°F. Grease two 10-inch springform pans. Beat egg yolks in large bowl. Add sugar, vanilla, and kirsch. Beat until creamy and light yellow. Fold the cocoa and flour into egg mixture. In a separate bowl with clean beaters beat the egg whites until soft peaks form. Fold in the egg yolk mixture. Pour batter into pans and bake about 20 minutes (test by pushing in toothpick—if it comes out clean, cake is done). Cool on racks and cut horizontally so you have 4 layers of cake.

To fill between the layers of the cakes:

1 can of tart cherries, drain and reserve juice	1/4 cup powdered sugar
1/3 cup sugar	1 teaspoon vanilla extract
2 tablespoons cornstarch	20 maraschino cherries
6 tablespoons or more kirsch or vodka	2 ounces of semisweet chocolate
1 quart whipping cream	

Combine cherry juice in small saucepan with sugar and cornstarch. Cook—stirring—until thickened. Add kirsch and cherries and let cool. In large bowl whip cream, powdered sugar, and vanilla until stiff peaks form. Assemble cake by putting about a half-inch of whipped cream on one layer of cake. On the next layer add the cherry-kirsch mixture. On the third layer top with whipping cream. Once all layers have been used, spread whipping cream over the whole cake and garnish with maraschino cherries and sprinkles of chocolate.

ZWIEBELKUCHEN (ONION CAKE)

Work 1/2 cup of butter into 1 3/4 cups of all-purpose flour, stir in 1 egg and 2 tablespoons salt to make a dough. Chill for 15 minutes. Fry 4 slices of diced bacon and sweat 4 medium onions, sliced thinly, for a few minutes. In a bowl, beat 1/2 cup whipping cream, 2 eggs, a bit of salt and pepper. Roll out pastry on an 11-inch greased pan. Spread bacon and onions on it, topping with cream mixture. Cover with foil and bake for 20 minutes; remove foil and bake another 10 minutes or until firm. Serve with chilled white Baden wine.

Swabian Noodles or Spaetzle With Cheese

2 1/2 cups sifted all-purpose flour	2 eggs, beaten
1/2 teaspoon salt	1/2 cup water

Combine flour and salt in a mixing bowl, making a well in the center. Add eggs and 1/4 cup water. Beat evenly until a stiff dough forms, gradually adding a little more water until consistency is thick, firm, and comes away easily from the sides of the bowl. Knead until smooth. Let stand in covered bowl for 30 minutes. Dampen pastry board with water, place dough on it, flour the rolling pin slightly, and roll out to 1/8-inch thickness or a little thinner. Heat a pot of salted water to boiling. With a sharp knife, cut off very thin slivers of the dough, transfer to a plate as it is cut, and push directly into rapidly boiling water. Do not crowd. Spaetzle will rise to the surface when cooked, in about 5 minutes. Remove with a slotted spoon, drain in colander. Add more slivers of dough to the boiling water, continuing until all is cooked. Then sprinkle with grated cheese. Recipe makes 4 cups, enough for 4 servings as a side dish, 12 servings if added to soup.

Chapter 2

𝔅𝔞𝔳𝔞𝔯𝔦𝔞

SPECIAL ASPECTS

The Bavarians have lilting dialects. As the local joke goes—two kinds of people exist in the world, Bavarians and those who wish they were. Some even acknowledge themselves as "odd" people, enjoying frothy beer; wild dancing to oompah-pah music; wearing short leather pants with wide suspenders *(lederhosen)*, low-cut dirndl dresses, and green hunting costumes with tilted hats. Such garb and behavior, as well as onion-steeple churches in green environs and fairy-tale castles towering over Alpine valleys, evoke traditional and rural images. Yet, their cities contain a modern, swift-paced world of automobiles and electronics. Since the 1960s, the conservative Christian Social Union has continuously dominated provincial politics, which helps to highlight the Catholic Church's influence and to mythologize the state's independent past and present.

REGIONAL TRAITS

The Free State of Bavaria is geographically the largest state (27,200 square miles; 70,548 square kilometers) with the highest mountain, *Zugspitze* (2,962 meters). There are 12.1 million "Texans of Germany," of which more than 10 percent are foreigners. Approximately two-thirds of the populace is Catholic. Internal migration to the cities, especially to expensive Munich, has not undercut continued identification with the countryside. Customs are upheld with traditional dress and festivals, especially May Day, church celebrations, and religious processions. The cultural heritage of Catholicism, represented by countless beautiful village churches with onion

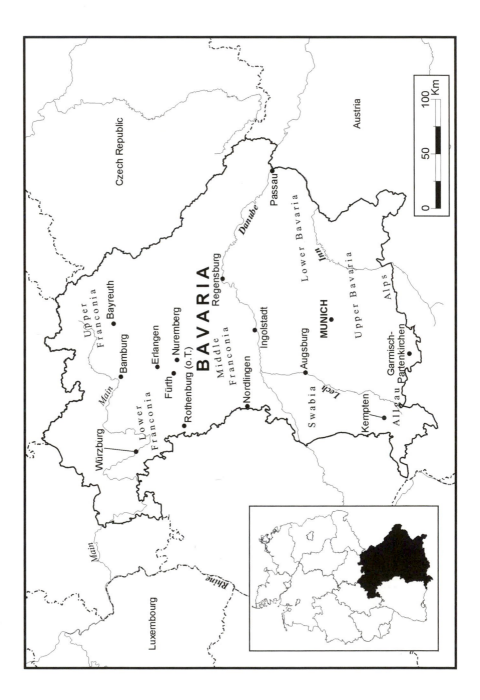

Figure 2.1
Bavarian Alps.

Source © Press and Information Office, Germany.

domes, draws numerous tourists. But the palaces and castles, many from the eighteenth and nineteenth centuries, attract even more. Lakes and varied countryside provide swimming, boating, and hiking opportunities. The Bavarians remain the most traditional of Germans, combining rustic folkloric habits and political conservatism with technological modernity.

The flag features the Wittelsbach dynasty's blue and white colors on an offset checkerboard. The coat of arms has the same pattern but is surrounded by small lions, held by two large lions.

GEOGRAPHIC FEATURES

The Alps in the south define part of the natural frontier with Austria. Austria and the Czech Republic share the eastern border. Saxony is just touched to the northeast, Thuringia is to the north, and Hesse to the northwest, while Baden-Württemberg is to the west. Nearly all the countryside descends from the Alps northward, but numerous rivers, such as the Lech in the west and the Danube in the east, cut large flat plains. The Bavarian Forest in the east and a series of glacial lakes in the south, just below the Alps, offer recreational opportunities. Most of the countryside is farmland, meadows, and forests with countless flower-bedecked villages perched near streams.

The subregions are divided according to the seven administrative districts (Upper and Lower Bavaria; Upper, Lower, and Middle Franconia; Upper Palatinate; and Swabia). More common in terms of identification by Bavarians are the historical subregions of Franconia (north and northwest), of Swabia in the west, and Allgau in the south and east. These are as much points of reference and identity for the inhabitants as the political state. Each of the latter areas has more geographic and historical unity than the political entity that combines them.

Figure 2.2
St. Kolomann's Church, Allgau, Bavaria.

Source © Press and Information Office, Germany.

Figure 2.3
Coburg market square, Bavaria.

Source Courtesy of the author.

HISTORY

The dynastic house of Wittelsbach ruled from 1180 until they were deposed in 1918. Expanding their territories over parts of the Palatinate and southern present-day Bavaria, by the seventeenth century they ruled a rough parallelogram bounded on the north by the Danube River, by the Lech in the west, the Inn in the east, and the Alps in the south. The realm they governed changed boundaries frequently until after the Napoleonic wars, when the present expanded configuration emerged. During the Napoleonic era, the Wittelsbachs had opportunistically shifted sides and in 1806 became monarchs (Maximilian I). The region, which this dynastic family consolidated, has a very long and complex history.

The tribal Celts left impressive gold, lead, and bronze artifacts from their civilization, many found at the archeological site developed at Manching. They also left their mark on the names and language of the region (Inn, Lech, and Isar all derive from Celtic terms). The Romans also influenced part of the southern area and left the remains of fortifications and villas. The archeological museum at Kempten displays some examples of these artifacts. The migrations of eastern tribes resulted in large population shifts and created the three main groups that permanently populated the area. These were the Bavarians in the south, Swabians or Allemanen in the southwest, and Franks in the north and northwest. Some suggest that the more than a million Sudenten Germans from Bohemia and other refugees after World War II became the fourth Bavarian tribal group.

In the medieval era much of the territory that later became Bavaria came under the rule of the Saxon kings, but by the thirteenth century a myriad of bishoprics, dukedoms, and other small states arose. Bamberg, Würzburg, and Augsburg became important religious centers. Ansbach, Bayreuth, and Nuremberg were significant handicraft and commercial centers. By the sixteenth century the Wittelsbach dukes dominated an increasing area with Munich as their base. Their court encouraged music, church building, and later baroque palaces. However, over the next two centuries the liberal elements of the Enlightenment had little influence. The Counter-Reformation had imposed a homogenous and repressive Catholicism illustrated by the dominance of Jesuits in higher education. Pockets of Protestantism remained in the north. The multitude of buildings so much prized in the present, aside from the few significant palaces and castles of the nineteenth century, emerged between the twelfth and the eighteenth centuries. Churches, cloisters, and small cities full of half-timbered buildings were the products of small bishoprics, free cities, and tiny principalities. The Wittelsbachs slowly came to rule over much of the central area and gained a rich inheritance from the small principalities that they incorporated into their realm.

Napoleon forced the secularization of the cloisters and church properties in 1803. He enlarged the Bavarian Wittelsbach realm and elevated it to a kingdom in 1806. The enlarged state survived the treaty negotiations in 1815 but then had difficulty maintaining its independence in the face of expansionist Habsburg and Prussian power. The powerful bureaucrat Maximilian von Montgelas modernized the state with administrative reforms, centralization, and economic liberalization. A constitution in 1818 ended absolutism but did not allow any significant influence by the populace. In the early nineteenth century Bavaria experienced the results of Europe's secularizing trends, including a rising illegitimate birthrate, geographic mobility, and political unrest. In 1832 attempts by students to raise pan-German national awareness encountered quick state repression. Economic depression and scandal about the monarch's mistress, the dancer Lola Montez, whom the king elevated to countess, tipped the balance toward revolution in 1848. The liberal rebels demanded constitutional reform, national unification, and an extended suffrage. They were defeated on all fronts in 1849, though a slow liberalization occurred over the next decades.

Bavarian society remained predominantly rural, with over 90 percent of the population in communities of less than 2,000 people at the end of the nineteenth century. Industrialization began to slowly alter some Franconian cities in the 1890s when Social Democracy (SPD) made important inroads, as did middle-class reformers such as Georg von Vollmar. Earlier, the Patriot Party had emerged to fight the liberalizing trends (secular schooling and separation of church and state) of the government. In 1887 the Patriot Party merged with the Center Party, which had appeared after German unification in 1871 to defend Catholic interests against the cultural and religious policies of the Bismarckian state as well as the liberal policies of Munich. The Center Party's conservativism remained especially strongly supported in the countryside where leagues of peasants and religious lay leagues ushered in populist politics. Some were influenced or dominated by clerics, others by university-educated individuals such as Georg Heim, whose appearance signaled an end to clerical domination. Some of the leagues had strong anti-Semitic overtones. At the end of the century, religious pilgrimages still drew far more participants than the socialist subculture of singing or hiking clubs.

The monarchs, especially Ludwig I and II (the mad king), engaged in museum and gallery building, which provided the basis for Munich's cultural importance, which by 1900 rivaled Berlin's. Ludwig I began rebuilding Munich into a monumental city of wide avenues, stately government edifices, and museums. Ludwig II's building spree in the 1880s included a series of palaces *(Linderhof, Neuschwanstein, Chiemsee)*, which have become known around the world. Under the Wittelsbachs, Bavaria proclaimed itself a "national" entity and emphasized regional loyalty. Even within the unified German state under Prussian leadership after 1871, Bavaria maintained its own troops, stamps, beer taxes, and railways. The support of Richard Wagner's Bayreuth opera house and festival by Ludwig II can be seen as part of the attempt to emphasize Bavaria's special ties to the medieval past but also to defend and to underscore an independent present.

In World War I the Bavarians suffered high casualties, especially among soldiers from the rural villages. That and inflation fueled resentment against Berlin. By 1918 war weariness led to support for the pacifism and radicalism of the Independent Social Democrats who had split from the war-supporting SPD. Under Kurt Eisner, the Independents overthrew the Wittelsbachs and proclaimed Bavaria a *"Freistaat,"* which is still its official designation. At first during the revolutionary transition period, the question of parliamentary versus council rule held public attention. The assassination of Eisner resulted in a leftward lurch, as anarchists and utopian communists (Carl Landauer, Ernst Toller) took over Munich and declared a council government. A communist group under Eugen Leviné, who proclaimed a dictatorship of the proletariat, displaced them. It deposed priests and terrorized the population. The national government refused to negotiate when foodstuffs ran out and sent in volunteer troops *(Freikorps)*. These *Freikorps* brutally fought their way into the city. In response, the Munich "red army" executed a number of "reactionaries." In revenge, the *Freikorps* murdered hundreds, including Russian prisoners of war and many Catholics wrongly believed to be with the leftists.

The loss of the war, then of the monarchy, and of symbolic as well as real powers after 1918 led to a more centralized German state, and the turmoil of the revolutionary period, increased social tensions. The situation helped foster separatist movements, followed by radical and racist revolt by groups such as the Nazis. The socialist and anarchist uprisings, with their attendant violence by both the extreme left but especially the right during early 1919, helped set the stage for growing and violent anti-Semitic movements, which established their bases in Munich. The Nazis had their start here in the early 1920s and tried to utilize anti-Berlin resentment in a *Putsch* during November 1923, for which they recruited the embittered war "hero" General Erich Ludendorff. Though Adolf Hitler's first attempt to gain power failed, the Bavarian state and judiciary tolerated his right-wing radicalism. Throughout the

1920s, conservatives generally ruled the Bavarian state in an authoritarian manner, as they underscored Bavarian independence. They followed inconsistent policies toward the extremes of the left and the right. They repressed the left but mainly permitted the Hitler movement free reign, including holding massive annual rallies at Nuremberg.

Once in power, the Nazis integrated Bavaria into their coordinated system of party control, which ironically centralized more decisions in Berlin. The Catholic Church initially cooperated with Nazi rule, especially since a Concordant (1933) with the Vatican acknowledged Catholic educational and institutional rights. Soon some personal and later institutional resistance to the regime occurred. By 1935 church leaders perceived the threat to Catholic youth organizations and began to distance themselves; by the late 1930s protest statements from Cardinal Michael von Faulhaber revealed the tensions between the old church and the new state.

The first concentration camp appeared in 1933 outside of Munich at Dachau and mostly housed communists, socialists, and liberals for "reeducation." Jews and other "undesirables" soon joined them. The Nuremberg Laws of 1935 denied citizenship and social rights to those not considered racially acceptable. Discrimination against Jews and so-called asocials and the attacks on synagogues in November 1938 found little opposition from the populace. The manner in which Jews were dispossessed and marched away in full view of their neighbors, as occurred with 800 in Würzburg during April 1942, has been much discussed by historians. By contrast, the group known as the White Rose (Die weisse Rose), mainly Munich university students and professors who lost their lives in 1943 for protesting the war, as well as the repressive and racist policies of the Nazis.

World War II bombing attacks hit industrial and administrative centers, especially Munich, Nuremberg, and Würzburg, but left much of rural Bavaria unaffected. Its agriculture, even its church properties, benefited from enslaved foreign—mostly Polish and Soviet—laborers.

In 1945 American troops occupied Bavaria. At first the conquerors feared Nazi resistance, but little materialized. Nazi symbols, such as Hitler's Alpine holiday retreat at Berchtesgaden, were closed or blown up. Nuremberg, where during the late 1930s Nazi party rallies gathered half a million faithful for shows of strength, was chosen for the trials of the Nazi leaders. The occupiers used questionnaires to determine who were Nazi criminal perpetrators and who were mere followers. However, some who had played important roles in the Third Reich were allowed to escape, often with Catholic Church aid and some with American complicity, because their expertise was sought against the Soviet Union or in developing rocketry.

Soon the Americans encouraged local political parties and elections within the reestablished state borders (aside from a part of the Palatinate, which went to the French zone). Bavarian politicians advocated a decentralized, federal state to maintain Bavarian traditions. Under American guidance, a constitution appeared in 1946. The Christian Social Union (CSU) and Social Democrats established themselves as the main political parties by 1947 and maintained their position within the German federation after 1949. Bavaria refused to sign the Basic Law, or constitution, of the new republic. The SPD ruled for two short interludes (1945 to 1946, 1954 to 1957). Otherwise, the champion of state's rights and conservativism, the CSU, has dominated Bavarian politics for over 50 years. Hans Erhard led CSU ministries from 1945 to 1954 and 1960 to 1962. After him Alfons Goppl (1962 to 1978) consolidated the CSU in all areas, except Munich. After that, the CSU repeatedly triumphed at the polls under the feisty Franz Josef Strauss—his secret ties to German Democratic Republic leaders and the financial manipulations of the fiefdom he dominated have emerged since his death in 1988. Max Streibl followed (1988 to 1993), and since then Eduard Stoiber has been the wearer of the regional crown. In 2003 his CSU succeeded in capturing 62 percent of the *Landtag* (state parliament) vote, which included support from all sectors of the populace.

The Bavarians, especially their politicians, see themselves as advocates for regional development. Their constitution emphasizes independence. They do not want interference from Berlin and have turned increasingly toward the idea of separate, strong regions in Europe. They advocate federal competition more than cooperation, though prone to forget that until the 1970s they received financial support from other states via the federal tax system. Bavarians constantly emphasize their difference from other parts of Germany as well as their singularity. They loudly repeat their intention to guard those traits.

ECONOMY

The success of the agricultural and industrial economy of Bavaria has attracted many companies to locate their headquarters at Munich, as well as brought tourists to its castles, churches, and palaces. One of the traditional trades, beer brewing, proved especially profitable in the early nineteenth century and in the immediate post-World War II period, though at present the industry's growth has slowed. The purity law of 1516 set the standard for German beer, which remains the norm. Though agriculture remains important, service industries and tourism are much more profitable. Added value for each sector at present is 1 percent for agriculture, 32 percent for industry, and 67 percent for services. The handicrafts received a boost from the nearly 2 million skilled eastern refugees who arrived after 1944. The shift to industrial production took place during the 1960s with the aid of foreign workers, mostly from southern Europe, and shifted to research and service industries by the 1990s. Strengths are in automobiles (BMW in Munich, Audi in Ingolstadt), aerospace, electrical (Siemens in Munich), insurance (Allianz in Munich), and publishing (*Burda, Bunte,* C.H. Beck). New economic strongpoints include the fashion industry, with such houses as Strenesse, located in Munich and Nördlingen.

At present nine state universities and 14 major institutes supplement 17 specialized colleges. Bavaria has become a leader in technological research especially in plasma, environment, and health, and with aviation and space at Oberpfaffenhofen. Leather pants *(Lederhosen)* and laptops is a much heard and fitting motto.

Bavaria has the lowest rate of welfare support and among the lowest rate of unemployment in Germany. It seeks to rewrite the terms of German federalism primarily to provide less support to the financially weaker states as well as to dismantle the welfare state. Its economy ranks as the equivalent to twentieth among the top exporting countries in the world.

Though agriculture is a small part of the state's economy, regional products such as cheese, pretzels, wine, sheep, pigs, and cattle are important. It has been claimed that agriculture is measured in the "economy of people's souls," or sentimental value. As in neighboring France, local fresh food is preferred. Agriculture has mechanized and become big business, despite the appearance of rustic rural piety with Catholic crosses and shrines at the corners of many fields and crossroads. Tourism is even bigger business.

An innovative approach to privatization of state property encourages cultural development. When state properties are sold, the profits go toward building new galleries, such as the *Pinakothek der Moderne* in Munich or the Museum for Art and Design in Nuremberg, and supporting established institutions, such as the *Germanische Nationalmuseum* in Nuremberg and the *Mainfränkische Museum* in Würzburg.

MAIN CITIES

CAPITAL

Munich is a city with over a million inhabitants in a region of over 2 million. It is one of the most significant cultural capitals of Germany. Its liberal urbanity stands in marked contrast to the conservative nature of the state's politics and rural hinterlands. Since the 1970s the mayors have mostly been Social Democrats.

Even before World War I, a famous Bohemian area existed in Schwabing and new art and lifestyles found many patrons. Simultaneously, modern artists' colonies, such as at nearby Murnau (Wassily Kandinsky, Gabriele Münter) provided pockets of challenge to the academy norms delineated by the state. By the late nineteenth century, the capital, as well as some of the industrial cities, developed Social Democratic and anarchist challenges to the dominant political conservativism. During the Weimar era, Munich was home to strong radical and leftist minority subcultures, which the Nazis nearly totally erased. Presently a depoliticized and consumerist "Scene," as the Germans say, is in an area called *Kulturost*, with endless pubs, bistros, cabarets, theaters, galleries, and museums.

As the capital city of a large state, Munich has many administrative offices. However, it is also an industrial and educational/research center. BMW and Siemens are among the large firms with headquarters here. The former is located in a set of round, high-rises of glass and steel. The technical university is considered one of the best in Europe. Space, medical, and electronic research facilities employ highly skilled personnel. All these groups with high incomes demand upscale cultural services. Sports, especially soccer, with F.C. Bayern's every play endlessly debated by the addicted fans of their "national" team, have popular support. Thousands of amateur sports clubs as well as the semiamateur spectacle of the 1972 Olympics attest to the fascination with sports and health. The stadium built for the Olympics, with a canti-levered roof hung over the field, has been much copied.

A ring outlines the center of the city where the medieval defensive walls ran. Though the walls were removed in the nineteenth century, the circular street pattern remains. It contains the identifiable double onion towers of the *Frauenkirche* near the *Marienplatz* with its neo-Gothic new city hall. The very large *Residenz*, or Wittelsbach palace, is to the north. Adjacent to the palace is the formal court garden, which abuts the rolling English Garden, one of Europe's largest urban parks.

Two exceptional sites outside the old city center are the *Deutsches Museum* of Technology on an island in the Isar River to the southeast and the collection of museums and galleries at the *Königsplatz*. The first is a showpiece of German inven-tiveness. This scientific center provides opportunities to learn about humans' abilities to move and to create, from early nineteenth century bicycles to locomotives, from Werner Siemens' electric dynamos to Otto Lilienthal's gliders. Conceived in 1903, it now houses some hundred thousand objects. By 2005 a set of re-created 1905 streets will depict the history of urban transport. A branch of the museum located at the city's international airport (Franz Josef Strauss) demonstrates the history of flight. Two private collections complement these displays. In a circular museum built as a spiral, BMW offers a look at all its motorcycle and car models. By contrast, Siemens encourages visitors to its electronics museum to experience old and new instruments and technological developments by hands-on activities.

Northwest of the city center is a series of galleries and museums on or near the *Königsplatz*. The *Alte Pinakothek* contains one of the world's best collections of medieval and Renaissance masters. The *Neue Pinakothek* holds nineteenth-century masterpieces, which go far beyond regional art. The *Pinakothek der Moderne* for twentieth-century art will complete the complex. Especially strong in Blaue Reiter holdings but also Franz Stück's erotic works in the *Lenbach-Haus*. These vast collec-tions make Munich a special cultural city.

Nuremberg (population 500,000) is a large industrial city with a central area surrounded by a nearly complete late medieval defensive wall. Enclosed within it is a fortress at one corner and the old town with many half-timbered houses. Along its ramparts are watchtowers and gates. Among the houses is that of Albrecht Dürer, the artist who superbly controlled his sketched and painted lines. Every hair on a rabbit or a beard seems real. Among his contemporaries was the poet and singer Hans Sachs, who helped foster Protestantism. However, the city is perhaps more identified with the annual Nazi Party congresses (from 1923 with interruptions to 1939), which were huge gatherings of up to half a million marchers. In 1935 the race laws, excluding Jews and others from German citizenship, were announced here. After World War II, the International Military Tribunals to expose and to exorcise Nazism were held here.

Before and during Dürer's era, Nuremberg was one of Europe's commercial crossroads and home of craft skills such as goldsmithing. It declined due to dynastic conflicts and warfare, especially the Thirty Years' War. Industrialization and the railways revived its economic fortunes. From the 1890s to the 1920s machine building expanded its workforce. Now it continues as an industrial and service center for the immediate region as well as seeking to develop electronic high technology for international markets.

Nuremberg's market square, with its wishing well in front of the *Frauenkirche*, provides an appropriate setting for the traditional Christmas market. The church's decorated gables fit with a square that becomes covered with stands serving mulled wine *(gluhwein)*, honey cakes *(lebkuchen)*, and sausage *(bratwurst)*. Every day many people come to watch the sixteenth-century clock, which opens to allow moving figures to appear and disappear at the stroke of 12:00. The city is also home to the clock with seven electors moving around the Kaiser. Among its special places is the *Germanische Nationalmuseum*, which displays medieval masterpieces, including Dürer works, toys, and antiques. Many foods and customs are described, including explanations of how they became part of German traditions.

Nuremberg's second main church *(Lorenzkirche)* contains finely carved altars in wood and in stone by Veit Stoss. In front is a fountain with ornate ironwork. Little dippers can be moved up and down and frequently result in many fun water splashings for those standing closely.

Fürth (population 109,000) is the site of the first German railway, which ran six kilometers from Fürth to just east in adjacent Nuremberg in 1835. Industries produced steam engines and glass in the nineteenth century. After 1945 the catalogue order firm Quelle and the radio company Grundig operated from this central base. Many patrician houses from the seventeenth and eighteenth centuries remain as does a twelfth-century Gothic church that has been extensively rebuilt.

Erlangen (population 103,000) is a university city with 30,000 students. The university, whose offices are located in a baroque palace, once the secondary residence of the counts of Brandenburg-Bayreuth, is closely allied with the local electronics industry. The so-called new city was built to house Protestant refugees from France and the Rhineland in the late seventeenth century. Just north of Nuremberg on the Regnitz River, Erlangen is part of an urban region of nearly a million people.

Augsburg (population 260,000) is associated with the rich Renaissance banking family, the Fuggers, who left such charities as a well-kept retirement home, the -*Fuggerei*. Perhaps the oldest subsidized housing by a private foundation, it accommodates those who fell into poverty by fate (rather than by drinking or gambling). The *Rathaus* square is dominated by the *Perlachturm*, or tower, with a functioning *glockenspiel* (chimes with figures) clock and the *Rathaus* itself. A very large Renaissance building, it has an opulent reception hall and ballroom *(Goldener Saal)*. The cathedral *(Dom)* escaped the bombing that destroyed half the industrial city. It contains original stained glass windows as well as altars painted by Hans Holbein. Masters of the baroque have their own gallery. Augsburg is rich in small museums: One is dedicated to Bertolt Brecht (his birthplace), another to well-displayed Roman artifacts, and one to earlier Jewish life and culture in an art nouveau synagogue.

Würzburg (population 130,000), with its many church spires and red roofs, is set beneath hills covered with vineyards that provide special wine, *Frankenwein.* A fortress and church are perched on a steep hill above the city. Some rougher areas on the edge of the city are overrun with concrete and advertising. They contrast with the central area, especially the renowned palace. The rich bishop who built it imported painters and sculptors from Italy to make his opulent palace the foremost among northern resident and diplomatic centers. Sweeping double staircases lead to large plastered rooms with figures emerging from the walls. One ceiling, for example, has the four then-known continents represented by women who surround a love scene. The palace was designed by Balthasar Neumann with frescos by G. B. Tiepolo and has attained a UNESCO world heritage designation. This remains a delightful small city with large parks and much green around its retirement homes.

Regensburg (population 125,000) was established in Roman times to help defend the Danube River. It prospered as an administrative (Imperial diets or *Reichstage*) and trading center before the Thirty Years' War. In World War II the *Altstadt* escaped bombing, so its meandering streets and stone bridges remind visitors of medieval times. Fine patrician Renaissance houses complement the scene. The old *Rathaus* contains a museum on Imperial meetings as well as a torture dungeon. Painter Albrecht Altdorfer and astronomer Johannes Kepler represent the strength of Renaissance prosperity transformed into culture and knowledge. A museum dedicated to Kepler is one among many. They include the carriage collection at the palace of the rich counts of Thurn and Taxis who made a huge fortune from their postal system. Others are the diocese museum, the city museum, and the East German collection, supposedly relating to post–World War II refugee homelands but including prewar paintings.

Ingolstadt (population 112, 000) is another walled city, home of the beer purity law of 1516, which eventually applied to all Germany and is now defended as the norm within the European Union. A walled medieval center *(Altstadt)* has been restored. In the eighteenth century the city became a military stronghold for central Bavaria, and some of its notable buildings as well as museums relate to that past. The Bavarian army museum is one of the largest. Quite different is the *Museum für Konkrete Kunst*, an offshoot of the Bauhaus, demonstrating industrial design. The university founded in 1472 is falsely identified with the fictional Frankenstein as its most illustrative graduate.

ATTRACTIONS

Many Bavarian cities were at some time the residential or administrative cities of rich bishops, local counts, or entrepreneurs. Hence, they boast countless palaces, charitable foundations, monasteries, and churches. Since these cities mostly remained small and nonindustrial, few suffered bombing in World War II. The many major centers that were bombed—some, such as Würzburg, so badly that moving the city was considered—have been restored.

Figure 2.4
Half-timbered early-nineteenth-century architecture, Bamberg, Bavaria.

Source Courtesy of the author.

The past is ever present in Bavaria, perhaps more so than in many other rural areas, villages, and smaller cities of Germany. Yet, an outside observer must ask to what extent has the prosperity of the late twentieth century brought indoor toilets and flowers to the Heidilike landscape of rural poverty and harsh living conditions? Many Lower Bavarian towns and villages proudly display exterior wall paintings with religious or local themes, but few people acknowledge their recent origins.

Much of the past, however, has been preserved in keeping with the respect for ancient buildings. For example, Bamberg has one of the most complete old city centers with half-timbered buildings. Some, such as the old *Rathaus* with exterior paintings, straddle the river. Off to one side, the huge Gothic cathedral dominates a hilltop. It contains the medieval "rider" whose lines appear to be so simple and clean that they approach an abstract modern form, in contrast to the detailed Veit Stoss carved altar.

This imperial and bishop's city is spread along the edges of the Regnitz River. A building on its banks contains the city archive, which displays special exhibitions. Frequently they relate to the witch persecutions, which accompanied the religious wars and reached their height in the early seventeenth century. Much of the city has been rebuilt and, aside from the small old section, is not very homogeneous. Yet, its old central city *(Altstadt)* has achieved a UNESCO heritage designation.

Bayreuth, known for the Wagnerian opera house, continues the tradition of staging Richard Wagner's massive productions. From the Imperial era through the

Figure 2.5
Slate-roofed housing, Bamberg, Bavaria.

Source Courtesy of the author.

Nazi era until recently, members of the Wagner family controlled the Bayreuth festivals. Long before the Wagner mania, encouraged and paid for by the Wittelsbach royal family, the residence city had a large palace and fine gardens as well as an opera house. The city still has extensive green space, though industry has eaten into the tranquility and the automobile is destroying some villa suburbs.

The subregions of Bavaria remain significant as tourist attractions. For example, the Franconian Swiss area offers a partly forested, hilly landscape of castles, caves, and small villages. Marked paths interconnect for hiking and opportunities for paddling, canoeing, and kayaking abound. Villages still practice communal baking and offer many festivals with folk singing and local rituals. Among the festivals are *Kurbisfest* (pumpkin fete), a harvest festival held on the first Sunday of October. At Prezfeld a huge *Kerberbaum* (tree) is set up by group effort accompanied by yodeling. At such times local dress *(Trachten)* and customs unify generations of a whole village and assure that traditions will continue.

The Franconian region varies within itself. At Iglostein castle ruins overlook a picturesque town. Local breweries such as at Papenstein insist on using hops from the area. Much folk singing extols the area: "we love our Franconian Swiss land." Local fruit, especially cherries and plums, are pressed and distilled in traditional ways, while the "blooming world" folk tune is sung. The poet Roland Tieck romanticized and the local poet Fritz Heuss extolled this landscape of water mills, castles, and caves.

The Alps have a special attractiveness as the highest points in the country, and they provide two significant opportunities: hiking with spectacular views and sites for winter sports. One of the main tourist attractions in the Alps remains the Romantic complex of buildings created by Ludwig II. He used the mountains as a background for castles such as *Neuschwanstein*. This remains the foremost nineteenth-century embodiment of medieval mythology in stone. Towering above deep mountain valleys, yet overlooking the undulating plains, *Neuschwanstein* propelled a medieval revival through Richard Wagner's operas. His lavish and long works, staged in the castle, employed mythologized medieval singing contests. The building of castles or rebuilding of medieval-style castles had started with the crown prince Maximilian, who in the 1830s had *Hohenschwangau* rebuilt from ruins.

Ludwig II built more modest and refined Wittelsbach palaces at Linderhof and Chiemsee. Others, such as *Hohe Schloss* at Füssen, appear in a more medieval setting, in a town with half-timbered buildings and a specially decorated church. The church, with its fan window, sits in a village of red roofs where the Lech River breaks out of the Alps.

Along the German Alpine Road one finds more than castles and palaces since the area originally developed through monasteries. One would have difficulty deciding which is the most representative church, that at Nesswang, at Seeger, at Speiden, or maybe Pforten-Berg? All have eighteenth-century Italian interiors with lines and images that contrast with the high towers of the simple exteriors. The cities of Kempten, Wanger, or Buxheim have similar churches and cloisters.

Among the multitude of beautiful cloisters with their churches and grounds, *Ottobeuren* stands out for its architecture. Spacious gardens, Romanesque archways, baroque church, decorated library, and Kaiser hall are in pristine, painted condition. Over 1,200 years old, the Benedictine abbey became a site of knowledge as well as an economic power. At the libraries of such cloisters much of the medieval heritage of church music developed. The monasteries helped preserve this rich cultural heritage, including the more secular *Carmina Burana* (songs from Beuren) at Benediktbeuren.

The medieval town of Nördlingen is very photogenic and appears in nearly every urban history book. It is the medieval round town par excellence. Today one can still walk around it in an hour. City halls with elaborately decorated gable ends occur frequently in Bavaria. Two of the most notable are at Amberg and Merkendorf.

In addition to the Mosel and Rhine valleys, the Bergstrasse (south from Darmstadt), and the Apline Road, the Romantic Road is among the traditional tourist routes in southwestern Germany. It received its official designation in 1950. It runs from the Main River valley to the Alps. Mostly it traverses Bavaria but does go into Baden-Württemberg. From Würzburg in the north to Füssen in the south, it goes through Bad Mergentheim (spa), Weikersheim (market and palace with knight's hall), Creglingen (chapel with carvings by Tilman Riemenschneider), to the walled city of Rothenburg. From Rothenburg it heads to Feuchwangen (altar by Michael Wolgemut and Franconian folklore museum), Dinkelsbühl (annual children's festival in medieval setting, Renaissance half-timbered houses), Nördlingen (round city), Harburg castle and Kaisheim (Cistercian abbey), to Donauwörth. Then the route follows the Lech River valley past Augsburg, Landsberg, and Ludwig II's castles (*Hohenschwangau* and *Neuschwanstein*). The Romantic Road combines much medieval, religious, and cultural heritage with pretty countryside, ending at the nineteenth-century mythological versions of medieval castles.

Perhaps the most typical Bavarian city for outsiders is Rothenburg ob der Tauber. The high stone, medieval wall that runs around the whole city, with its many large gates, is almost intact. Billboard advertising is forbidden. The Renaissance patrician houses and the half-timbered structures inside the walls transport the visitor to another time. The religious inspiration of that time, expressed in the linden wood altars carved by Tilman Riemenschneider, is perhaps lost on the visitors. They seem to prefer to hear how the mayor drank five liters of beer in one gulp to save the town from looting and destruction during the Thirty Years' War. A special museum is the *Kriminalmuseum*, with collections about crime, torture, and punishments, as well as the social history of robbery, theft, and deviance.

Bavaria does not lack the half-timbered towns so prevalent elsewhere. Miltenberg has many with bent or rounded designs. Bamberg, Nuremberg, and Rothenburg all

Figure 2.6
Half-timbered town hall, Staffelstein, Bavaria.

Source Courtesy of the author.

have their own patterns. But special is the tiered set of half-timbered houses in Memmingen. Its seven-roof house is the most famous. The tiered finance building and the *Rathaus* (city hall) on the market square are next to similar half-timbered structures. Others can be found in towns such as Staffelstein. A more simple style is evident in the peasant cottages, some of which have been brought together as a *Bauernhofmuseum* (farmyard museum) at Illerbeuren. Half-timbered houses, sheds, and stables from the sixteenth to the nineteenth centuries are on display, along with gardens and sheds.

Special to Bavaria are the painted exteriors, most with religious themes, on the buildings in the towns of the south. Whether in Garmisch-Partenkirchen or in Obergammergau but especially in the villages, the eye encounters a profusion of color and forms.

In great contrast to the religious piety of the Catholic Church, is its history as a repressive instrument of the lords and as a controller of large territories. An under-class of robbers and social bandits emerged that have been immortalized in Roman-tic lore but reflected a harsh reality. The robber museum at the *Bauernhofmuseum* (farmyard museum) Jexdorf at Fürstenfeldbruck examines the many sides of this question. Placards and documents depict the disciplining role of the church, as well as including examples of priests who sided with poor parishioners. The earlier revolts of peasants who staged a series of uprisings against tithes and feudal burdens from the 1490s to the 1520s were brutally repressed with the blessings of the churches. A plaque, for example, at the Würzburg fortress *Marienberg* acknowledges these social disasters in which thousands of peasants were brought to summary injustice, legit-imized by church officials.

CULTURAL ATTRIBUTES
——————— AND CONTRIBUTIONS ———————

VISUAL ARTS

From the many medieval altar painters to the stone carvers of the medieval cathe-drals to the abstracts of Paul Klee and Wassily Kandinsky is a long way, but all are part of Bavarian cultural heritage. Veit Stoss, Peter Vischer, Tilman Riemenschneider, and Erasmus Grasser are among the best-known sculptors. Similarly, little connects the etchings and portraits of Albrecht Dürer, Matthias Grünewald, or Lucas Cranach with the Provo-proT (provocative theatre) of Alexij Sager, who calls himself an action artist. Bavarian galleries, especially the ones in Munich, contain representatives of all international, German, and local styles.

The cloisters and churches are highly decorated. Johann Schmutzer and Cosmas Asam are among the many stucco and ceiling experts of the seventeenth and eigh-teenth centuries. Architects who mostly made reputations working on churches include Dominikus Zimmermann *(Wieskirche)*, Bathasar Neumann (Würzburg palace, *Vierzehnheiligen*), Johann Fischer *(St. Michael, Munich)*, and François de Cuvilliés (Munich court builder).

The Bavarian school of painting began in the mid-nineteenth century and challenged traditional academic motifs. Especially noteworthy are the works of Hans von Marees, Wilhelm Leibl, Anselm Feuerbacher, and Arnold Böcklin. Earlier, Wilhelm von Kobell and Moritz von Schwind were part of the Munich School and the Romantic movement. Also identified with Munich were Wilhelm Trübner and Karl Schacht. Part of the impressionist and postimpressionist modern movement centered at Munich (Franz von Lehmbach) and by the beginning of the twentieth century had become home to the most radical departures at the artist colony of Murnau (Kandinsky, Gabriele Münter, Franz Marc).

In the twentieth century Rainer Fassbinder (1945–1982) created an almost endless series of films about postwar Germany. As part of the New German Cinema, the acceptance of his provocative works in Munich demonstrated how modern the city had become by the 1960s. It also reflected the emergence of a film and television production system after World War II.

LITERATURE

Many well-known writers have been based or passed part of their time in areas of Bavaria. Hans Sachs (1494–1576) of Nuremburg is in every literary textbook. Jean Paul (1763–1825), the poet, sometimes used local themes or settings. Hans Thoma (1839–1924) offered local color in his stories about simple peasants, but sometimes his work takes on a racist element. By contrast, his contemporary, Frank Wedekind (1864–1918), made a reputation shocking the bourgeoisie with plays about female sensuality and homosexuality, such as *Lulu* and *Spring Awakening*. Karl Valentin's (1882–1948) sharp wit fit more with Munich than with its hinterland. Patrick Süskind (1949–) achieved international fame with his rich descriptive writings about simple themes, such as perfume, pigeons, or double bass.

MUSIC

Can anyone get away from Richard Wagner (1813–1883) and his sometimes-bombastic operas when mentioning Bavarian music? More refined is the work of Johann Pachelbel and Franz Liszt. Few outsiders would know Bavaria's national anthem was composed by Konrad Kunz in the mid-nineteenth century. What of the choral music, which came from the cloisters? Certainly church and folk music are very prevalent with local choirs and singing associations. For instance, at village festivities in the Franconian Swiss area, yodeling and local refrains accompany setting up fertility trees. The refrains of "In Munich stands a Hofbrauhaus . . . where many a jug went down . . ." may be offered mainly to tourists, but regional television shows also seem to succeed with the old standbys. Yet, modern versions of folk music by such groups as the Wellküren, FSK, and Biermösl Blosn illustrate that traditions can evolve and the results accepted. Throw That Beat in the Garbage can! a popular group of youthful singers, employs Franconian charm with songs about love and everyday children's objects, such as, "You only think of me, when there's no program on TV." They also demonstrate how English is making inroads into everyday speech.

Classical music is strongly supported, and every major city has an orchestra with Munich having the greatest variety and the main opera house.

CUSTOMS AND FESTIVALS

Wearing traditional clothes is not restricted to special events, since green-gray clothes trimmed with red appear everywhere. But local costumes *(Trachten)* are generally reserved for festivals, and those occur everywhere during the summer. Bands, processions, and street decorations are normal on festival days. Any excuse, from defeating the Swedes to racing oxen, will do. One authority has counted 3,913 festivals. Some, such as the Hofer film festival and the Donaueschding music days, like the Renaissance days at Neuburg on the Donau, are fairly recent inventions. So is the best known. Munich's Oktoberfest started in 1812 and has become the biggest two-week celebration in the world with about 20 beer tents and more than a million beer-swilling and dancing participants. In Bavaria, generally, folk singing, dancing, and music remain vibrant. Local dialects are cultivated in the subregions. A somewhat different type of celebration is in the Spessart, in the northwest. People dress up in rough clothes, with pointed hats and fake beards. They sing the folksong "in the forest are the robbers, the robbers . . ." with reference to a time when poaching and thieving were necessary to survive because the lords had cut off access to ponds and forests.

To experience Bavarian public celebrations, one needs to go to the villages during religious celebrations such as Easter. The Obergammergau Passion Play is the largest, with processions and crucifixion. Even though it is not the only event of its kind, it is still special. At least 4,000 villages have Good Friday processions, solemn, dignified affairs led by robed priests with symbolic crosses. A special procession at Chiemsee takes place on Corpus Christi. Streets are strewn with hay and trimmed with flowers. Boats are decorated and these move from altar to altar at the water's edge. By contrast, colored Easter eggs hanging on trees or bushes have revived a pagan fertility festival. The Bavarian tradition of "windowing" is also sometimes related to fertility. A young man serenades or talks to a beloved through a window and sometimes is allowed to climb a ladder and stay with her for the night. Windowing at more than one window has its consequences.

Every four years most of the Lower Bavarian town of Landshut re-creates the 1485 marriage of George the Rich with a Polish princess. The site is fitting with the medieval background of a small city that has an Italianate palace. The setting is strikingly picturesque with a massive castle on a high hill in the town's center.

LEISURE AND SPORTS

Some Bavarians, especially coaches, assert that soccer is the essence of Bavarian life. FC (football club) Bayern Munich has won the German title more than any other team. Its star player, Franz Beckenbauer, led them to league, European, and world championships. In a new role he is organizing the next World Cup, which will be held in Munich during 2006 in a flexible and translucent-shell stadium.

Hiking is a much-loved activity, especially in the Alps. Marked paths *(Wanderwege)* traverse the state. Each region seeks to draw tourists to its landscape. Some market special church visits with spas; for example, the baroque opulence of *Vierzehnheiligen* at Kloster Benz is often combined with warm-water treatment. Here one can loosen the muscles stretched taut during the hikes through forests and around small lakes (sometimes homemade fishing ponds) to the remains of some cloister, church, or village. The country's largest nature preserve, *Naturpark Ahltmuehl*, is on the river of the same name. It offers trails for cyclists and horse riders as well as hikers.

CIVICS AND REMEMBRANCE

The Bavarian state proved slow to deal with its Nazi past. However, at present, its office for political education provides information on concentration camps such as Dachau outside Munich. That had long been a site of remembrance, but only in the 1980s did it receive sufficient support for a large educational program of seminars and publications. By contrast, information and publications regarding the history of the Free State of Bavaria and about federalism have been strongly supported themes since the 1960s. The history of Bavaria usually emphasizes its struggle to remain independent (of Austria, of Prussia, of central interference) as well as local and regional traditions, history, and culture.

Perhaps the initial reluctance to deal with the Hitler regime was due to the Nazi party's origins in Bavaria. Instead, much emphasis was placed on Catholic suffering and resistance. In recent times, a more balanced account has been provided, partly through the results of oral history projects. Though the formidable and innovative research of the Institute for Contemporary History in Munich started to influence the academic world in the 1960s, the historical insights and findings were only popularized later.

Landeskunde studies (a combination of geography, history, and customs) have always been strong in Bavaria. Sometimes almost propagandistic but mostly very informative materials are provided to the public by the state offices, with the office for political education directly under the prime minister. If one compares the handbooks offered to schools and libraries in the 1960s to the historical studies presented during the 1990s, the increased sophistication, a plurality of views, and continued insistence on Bavarian difference, are notable. The idea that Bavaria served an historic "*Mittlerfunktion*," utilizing its location in the "center of Europe," is underscored.

CUISINE

Due to Oktoberfest, with its huge one-liter beer steins, some foreigners think that beer is the staple Bavarian food. As everywhere in Germany, beer is lightly taxed because it is considered a nutrient (locals refer to it as liquid bread). Bavarians are proud of the many varieties and tend to drink specialty brews (Kulmbach dark, Augustiner), including wheat-based beers or oddities such as smoked beer from

Bamberg. Bavarian beer is mostly lighter and sweeter than northern beers because fewer hops are used. Wine has been replacing beer as the evening drink, however, especially among the middle classes, though in some areas, such as Franconia, wine has competed with beer as the traditional drink since Roman times.

As expected for a large region with diverse terrain, food is quite varied. Traditional dishes can be found both in restaurants and at home, especially in the rural areas. Munich, with *weisswurst* (white sausage), made from veal and calves' brains, and Nuremberg, with its thin *bratwurst*, illustrate that sausage comes in as many varieties as bread and beer. *Leberkäs* is a liver paste that is cooked in large batches. It is to be eaten hot and is usually sold at market booths. A traditional meal in Bavaria might include a soup such as oxtail, a pork roast accompanied by potato dumplings, and cabbage with bacon, white wine, and apple slices. Today, lighter and fast food is common, influenced by foreign workers who popularized pizza and fries.

Gourmet food is becoming more popular. Those who record the assignment of Michelin stars to restaurants note the increased number in Bavaria. Food tends to be more natural because of fresh, local ingredients. Bavarians think urban northerners, like those in cosmopolitan Hamburg, have false airs about their food.

Ox Tail Soup *(Oxenschwanzsuppe)*

Sauté 2 pounds of ox tail or 2 veal tails with 1/2 cup sliced onions in oil or butter. Put in large pot with 6 cups water and pinch of salt, bring to boil, and simmer for 2 hours. Add 1/4 cup diced parsley, 1/2 cup diced carrots, 1/2 cup diced celery, a bay leaf, 1/8 cup herbs de Provence (thyme, marjoram, and basil), as well as some peppercorns. Strain this stock, saving meat, chill, and take off fat. Reheat stock adding meat and seasoning. Add 1/2 cup dry sherry just before serving.

Bavarian Pork Roast

Pork should be deboned to about 3 pounds

1 tablespoon pepper	2 tablespoons of caraway seeds
5 tablespoons butter	1 tablespoon of marjoram
2 cups onions, diced	1/2 cup water
8 cloves of garlic, sliced fine	

Preheat oven to 350°F. Slice roast into 6 to 8 pieces and pepper both sides. Melt butter into large roasting pan, put meat in pan and cover with other ingredients and bake for about 2 hours. Turn meat over and bake for another hour, adding water if necessary.

Chapter 3

Berlin

SPECIAL ASPECTS

Berlin is known for caustic-tongued people, rich cultural choices, and spectacular public and private buildings. A green and expansive city, Berlin is filled with history. There are many memorials to the suffering of the 1930s and 1940s. The post-1990 Reunification capital seeks to acknowledge the past and build a sparkling new future, but it remains heavily dependent upon subsidies from the country it represents.

REGIONAL TRAITS

Berlin, population 3.5 million and 889 square kilometers, is the largest city in Germany and the country's capital since 1990, as it had been from 1871 to 1945. The city-state is located within the state of Brandenburg on the rivers Spree and Havel approximately 120 kilometers from the sea. Very wide and long, straight streets, some dating back to the eighteenth century, provide major traffic arteries as well as an atmosphere of physical openness. A well-organized transportation system of two major airports, light rail system, subway, and expressways leading into and circling the city helps to move people into and around an expansive urban complex. Some high-technology industries, administrative services, and industrial plants provide employment, with the western sections more prosperous than the east. Berlin is home to Germany's largest single concentration of industries: tool-and-dye making, electrical components, and chemicals, such as pharmaceuticals and fertilizers. However, since 1990 a process of de-industrialization, especially in the east, has been under way, and only one major firm, Schering, has headquarters here. One analyst

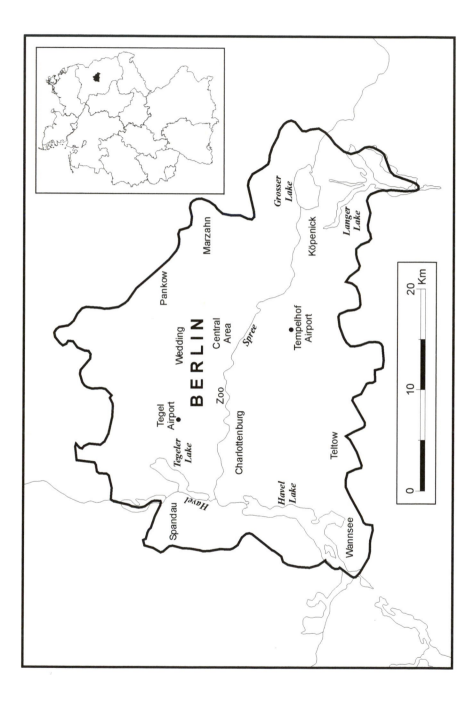

noted that the era when Berlin was an industrial, banking, insurance, service, and newspaper metropolis is past and unlikely to recur. The decline of federal subsidies has saddled the city with huge debts and made it difficult for Berlin's industries to compete in Western markets. This situation has been only partly balanced by the increase in administrative employment. Other parts of the country resent its opulence and competition for funds.

Berlin is a cultural city with more museums, theaters, galleries, and bistros than most urban centers. Some spectacular buildings were erected after World War II, especially since the fall of the Berlin Wall in 1989 and the redesignation of Berlin as Germany's capital. The city has numerous historic buildings, mostly from the pre-World War I Imperial era, but some palaces and churches go back beyond the eighteenth century. Most had to be restored, or reconstructed due to wartime bombing, and some still show the effects of the city's tumultuous history. Whether the architectural and cultural abundance will draw enough tourists to support the hotels and infrastructure costs remains an open question. The city's debt stands at 50 billion Euros and is accelerating, while its economic growth has been in decline and unemployment is nearly 20 percent. Many people live in poverty, despite the fact that the state spends far more money per person on housing, city building, police, family support, interest payments, culture, and universities than other cities. Despite receiving a third of all federal transfer funds, Berlin has not reduced its administrative costs.

The city is shaped like a slightly rightward-tilted triangle with a base of approximately 45 kilometers and a height of 40 kilometers. The west side is defined by the Havel River and its lakes running northward, while the Spree runs west-northwest, cutting the triangle almost in half. The flag and coat of arms show a bear on a shield topped by a crown to symbolize the city's strength and relationship to its Saxon and later Prussian rulers. The city contains 12 districts, previously 16, based on earlier villages and parishes, which merged in 1920. Some residents identify with their own district as much as with the larger city. Some districts, such as Kreuzberg and Köpenick, have their own special characteristics. Much of the large Turkish population lives in the former; the latter retains a rural atmosphere. Despite their rough appearance, parts of Kreuzberg and Prenzlauer Berg have become popular areas for bistros and the youth "scene" or "in" places to be while the western suburbs of Wilmersdorf, Charlottenburg, and Grunewald remain desirable residential areas.

GEOGRAPHIC FEATURES

Low plains and sandy soils on the edge of the Spree River originally led to the development of two fishing towns at a trade crossroads. The city has spilled over the flat countryside. The largest hill, *Teufelsberg*, is a mound created from wartime rubble. Surprisingly green, the city-state includes many large lakes, forests, zoos, and parks, as well as the urban center with its historic buildings. One-third of the territory is undeveloped, while the many canals and waterways are crossed by over 200 bridges.

Local Berliners, or those pretending to fulfill the local stereotype, are known for their cheekiness, frankness, and toughness. The oft-heard phrase, "Berlin, despite all, remains Berlin," attests to local loyalty and survival traits. Another, "I have a suitcase in Berlin," signifies the desire of emigrants or visitors to return. Past and present visitors repeatedly comment on the city's dynamism and restlessness. The city has always drawn foreigners. In the fifteenth century Jews began a love-hate relationship that has lasted to the present. Each century brought a new group: in the sixteenth century Dutch traders, in the seventeenth century persecuted Huguenots from France, in the eighteenth century enterprising Scots and Polish aristocrats, in the nineteenth century Polish laborers. In the 1920s many Russian émigrés arrived; during World War II slave laborers, mostly from eastern Europe, populated the factories. After the 1950s, many ethnic groups from southern Europe did menial work, but some also engaged in commerce. At present, nearly 12 percent of Berlin's population is of foreign extraction; Turks (120,000), former Yugoslavians (80,000), Poles (50,000), Russians, Greeks, and Italians predominate. A vibrant and growing Jewish community has been reestablished. By the 1980s, Germany's liberal asylum laws brought diverse refugees from every trouble point on the globe, especially Asia and the Middle East. This ethnic mixing and the constant migration of "Germans" from eastern areas, where many had settled in what was once considered German territory or cultural homelands—Silesia, Sudetenland, parts of Russia, Romania, and especially Poland—makes it difficult to say who now is a Berliner and what their unique traits are. However, the local dialect with harsh *ick* for *ich* (I), or *j-hut* for *gut* (good), announces the authentic article (even if only here a generation or two).

A hallmark of the last century of Berliners' experience is ideological conflict. The working-class movement achieved great strength during the Imperial era, despite the militarism of the Brandenburg-Prussian state. Social Democracy (SPD) became the largest political party with a majority of voters before 1914. However, that movement split during World War I, and Communism challenged Social Democracy in the 1920s. Both of the labor parties were destroyed by the racist Nazis in 1933. After World War II the Communists ruled with Soviet support in the East, while Social Democracy dominated the Western parliament. Mayors such as Ernst Reuter and Willy Brandt made West Berlin into a Social Democratic stronghold. Additionally, it became a symbol of freedom when supplies were airlifted during the 1948 to 1949 Soviet blockade and once the Berlin Wall divided East from West after 1961.

By the 1980s the Christian Democrats and the Greens challenged and changed the political pattern in the West. After Reunification, the Christian Democrats received the most electoral support, but scandals undercut their lead and the Social Democrats have pulled even with them. For one term at the end of the 1990s, a coalition of the CDU and SPD ran the city. The continuing strength of the Social Democrats and the Party of Democratic Socialism (PDS; liberalized Communists) and the increasing number of Greens made creating coalitions difficult. At present a SPD/PDS coalition under Klaus Wowereit of the SPD is seeking to address the city's problems, but party scandals have not helped credibility.

The city has repeatedly had charismatic and capable leaders—Ernst Reuter and Willy Brandt of the SPD to Richard von Weizsäcker and Eberhard Diepgen of the CDU. Some have moved from Berlin to important national offices.

HISTORY

The city's founding can be dated back to the thirteenth century. Berlin, east of the Spree, and the other village, Cölln, on the west, date back to 1244 and 1237, respectively. They were federated in 1307 but functioned in parallel until 1709. By then Berlin had become an administrative and military center. Both sides quickly began their expansion into the surrounding countryside. During the fourteenth and fifteenth centuries Berlin participated in the Hanseatic League of north European trading cities. In the fifteenth century the city's fate became tied to that of the Hohenzollern dynasty, which ruled surrounding Brandenburg and Prussia. The Hohenzollerns built immense fortresses, residences, and palaces in Berlin or in nearby Spandau and Potsdam, and Berlin became a court, administrative, and military center.

At the beginning of the nineteenth century, Berlin was a moderate-sized city with 200,000 people engaged in small manufacturing, trade, state service, and military functions. Industrialization expanded the city's boundaries greatly during the mid- and late-nineteenth century. Its population increased to over 900,000 by 1871 and to almost 2 million in 1890. The spectacular population increase can be seen in Wilmersdorf, a suburb that in 1890 had 5,000 inhabitants but by 1910 had 110,000. By 1910 there were 3.7 million people within the greater Berlin area.

In 1881 Berlin became a city-state separate from Brandenburg and developed modern sewage, electrical, and traffic systems. The huge apartment blocks known as "rental barracks" pockmarked the suburbs, where factories extended over large areas. For example: Siemens-Stadt, or Siemens-city, covered many blocks. Borsig's locomotive and German General Electric Company (AEG) factories hinted at feudal work relations by having castle gates as main entrances. The AEG, soon to be Germany's and eventually one of the world's largest electrical-component producers, later hired the modernist Peter Behrens to design glass and steel buildings along simple lines. Berlin led Germany in the new chemical and electrical industries, exemplified by Siemens' growth from a small telegraph company in 1847 to an international electricity giant by the 1890s. The city's planners quickly applied these new technologies to street lighting and transport, for example, electric trams in 1883 and an underground by 1902.

World War I impacted Berlin in two ways. The vibrant cultural life expanded, causing even more scandal and furor in the 1920s than in response to the modernist movement after 1890. At the turn of the century the autocratic and erratic Kaiser Wilhelm II still tried to determine art tastes, despite museum and gallery directors who sought to attain an international reputation with collections representing all European cultural trends. In the 1920s, experimental films, circuses, boxing and bicycle matches, cabarets, and very political art, such as Dada, proliferated. The middle class and conservatives denounced much of it as decadent. Weimar culture in Berlin became almost a code word for modern art, architecture, semi-pornographic nightclubs, and politicized theater. Its brilliant scientific research—including that of Robert Koch and Albert Einstein—and literary abundance won Germany more Nobel Prizes than any other country. Except for sports, the Third

Reich terminated this renaissance of experimentation and imposed stifling conformity and censorship.

In 1920, the addition of outlying villages and suburbs, such as Dahlem and Spandau, brought together 4 million people into greater Berlin. That created the present topographical configuration of the city. After 1929 the world economic depression caused massive unemployment; 600,000 persons out of work by 1932 brought a reversal of material wealth. The unemployed resorted to bicycles instead of trams and tent cities on the lakes to avoid rents. Conflicts among the main political rivals—Social Democrats, Communists, and Nazis—led to riots, even deaths. After January 1933, under their local district leader Joseph Goebbels, the Nazis destroyed their ideological opponents' organizations and drove their leaders into jail, exile, or death. For instance, in June 1933 the SA (Sturm Abteilung; storm troops) murdered hundreds in what became known as *Köpenick*, or "blood" week.

Adolf Hitler's regime ended the independent administration of the city and rebuilt parts of the city center. Berlin was to be more than the capital of a revived Germany; it was to be a showpiece for a New Order. Rearmament helped restore prosperity. Monumental make-work projects included stadiums and government offices. The 1936 Olympic Games in Berlin drew attention to the Nazis' insistence on orderliness and organization. However, behind the parades and propaganda façades, a controlled society excluded and punished liberals, Marxists, Jews, gypsies *(Roma),* pacifists, and homosexuals. Those who had been so much a part of the special aspects of this cultural and scientific center during the pre-1933 era were repressed and exiled.

New neoclassic buildings, such as the Reich Chancellory, represented Nazi grandeur. Most of it disappeared in rubble during the Allied bombing from 1942 to 1945. More than half of Berlin's buildings became uninhabitable. The population declined to near 3 million by April 1945 when the Soviet army shelled, raped, and looted its way to the city center in revenge for Hitler's actions in Eastern Europe, especially in Poland and the Soviet Union.

After military defeat and unconditional surrender, Berliners found themselves inside Soviet-occupied eastern Germany. Starting in mid-1945, an Allied Control Council ruled a city divided into three, then four sectors. For a short while, joint rule by Britain, France, the United States, and the Soviet Union withstood the strains of the cold war. But Berlin quickly became an international focal point as each side sought to determine the city's fate. In early 1948 the Soviets withdrew from common rule, and in June the Western powers insisted that currency reform would be introduced as in their western zones. The Soviets blocked the three main land access routes to West Berlin. The Western countries responded with an airlift of coal and foodstuffs to supply 2.2 million Berliners in the western sectors. This effort turned Berlin into a symbol of freedom as opposed to one of Nazi repression. The Soviets lifted the blockade after nearly a year, but diplomatic crises continued over the status of the increasingly split city. On August 13, 1961, the East German government began to erect a wall to surround all of western Berlin. For 28 years it divided families and friends. The German Democratic Republic designated eastern Berlin the capital of its state, a title with little meaning.

Though the East Berlin rulers tore down the remnants of the Hohenzollern palace—which is slated to be rebuilt—by the 1980s they had rebuilt much of the city's historic center at *Unter den Linden* and *Alexanderplatz*. At the latter they constructed a huge television tower with modern boutiques and cafés, high-rise hotel, large department store, and meeting places with fountains and murals as on the House of Teachers. In contrast to such showcase areas, including newer ones at *Stalinallee* and *Leninplatz,* much of the East Berlin population lived in cramped housing or in prefabricated apartment blocks. Some experiments with social housing in outlying areas on both sides of the Wall ended in isolated, concrete communities. During the 1960s and 1970s West Berlin's center, especially the *Kurfurstendamm* (slang: *Kudamm*), offered a tiny area as a showcase of capitalism. In reality, the western part of the city stagnated and lived off subsidies. Some firms, such as Siemens, moved their headquarters to Munich while others, such as the drug giant Schering and the newspaper publisher Alex Springer, emphasized with new buildings that they were in Berlin to stay. Much dilapidated housing served the so-called guest workers from southern Europe. They did the labor-intensive jobs the native Berliners and young West Germans, who escaped conscription by living in West Berlin, thought beneath them. On both sides of the Wall the famed universities and technical colleges continued to draw numerous students. The Free University, created in West Berlin because the Humboldt University was under eastern control, became the seat of

Figure 3.1
Philharmony and Potsdamer Platz with Sony and federal railway office buildings, Berlin.

Source Courtesy of the author.

extensive student revolts in the 1960s. Since Reunification in 1990, Berlin has regained its status as one of Europe's preeminent centers of higher education, especially in the humanities and social sciences, with nearly 100,000 university students.

After the collapse of the Wall and Reunification, Berlin became an accessible city. However, only with its designation as the German capital has a building boom altered the whole central city. Renovation of an old infrastructure on both sides of the former Wall is still under way. Indeed, some of the most interesting developments have occurred exactly where the Wall previously stood, for example, at Potsdamer Platz. Imaginative glass buildings with plastic canopies hang over the central square hallmark, the Sony complex. Nearby a whole new set of museums and galleries has been added at the *Kulturforum,* where the New National Gallery and the Philharmonic once stood alone in modernist splendor. The *Reichstag,* the central part of which burned in a controversial fire during February 1933, has a special glass cupola with viewing platforms, which emphasizes the transparency of the new state and society. The Brandenburg Gate—through which victorious troops have marched since the late eighteenth century—has been refurbished. The Museum Island, with its numerous galleries and museums, is a United Nations historic site. Most of its buildings are being renovated or enlarged.

At the end of the twentieth century Berlin became known as the city of cranes. A complex of government buildings abutting the *Wilhelmstrasse* is transforming the old administrative center. The old oyster-shaped congress hall built by U.S. funds in 1957, which collapsed in 1981, has been rebuilt as a house of world cultures. But it appears puny beside the immense *Bundeskanzler Amt* (federal chancellory), which stretches its huge arches and glass walls as though grasping for power. From the *Reichstag* cupola one can see the extent of the new legislative as well as administrative state buildings.

The rebuilding has not changed one of the city's major traits: Berlin has many focal points—governmental near the *Reichstag* and Brandenburg Gate; commercial at the Sony complex, *Alexanderplatz, Kurfurstendamm,* and *Unter den Linden;* cultural on the Museum Island, Dahlem, and Charlottenburg. The city is very spread out, and each area has its own special elements.

Since the late eighteenth century Berlin has been rich in culture and educational institutions. Like other capital cities, it sucked the talent out of the provinces and gathered huge collections of artifacts in the name of the state or nation. By the late nineteenth century, Germany obtained antiquities from the whole world but especially from Egypt, Persia, the Pacific Islands, and Africa. Those riches are on display in the extensive gallery and museum complexes spread out around the city.

What identity emerges out of this difficult and diverse history? The wall inside people who have been socialized in different ways in East and West has replaced the Wall that physically divided people from 1961, or 1949, to 1989. West Berliners have lost some *schnautz* (caustic assertiveness) as they seek to be pluralistically modern, respectful of the past of Nazi and cold war victims but still wanting to build a showy new future. East Berliners have in some cases retreated into new niche societies of family, parish, or limited social relations tending their tiny garden allotments

Figure 3.2
Potsdamer Platz, interior of Sony complex, Berlin.

Source Courtesy of the author.

(kleingarten). The East/West divide remains very evident in the city: The buildings, the street lighting, the clothes people wear, and even the levels of street cleanliness hint at which part one is observing. Many East Berlin restaurants offer traditional German fare at lower prices with a rougher edge than those in the western parts.

The city's role as gateway to the east, due to the additional members being added to the European Union from eastern Europe, is emphasized. Sometimes much is made of the Prussian cultural heritage and the city's needs as capital. Certainly, it has become increasingly multicultural, in people and outlook; many of the new buildings emerged from the imaginations of British or American architects. Yet, whether Berlin can offer more "Big City Magic" than Hamburg or Munich is questionable. What it does have is special architecture, showcase places, and a high degree of cultural vibrancy, for those who can afford them. The extent to which those consequences of size, administrative role, and heritage touch the average Berliner must remain open, especially as state debts increase and discussions about merging with Brandenburg continue.

ATTRACTIONS

As with most large, capital cities, the historical sites and special places are almost endless. *Alexanderplatz*, known as Alex, is a crossroads where the subway, light-rail, and the railways have abutting stations. This comprises a huge square containing a circular clock showing the time for the main cities of the world and a fountain of world peace. A high-rise hotel, 365-meter television tower, department stores, and a series of new office towers are supposed to surround the square.

The 10-kilometer *Avus*, just off the *Grunewald* (green forest), served in the 1920s and 1930s as one of the main race car tracks in Europe. The main Botanical Garden, with huge glass houses and a historical museum—proclaimed the world's best by a garden expert—is in Steglitz, but parks abound near every major dynastic building, such as the Charlottenburg palace. The *Tiergarten* is more than a zoo; it is one of Europe's largest city parks and forests, the latter recovering from postwar cutting when coal supplies ran out. Another is the *Grunewald*, with winding paths and a former hunting palace serving as an art gallery. Nearby is the Olympic Stadium from the 1936 games.

Much of the area near Unter den Linden was designed by Karl Friedrich Schinkel, and his *Neue Wache* (new guard house) and museum buildings remind one of his earlier influence. The Red *Rathaus*, or red-brick and later socialist city hall; the restored St. Hedwig's cathedral modeled on the Pantheon in Rome; and the restored New Synagogue in Oranienburger Street attest to the variety of styles in the middle of Berlin. The two restored cathedrals on the *Gendarmenmarkt*, German and French, are a reminder of the influx of refugees.

Many visitors to Berlin saunter through the huge columns of the Brandenburg Gate. From it they may wander north to the renovated *Reichstag*, a building dating back to 1900 but with a recently added glass dome. A walk up an inclined circular corridor in the dome allows views of Berlin that clearly illustrate the city's multitude of distinctive buildings including the New Chancellory. Within a good walking distance through the *Tiergarten* is the *Siegessaulle* (Victory Column), commemorating the victory against France in 1871. From its circular top one can see over the president's new glass oval administration building and his official palace to the old congress hall and new chancellory.

Figure 3.3
New Chancellory, Berlin.

Source Courtesy of George Buse.

Near the *Kurfurstendamm,* the main shopping street of the former West Germany, the heavily bombed Kaiser-Wilhelm Memorial church contains some of its late-nineteenth-century mosaics. Most of the edifice has been left in ruins as a reminder of war, a monument made more notable by its new angular sections constructed out of stark glass cubes. Just to the east is the Europa-Center, with its ever-turning Mercedes symbol. Adjacent is the *Kurfurstendamm* and *Budapester Strasse* for upscale shopping opportunities and cafés seeking to re-create Berlin's earlier elegance.

The radio tower, which became operative in 1923 as a mini-Eiffel tower, is next to the large congress center in the suburb of Charlottenburg. Its metal box shape is fronted by a huge abstract sculpture. The main site in Charlottenburg is the palace, with its circular three-story teahouses across the street and huge park behind it. Like many large cities, Berlin has many interesting cemeteries *(Dorotheenstädtischer, Judischer, Hugenotten),* an International congress center, and much striking architecture as new embassies and industrial headquarters vie with each other. Earlier, especially in the postwar rebuilding, international competitions created unique quarters, such as the *Hanse Viertel,* with its colorful, international mix of apartments, and near the presidential palace, the Belvedere, a congress hall shaped like an open oyster. In architecture, as in theater, Berliners see their city as a *Weltstadt* (world city). The *Kulturforum* area with *Philharmonie* (Philharmonic) and new galleries, including the

Kunstgewebemuseum, underscores the cultural as well as architectural richness of the new. Among the old are the castles and palaces: *Schloss Bellevue*—seat of the federal president; Charlottenburg palace; Spandau citadel from the seventeenth century. The monument to fallen Soviet soldiers in Treptow is impressive if only for its size.

That Berlin has large stretches of sand beaches, as on the Wannsee, will surprise those who do not know that this vast urban center contains many lakes. Farther on its outskirts and used by Berliners for weekend excursions lie the Potsdam palaces and gardens of Frederick II (1740–1786) and his successors, especially *Sans Soucci,* with its *Orangerie, Neues Palais,* and huge parks, but also the Spree countryside.

As with most large cities, Berlin's major attraction for many is simply the variety of street scenes, including the remains of its infamous Wall and graffiti, the pubs, and choices of food and entertainment.

CUSTOMS

Many months of the year are dedicated to special cultural events, such as the *Berliner Festspiele* for theater and ballet. Each January the *Gruene Woche* (green week, the world's largest agricultural fair) seeks to make Berliners and guests aware of food-stuffs. The Six-Day (bicycle) Race continues a tradition of all-day-and-night racing, which dates back to the 1920s. Each February witnesses the international film festival; May offers more theater events and October, festival weeks; November, much jazz; and the Berlin Gay Days, or Love Parade, of June has become widely known and attended.

CULTURAL ATTRIBUTES
—————— AND CONTRIBUTIONS ——————

VISUAL ARTS

At the turn of the twentieth century, two artists captured elements of daily prewar Berlin: Heinrich Zille and Hans Baluschek. In Zille, the lower class of Imperial Berlin had a comic sketcher of daily life. Examples from this more-ironic German equivalent of Norman Rockwell are found in few galleries but in many bookshops. Baluschek tried to capture the realities of industrialization—poverty and its impact on women. Simultaneously, he presented in graphic prints the vagabonds, prostitutes, and drunks peopling the metropolis. An earlier street-scene artist, Daniel Chodowiecki, captured the variety of artisan trades and characters of the eighteenth century.

A court painter known for his historical portraits during the Imperial era, Adolph Menzel now receives fewer accolades than the outsiders of that era. Those were the Secessionists, led by the impressionist Max Liebermann, who challenged official academy styles. He had his studio in Berlin after the 1890s but often preferred such places as Amsterdam or his Wannsee villa surroundings as themes for his paintings. At Ferch, younger Secessionists created an artists' colony focusing on Havel landscapes. Simultaneously, Käthe Kollwitz (1867–1945) attained fame for her pacifist and radical prints. Both Liebermann and Kollwitz would suffer dismissal and disparagement under the Nazis.

From 1910 through the 1920s, Ernst Ludwig Kirchner brought much of the elegance of the city to his paintings, which captured the hectic lifestyle of the upper classes, including their girlie-show haunts. In the Weimar era, Otto Dix, Georg Grosz, and John Heartfield took this nouveau riche group down many pegs and exposed its hypocrisy with poignant sketches and political cartoons. The Nazis supported mostly politicized or historical and mythological art and excluded or confiscated much of what they designated "decadent" and foreign art, from the impressionists to the cubists.

The work and careers of sculptors such as Georg Kolbe and Fritz Cremer illustrate twentieth-century stylistic trends and political interventions in artistic creativity. Kolbe's *Dancer* from 1912 is a delightfully delicate and evocative piece, while his huge works from the 1930s demonstrate the demands of Nazi monumentalism. Cremer's memorials to war experience illustrate his preparedness to adapt to Nazi prerequisites and later to adjust to East German socialist realism. However, his works in honor of those who resisted or suffered under fascism deeply reflect victims' suffering, and he courageously supported East German dissidents such as Wolf Biermann.

Among noted post–World War II artists, Georg Baselitz (1938–) taught at the art academy in Berlin after some controversial exhibitions. However, more of Anselm Kiefer's (1945–) historical works, displayed at the Hamburger Bahnhof contemporary gallery, have found their appropriate home in Berlin.

LITERATURE

Alfred Döblin's *Alexanderplatz* (1929) is for some the representative Berlin novel. Döblin used the hectic life around one major square as a setting and combined it with the speech of the local underworld and unsavory characters. His story captured the difficulties of being moral in a city full of temptations and questionable people. Just as Döblin's work overlapped with the political turmoil of the Weimar era, Heinrich Mann's works had earlier reflected and challenged the Imperial regime. His socially critical novels, such as *Der Untertan* (*The Subject*, 1914) and *Professor Unrat* (1905), respectively illustrated the political consequences of a cowering social climber and the degradations of class snobbery. The latter story of a respected teacher losing his emotional self-control over a pretty barroom woman, and thus falling down the social ladder to become a deranged clown, attained renown in the late-1920s film version, *The Blue Angel*. Marlene Dietrich's legs figured predominantly in that film, and she still captivates Berliners, as plays about her attest.

Among the many noteworthy writers who made Berlin their home as well as their subject matter, a few stand out. Bertolt Brecht has been termed the twentieth century's Shakespeare. Of his many imaginative theatrical pieces, *The Three Penny Opera* perhaps captured 1920s Berlin the best. Filled with ribald songs and questionable morality—pimps and prostitutes serve as the main characters—it hints at parallels between street life and decadent politics. Actresses such as Helene Weigel and Lotte Lenya brought Brecht's plays to life. The Berliner Ensemble continues to present his socially critical ideology. Max Reinhardt's theater innovations—circular and mobile stages—fit well with Brecht's linguistic flair. From this era a number of people, who still seem to be with us, emerged in the cabaret and musical mixes. Josephine Baker, the nearly nude African-American dancer, who simultaneously had captivated the elites of Paris, stands out. Similarly touching the edge of decadence or pornography were the endless revues of seminude dancing girls in the huge *Friedrichstadtpalast*. No wonder Beate Uhse could establish her Erotik Museum here in 1987 after her success with sex shops in postwar Germany.

In recent times a few authors have been especially identified with Berlin, its history, and its difficulties. Uwe Johnson (1934–1984), who lived in West Berlin from 1959 to 1974, published *Jahrestage (Anniversaries)* (1968–1983) in four volumes about a family's experiences with Nazism and the division of Germany. An earlier work, *Speculations about Jacob* (1959), explored the theme of an East Berlin railway worker in love with a western woman. Jurek Becker (1937–1997), like Johnson, remained sympathetic to the situation of people in eastern Germany, despite his own difficulties with the regime. He had spent his youth in concentration camps. His *Jacob the Liar* (1968), recently an international film success, tells the gripping moral story of someone lying to create hope for others. Both Johnson and Becker had to leave East Berlin because they criticized the regime. Another dissenting East Berliner, the poet Wolf Biermann (1936–), was exiled to the West in 1976. Biermann employed Prussian symbols to satirize contemporary East German authoritarianism in *Preussischer Ikarus*. Christa Wolf (1929–) and Peter Schneider (1940–) focused some of their stories on the creation and meaning of the Berlin Wall, the former with *Nachdenken über Christina T.* (1962). Her protagonist has to decide on which side of the barrier to stay. Schneider, in *The Wall Jumper* (1983), allows his main character to imaginatively hop back and forth. Wolf became the best-known East German and East Berlin writer and has been maligned since Reunification as a Stasi agent (GDR secret police), but maintained her poise in the face of the accusations.

Many local authors have explored aspects of Berlin. Joseph Roth was among the journalists whose reporting during the 1920s brought the world to Berlin and Berlin to the world. The class and ideological conflicts of the city's political and social life during the same era can best be found in the writings of Kurt Tucholsky's *Weltbühne* articles. At present, among the most successful is Horst Bosekzky, whose historical novels autobiographically detail the social conditions at the end of the war and in the postwar era. Hundreds more have published memoirs or written about Berlin.

MUSIC

A long tradition of state support for the arts, especially music, theater, and opera, exists from the eighteenth century flute-playing monarchs such as Frederick II of Prussia to the present. During the cold war, East and West Berlin competed using culture to showcase their societies. Wilhelm Furtwängler and Herbert von Karajan at the Berlin Philharmonic held onto their posts through various regimes from the 1930s to the 1960s. That house, with its fine all-around the orchestra seating, is still among the world's best places to hear classical music. The Berlin Radio Orchestra, Kurt Weill's compositions, and Bertolt Brecht's lyrics made Berlin internationally known during the 1920s. Brecht and Weill attained fame mostly through the irreverent *Three Penny Opera*, which encountered censorship in 1927 and closure in 1933. Modern music, meaning nearly anything since Gustav Mahler (1860–1911), nearly disappeared during the Nazi era but came back forcefully by the 1950s. By then American jazz, which had started to make inroads in the cabarets and pubs during the 1920s, was competing with classical music. Among the young, folk and then British and American rock music predominated after the 1960s, dutifully followed by every "international" trend. However, at carnival time somehow German folk and bourgeois sociability (*Gemütlichkeit*, or feel good sentiments) triumph.

FILM

By the late 1920s Berlin directors (F.W. Murnau, Fritz Lang) had produced many of the films that have become classics for innovations in lighting, camera angle, and acting. Among them: *Metropolis* with trudging robots, *M* (for murder) with Peter Lorre, *The Last Laugh* with Emil Janning, *The Blue Angel* with Marlene Dietrich and Emil Janning, *The Three Penny Opera* with Lotte Lenya. The Nazis used films mainly for propaganda, just as the Imperial regime had done during World War I. Since World War II, at Babelsberg west of Berlin, the old UFA (Universal Film) studios were employed by East Germans to create documentaries and narrative films. Some are making a comeback.

In West Berlin, Wim Wenders (1945) became known for his avant-guarde creations such as *Wings of Desire (Der Himmel über Berlin)* 1987, employing many of Berlin's buildings as symbols. His work became representative of the New German Cinema of the 1970s. Many more examples could be listed, but one success of the post-Reunification era is *Goodbye, Lenin* (2003) showing that the debate over the destruction of eastern society by western norms is not finished. Otherwise, the glitz and consumerist influence of Hollywood is evident in Berlin films and their film festival *(Berlinale)*, aside from the Teddies, the awards offered for gay and lesbian productions.

THEATER

Cabaret and theater have been especially vibrant in Berlin. More than 50 public and private institutions in East and West Berlin once made it a formidable center, drawing talent and creating imaginative staging of classical authors such as Goethe, Schiller, or Shakespeare and more recent fare. Though the Schiller Theater closed in 1993 and the generous subsidies have been reduced, the theater scene remains strong. What other city can offer a National Theater, *Volkbühne, Komödie, Schaubühne, Theater am Kurfurstendamm*, Brecht Berliner Ensemble *(Theater am Schiffbauerdamm)*,

Renaissance Theater, *Komische Oper*, numerous varieté-style ensembles, and many cabarets such as the *Diestel*?

OPERA

Reflecting the earlier division of the city, its rich choices include the German Opera Berlin in the western part of the city, the German State Opera in the east, and the Comical Opera in the center.

MUSEUMS AND GALLERIES

Reunification enabled Berlin's 17 state museums to restore their collections by exchanging pieces of art previously scattered between East and West. European art, crafts, and artifacts of all eras and many countries can be found in Berlin's numerous and high-quality galleries. The Painting Gallery (at the *Kulturforum*) and the (old) National Gallery offer classical painting and sculpture from European medieval to late-nineteenth-century impressionism. These are among the richest collections in the world of artists such as Dürer, Holbein, Rembrandt, Caspar David Friedrich, Feuerbach, and Max Liebermann. The collection of engravings in the Graphic Cabinet is among the best anywhere. The New National Gallery, designed in huge glass rectangles by Mies van der Rohe, mostly features twentieth-century German art, but the post-World War II collection is international.

The Alte Museum, known for its superb Pergamon Altar from Greece and its huge, gold-and-blue-tiled Isar gate, or processional route from Persia, contains mostly Greek, Roman, and Middle Eastern sculptures and objects. The fine Egyptian collection is in one of the remodeled guard barracks next to the Charlottenburg palace (though scheduled to move to the Museum Island). It features Queen Nefertiti, a beautiful bust of inexplicable elegance, and the "Berliner green head" in granite. The collection is extensive, including jewelry and religious and children's artifacts. Across the street is the Berggruen collection of Picasso and his times featuring Pablo Picasso, Paul Klee, Henri Matisse, and Alberto Giacometti. Next door is a private art nouveau exhibition. The palace itself houses the well-displayed prehistory collection. Less well known is the Georg Kolbe museum. His house, studio, and garden have been turned into a large museum for his own sculptures as well as exhibitions.

Among the newest museums and receiving much attention for its striking architecture is the Jewish Museum, designed by Daniel Libeskind. It presents 500 years of Jewish history in a large angular building that has become a very popular attraction for its appearance—broken walls—as well as its contents. The presentation—moving from multimedia to artifacts, from personal letters to public policies—is as imaginative as the building. Another popular site is the I.M. Pei addition to the Berlin Historical Museum. Its round glass entrance is perhaps more spectacular than the exhibits.

After a decade of debate on form and location, the Monument to Europe's Murdered Jews is being built close to the Brandenburg Gate. It comprises 2,751 five-meter pillars buried to varying heights to express the meaninglessness of the

Holocaust, according to its architect Peter Eisenman. Many other places of remembrance (Topography of [Gestapo] Terror, Airlift Monument, Eternal Flame, Wannsee villa) commemorate Berlin's turbulent history, especially its wars and Holocaust-related sites. *Plötzensee* offers a historical site reminding of the terror employed against those who opposed Nazism. Many plaques and markers identify the Berlin Wall and those who died trying to cross it. The uprising on 17 June 1953 has also been memorialized to honor its victims. The positive actions of those who protested against the Wall and the regime similarly have been acknowledged with plaques and markers.

In the suburb of Dahlem, the Ethnographic Collection provides insight into the customs, cultures, and arts of the peoples of the Pacific, Africa, and Mexico. Many exhibits relate to German colonial or exploration enterprises and are therefore strong in artifacts from Papua New Guinea and other South Sea Islands, as well as Cameroon and East Africa. The Brücke archive and collection has its own gallery in the suburb of Wilmersdorf.

In addition to the above major holdings, Berlin, with a total of 128 museums, has many small ones. Examples include an excellent one on the history of sugar, on phonographs, many on local history, on former Chancellor Willy Brandt, on the air force, and music. Arts and crafts have a new spacious home in the *Kulturforum*, and very contemporary art and installations (media and video happenings) can be found at the Hamburger Bahnhof or the Berlin Guggenheim. Larger special collections include the Bauhaus archives; the technological museum; the state museum for regional history; Allied museum; and, specific to the Berlin Wall, the museum at Checkpoint Charlie.

CIVICS AND REMEMBRANCE

The Berlin office for political education provides information and sessions on democracy, parliament, and political parties. It also seeks to foster an understanding of history, especially of the Nazi era. It works with many special-interest groups to maintain and to acknowledge sites of repression and terror. Berlin has an almost endless series of public plaques, statues, installations, and museums relating to the Third Reich and the Holocaust. These include: Memorial for the Murdered Jews of Europe, Central Memorial for the Victims of War and Tyranny *(Neue Wache)*, Topography of Terror (Gestapo, SS, and police), and *Rosenstrasse* sculptures showing a variety of human motives (where Jewish women protested publicly against the deportation of their husbands). A guide lists 13 major memorial sites plus hundreds of smaller sites relating to resistance, systems of oppression, concentration camps, prisons, as well as places where important events such as the Wannsee conference took place.

The memorial sites include the concentration camps in Brandenburg, which were inhabited by victims from Berlin. The office for political education offers programs to keep students aware of the problematic past. Some sites and museums relate to postwar events: an eternal flame to memorialize expellees from the east

(Vertriebene at Theodor Heuss-Platz), Airlift Memorial at Tempelhof airport, and the Karlshorst command center of the occupying Soviet military.

CUISINE

Traditionally beer (Schulteiss was one of Germany's largest brewers) is combined with smoked pig hocks *(eisbein)*, sauerkraut, pureed dried peas, potatoes, and sausages. Presently, the normal fare is *döner kebab* (a pita sandwich with sliced beef or chicken and greens), pizza, and burgers, while Italian, Spanish, Greek, and Thai delicacies appear in the many specialty restaurants. Wine is replacing beer as the main beverage, and *schnapps* (strong spirits) are still taken along with beer by some locals. The Huguenots introduced *Berliner Weisse,* a special light beer into which a raspberry or other sweet concentrate is added in a large bowl-like glass to create a summer cooler.

TRADITIONAL EISBEIN

1 large can or jar (28 ounces) of sauerkraut	1/2 teaspoon black pepper
4–5 garlic cloves	2–3 pounds smoked pork hock
1/4 teaspoon allspice	1/2 cup of dry white wine or water
2 bay leaves	

Preheat oven to 400°F. Mix sauerkraut with cloves, allspice, bay leaves, and pepper. Place pork in large baking pan, surround with sauerkraut mix and pour in wine or water. Turn heat down to 350°F and allow dish to steam for at least 2 hours. Check every 20 minutes; if all wine or water evaporates, add more.

Serve with boiled potatoes, puréed peas, and mustard. Sometimes soft sausages are added to the pork and sauerkraut for the last half hour of cooking.

Chapter 4

𝔅randenburg

SPECIAL ASPECTS

A local poem reads

Wald, Sand und Heede	Forest, sand and heath
Sind des Maerkers Freude	Are the Markers' joy
Wald, Heide, Sand	Forest, heath and sand
Sind sein Vaterland	Are his fatherland

The Mark (or fortified region) Brandenburg—sometimes termed the Mark—amounted to the military sandbox of Europe, supplying Prussian kings with soldiers. It has become a tourist destination and rural escape from Berlin's asphalt and concrete, which it completely surrounds. Potsdam's collection of palaces, the city of Brandenburg's churches, and Cottbus's artisan houses provide small urban focal points for a populace comprised mostly of farmers and artisans. The region has no middle. In 1992 a plebiscite rejected merger with Berlin. Perhaps that amounted to a rejection of the centralism and dominance by the Berlin of earlier eras or perhaps that the populace had survived fairly well before Reunification in 1990. Since then a post-Prussian, post German Democratic Republic future is being sought by identification with a rural landscape.

REGIONAL TRAITS

With 2.5 million inhabitants, most dispersed in rural towns and villages, Brandenburg is the fifth largest state (29,479 square kilometers, or 11,218 square miles) and among the least urban regions. After a sharp decline and then a slow

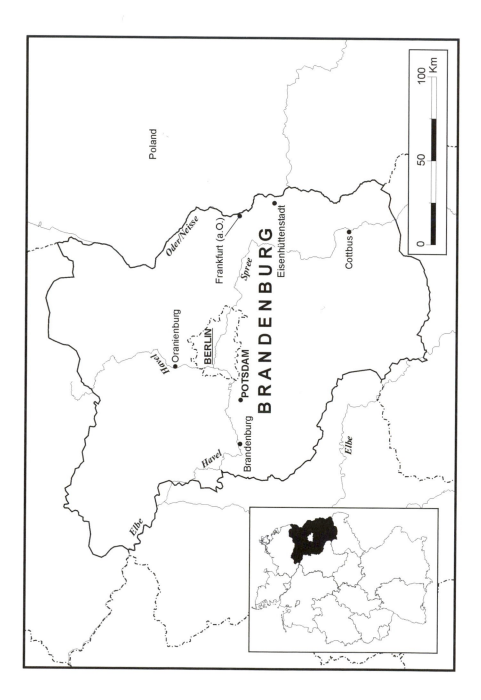

Poland

Oder/Neisse

Frankfurt (a.O.)

Spree

BRANDENBURG

Eisenhüttenstadt

Cottbus

Oranienburg

Havel

BERLIN

POTSDAM

Brandenburg

Havel

Elbe

Elbe

0   50   100   Km

increase during the 1990s, the population fluctuations seem to have stabilized. The Elbe River touches the northwest and runs through the southwest corner. The Oder/Neisse rivers divide Brandenburg in the east from Poland and from former German lands such as Silesia. To the north and northwest is Mecklenburg–Western Pomerania. The Havel and Spree rivers drain toward the Elbe in the west and from south of Berlin. Saxony is to the southwest and south. Three main cities provide administrative bases: Cottbus in the southeast, Potsdam in the west, and Frankfurt/Oder in the east. The Sorbs, an ethnic minority of about 60,000 Slavs whose minority rights are anchored in the constitution, live in the forested areas of the southeast and have retained their own customs and language.

The flag and coat of arms show a red Prussian eagle on a white background.

GEOGRAPHIC FEATURES

The sandy low plains provide average agricultural soil. Many small lakes, meandering rivers, and diverse forests (pine, birch, and beech) add variety to the slightly undulating landscape. Some heights of land or plateaus in the northeast break the rolling plains, but heaths, pasturelands, and sandy terrain prevail. In a few richer agricultural areas, such as the Spree Forest, marketing garden vegetables is a mainstay. Coal, mined in open pits, exists on the southeast border with Poland, but its extraction has become unprofitable.

Subregions include Havelland (west), Flaeming (southwest), Uckermark (northeast), Barmin (east central), Prignitz (northwest), Ruppin (central north), Spreewald (south central), and Niederlausitz (southeast). These landscapes overlap or meld into each other. Transportation improvements continue to erase their historical significance, though locals remain attached to them and ascribe special traits to the people and the landscape of each area.

HISTORY

Sand and water always have been crucial to Mark history. By the sixth century the region supported dispersed Slavic tribes who mostly hunted but also cultivated the soil and fished. The archaeological museum at Wünsdorf has organized and recorded many of the prehistoric urns, tools, and settlement patterns. The movement of Slavic people and goods can be followed via gravesites and weapon finds.

By the ninth century Charlemagne began to extend his realm into the region, noting that waterways eased movement. During the early period of Christianity, from the ninth to eleventh centuries, many clashes occurred over land and values. A Catholic bishopric existed by 948. By 1151 Albrecht the Bear, a capable Saxon king, held the sparsely settled area.

The concept of "Mark" meant a duty to fortify; thus, a series of fortifications spread eastward. Cistercian monks successfully developed cloisters, as at Seehausen. Some trading cities were able to extract rights of near independence from the regional rulers. Such urban centers even developed water systems, using hollowed timbers. The various rulers of the small territories hoped to reassert control, however. One such ruler appeared in the late fifteenth century, as Zollern counts from southwest

Germany gained part of Brandenburg's territory. They came with high status—the right to participate in electing Imperial emperors. They would eventually use their base to build the imposing military and bureaucratic state of Brandenburg-Prussia. Simultaneously, the eastward colonization by German and Flemish settlers continued so that only in the Spreewald area did the Slavs retain a majority. The present Sorbs are their descendants.

The Reformation debates impacted slowly on the region. Only in the 1540s did the Protestants win the religious struggles. Complicated by dynastic and economic clashes, those religious conflicts caused turmoil for the next hundred years culminating in the devastation of the Thirty Years' War. The rulers of Brandenburg restored order and extended their control by more authoritarian, militaristic rule that consolidated serfdom and gave the landholding aristocrats privileged positions within civil and military society.

Brandenburg is associated with the Hohenzollern dynasty and the East Elbian large landowning aristocracy, the Junkers. From the fifteenth century to 1918 the former ruled an expanding Brandenburg-Prussia, as dukes, princes, and finally as monarchs. The aristocrats provided support from their manor houses as haughty feudal lords and as a military caste providing officers. Aside from royal estates, where serfdom ended in the mid-eighteenth century, a harsh personal regime of peasant obligations and Junker privileges continued well beyond the official end of serfdom in 1811. Numerous successful, but financially draining, wars depended upon the monarchs and aristocrats exploiting serfs and peasants as cannon fodder and as taxpayers. By the time of Frederick the Great (1740–1786), Brandenburg-Prussia had one of Europe's largest standing armies. By marriage and warfare he continued the territorial enlargement of the realm that his predecessors had initiated. During the eighteenth century the military and bureaucratic state codified the realm. Its officials very thoroughly examined and defined Prussia and the new territories gained from Austria and Poland, such as Silesia, South Prussia, and New South Prussia. The maps, the detailed descriptions, and systematic accounting, with regulations for every trade and city activity, served military purposes, but it required a highly trained, dedicated group of administrators. This educated elite versed in cartography, ethnography, and agricultural understanding oversaw a finely regulated system. In addition to serving the military purposes of the state, this elite contributed to the culture of the European Enlightenment. A few examples: Voltaire spent three years in the discussion and music circle of Frederick II's court. The classical authors, such as Fredrick Schiller, wanted to serve at the Berlin court because its theater and intellectual life were so vibrant.

However, Napoleon proved that the military side of this state had decayed. By 1800 it had an aging officer corps, a lack of understanding of advances in artillery, and an absence of espirit de corps. After a series of victories in 1806, Napoleon occupied most of Brandenburg and forced it to pay heavy reparations into the French treasury. Until 1812 it remained under French occupation and influence.

During the nineteenth century migration from the rural areas to Berlin and to the west, including across the Atlantic, limited the population growth of Brandenburg.

Novel, late-eighteenth-century agricultural products, such as sugar beets and potatoes, became staples of the local diet. Agricultural work, though partly mechanized,
remained marked by hard labor. Simultaneously, distilling grains into *schnapps*
became especially important for the East Elbian landowners' finances. Their estates
were often indebted despite the manner in which they overworked and mistreated
servants and day laborers, who had almost no protection under Prussian law. In
1847, when food shortages and inflation made them desperate, some peasants and
workers rioted to obtain potatoes.

Until 1918 the lower classes had no political representation, since Prussia had a
three-class voting system. As a result, in the late nineteenth century peasants and
workers increasingly turned to organized left-wing politics. Once industrialization
spread to the Brandenburg cities near Berlin, it created horrid housing and working
conditions for the working class. For instance, in response to the population increase,
housing speculators were allowed to expand the system of huge rental barracks with
up to 14 persons to a room into Brandenburg. As the only group opposing social
malice, the emancipationist ideology of Social Democracy spread far beyond Berlin
by the 1890s. The outspoken radical, Karl Liebknecht, even attained election to
the *Reichstag*—unlike Prussia it had universal male suffrage—from the Potsdam area
by 1912.

In contrast to the lower class, the middle-class of Brandenburg had already
attained an awareness of their area by the 1860s. Railways made discovery of the Mark's
traits more possible, but those only connected the major cities. Through writings and
painting, intellectuals helped move the regional self-understanding onto a new level
and made the hinterland more visible. Theodor Fontane (1819–1898) published his
Wanderungen (wanderings through the Mark Brandenburg, 1860s) and helped the
middle class to know about life in the villages and to notice the landscape. Earlier the
landscape artist Carl Blechen (1798–1840) romanticized the forests, lakes, and open
fields. Karl Schinkel (1781–1841), in addition to creating museums to house the treasures of the region, raised concern about the state of heritage buildings such as churches
and cloisters, but especially the village church at Grossmutz. At the end of the century
the writer Robert Mielke dedicated himself to the old villages and farms. He described
the farmhouses, their decorations, and building styles. At Ferch an artist's colony
painted impressionistic landscapes. By the beginning of the twentieth century, more
than Prussian militarism provided a basis for identification with the Mark.

World War I drastically affected this rural region. Though sales of agricultural
goods increased and prices rose, the number of war dead and the lack of reforms to the
Prussian political and social system heightened social tensions. Protests against the war
and strikes against food shortages and inflation culminated in revolution in late 1918.
It swept away the monarchy and the feudal laws regarding domestics and day laborers.

With a republican and democratic constitution, Brandenburg-Prussia, under
the leadership of the moderate Social Democrat Otto Braun, became one of the
democratic pillars of the Weimar Republic. However, most of his support came from
Prussian areas other than Brandenburg. Indeed, in Brandenburg during the Weimar
Republic, the declining prices on the world grain market further undercut the rural

landowners, despite state subsidies. Many moved from conservative to right radical politics, including the Nazis. The latter promised them a better future, though most aristocrats saw that future in terms of a past when they had been unchallenged lords on their estates and dominated state institutions. The peasants suffered but had little influence because they remained unorganized and did not have representation at the top of the state, such as the Junker Paul von Hindenburg, who secretly and publicly received state subsidies for his and other large estates.

In July 1932 President Hindenburg legitimized a coup that deposed the government of Prussia and installed a dictatorial commissioner. When the Nazis came to power through Hindenburg's appointment of Adolf Hitler to lead a coalition government in 1933, Hermann Goering headed Prussia and controlled its police for Nazi purposes, including the destruction of left-wing parties. In 1934, Brandenburg was melded into the Nazi district system with little opposition.

Repression became the Nazi norm for anyone not considered loyal. The Sachsenhausen concentration camp opened in 1933, near Oranienburg, mostly serving Berlin. Communists, Social Democrats, and liberals were sent for "reeducation." Later, Ravensbrück became the main camp for dissenting women, while the first experiments with gassing the mentally ill took place just north of Berlin.

During World War II, Brandenburg cities such as Potsdam suffered from bombing, and much destruction came from ravaging armies and artillery attacks. In 1945 the Soviets occupied the region, and the Allies outlawed the state of Prussia in early 1947. By then the Soviets had instigated a popular land reform that dispossessed most of the big landowners. It created Brandenburg as a separate state from former Prussian provinces. In 1952 the German Democratic Republic (GDR) eliminated the traditional states and the "Mark" disappeared into three administrative districts.

With Reunification in 1990 Brandenburg reappeared, but the collective agricultural holdings were reorganized or sold. GDR products were devalued, but within five years agriculture had stabilized and industrial closings halted. Subsidies from the West to rebuild infrastructure of roads and communications, however, could not prevent mass unemployment. It remains at 20 percent, despite early retirements and migration to the West. Women, who had received special social support and had participated actively in the GDR labor force, especially experienced new difficulties under the terms of Reunification. They lost abortion rights, direct support for large families, and time off for family related work. But mostly they lost workplaces.

The constitution approved by plebiscite in mid-1992 has special aspects, which illustrate that it partly emerged from the roundtable discussions following Reunification. Plebiscites and citizens' initiatives are written into it. Basic rights include housing and employment. The environment has to be protected. Fostering good relations with Poland is a state task, not merely a wish. The communal self-government emphasizes citizens' active participation; numerous mayors have been deposed.

At first, middle-of-the-road coalitions led by the SPD dominated the political state re-created in 1990. The Social Democrats have led all the cabinets since Reunification. Manfred Stolpe, served as prime minister from 1990 to 2002, when he joined the federal cabinet responsible for transportation and rebuilding the East.

Before 1990 he had been head of the evangelical church in the GDR. Social Democracy continues to be the leading party with 37 percent of the vote in the 1999 elections, compared to the Christian Democratic Union's (CDU) 25 percent and the Party of Democratic Socialism's (PDS) 22 percent. Since 2003 the re-elected left coalition of SPD and PDS has been headed for the SPD by Matthias Platzeck, long-time advocate of ecological improvement.

The rural landscape and living down the Prussian past—especially finding a conciliatory relationship with neighboring Poland—have become the crucial elements in the regional identity fostered by the state.

ECONOMY

Agriculture is decisive but so is the proximity to Berlin, with nearly three times more population than the whole state of Brandenburg. Some industries exist in the larger cities such as Brandenburg (machinery), Eisenhüttenstadt (steel), and Eberswalde (machinery). But many could not withstand the economic shock of competition in western markets. Brown coal mining had employed many and has been nearly completely shut down. During the 1990s rural unemployment soared and has remained near 20 percent as the collective farms were transformed into individual holdings. Though productivity and export values have improved through trade with Eastern Europe, employment opportunities have not increased. Women especially have been disadvantaged in the new economy. Tourism has been encouraged and has increased, though slowly.

Education and research have been encouraged by subsidies to help move the region toward a service society. Occasionally, researchers discover the meaning of globalization. One doctor at Teltow discovered a way to regrow parts of bones and needed capital to commercialize his medical innovation. A group of Americans leveraged him out of his discoveries as well as out of the firm.

Three universities (Potsdam, Cottbus, and Frankfurt-Oder) foster self-understanding, good relations with Poland and Europe, as well as support research centers. Potsdam's film college and an earth sciences research center point to ventures with employment potential. Cultural institutions such as theaters, museums, galleries, and orchestras relate to both the universities and the tourist industries but often prove costly.

MAIN CITIES

CAPITAL

Potsdam (population 140,000) served as one of the main garrison cities under the Prussian kings, with military churches and barracks predominant. Heavily bombed during World War II, few half-timbered structures remain but many brick military barracks and administrative buildings survived. The renovated huge cathedral

Figure 4.1
Friendship Garden, Potsdam, Brandenburg.

Source Courtesy of the author.

(Dom) and church towers compete with a few hotel towers on the skyline of a very green city. In addition to having Frederick the Great's complex of palaces (*Sans Souci, Orangerie, Neue Kammern, Neues Palais, Commers,* and his nephew's *Charlottenhof*) and gardens at *Sans Souci* on the edge of the city, it also has *Cecilienhof,* the former crown prince's palace, and many city parks. Just outside is Germany's Hollywood at Babelsberg, where documentaries and feature films have been produced for a

Figure 4.2
Cecilienhof palace near Potsdam, Brandenburg.

Source Courtesy of Inter Nationes, Bonn, Germany.

hundred years. The Hohenzollern palace is to be rebuilt on the *Altmarkt* (old market) as a tourist attraction. Many of the buildings, including the Imperial stables, have been renovated near the *Neues Markt* (new market). Some house the regional museum devoted to Brandenburg history, some a major film museum, and others historical research institutes.

Potsdam is an administrative and small-industry center with extensive cultural offerings (theater, music, film, small university). Tourism is important, luckily well supported by the legacy of buildings left by the Prussian monarchs. In addition to *Sans Souci* they left the *Nauener Tor*, Nicolai Church, many garrison buildings, and a small Brandenburg *Tor*. In addition the *Einstein Turm* and *Wasserwerk* (water tower) in the style of a mosque are complemented by a Russian colony's onion-steepled churches and decorated, wooden houses. The renovation and rebuilding of these structures illustrate how much investment has been undertaken since Reunification.

Cottbus (population 123,000), the main city of the Lower Lausitz area on the Oder River, dates from 1156. Textiles have been produced here since the Renaissance. The railroad center, added in the late-nineteenth century, helped diversify the economy. The old city center contrasts with the concrete prefabricated buildings of GDR days. The remains of a fortress, a cloister, and many artisan houses are a reminder of a rich commercial past. The gallery for regional art *(Brandenburgische Kunstsammlungen)*, founded during 1977 in a renovated Diesel factory, offers Renaissance masters and contemporary works, including photographs and posters.

Frankfurt an der Oder (population 80,000) is special as Germany's largest city on the border with Poland. How its trade and commerce will fare when Poland becomes part of the European Union is an open question. It could profit, but few inhabitants speak Polish while many Poles speak German. The attempt at the Viandrina European University to foster a bilingual and pan-European outlook has been limited. It does seek to conciliate the conflict-ridden past and to develop a more positive future in Polish-German relations. Cultural offerings have been expanded, for instance, a Franciscan monastery church in the baroque style has been rebuilt into a modern concert hall. Carl Bach (1714–1788) served as organist at the church that contains the country's oldest functioning organ. Perhaps the most impressive building, in a well-kept city center dating to the medieval era, is the city hall. Mostly destroyed by bombing and rebuilt by 1978, it is one of the largest and oldest built in the so-called brick baroque style with a series of towers and three round windows dating from Hanseatic days. The golden herring on the south gable from 1454 represents the trade in fish, which reached from the Baltic to Austria. The Heinrich von Kleist Museum is located in a beautiful garrison school built at the end of the eighteenth century. One of Germany's and Europe's oldest public parks, designed in the 1840s by Josef Lenné, covers part of the medieval city walls.

Brandenburg (population 75,000), a thousand-year-old city that gave the name to the region, is in the central western area close to many rivers and lakes. Water determined the pattern of development with the main cathedral on an island of the Havel River. An attractive central city dates from the medieval era with beautiful churches, especially the St. Catherine church with a side façade of towers and windows. A set of entrance gates at each side of the city reflects its former military purpose. Ruins of cloisters on the Havel are used for music concerts and festivals. The cathedral and city museums are complemented by an industrial museum, which contains a Siemen-Martin blast furnace.

ATTRACTIONS

The quiet solitude of little lakes at a short distance from hectic urban life is made more interesting by numerous manor houses, palaces, and churches dating mostly from the fifteenth to the nineteenth centuries. A series of nature preserves has been established to help ecotourism. Canoe and punt rides on the streams of the Spree Forest or on the many canals are favorite activities. The Sorbs of this area still appear in local costumes, their houses are decorated, but they mainly work at food processing producing semi-industrialized products such as *Spreewald Gurken* (pickles).

The Ruppiner Land is an area of lakes, canals, and rivers northwest of Berlin. Defined by Oranienburg, Neuruppin, and Furstenberg, the area contains many walking and bicycle paths. Not far from Neuruppin at the battleground of Fehrbellin, the Prussian duke Frederick Wilhelm I defeated the Swedes who outnumbered the Prussians two to one. Monuments to that battle are at Fehrbellin and Hakenberg. In

Neuruppin, Theodor Fontane's birthplace, he is honored with a statute. Rheinsberg palace is built on one of the most important defense works just north of Brandenburg. In the late sixteenth century a castle with moat replaced the previous one destroyed by fire. Frederick William I bought it for his son in 1733 and had it rebuilt into a baroque palace. From 1736, until he became king in 1740, Frederick II lived in the palace, which he gave to his brother in 1744. This is the star palace of the region and many local and Berlin authors, such as Kurt Tucholsky (1890–1935), employed its setting in novels. The gardens, started by Frederick in 1736, served as a model for Sans Souci. An orangerie, grottoes, and monuments to the royal family made the garden into a place for walking and reflecting.

Southwest of Berlin (Fläming), imaginative tourist promoters have built a three-meter-wide 100-kilometer circular track for in-line skaters and bikers. They hope it will be for skating what winter resorts such as *Oberhof* are to skiing. They have coordinated overnight stays with hotels along the route. The restored Cistercian cloister at Zinna is nearby.

East of Berlin at Buckow, in surroundings ideal for hiking, is the Brecht/Weigel house to which the playwright and actress retreated in the 1950s. Much earlier in the far southeast an eccentric aristocrat, Count Ludwig von Pückler, spent his fortune to build some of the largest sculpted gardens at *Schloss Branitz* (at Cottbus) and especially at *Bad Muskau*. During the 1780s he helped develop the art of garden landscaping in Germany. Two other well-restored palaces are *Neuhardenburg* and *Wusterhausen*, the latter having been Frederick Wilhelm's hunting lodge.

The small lakes of the glaciated landscape provide an attraction close to Berlin but also in more distant parts of Brandenburg and Mecklenburg. By the late nineteenth century, these became an escape from the city. During the 1920s and again in the GDR era, many small colonies emerged. At Leipnitzsee, for example, small gardens and camping places offered a simple lifestyle out of which summer communities emerged. Due to access limited to a ferry, and with the Berlin Wall shutting out West Berliners, such well-treed places were not overrun and did not take on a painted prettiness typical of so many Western resorts. Some beaches have nude bathing. Many have been invaded by the "Wessies" since Reunification. Some, such as *Bad Saarow*, have become golf and spa retreats. More in keeping with the history of the region are the various places that seek to memorialize the attempts at flight by Otto Lilienthal, whose batlike contraption achieved 15 meters at Drewitz by Potsdam in 1891. In 1896 at Stölln he crashed and died of his injuries. A museum centered on flight is to be created there as well.

The small towns and villages contain diverse and sometimes surprising attractions. *Museumsdorf Glasmütte* has a display of the Thermos, which Franz Burger invented in 1903 and patented under that name in 1924. Neuzelle has a Cistercian cloister with tall church steeple and half-timbered houses. Its cloister church is considered an exquisite example of baroque. The inside of the church contains many angels and other carvings. Eisenhüttenstadt may have a large steel plant, but it also has one of the oldest original Cistercian monasteries of Europe. Completed in 1300, the grounds as well as the buildings have been maintained. Brick is everywhere in castles, in half-timbered houses, but especially in Brandenburg city halls and churches. A brick museum at Mildenberg illustrates how they have been made since the fifteenth century.

As in most other regions, Brandenburg has an open-air museum to illustrate work and life on the land. The *Freilichtmuseum Altranft* is a village placed under heritage protection. The smithy, school, and storage sheds have been preserved, but perhaps most instructive are the demonstrations of baking, basket making, and grain grinding by windmill.

A different attraction is an attempt to transform the wastelands left by open-pit mining into ponds and lakes for recreation as well as sculpture gardens as at Pritzen. An imaginative attraction is the world's largest instrument for scrapping coal, which has been decorated and lit up. This 500-meter bridge of steel at Lichterfeld near Finsterwalde is known as the "lying down Eifel tower."

The greatest tourist draw is Sans Souci, Frederick the Great's complex of palaces and gardens near Potsdam. First he had his favorite architect, Georg von Knobelsdorf (1699–1753), built an elegant and modest baroque residence intended only for discussion evenings with male friends. Since he needed more space for his paintings, he built the New Gallerie, for guests, the Chambers. Then he had a very large building, the Orangerie, created to protect trees during winter. The gardens in front of these buildings were sculpted with vines, figs, and tree plantings. The symmetrical pattern leading up the front of the main palace is broken at each side by big trees and hedges with antique sculptures spread among them. Since Frederick thought of himself as following in the tradition of significant kings and emperors, he had Roman ruins and Chinese teahouses constructed in the extensive grounds. The plantings and park extend over many square kilometers. The formal gardens were landscaped with hills and trees so as to isolate the parts from each other. Having won a series of wars and elevated Brandenburg-Prussia to one of the decisive states of Europe, Frederick emulated Louis XIV and built his own version of Versailles, the New Palace *(Neues Palais)*, after 1763. It contains grotto halls, mirrored reception rooms, and suites for visitors. Since his nephew, Frederick William IV, did not like the style of these monumental buildings, he built *Charlottenhof* in a simpler more classical style in one section of the gardens. At the end of the nineteenth and early twentieth centuries, Wilhelm II frequently used the New Palace but had it modernized with heat, running water, and elevators. Straw and chamber pots had been the previous toilet facilities in the palaces, which were intended as summer residences or country houses. The whole complex provides rambling space, concert grounds, and splendid views, though only a windmill remains of the rural landscape into which Frederick planted his pleasure palaces.

Just northeast is *Cecilienhof,* the former palace of the Prussian crown prince. It served as the venue for the Potsdam conference in 1945. Winston Churchill, Harry Truman, and Josef Stalin met to decide the shape of central Europe, especially Poland and Germany, in the postwar world. It houses a museum showing pictures and documents about that historic meeting. In contrast to the emphasis upon the elite in

Figure 4.3
Eighteenth-century Chinese Tea House, Sans Souci, Potsdam, Brandenburg.

Source Courtesy of George Buse.

so many palaces is the special Documentation Center of Daily Life, dedicated to collecting objects from the GDR era. Some 50,000 items illustrate the innovative as well as the mundane. From flags to furniture, from canned goods to toys, the GDR as experienced by the average person has been placed on display to evoke reflection more than nostalgia at Eisenhüttenstatt.

CUSTOMS

The Sorb minority in the Spree Forest area wear colorful traditional garb, even to serve tourists on boat rides. In Werder, outside Potsdam, the blossom festival has served cider and fruit wines since 1879. Many Berliners come out to see the apple orchards in bloom and to drink copiously. Easter and Christmas provide the main annual celebrations, the former with the usual eggs and chocolate, the latter with food markets. Youth inauguration (*Jugendweihe*, similar to a secular confirmation) remains popular since its origins in GDR days. Carnival, each February, with dancing, processions, and poking fun at politicians, became an annual event by the 1980s but has gained renewed strength since Reunification.

In the 1920s, some village festivals reverted to the festivals of earlier times, such as the *Belziger Huhnreiten* (chicken riding). Males on horseback tried to turn around a wooden rooster on a post. The heavy workhorses were excited by an overseer and hence jumped forward so that the rider frequently was dumped. Then a doctor dressed like a clown helped the downed rider with many medicinal drinks. The winner received a tablecloth. After more prizes, the whole company went to the village square and ritualized bowling preceded dancing. Such celebrations have mostly ceased. Attempts to revise others, such as tobacco blossom festivals, are under way at Vierraden near Schwedt.

CULTURAL ATTRIBUTES
AND CONTRIBUTIONS

VISUAL ARTS

Local painters such as Alexander Kircher and the Havel impressionists at the end of the nineteenth century made inhabitants more aware of the land and seascapes around them. An artist colony at Ferch in the 1890s supported the Berlin Secessionist's challenge to the norms of official academy styles. Eugen Lindenberg and Max Schroder tried to evoke a serene landscape of unspoiled nature, especially waterways.

LITERATURE

Theodor Fontane is perhaps the best-known local author due to his *Wanderings through the Mark*, composed after extensive foot and horseback tours during the 1860s. A more recent author, Ehm Welk, who experienced Nazi concentration camps, wrote about life on the land in *Heiden von Kummerow*. The Uckermark literary society honors his memory at Angermünde. The postwar poet, Peter Huchel, who for many years edited the critical GDR magazine *Sinn und Form*, wrote lovingly about his homeland, which he left under duress in 1971. Franz Führmann, another GDR writer who appreciated the *Markisch* landscape and wrote about it in clear language, is commemorated at Buchholz.

CIVICS AND REMEMBRANCE

Ravensbrück and *Sachsenhausen* at Oranienburg—these concentration camps have also become attractions, for educational and reflective purposes. Ravensbrück served as the main camp for women who had opposed and resisted Nazism in Germany and Europe.

The state office for political education offers many publications on regional history and parliamentary democracy. The historical accounts emphasize the Prussian past but go beyond the military expansion of the state to emphasize lifestyles of common people, as well as showing who made a wider audience aware of the Mark during the nineteenth century. Tours of concentration camps and seminars regarding intolerance toward minorities are part of the educational program. If the first activity fosters regional identity, the second seeks to force reflection on the burden of the Nazi and GDR pasts. The assumption is that both need to be better understood to prevent a recurrence. Much effort goes into developing active citizenship.

Many sites relating to repression by and resistance to both Nazi and GDR dictatorships have been identified with plaques, and some have been made into museums. The series of special labor and punishment camps in which the Soviets killed many in the immediate aftermath of World War II have been identified, for example, at Mühlberg, at Weesow near Werneuchen, at Pritzwalk, and at Potsdam. Mass graves have been marked (at Jamlitz and at Schmachtenhagen near Oranienburg). Some of the Soviet camps were located in those that the Nazis had used, for instance *Sachsenhausen*.

The foundations that operate the concentration camps such as *Sachsenhausen* and *Ravensbrück* provide educational tours and seminars. The office for political education is very active with seminars and program for schools. Those have a social as well as a educational intent—to raise citizens who question and who participate but who are well informed.

CUISINE

A local poem reads:

Kartoffeln und Gruetze	Potatoes and grits
Feuersteene und Sand,	Firestone and sand
Sind die Elemente	Are the elements
Vom Brandenburger Land	Of Brandenburg land

The reality is not quite so basic, though potatoes figured large in the local cuisine, once accompanied by *schnapps* from grains. Cider and fruits remain favorites, and smoked fish from the rivers is still sold at local markets. In addition to the great variety of local fish, a special vegetable is returning to the regional table. Napoleon, among others, liked *Teltower Rübchen* (roots, somewhat like a parsnip), which are rich in vitamins. An annual festival is seeking to spread awareness of a vegetable that can be pureed, fried, caramelized, and deep-fried.

Game meats such as wild boar and deer are popular with the elite, while ground meats *(Buletten)* are more common. A traditional dish is *Königsburger* meatballs *(Klops)* served with capers in a cream sauce accompanied by fried or boiled potatoes. One dish, *Klemmkuchen* (literally, clamped cake) has a long history since it came with Flemish migrants. It is a flour-based waffle or crepe baked over a fire in a long-handled hinged iron. Another item, *Knieperkohl,* is termed a national dish in the northwest, the Prignitz, but is a variant of sauerkraut. White cabbage, kale, and brussels sprouts are mixed with pork and served with potatoes.

Stuffed duck or goose is frequently served on festive occasions. This recipe is a modern variant.

Duck Stuffed with Sauerkraut

1 medium onion diced	4–5-pound duck
20 cloves of garlic, sliced	5 slices of bacon or *Speck*, diced
2 medium carrots, grated	
1/2 pound of sauerkraut (can be can of wine-soaked)	

Preheat the oven at 375°F. Sauté the onion and Speck, add garlic, carrots, and sauerkraut and let steep for about 20 minutes. Stuff the rinsed duck with mixture, packing fairly tightly in main cavity and neck. Fold skin over and pin shut with skewers. Place the duck on a rack so duck is above roasting pan and fat drips away from carcass. Roast for 1.5 hours and check if done (160°–170°F, on meat thermometer or when wings pull away readily).

After letting duck rest for 10 minutes, spoon stuffing into serving bowl. Carve duck. Serve with potatoes (scalloped or fried with little pieces of bacon) and side dish of vegetables, such as broccoli or cauliflower.

Chapter 5

𝔅remen

In the Free and Hanseatic State of Bremen, local people have been stereotyped as reserved but calculating entrepreneurs. The city-state values its long independence as a small republic and its identity as a trading center. The carefully preserved city hall, large cathedral, and the moat surrounding the core city emphasize a glorious past as opposed to the debt-ridden present. Pride in previous achievements is combined with bold moves toward the future—a science center, two small universities, and a mixed state-private economy—plus the comfortable lifestyle of a midsized city. Locals claim that in Bremen everything is different, while visitors see it as manageable *(Überschaubar)*. Bremer enjoy their city's amenities and their region: A 2003 questionnaire found 96 percent liked living there.

Native Bremer speak Low German, *Plattdeutsch*, though nearly everyone is capable of High German. Integration of outsiders has been a constant issue for this port city since the mid-nineteenth century. Migrants from the immediate hinterland and Polish workers came to work in crafts and industries. These were followed during World War II by slave laborers, then German refugees from the east—nearly 20 percent of the population by 1950. Since the 1960s, waves of immigrants—so-called guest workers—from southern and eastern Europe have been succeeded by asylum seekers. Approximately 10 percent of the Bremen population comprises noncitizens from other European and Asian countries.

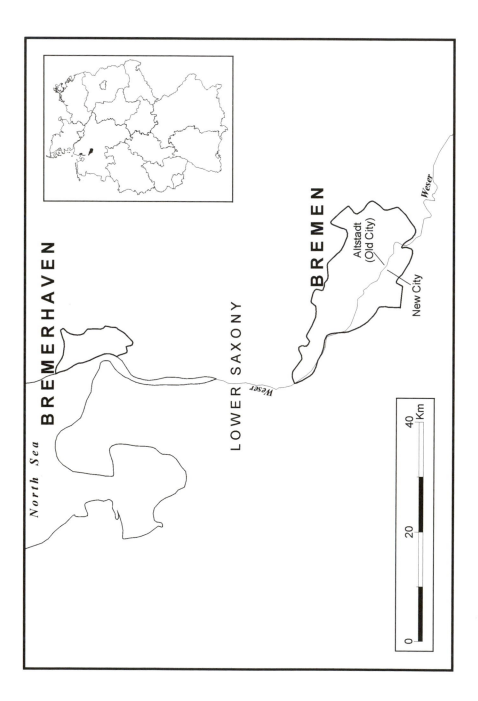

North Sea

BREMERHAVEN

BREMEN

LOWER SAXONY

Weser

Weser

Altstadt
(Old City)

New City

0   20   40
Km

REGIONAL TRAITS

The Free and Hanseatic State of Bremen is a city-state comprised of Bremen and Bremerhaven with a population of 680,000 and an area of 404 square kilometers. The second-oldest republic in Europe is located on the Weser River about 60 kilometers from the North Sea, while its subcity, the port of Bremerhaven, is on the seacoast near the mouth of the same river. Lower Saxony surrounds Bremen and Bremerhaven.

GEOGRAPHIC FEATURES

Sandy dunes and marshes surround the two cities within the lowlands of the state of Lower Saxony. Some 170 kilometers of dykes defend the cities against flood tides. The weather is wet, windy, and sometimes chilly. The flag is known as the "bacon" flag because of its red and white stripes.

CAPITAL

The city of **Bremen** is surrounded by Lower Saxony and is the economic and cultural hub for the surrounding towns and villages on both sides of the Weser River far beyond its political boundaries. It has a population of 550,000 and an area of 327 square kilometers.

HISTORY

An imperial privileged city since 1186, some 400 years after being founded as a bishopric, Bremen became known in the eleventh century as the Rome of the north for spreading Catholic Christianity, especially in Scandinavia. As a member of the Hanseatic League, for centuries Bremen merchants traded along the coastline of Europe from Spain to Russia. During the Reformation era, Bremen joined the Protestant, and later Calvinist, cause. It became an independent Imperial city in 1646, though some areas remained under Swedish and Hanoverian influence. Occupied during Napoleon's empire, for a short time after 1810 it became a department of France.

In the late eighteenth century the trade pattern changed more to the trans-Atlantic routes, and by the mid-nineteenth century Bremen became known as continental Europe's point of debarkation for emigrants. By the late nineteenth century the fiercely proud city-state developed large parks, many cultural amenities, and became known for its attractiveness. Decaffeinated coffee originated here in 1906, and its inventor, Ludwig Roselius, became an influential patron of local artists, such as Paula Modersohn Becker, Bernard Hoetger, and Heinrich Vogeler. He supported architects working in international styles, though he later strongly supported racist nationalism, including Adolf Hitler. Politically, an oligarchy of shippers and lawyers dominated until 1918.

After the 1880s, industrialization changed the nature of the local economy and society. Factories for jute, wool, steel for ships, and new wharfs increased the in-migration of laborers. By 1910 the population of the city reached 247,000 (310,000 for the city-state), compared to 83,000 in 1871. Labor leaders organized trade unions and a dynamic Social Democratic movement. Both groups fought the long hours and dangerous conditions of work in artisan shops and industrial factories, especially ship-building and textiles. They pointed to the slum housing conditions and limited polit-ical rights. During the World War I that labor movement split, and eventually the Communists, based in the large factories, proved to be among the strongest resistance to Nazism. By then the local economy depended heavily on shipbuilding and state sub-sidies for industry. The Depression of 1929 hit especially hard in Bremen, and the mid-dle class readily accommodated itself to Hitler's authoritarian regime.

From the turn of the century to the Nazi era, when the labor movement had great strength, and again in the 1960s, with student unrest and the women's movement, Bremen had a reputation as a place of radicalism. That radicalism existed primarily among those without political influence. Until 1918 Bremen was ruled by lifetime senators. Thereafter, a small elite from the same oligarchy of shippers and lawyers who saw themselves as liberals (economically) and operated conservatively (politically), but could prove to be quite progressive or at least tolerate a great variety of modernist movements (culturally), held power. During the 1920s the reformist Social Democrats cooperated with the reigning liberals and after 1945 became the dominant political party. They fostered a moderate program of social and economic reform—investment in housing, education, and culture—under Allied tutelage.

When the British occupied Bremen after World War II, Bremen nearly disap-peared as a separate state. The British had thought of integrating the Bremen republic into Lower Saxony, but because the Americans needed a supply port, Bremen became part of the American zone of occupation. The city-state had lost Bremerhaven during the Nazi era to its rival Oldenburg, but in 1947 Bremen and Bremerhaven were offi-cially reunited into an independent state. During the process of creating the federal republic of Germany, Bremen's independence again was threatened, and the federal constitution of 1949 left open the possibility of border alterations. In 1953 and 1954, a commission examined the capability of small entities such as Bremen to carry out administrative and cultural tasks according to the constitution. The commission con-firmed Bremen's separate status.

World War II transformed Bremen politically and economically. It was among the most bombed cities in Germany; its industry relied heavily on slave laborers. The Allies insisted that the port and shipbuilding not become operative until the late 1940s. In 1947 its Land status was restored and in 1949 confirmed in the federal constitution. Soon postwar reconstruction of infrastructure such as the port and wharfs, shipbuilding, auto manufacture, and housing brought an economic boom. Until the early 1960s, Bremen had more than 20,000 people working on the wharfs and another 20,000 producing automobiles. The boom ended in the 1960s. Until that time Bremen had been among the richest German states, and its new elite fiercely underscored its independence by emphasizing its regional identity as well as by encouraging federalism and local pride in historic achievements.

In the late 1960s and early 1970s, supported by many radicals and social critics at the small new university (founded in 1971), some parts of the city developed casual lifestyles, which challenged a staid and conservative society. A large antinuclear movement, a strong feminist community, and numerous pacifists revived the radicalism formerly identified with left-wing labor. The Greens elected their first parliamentarian here in 1979.

The 1970s and 1980s brought high unemployment and economic difficulties, though the highly indebted state has made the shift to a service economy and high-tech industries. The university has slowly been transformed into a reputable, if not as lively, institution with some strong research areas. Nearly 30,000 university and college students add much to the local economy as well as to the increasing number of research centers.

As part of their policy of decentralization, the Allies insisted on no media monopoly. Hence, Bremen obtained a radio frequency and produces high-quality radio programs. It also developed a regional television station. One author noted that the subject of financial equalization payments are discussed frequently and defended by the Bremen media, since Bremen receives substantial support from the federal government transfer system.

Social Democracy (SPD) has been the dominant postwar political party, though the Greens and recently the Christian Democratic Union (CDU) have been challenging its dominance. Wilhelm Kaisen served as Social Democratic mayor from the end of the war through the 1950s and attained majorities for the party. Bremen became known as a left, or radical, city where in the immediate postwar years Communists participated in the government. During the cold war they were excluded, but during the counterculture and radical politics of the 1960s, Bremen experienced many sit-ins and protests. In the 1980s, the peace and feminist movements dominated the left and reformist causes. By the 1990s, split votes between the conservative Christian Democrats, the liberal Free Democrats, and the Green ecological party forced coalitions on the Social Democrats. At present a coalition of the two dominant parties, the Social Democrats and the Christian Democrats, underscores the concern to find political solutions to the economic difficulties of the small city-state. The coalition was reelected in 2003 under the Social Democratic leadership of the popular Henning Scherf, making Bremen the only German state that has had a Social Democrat political leader since World War II.

Whether Bremen can afford to remain an independent state, as a dwarf within the German federation, remains an open question. Certainly the Bremer like their little city and identify with its historical role as an independent commercial center.

MAIN CITIES

Bremerhaven (population 130,000). Located on the eastern seacoast where the Weser River meets the North Sea, the city comprises 77 square kilometers, a long sliver of land with many of the largest wharves of Europe. A new expressway tunnel has improved connections to the hinterland. The weather is windy, wet, and cool. Container shipping is the mainstay. More than 800,000 vehicles leave Europe via Bremerhaven each year. The Alfred-Wegner Institute for marine, polar, and climate research continues a long tradition of scientific exploration and expeditions, especially in polar regions.

Bremerhaven was founded in 1827 with the purchase of seaside land by Bremen. The Weser's silting made oceangoing traffic to Bremen itself difficult for newer, bigger vessels. Large state-subsidized wharves and dockyards in Bremerhaven served Bremen merchants' shipping, shipbuilding, and luxury liners. Nearly half the German fishing fleet is harbored here. Though the Weser would later be dredged and restore access to Bremen by oceangoing vessels after 1888, Bremerhaven remained the main port for the outflow of emigrants, industrial products from other parts of Germany, or reworked goods such as roasted coffee. The inflow comprised staple goods such as tobacco, sugar, cotton, wool, petroleum, coffee, and rice. For a short time Bremerhaven was integrated into the Nazi district Nordwest and renamed Wesermunde but in 1947 again became part of the city-state of Bremen.

ECONOMY

Transhipping of vehicles, shipbuilding, brewing or roasting (beer, coffee, cocoa), fish and agricultural products, and aeronautics provide the main occupations. Some 40 percent of the population works in trades related to the port, which is second only to Hamburg's in size and importance. Importation of raw materials has hallmarked Bremen trade, especially in timber, copper, wool, cotton, coffee, tobacco, cereals, and cocoa since the 1830s, when it began to ship out millions of emigrants. By the 1850s the shipping lines shifted from sail to steam, especially on the profitable trans-Atlantic route. In 1857 a merger of firms created Norddeutscher Lloyd, which became one of the world's largest shipping lines, and Bremen wharfs produced among the biggest passenger ships. In 1970, after a decline in shipping and shipbuilding, Lloyd merged with its Hamburg rival, Hapag, to form Hapag-Lloyd. During the 1950s and 1960s, automobiles, steel, and electronics supplemented shipbuilding and port activities. Each of the major companies, Borgward in automobiles and Weser and Vulkan in shipbuilding, has gone under between the 1960s and 1995. Mercedes is one of the largest employers.

At present, high-tech industries, research in ecology, and marine-related matters, as well as fine arts and music, supplement the traditional economy related to staple imports. Approximately 10 percent of Germany's export trade, especially automobiles, wine, and industrial products, go through Bremen ports. The commodity exchange and tourism continue to be stable elements in a tenuous economy. A science center shaped like a whale and a second, private university, founded in 2001, are among the efforts to boost its tourist, service, and research sectors. Space research, a Disneylike space amusement center, and laser and marine research have all been encouraged by state investments. However, unemployment remains the highest among the western states.

CULTURAL ATTRIBUTES
AND CONTRIBUTIONS

VISUAL ARTS

The little artists' colony north of Bremen, Worpswede became nationally known when two painters from this tiny village won prizes and sold naturalist landscapes at the Munich exhibition of 1895. Fritz Mackensen had discovered the area's special attributes in 1884 and invited painter friends Otto Modersohn, Hans am Ende, Fritz Overbeck, and Heinrich Vogeler to join him. In 1895 they termed themselves the Artists' Association Worpswede, which only lasted until 1900, but its influence continued. Two special persons associated with the group attained national and international stature: Vogeler and Paula Modersohn Becker. Vogeler's art nouveau designs made him rich, and he established a meeting place for artists at his tiny villa, *Barkenhof*, reconstructed from a farmer's house. In the Weimar era it became a commune and refuge for the politically persecuted; later it became an educational center and children's home. Modersohn Becker's art, expressionist and tending toward the abstract, remained unknown to friends and relatives during her tragic short life. She died at 31 in 1907, just after giving birth, and had completed a thousand paintings and sketches, including some 30 self-portraits. Her multitude of styles in the self-portraits and her still life employing symbolic abstraction made Modersohn Becker Germany's foremost female artist of the early twentieth century, comparable to Käthe Kollwitz.

The Kunsthalle, a private gallery for self-education by the well-to-do, became a public gallery in the 1890s and houses a fine collection of German renaissance art (Albrecht Dürer, Lucas Cranach), as well as late-nineteenth century and early twentieth century examples of German and European styles. The *Übersee* (Overseas) Museum contains cultural objects from former colonies, from traders, and from expeditions of scientific exploration. The ethnography and anthropology of Africa, including, 2,000 skulls, and of the Pacific is strongly represented. The Focke (Regional) Museum houses mostly artifacts from Bremen's history. The Morgenstern Museum in Bremerhaven is a natural history and regional museum on aspects of fishing and fish processing, including model fish shops.

LITERATURE

Only a few figures of national or international stature were born, settled, or worked for a long time in Bremen. The artists' colony nearby in the village of Worpswede drew many seeking rural tranquility and artistic/communal experimentation. In 1899 the poet Rainer Maria Rilke visited and soon returned to live in a neighboring village. The serene landscape of moors populated with twisted birches and solid peasants inspired some of his poetry exemplified in *The Book of Pilgrimage (Das Buch der Pilgerschaft)*. He sometimes worked with Carl Hauptmann, another playwright and poet inspired by this adopted homeland. In 1900, Rilke married a member of the artist colony, the sculptress, Clara Westhoff, and the two went to Paris to work with sculptor Auguste Rodin in 1902. Earlier, from the 1830s to 1850s, the ethnologist Johann Georg Kohl penned widely read accounts based on his travels and experiences among many European and eventually North American people. For much of the late-nineteenth century Arthur Fitger ruled as Bremen's "pope of taste" though his poetry, literary critiques, and his paintings have mostly been forgotten. The inspiration of the moor landscape can be seen in the works of many authors who were drawn to Worpswede. Manfred Hausmann came in 1927 and stayed until 1950, writing his bestseller *Lampioon Kisses Girl and Small Birches (Lampioon küßt Mädchen und kleine Birken)*. Another Bremen *Heimat* (homeland) poet, Wilhelm Scharrelmann, made the moor landscape central to his children's books, such as *Katen in the Devil's Moor (Katen im Teufelsmoor)*.

CUSTOMS

Each February a special meal *(Schaffermahl)* is served in the upper *Rathaus* with a ritualized set of courses. Guests from outside Bremen can be invited only once in a lifetime. The various parish and small villages continue to hold traditional shooting matches, some dating back hundreds of years. These involve much fanfare, processions, and parades. The two-week-long so-called free market *(Freimarkt)* is a fair dating back to 1035. Such social events complement extensive music and theater offerings in the classical tradition. The churches and a hall with special acoustics, *Die Glocke*, are the main music venues.

Sports, especially professional soccer, are popular as is hiking and biking in the moors.

ATTRACTIONS

The stone statue of Roland with shield and coat of arms, which replaced a wooden one, is located on the main market square and dates from 1404. He symbolizes the freedom of the city. Behind him are the Renaissance façades on the *Rathaus*, built in Gothic style in the early fifteenth century. On the same square is the *Schütting* (chamber of commerce tax collecting house). These and some elegant commercial half-timbered houses are among buildings carefully restored after World War II bombing destroyed many historic edifices. Close by is the large late-medieval cathedral with six mummies from the seventeenth and eighteenth centuries. A narrow passage leads from the market to the *Böttcherstrasse*, with art built into the walls of the walkway. A complex of buildings and galleries offers a variety of styles. The *Roselius-Haus* offers part of the collection of objects and tapestries of the Bremen patron of the arts, Ludwig Roselius, the inventor of decaffeinated coffee. The *Atlantis-Haus* contains a modernist dome also designed by the architect Bernhard Hoetger, and the Paula-Modersohn-Becker-Haus contains much of her art. Toward the river is the *Schnoor* quarter, once a slum and sailor hangout inundated by spring floodwaters. The tiny high-gabled houses are now home to craft shops in what is considered quaint and rustic surroundings. Many of the rich shipping and industrial

Figure 5.1
City Hall (seventeenth century) and Roland statue, Bremen.

Source © Press and Information Office, Germany.

families' villas along the old moat and the main park illustrate well the styles and high income levels of the elite during the nineteenth century.

In Bremerhaven the Columbia wharf and ship terminal provide the main attractions in the city. Promenades on the Weser River offer observation points for ship traffic and the 100 foot lighthouse. The theater in art nouveau style (1911), and churches and monuments dating back only to the mid-nineteenth century underscore the newness of the city.

The National Maritime Museum offers the history of the German merchant marine and the navy, including luxury liners from sail to steam. Every type of ship sailing German waters is represented, including illustrations of conditions on board. A special draw is a Hanseatic cog or shipping vessel, dating from the 1380s, recovered from the Weser bottom. Surprisingly large, it has been superbly restored and is known as the world's best surviving plank ship from that era. A submarine museum provides a tour of a World War II U-boat. The open-air museum too is related to the sea and shows a variety of old ships, from whaling vessels to fire boats and tugs.

CIVICS AND REMEMBRANCE

The state office for political education provides information, books, and seminars fostering tolerance of foreigners, understanding of parliament and political parties, plus local history. Examples from the recent program of lectures and presentations include remembrance of the victims of National Socialism and information on treatment of gypsies *(Sinti* and *Roma)*. School programs focus on understanding foreign cultures so as to avoid the antiforeigner attacks of the 1980s and 1990s.

Recently, there has been much emphasis on acknowledging the Holocaust. Memorials identify where a synagogue was burned and Jews murdered on November 9, 1938, and slave labor and concentration camps near the city, such as *Missler* and *Valentin*, a huge submarine bunker built mostly by foreign workers at Farge. Former slave laborers from Poland have been invited to visit the city to recount their experiences especially to young Germans.

CUISINE

Fresh fish is the staple offered in a variety of types and ways, including the traditional marinated herring eaten with green beans.

The dish eaten in winter is *Kohl* and *Pinkel* (finely chopped kale cooked with onions and lard accompanied by sausages, some grits filled), served with boiled as well as fried potatoes. Such traditional food is hearty and accompanied by beer, especially the dominant local brew, Beck's, and wine. Bremen's *Rathaus* offers the world's largest and finest selections of German wines. Vegesack, a Bremen suburb, is known for its *matjes herrings*, marinated filets.

KOHL AND PINKEL (KALE AND SAUSAGE)

2 pounds curly kale (tastier if it has been frozen)	salt to taste
1/3 cup lard	4 smoked pork chops
1 medium onion, diced	pepper to taste
1/2 pound bacon, diced	1 tablespoon rolled oats
1 pound pork and grits sausage	

Wash kale and trim away stalks, blanch in boiling water, and drain. In large saucepan melt lard, sauté onions, add kale, bacon, sausage, and salt. Add pork chops and cook covered over low heat for an hour. Season to taste with salt and pepper. Add rolled oats to thicken in last 5 minutes. Serve with boiled potatoes, though usually fried ones with *Speck* are also offered.

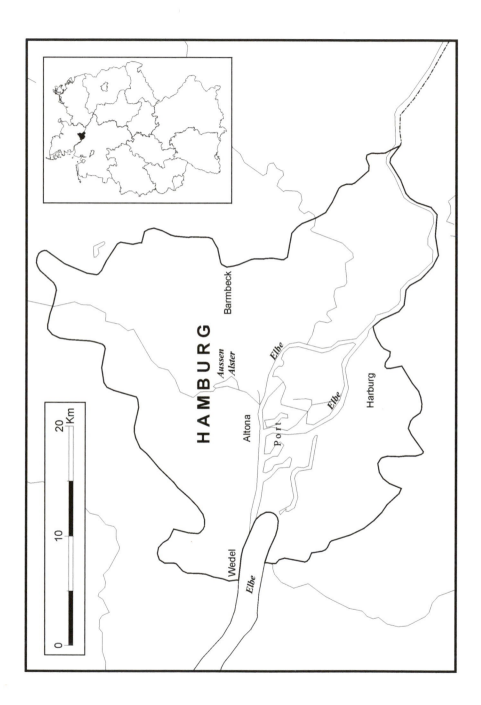

Chapter 6

𝕳𝖆𝖒𝖇𝖚𝖗𝖌

SPECIAL ASPECTS

The people of the Free and Hanseatic City of Hamburg are seen to be independent and cosmopolitan, and sometimes thought to be like the English. Trade and water previously determined Hamburg's fortunes; air has become more important since communications, electronics, and high-tech aircraft are the commerce of the present. The locals are proud of their city and its cultural institutions and claim that Hamburg is the richest and most productive city in Europe. Much green space and investments in culture, especially the tradition of high-quality music, drama, and arts, has sustained local pride.

REGIONAL TRAITS

The second-smallest state by size (area 755 square kilometers), Hamburg as a city-state has lost population to its surrounding suburbs since the 1970s. Its current population is 1.7 million. With many Lower Saxon towns to the south and Schleswig-Holstein towns to the west, Hamburg's metropolitan region encompasses more than 3.5 million people within and outside the city-state. Approximately 15 percent are foreigners. Approximately 100 kilometers from the sea on the Elbe River, Hamburg is Germany's largest overseas trading center and second largest city after Berlin. The coat of arms and flag have a white castle portal on a red background, signifying Hamburg as a gateway to the world.

Native Hamburger speak Low German, *Plattdeutsch*, though nearly everyone is capable of High German. Integration of outsiders has been a constant issue for this port city since the mid-nineteenth century. Migrants, including Poles and Danes, came from the immediate hinterland to work in crafts and industries. These were followed during World War II by slave laborers, then German refugees from the east—nearly 15 percent of the population by 1950. Since the 1960s a wave of immigrants—so-called guest workers—came from southern and eastern Europe. During the 1980s a wave of asylum seekers appeared. Approximately 15 percent of the Hamburg population comprises noncitizens from other European and Asian countries.

Does any regional identity emerge for this prosperous trading city? In 1959 the state printed a book for school students, which began with a poem by Wolfgang Borchert:

> Hamburg!
> That is more than a pile of stones, roofs, windows, carpets, beds, streets, bridges
>   and street lights.
> That is more than factory chimneys and cars honking
> More than gulls' laughter, street car screeching and the thunder of the railway
> That is more than ships' sirens, cranes' cries, cursing and dance music
> Oh, it is endlessly more
> It is our will, to be.
> Not anywhere, not any way,
> But here, and only here, between Alster lake and Elbe stream
> And only to be, as we are
> We, in Hamburg.

Though the fear of survival is gone, the poem may still express important elements of regional identification in just being and having a home port in a stormy world.

GEOGRAPHIC FEATURES

The city is built over low marshy, sandy plains but contains two large basins *(alster)* around which it expanded, especially in the nineteenth century. Previously, the city limits stayed within the medieval walls along the northern riverside. The city-state, shaped like a jagged triangle, is surrounded to the north side of the Elbe River by Schleswig-Holstein and to the south by Lower Saxony. Hamburg, in a manner similar to Bremen and Bavaria, nearly kept its traditional boundaries in the post–World War II restructuring of Germany. But changes occurred because it kept the suburbs added in 1937, Altona in the west and Harburg to the south.

The cityscape comprises bridges and cranes along the river port. With more than 2,300 bridges (more than Amsterdam or Venice), Hamburg is often termed the Venice of the north. Traffic congestion is serious, since the wide river and many canals impede the creation of main arteries.

HISTORY

Hamburg's development has been related to its port, though at first the town served as a center of Christian missionary activities. The bishopric established in the ninth century amounted to a fortress *(burg)* in a depression *(hamma)*. Soon commercial, craft,

Figure 6.1
Inner Alster, Hamburg.

Source © Press and Information Office, Germany.

and trading houses surrounded the *burg*. Due to Viking and Slavic raids, as well as conflicts between the secular and religious powers, the town remained smaller than neighboring Stade, downstream on the Elbe. Lübeck, on the Baltic coast, outpaced Hamburg as the northern continental mercantile center.

In the twelfth century, with the building of protective walls, Hamburg began to prosper, especially once a group of merchants created a "new" center west from the bishop's "old" city. In 1300, the town of approximately 5,000 inhabitants became a member of the Hanseatic League of north European trading cities. Fish, grains, linens, and many agricultural products—moved from between Russia and Spain, from the Elbe River hinterland to Scotland—were a hallmark of Hamburg's profitable commerce.

Organized in parishes dominated by church spires, each area of the city had its own dominant group of craftsmen or traders. After many debates, the Lutherans prevailed in the Reformation struggles of the 1530s. Though encouraging some cultural activities such as church-related art and choral music, the religious leaders exercised such an intolerant rule that it partly inspired Gotthold Lessings' play *Nathan der Weise (Nathan the Wise)* (1779), advocating religious tolerance.

Hardly touched by the Thirty Years' War, Hamburg prospered due to trade in colonial goods and artisan products. For example, in 1780 8,000 people in 800 establishments were employed in refining cane sugar imported from the Caribbean.

The city grew to more than 100,000 inhabitants by the middle of the eighteenth century. Its population began to pour out of the defensive walls as this medium-sized city-state's trade attracted craftsmen and traders from the Netherlands, France, and German hinterlands. The upper middle class, rich traders and well-to-do clerics and lawyers, supported a high culture of opera, music recitals, and theater. This prosperity was interrupted by the French revolutionary and Napoleonic eras. At first smuggling and shipping under a neutral flag aided trade, but then taxation, confiscation, and occupation drastically undercut it. Napoleon annexed Hamburg as a department of France from 1810 until 1814.

During the nineteenth century, with increasing trade, especially exporting grains and trans-shipping of British industrial goods, Hamburg's population soared. The protective walls were dismantled. From less than 200,000 in the 1820s, the population exceeded 1 million before World War I. By 1860, less than 60 percent of the population had been born in the city-state. The unregulated urban growth resulted in slum housing, limited sewers, and no water filtration systems. In 1842 a three-day fire razed a quarter of the old city, and in 1892 a cholera epidemic killed nearly 10,000 people in six weeks. Such events illustrated the consequences of a bourgeois, amateur administration focusing resources solely on trade. Between the 1860s and 1880s, harbor expansion and modernized wharfs impacted the city's composition. Lower-class housing was destroyed to create a "storage city" (Spicherstadt). During this era, an oligarchy of lifelong senators and a restrictive voting system limited political participation to a small elite, though Social Democracy and militant port workers challenged their rule with strikes and protests.

The Baltic–North Sea canal opened access to northeastern European markets after 1895, and the Boer War brought great returns to Hamburg's commerce. By 1914, Hamburg's premier shipping line, the HAPAG under Albert Ballin, became the largest in the world. Saltpeter from Chile and passengers on the Atlantic were among the many profitable goods moved. In the late-nineteenth and early twentieth centuries, the multitude of small traders and shippers' countinghouses began to be replaced by large office buildings, many fronting the inner and outer basins. A few architectural gems, such as the Dovenhof and Chilehaus, survived the bombing of World War II. The bombing aimed to devastate the naval and aircraft industries but also to break civilian support for the war effort; it involved incendiary bombs that unleashed a firestorm in 1943. Some 100,000 people died during World War II, including approximately 50,000 in concentration and labor camps near Hamburg.

The 1929 depression had already undercut Hamburg's prosperity, including the functioning of the democratic political system created after the Revolution of 1918–1919. Though Social Democrats ruled in conjunction with liberals during the Weimar era, the city was considered "Red" because, as in Saxony, the Communists had some support and even attempted an uprising in 1923. A strong labor movement offered resistance to the National Socialists, but the middle class and elite showed few qualms about cooperating with the Nazis, who took over the city in 1933. Already by 1932, the Nazi fanatics had become the largest party in the city's assembly. As elsewhere, one-party rule replaced parliaments. Armaments production was fostered. Dissenters were jailed, and the large Jewish minority suffered many forms of discrimination, including loss of property, destruction of synagogues, and eventually loss of life. Many emigrated before the deportations and deaths of the world war. A major concentration camp at Neuengamme held Marxists, socialists, liberals, and Jews. Many subcamps organized forced labor by Poles and Soviets.

British troops occupied Hamburg in April 1945 and installed a Social Democratic-led provisional government. Little opposition existed to Hamburg's re-creation as an independent state of the federation established in 1949. In 1946, the British occupation forces allowed the democratic constitution of 1921 to be restored. In 1953 and 1954, a commission examined the capability of small states such as Hamburg to carry out administrative and cultural tasks according to the federal constitution. The commission confirmed Hamburg's separate status.

The constitution of 1921 served as the model for the new one passed in 1952. After the rebuilding and reestablishment of trade ties, Hamburg became one of Germany's richest regions. The Social Democrats dominated the parliament, with majorities in the 1957, 1961, 1966, 1970, and 1978 elections. By the late 1980s, the Christian Democrats and Green party challenged the Social Democrats, who had provided every mayor from 1945 to 1982. After the 1997 elections, the Social Democrats combined with the Green ecological party to form a tenuous coalition. In 2001 a revived, tiny liberal party, plus a new conservative state party, combined with the Christian Democrats to form a coalition. In 2004 the Christian Democrats won a narrow majority, and the Social Democrats suffered a postwar low. However, at present no party dominates the political arena, hence few social improvements are expected.

ECONOMY

Clearing rubble, rebuilding the harbor, and providing housing were the first tasks after the war. During the 1950s, the Senate used large state subsidies and deficit financing to build housing and develop infrastructure. After the worst flooding in centuries during 1962, new dykes and floodplain controls were built. Those large projects helped employment, but the economy also boomed due to revived trade patterns. Shipbuilding, shipping, and exporting the products of German mills, such as automobiles, restored Hamburg's trade. By the 1960s, service industries and airplane manufacture (later the Airbus) supplemented port activities. However, processing raw materials from abroad continued to be the main base of the economy. By the 1980s, Germany's highest personal incomes were matched with the highest unemployment rates.

By then Hamburg had become Germany's premier media and publishing center—17 of 21 news magazines with over 1 million circulation are published in Hamburg and some 6,000 firms are active in this sphere. The city is home to many radio, television and multimedia electronics firms. Daily *(Bild, Die Welt)* and weekly newspapers *(Die Zeit)*, weekly journals *(Der Spiegel)*, and many special-interest journals

(Hör Zu, Stern) continue to be published here. The newer technologies of video and computer games have been added. Music production studios as well as television and radio interact. Hamburg is a rich city that has successfully combined being Europe's second-largest container port and a center of financial, industrial, and social services.

Simultaneously, Hamburg remains the banking and insurance center for northern Germany. Finance and service industries have become especially strong. Banking, insurance, and the stock market keep expanding. A large number of consulates represent countries with which Hamburg trades. Some 6,200 exporting firms have offices here, including some 1,700 from industrial firms. Foreign investment is strong. The world's largest catalogue order company *(Otto Versand)* operates from here.

However, the city has social problems from unemployment, drug use, and economic inequality. Indeed, many people only work in Hamburg and live outside it, thus undercutting its tax base in favor of the surrounding countryside. Strong professional sports clubs and cultural industries do not employ many people. Restaurants and pubs do, but those are low-paying jobs. Among those receiving welfare or social support, more than 25 percent are foreigners. That is the group that supplies most of the population increase, but to service it—for example, with educational opportunities—is costly.

CULTURAL ATTRIBUTES
——————— AND CONTRIBUTIONS ———————

VISUAL ART

Hamburg's church art and seventeenth-century Netherlands-influenced paintings reflect major European styles. Later, only a few major artists, such as the Romantic Philipp Otto Runge, worked or came from Hamburg. However, the *Kunsthalle* collection, especially as developed by Alfred Lichtwark (from 1886 to 1914) and Gustav Pauli, provided Hamburg with one of the foremost galleries of impressionists and postimpressionists, including many works by Max Liebermann. Simultaneously, Justus Brinkmann developed a major art nouveau collection in the *Museum für Kunst und Gewerbe* (design museum), which contains objects from many eras. After World War II, the cigarette manufacturer and art patron Hermann Reetsma donated the Barlach-Haus, which displays many of Ernst Barlach's expressive etchings, drawings, and sculptures.

LITERATURE

In the eighteenth century, many enlightened authors such as Friedrich Gottlieb Klopstock wrote texts that became part of the German classic tradition. Newspapers such as the *Hamburgische Correspondent* contained literary contributions and sold all over Europe. By contrast, Gotthold Lessing had little success with his dramas and left Hamburg in 1770. Publishing, however, remained strong with houses such as Campe, which printed Heinrich Heine, Ludwig Borne, and Friedrich Hebbel. In the twentieth century, Richard Dehmel, Willy Bredel, and Wolfgang Borchert received much notice and many book prizes, though only Bredel used local landscapes and themes. Borchert, who sought to help the postwar generation understand World War II, appreciated the city's diversity.

MUSIC

Hamburg had the first German public opera house in 1678 though guides to operas had been printed as early as 1657. In 1721, Georg Philipp Telemann became church music director, and he composed here for over 46 years while expanding music offerings in the city. After Telemann's death, Carl Bach performed many of his father's works. By contrast, Johannes Brahms and Gustav Mahler stayed less than a decade despite some public support. The state opera has a solid reputation; locals insist it is world-class. The philharmonic and the radio orchestra have been able to draw known directors. The Beatles had their start here, and at present the music scene is very varied. Jazz and pop are part of the bistro world, which is very extensive.

ARCHITECTURE

Few pre-twentieth-century buildings remain due to the firebombings during World War II. One hallmark of the skyline is St. Michael church, with its copper-green dome that dominates the old city. During the late nineteenth century, when the city was prosperous, many spectacular buildings were erected. One is the new town hall (1897), built in the Renaissance style. Like the *Speicherstadt* (storage city), these edifices are popular tourist attractions. They were the result of extensive town planning under Fritz Schumacher (1869–1947), who became *Baudirektor* (city planner) in 1909.

THEATER

Hamburg has had a strong tradition in drama since the publication of Lessing's work in the late eighteenth century. At the end of the nineteenth century, Baron von Berger headed the *Deutsches Schauspielhaus* (German Theater). He staged innovative theater productions, including *Hedda Gabler* by Henrik Ibsen and *Rose Bernd* by Gerhard Hauptmann. In 1906 Leopold Jessner took over the Thalia Theater, where he directed provocative plays such as Frank Wedekind's *Erdgeist* and *Pandoras' Box*. Later in the twentieth century, two actors attained international fame, or infamy, due to their skills and political opportunism under the Nazis and their ability to continue their craft afterwards: Gustaf Gründgens and Elisabeth Flickenschild known for their performances in *Faustus*. Hamburg's theater tradition has remained strong and original to this day. The *Deutschen Schauspielhaus* repeatedly wins theater of the year. It and the Thalia Theater are accompanied by some 40 smaller ones, including the modern *Kulturfabrik*.

ATTRACTIONS

The Sunday fish market has become a beer and shopping attraction for nearly every commodity, while the St. Pauli red-light district tries to match Amsterdam's prostitution displays. A 400-meter tunnel under the Elbe, constructed in 1907, connects St. Pauli with the old city. The dykes along the Elbe provide walking and biking opportunities, while the automobile has made Lower Saxon heaths and Schleswig-Holstein coasts easily accessible since the 1960s. The Hagenbeck Zoo, created in 1907, keeps animals in more natural settings and is one of Europe's premier collections.

Tourists tend to head for the haunts where the Beatles first sang in local basement bars. British youth, before and after soccer matches, head for the seamier side of St. Pauli, with its *Reeperbahn* of endless bars (now without sailors). Some go to the same *Reeperbahn* area for the prostitutes in a well-marked and policed area. Among many "good" *Burger* (citizens), it is customary to lead visitors there for a stroll and a voyeuristic peek. Songs with hints at naughtiness, especially about the rougher part of St. Pauli (*St. Pauli, St. Pauli bei Nacht . . .* [St. Pauli, by night . . .]) are more sung than acted upon.

Hamburg is especially rich in museums. Its city museum goes from prehistory to the present; the ethnological museum is especially strong on the South Sea areas, where Hamburg traded. A toll museum presents the history and impact of customs on goods and people. The spice museum offers hands-on experiences, while the communications museum fits well with the city's role as a media center. An Afghanistan museum educates about one of the trouble spots of the world. The Johannes Brahms commemorative museum illustrates his creativity in music while the Ernst Barlach museum, on the edge of the city, demonstrates the versatility of that artist and dramatist. Especially informative is the museum examining the theme of work. It demonstrates changing laboring and, to a lesser extent, living conditions since early industrialization. The Bucerius foundation offers art via major exhibits at its gallery. Old ships anchored in the harbor allow exploration of sailing and handling of goods.

The city appears new because so much building took place after the firebombing of World War II. In the 1980s, glass and steel took over from concrete, and buildings rose higher due to space limitations. Many glass-covered buildings, such as the *Berliner Bogen*, a huge structure like a football field covered over with a glass dome, and the so-called Smart City of glass hung over a minimal steel structure, become almost eerie in their translucence at night.

CUSTOMS

A former chancellor, Helmut Schmidt, popularized a little blue sailor's hat for his home city-state, but it is not as prevalent as the customary street greetings. Locals and tourists spend much time in the *Schanzenviertel*, a quarter that offers shopping and fresh produce in a trendy, rundown area with many bistros, coffeehouses and folk clubs. On Sundays, local families stroll the parks and stop for cake and milk-coffee. Each year, around May 7, Hamburg celebrates its harbor with tours and the anniversary of the mythical granting of freedom to the city. A botanical garden, *Planten un*

Blomen—the name reflects the slowly disappearing Low German dialect—contains special fountains and offers music throughout the summer. One of Germany's largest carnivals is staged in February. Fireworks accompany the monthlong music, theater, and dance spectacles of the *Alstervergnügen* (enjoyment on the lake), which has been celebrated since 1650.

The prosperity and perhaps the family relations of the city-state may be reflected in statistics relating to dogs. Ninety-four veterinarians, 16 clinics, one ambulance, two taxi companies, three hotels, 16 training institutes, 45 beauty salons, eight cemeteries, and two homeopaths attend to the needs of canines.

CIVICS AND REMEMBRANCE

Though mostly supported by the private foundation of the Reetsma tobacco fortune, the Hamburg Institute for Social Research has publicized much local history, especially about the Nazi era. Recently, it exposed the war crimes of the German military *(Wehrmacht)* with photographic evidence, and the exhibition later traveled throughout Germany.

The city has supported public education about concentration camps by maintaining *Neuengamme*, one of the main concentration camps created in 1933 on the site of an old brickworks, plus identifying some of its 80 subcamps with plaques. Two of the subcamps, *Bullenhauser Damm*, where tuberculosis experiments were conducted on Jewish children, and *Plattenhaus Poppenbüttel*, where female Jews were interned, have become memorials. The many places at which slave laborers worked in war industries have also been identified with plaques and information sessions have been held about them. From an opposite perspective, a recent debate initiated by new literary and historical accounts of urban destruction through Allied bombing focuses partly on Hamburg. A firestorm in 1943 from Allied phosphorous and incendiary bombs destroyed the entire central city and killed thousands of civilians.

The local office for political education has handled regional history in a special way. In the 1960s, emphasis focused on Hamburg's ability to survive, despite major disasters. Five were usually identified: the French occupation in 1806, with destruction of its commerce; the massive fire of 1842; the cholera epidemic of 1892; the loss of World War I with the destruction of maritime shipping; and, finally, the bombing destruction of World War II. The office repeatedly points to the local tradition in democracy, the constitution of 1921 and how it came into being. In addition, it is one of the few offices that has and continues to emphasize the contributions of Social Democracy and the strong local labor movement in fostering German parliamentary democracy. In doing so, it has identified historical role models, such as local Social Democratic parliamentarians.

CUISINE

Eel soup is a traditional dish, but novelties such as Turkish pizza—thin crust with red cabbage, cucumber, tomato, plus meats—illustrate the contemporary influence of foreign workers and international culture. Traditional drinks, such as clear spirits and beer, the latter sometimes mixed with soda, are being replaced by wine. A refined popular dish, served in the best restaurants, is stuffed baby chicken, *Stubenküken*. The name comes from the times when baby chicks were allowed to run around inside cottages to keep warm on cold days, but some were eventually popped into an oven. Now they are stuffed with mushrooms, livers, onions, and breadcrumbs, plus spices. Eel and fish are frequently served "blue" that is, boiling vinegar is poured over the cleaned eel. Then the eel is immersed in boiling water containing salt, lemon, and greens, such as parsley or celery, with reduced heat for about 10 minutes. This is served with salted potatoes and clarified butter.

Hamburg Eel Soup

1 eel of about 1 1/2 pounds	1 small onion
2 tablespoons coarse salt	1 bay leaf
1 quart water	3/4 tablespoon vinegar
some peppercorns	2 diced medium carrots
mustard seeds	a few diced celery stalks

The eel should be cleaned and skinned, then rubbed with coarse salt. In a big saucepan, bring water to boil and add ingredients, simmering for half an hour. Pull out eel and cut into 3″ pieces. Strain broth and then return eel to pot. Sometimes 1/2 cup of prunes is added and the soup is garnished with fresh basil.

Chapter 7

$\mathfrak{Hesse}$

SPECIAL ASPECTS

The Hesse region is a combination of small villages with an ultramodern banking capital (Frankfurt). The 1980's television series *Heimat (Homeland)* used a Taunus village to represent common peoples' experiences during the twentieth century. The popular, long series of episodes, offering an image varying greatly from the stereotypical, even ran on public television in North America. In it the Hessen hinterland served as the backdrop to the idea of a land with which people identified as they experienced the changes they mostly did not create (motorcycle, automobile, autobahn, migration to the urban centers, Nazism, war, and postwar modernization). They experienced, they participated, and they survived.

Against that historical, almost nostalgic, image must be placed the region's progressive education and social modernization after World War II. Long located at the edge between competing Catholics and Protestants, religious differences mean little to the region at present. Instead, being on the edge between the country and the globe is where the tension lies.

Simplicity and hard work are much prized by locals, who claim to be resolute in tough times. Difficulties are supposedly faced with a biting sense of humor. If Thuringia claims to be the country's "green" heart, Hessians sometimes claim to be its "quiet" heart.

REGIONAL TRAITS

This midsized state of 21,100 square kilometers contains just over 6 million inhabitants with nearly 10 percent foreigners. Forty percent of the region is forests, including many old oaks, some threatened by acid rain. Forests predominate in the

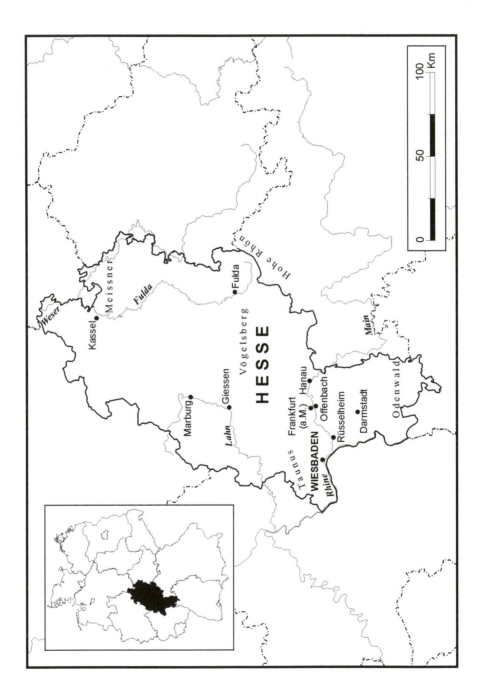

north, industry and urban centers in the south. To the west is Rhineland-Palatinate, to the north North Rhine-Westphalia and Lower Saxony, to the east is Thuringia, and to the southeast is Bavaria, while the south just touches Baden. This region is the main crossroads in western Germany. The Frankfurt, Wiesbaden, Darmstadt triangle is a maze of autobahn and railways. The flag and coat of arms is a griffin with diagonal red and white stripes against a blue background.

GEOGRAPHIC FEATURES

The Rhine and Main rivers remain significant for transporting heavy goods. The Rhine forms part of the western border in the southwest. The Main River, like the Lahn, cuts across the region westward to join the Rhine, while the north is drained by the Weser and its tributaries, the Eder (subtributary Schwalm), Fulda, and Werra rivers. Hessen's Rhine-Main ports have been superceded in economic importance by roadways and airways, which defy geography. Major autobahns intersect near Frankfurt and the western lowlands. The Frankfurt airport keeps taking up more land and remains central Europe's leading international landing spot. The Weser River forms part of the northern border of the state, which has some hilly regions such as the Meissner and Reinhardswald uplands. Most of the hilly area is in the south, formed from volcanic eruptions. Uplands include the Taunus (southwest), Vogelsberg (central east), Rhön (east), and Odenwald (far south), with heights just under a thousand meters (3,000 feet). On the border with Bavaria is the Spessart.

HISTORY

"Great" Hessen, as it has been termed, began as the dream of some politicians in the nineteenth century and was discussed after the Revolution of 1918. The Americans, at first reluctant, later helped it become a reality after World War II with a constitution signed in December 1946. The territory included a combination of Hesse-Darmstadt and parts of Prussian provinces (with some Hessian territory going to Rhineland-Palatinate). Attempts to reverse the merger process via plebiscite failed in 1956. The region, which became the political state, has a varied history that sometimes has been patched together into one narrative. However, it also can be seen as pieces developing separately.

Hessen, as a crossroads from north to south along the Rhine River and east to west along the Main River, has rich evidence of prehistoric inhabitants, especially in the form of defense works. The state heritage office responsible for preserving artifacts occupies a large palace at Wiesbaden-Biebrich. Archaeological excavations have received much support and have dug up Celtic remains at Bad Nauheim and ceramics at Nieder-Mörlen. Carefully worked tools, artwork, vases, and jewelry have been found at grave sites, such as at Glauberg. The animal and human designs are startling in their simple beauty. One lifesize cult figure of sandstone shows an early Celtic warrior, with exceptionally clear, almost abstract lines.

In the Roman and early medieval era, earthen and wood defense works sought to protect transportation systems on the Rhine and other rivers with their many settlements. The migrations of people and the wars over territory left many battle sites that reveal the high level of armaments technology. The Romans built earth and wood walls (limes) against the eastern migrants and warriors, but they also cultivated vineyards. During the Christianization by various monks such as Boniface, who is buried at Fulda, the *populus Hassiorium* (people of Hessen) were first mentioned (738) in relation to those living near Kassel.

In the Carolingian Empire, the cloisters at Fulda, Hersfeld, and Lorsch became the decisive economic and cultural supports for the Christian missions. A bit later, Northern Hessen experienced a series of wars in which the Saxon kings extended their realm toward the east. The administrative unit *Gau*, which attained infamy under the Nazis, dates from this era.

In the ninth century, Hessian counts united some of the Rhine/Lahn area and, under the Conradini family, held most of the present-day region. They built a series of churches, including the superb Romanesque examples at Limburg and Wetzlar. By the twelfth century, through intermarriage, they claimed to be a princedom. Frankfurt had by then become the place where emperors were crowned and trade fairs held. Large castles defended the Rhine/Main area, though Marburg eventually had more political importance than Frankfurt. The Marburg castle also served as the cultural center for the region. However, many dukes and counts controlled smaller parts of the realm, which continued to have independent bishoprics and cities.

Among all the petty principalities and fights for succession to various territories, Philip the Generous stands out as the main Earl of Hessen. He converted to Protestantism and used the gains from the dissolved monasteries to found schools, charities, and hospitals. At Marburg he established the university where Luther, Zwingli, and Melanchton debated the fundamentals of revised Christianity in 1529. For a short time he provided unity to a region that is almost the configuration of the present state. His successor built Hanau as a residence city with a fine palace, *Philippsruhe* (now a paper museum). However, the religious wars devastated the area and continued to do so through the Thirty Years' War after 1618. The region became a patchwork according to the religious beliefs of the ruling princes. Hence, Fulda remained Catholic while Hersfeld became Protestant. Many people moved into and out of the area due to their religious convictions, including Huguenots from across the Rhine who came to Homburg and Darmstadt.

In the eighteenth century, the Hessian princes and bishops built the typical baroque palaces of the era. Each small principality tried to prove itself the cultural equivalent of the larger states, especially in imitating French models in buildings and court styles. For instance, at Fulda the abbey was rebuilt as palatial residence, while at Weilburg, at Wiesbaden *(Biebrich)*, at Hanau *(Philippsruhe)*, and at Kassel *(Wilhelmshöhe)* a series of new edifices demonstrated the princely ability to tax the peasants and traders. Some of the peasants were forced into the military and sold as mercenaries, serving in the British attempt to repress the American colonies. Others sought a different future through emigration, especially to Russia and the United States.

The French Revolution and Napoleonic era had a profound impact on the region. It ended many of the small states and created a confederation of Rhineland states dominated by the French. The duchy of Hessen became a princedom. Napoleon's brother ruled from Kassel as King of Westphalia and exacted heavy taxation. However, legal reforms introduced equality before the law, including for Jews. Liberal demands for constitutional controls on rulers hinted at the struggles to come. During the early nineteenth century, students and pastors demanded an end to aristocratic rule as well as a national territorial unity. The three main principalities that had survived the Napoleonic restructuring, Darmstadt, Hesse-Kassel, and Nassau, prefigured the present configuration of the state.

The Revolution of 1848 emerged out of the same difficult social conditions, as elsewhere in Central Europe: liberal demands for constitutional reform and national aspirations. However, since the National Assembly met at Frankfurt, attention focused on Hessen. But the revolutionary tide quickly reversed and the previous principalities were reestablished. The National Assembly at Frankfurt was disbanded with little achieved, though feudal aristocratic privileges had been terminated.

Outside influences decided the region's configuration again after midcentury. National unity came in an unexpected form as Prussian troops in 1866 occupied, then annexed, much of Electorate Hessen and combined it into a Prussian province (Hessen-Nassau) within the North German Confederation. The Grand Duchy of Hesse-Darmstadt remained semi-independent within the German-Prussian Empire created in 1871.

Industrialization and urbanization during the last part of the nineteenth century increased mobility and modernized attitudes. Jewish intellectuals and businesses prospered, especially in Frankfurt as publishers and professors. Simultaneously, Social Democracy built an organized challenge to the liberals who began to control the city parliaments. They also challenged the princely rulers, who continued to limit popular sovereignty. World War I ended the blocked reforms, and the Revolution of 1918–1919 brought a *Volksstaat* (people's state) Hessen with its capital at Darmstadt. Under the Social Democrat Carl Ulrich, Hessen included parts of the Palatinate as well as the present territory except the Prussian province administered from Kassel. Though the Social Democrats ruled during the 1920s, they could not retain popular support, especially once the Depression of 1929 undercut employment. The large automotive subsidiary of General Motors, Opel, at Rüsselheim, for example, drastically reduced its car manufacturing workforce. Already by 1931, the Nazi party had the strongest caucus in the regional parliament. In 1933 the Social Democrats were forced out of office and the state coordinated with Nazi party districts *(Gau)*.

In the Nazi period Frankfurt became the head of the Gau Hesse-Nassau in the south, while the Gau of Princely-Hessen had its headquarters at Kassel. The destruction of parliamentary democracy was accompanied by placing leading Communists, Social Democrats, liberals, and dissenters into concentration camps. The Nuremberg racial laws of 1935, the pogroms of 1938, and Aryanization of businesses destroyed Hesse's large and prosperous Jewish communities. During World War II the cities, especially Frankfurt, Kassel, Darmstadt, Hanau, and Offenbach, suffered extensive bombing damage.

The Americans occupied most of the region during March and April 1945. They unified the territory, which became the present state of Greater Hesse. They helped create a parliamentary government that had to address the rubble and destruction left by the Nazi regime. The political rebuilding began with reestablished political parties (Social Democrats [SPD], Christian Democratic Union [CDU], liberals, and Communists) and local elections. Leftist and Socialist tendencies had strong support in the communal effort of overcome Nazism. Those who had aided the regime were to be punished. Structural changes to the economy were introduced to limit the influence of wealth, and socialization and land reform were to be introduced. Plebiscites confirmed that the populace agreed to radical measures, including dispossession of Nazis and redistribution of land, but those were blocked by the Allies.

In Hessen, the 1950s and 1960s saw a successful physical rebuilding as automobile and chemical industries joined banking and commerce in record economic growth. Simultaneously, consumerism remade the labor world with foreigners replacing Germans at menial tasks and on the assembly line. Under Social Democratic leadership, a transformation of the educational system placed Hessen among the most progressive states. However, as elsewhere, denial of the Nazi past continued into the 1960s when spectacular trials of some of the perpetrators took place in Frankfurt (1963). This was reinforced by university student protests that pointed to the continuation of Nazis in prominent positions. They insisted on placing the democratization of institutions on the agenda in the late 1960s.

During the immediate postwar rebuilding, the SPD and CDU cooperated. But from 1951 through the 1970s, Hesse remained a SPD stronghold. The SPD pushed through many educational reforms and modernized society. However, the CDU, under Alfred Dregger, attacked the increasing state direction and raised its profile from 26 percent in 1966 to 47 percent of the regional parliamentary vote in 1974. Despite the CDU electoral increase, by 1985 Hessen had the first SPD-Green coalition, which foreshadowed the national government of 1998. Meanwhile, Hesse had turned back to the CDU in 1987, which first led a minority government with the liberals (FDP) under Roland Koch. He consolidated the CDU position and attained a majority in the 2003 elections; now the CDU rules on its own.

Does this history of plurality of governments, of strength of village associations, of principalities with courtly residences, and of cities with modern flair lead to a new cosmopolitanism? As one of the continuously prosperous and richest regions, can Hessians be casual about the high rate of foreign investment, the ecological costs of economic growth, and declining industries? The rise and integration of the Greens, the continuation of local traditions (even in the form of garden dwarfs), and the strength of the financial and chemical sectors indicate that the quiet heart may have achieved a balance between creating workplaces and maintaining the region's identity.

ECONOMY

Aside from the Rhine-Main and Kassel areas, at the end of the war Hessen mostly comprised an agricultural and poor region. In 1950, 23 percent of the population worked in agriculture and forestry; in 1960, over 13 percent; and in 1970, 8 percent; but by 2000, less than 2 percent. The service sector has doubled from 20 percent to 43 percent, while industry, with 50 percent in 1965, has dropped back to 30 percent by 2000. Part of the modernization program of the SPD during the 1950s and 1960s included investment and credits to farmers, building communal offices, and spreading educational institutions across the rural areas. Hessen thus equalized rural and urban opportunities. State planning included fostering youth and retirees, as well as sporting clubs. By 1965 a "great Hessen plan" sought to coordinate social and economic policies, while the economy grew at about 6 percent per year. Georg August Zinn of the SPD is seen as the father of this successful effort to coordinate state and private enterprise. His successor, Albert Osswald, consolidated his reforms.

During the 1960s, university students demanded more political reforms, and by the 1980s, many in the middle class sought a halt or reversal to state-led planning and direction. However, during the 1970s, the structures of the universities were opened to public input, and at Kassel a comprehensive university combining technical and theoretical subjects emerged. The high financial costs of all these social measures were contained through computerization and by reducing the number of administrative units.

The symbolic break with state direction and planning probably came with the attempt to expand nuclear energy. The atomic reactor at Biblis became the focal point for antinuclear protests during the 1970s. Similarly, despite strong, sometimes violent protests, the government moved to expand the Frankfurt airport. The Greens gained much support for advocating limits to growth and to ecological destruction, but when they attained positions in government after 1985, they saw the need to accept compromises so as not to undercut employment.

Meanwhile, the banking, car manufacturing, chemical, and drug sectors continued to expand. Hoechst chemicals, Opel cars, E. Merck pharmaceuticals, Linde refrigeration, and many smaller auto parts manufacturers and the banking sector made the Rhine-Main region crucial to continued prosperity. In the Frankfurt area alone, which has the German federal bank and European central bank headquarters, 70,000 work in the banking sector. Trade fairs for automobiles, textiles, and specialty products, especially the international book fair, continue a long tradition at Frankfurt. Public relations firms, insurance companies, stock market services, and consultants make Frankfurt the most concentrated financial and service center of the country. Publishing is strong with newspapers such as the *Frankfurter Allgemeine* and *Frankfurter Rundschau* dailies and especially because of the book trade (Suhrkamp, S. Fischer, Campus). Hesse Radio is also located here.

The state has reputable universities and research centers. Marburg has a software development center, Giessen a transfer systems center, Wetzler has optics, while Kassel is strong in environmental issues.

MAIN CITIES

CAPITAL

Wiesbaden (population 260,000). The former residence city of the dukes of Nassau reveals its princely past with spas, casino in a palacelike temple, and a large state theater. The present is more evident in the huge and unattractive Rhine-Main Halle entertainment ensemble. Ugly parking garages have not solved the traffic congestion. The automobile even threatens to overrun the villa areas. As an administrative city, Wiesbaden has many office blocks, cafés, and champagne bars. The façades of the Imperial era have been maintained or rebuilt and are accompanied by many green spaces with fountains and statues. A very tall, neo-Gothic brick church dating from the late nineteenth century marks the center near the market square. Nearby, along the main avenue, north from the railway station, are Rhine-Main Halle, the main churches, the templelike spa, casino, and state theater, plus the huge spa park. The largest number of villas dating from the Imperial era stretch up toward rolling hills covered in vineyards. Also in the hills is a memorial church with five gold onion towers built by the Duke of Nassau for his beloved Russian princess, who died giving birth in 1845.

Some small research-related industries, tourism in casinos and spas, and administration employ most people. The main federal office of the criminal police employs some, 4,000 people but is being moved to Berlin, over objections of the Wiesbadener.

The conservative populace of Wiesbaden comprises mostly bureaucrats and retirees. Hence, it is surprising to find a large collection of expressionist art, especially the forceful colors and stylized portraits by Alexej Jawlensky, in the Hessen Museum. Also very modern and large is a specialty medical clinic, modeled on the Mayo system, organized to assure early diagnosis. Yet tradition is strong. Carnival halts work for nearly a week, even if many go across the Rhine to the larger one in Mainz. Each June Wiesbaden celebrates a huge festival with products from the area: champagne, duck, and Rhine wines.

Frankfurt (population 650,000). The airport, autobahn links, and railways move more people and freight than any other place in central Europe. The Frankfurt air terminal employs more than 40,000 people. Among the goods moved is money. Known as Mainhatten, the city center is dominated by skyscrapers, which filled the holes left by World War II bombing. Frankfurt, long a strong financial center and once home to the Rothschild banking family, became the financial capital of Germany in the 1950s and seeks to play the same role for Europe. About 150 German and nearly 300 foreign credit institutions have offices here. Some 170 insurance companies complement these. In addition, publishing; machine building (auto parts); and chemicals, especially the huge Hoechst firm (30,000 employees, but declining), balance the employment picture. Frankfurt has been an important trade fair city. Post-1945 it became the main book fair center of western Germany. Its international automobile exhibit *(Internationale Automobil-Ausstellung)* is among the main showcases for new designs and technology in the world.

Figure 7.1
Frankfurt am Main, Hesse.

Source © Press and Information Office, Germany.

In the small old center, the *Rathaus* (city hall) square, are some rebuilt half-timbered houses and the *Römer*, where German emperors were elected in the early modern era. The *Paulskirche* (Paul's Church), where the national assembly met in 1848 to 1849 to write a liberal constitution, is another historic site, Johann Wolfgang von Goethe's birthplace and sites relating to his youth have become literary pilgrimage spots. Museums for modern art as well as city artifacts are common.

The growth of the middle class during the nineteenth century is symbolized by the restored opera house, first opened in 1880. Related to the liberal and later Social Democratic outlook of many Frankfurt intellectuals is the large university that has long been strong in critical humanities subjects. Many of its philosophers and social scientists (Franz Neumann, Otto Kirchheimer, Herbert Marcuse) radicals and Jewish, had to emigrate after 1933. The School of Social Research became the New School in New York City. When reestablished at Frankfurt, its leaders, such as Juergen Habermas, showed themselves not as progressive as might have been expected when university students revolted against authoritarianism during the 1960s.

Only a few signs of the medieval wall or the pre-1848 Jewish ghetto remain. More known is the popular drinking area across the river in Sachsenhausen. Apple wine paradise *(Äppelwoiparadis)* hints at the special brew, which, with much local beer, is consumed in bistros where foreigners sometimes outnumber locals.

Offenbach am Main (population 110,000), Frankfurt's neighboring city, suffered drastically from bombing and continues to suffer the barbs of Frankfurters. The leather industry once served a world market, and a museum illustrates its past. The German weather service has its main office here.

Darmstadt (population 140,000) is a residence city that has become an educational and research center (space and speech projects). The technical college has university status. Gardens and palaces in baroque and rococo abound, but most noted is the complex of buildings related to an art colony on the Mathildenhöhe. A series of elongated floral façades demonstrate exterior application of *Jugendstil,* or art nouveau. A Russian chapel (1899) hints at the background of one part of the Hesse-Darmstadt princely family. Retired bureaucrats enjoy the cultural life and closeness to Odenwald hiking.

Kassel (population 195,000) is the only large city in the north of the state. Heavily bombed, the city was rebuilt in concrete with an eye to automobile traffic patterns. Though its original university did not last, the early modern era court fostered knowledge. The philosophical travel writer who accompanied James Cook to Australia and later political radical, Georg Forster, taught here. The Brothers Grimm created their many-volume dictionary of the German language and gathered fairy tales in the region. The theater (1604) and museum (1769) are the first continuous institutions of their kind. The present technical university seeks to compete in many research areas.

Surrounding Kassel are a series of castles and palaces with parks. The most well known is *Wilhelmshöhe,* where Napoleon's brother resided when Kassel served as capital of his Kingdom of Westphalia and where the German general staff established itself at the end of World War I.

Smaller cities, such as Hanau, Giessen, Marburg, or Rüsselsheim (all with populations over 70,000), have specific functions: nuclear energy centers, university cities, wine or automobile producers. Marburg has the elector's palace *(Markgrafenschloss)* towering over its steep streets. Once a Thuringian fortress, it became a residential palace. The university, like the one at Frankfurt, has been associated with left-wing and radical perspectives. Giessen, by contrast, has fostered many eminent scientists, such as Wilhelm Röntgen (X-rays). Justus von Liebig's laboratory has

Figure 7.2
Half-timbered facade, Marburg, Hesse.

Source Courtesy of the author.

become a museum, and the botanic garden dates from 1609. Rüsselsheim is dominated by Opel's automobile assembly plant.

ATTRACTIONS

Tourism equals income, and the locals know the importance of hanging on to those who come to Frankfurt with the intention of only passing through it. The city has a tiny *Römer* area of half-timbered houses and a trendy bistro area, with lots of *Apfelwein*, across the Main River. The romantic Bergstrasse leads past Darmstadt into the Odenwald. Sleeping Beauty's palace *(Dornröschenschloss)*, at Sababurg near Trendelburg in the far north (not far from Kassel), offers children a version of what is in the fairy tale without becoming Disneyland.

The Rhine River draws many tourists. Little rustic villages have become rarer, but tours along the winding wide valley remain popular by boat as well as by bike. Looking as though she seeks to protect the vineyards is the huge *Germania* statue atop the Niederwald monument above Rüdesheim. Built to commemorate the re-creation of the German Reich, in 1877 to 1883, the patriotic symbol of peace and war can be climbed, or one can take a cable car.

Away from nineteenth-century national fervor is the international art venue. Kassel has established itself as one of the world's premier sites for presenting the newest visual artistic trends with documenta, held every four or five years, for 100 days, since 1955. After initial local skepticism, eye-opening exhibits and installations revived modern and contemporary art after the shroud of Nazism. Abstract works by American painter Jackson Pollack or installations by Josepf Beuys publicized and perhaps popularized abstract and event-related art. Certainly it made German contemporary work known in the world and brought the foremost foreign works to Germany. Also at Kassel, as though underscoring the impermanence of all creations, a special museum deals with death in the form of masks, crucifixes, grave monuments, and documents relating to it.

In contrast is homegrown artwork, which has also attained international stature. The cloister at Lorsch is one of the best-preserved Benedictine monastery complexes, including the abbey church (founded in 772, rebuilt in the Gothic style). Its king's hall and the Carolingian gate are its trademarks: open arches in white and dark stone with a main building set above them in a matching pattern. This complex has UNESCO heritage status, as does the fossil site at Messel near Darmstadt, where images of 50-million-year-old mammals are imprinted in stone.

Another aspect of cultural development, closely associated with the region, is the abundance of half-timbered buildings. Hessen can claim many special ones, especially in a combination of black timbers against white fields. The timbers have been used in so many ways that they are difficult to describe. For example, a square house in Frohnhausen has a heavy vertical outer edge, four rows of solid horizontal beams, with supports at a diagonal near the corners. The square roof has a square small central lifted piece above it that culminates in a square tower. The Junker tower in Neustadt has a round stone base, horizontal timbers going in parallel around the building, with two light lines and two heavy ones, then a crisscross pattern under the round roof. Four small round corner towers jut out of each side. These towers have long roof peaks and on their sides repeat the pattern of the timbering. Some village churches, for example the church at Wagenfurth, have a small base, then with arched timbers become larger with each level. Hanau, Melsungen, and Bad Hersfeld have many commercial and administrative buildings done in a variety of such styles.

Bad Homburg, not far from Frankfurt, is a combined castle, palace, park, and spa. The palace built over the castle is in excellent shape because it served as the summer residence for the Prussian monarchs. Wilhelm II had a hand in designing the nearby Savior's Church *(Erlöserkirche)* and employed mosaics and marble in a similar fashion to the Memorial Church *(Gedächtniskirche)*, which is now a preserved ruin in Berlin. Not far away in the Taunus is a reconstructed Roman fortress with museum at Saalburg. Roman military architecture is evidenced by a fortified bridge and the type of walls delineating the empire's territory. Wilhelm II started the restorations during the late nineteenth century.

Fulda, center of Catholic strength as the seat of an archbishopric, has a long heritage. Its large Romanesque cathedral dates from the early medieval era. The bishop's palace hints at the secular interests of the courts held here. Another Romanesque church is well known and easily seen from the expressway. Limburg on the Lahn River had its pretty church renovated to its stark original colors. Its superb symmetry and exquisite carvings fit well with the height of land on which the church is located. Another well-maintained medieval set of edifices is the cloister at Eberbach, which produces fine wines. It is part of the state system of vineyards.

To see how peasants lived in this region a collection of houses, barns, churches, and storage buildings have been brought together near Anspach as an open-air museum *(Freilichtmuseum)*. This *Hessenpark* displays crafts and agricultural processes from the fifteenth to nineteenth centuries.

The Odenwald is among the most used hiking and driving area along the Romantic route south of Darmstadt. Just west is Lorsch, with Michelstadt to the east, while Weinheim is on the route south. All have notable buildings, such as the half-timbered market square at Michelstadt with its fountain, but they should also be noted for the wooded settings and rolling countryside.

CUSTOMS

Carnival, *Apfelwein* (apple wine), and hiking provide the basis for organized and nonorganized celebrations in small and large groups. But village festivals, such as sharp-shooting competitions, association festivals, May Day, and religious holidays, provide the main occasions to display local dress *(Trachten)* and to participate in raising fertility trees or demonstrating semimilitary prowess, including, of course, drinking ability.

Before the nineteenth century the poor had few alternatives, aside from theft and poaching, to survive the repression of robber barons. The latter had closed large territories to fishing, hunting and wood gathering by commoners. In the Spessart area, much of which overlaps into Bavaria, this banditry is remembered by dressing up in torn clothes, fake beards, and peaked hats.

An invented tradition is the *Hessentage*, for which cities and towns must compete. Hessen Prime Minister, Georg August Zinn, started the initiative in 1961 to encourage knowledge about the state among its population. He offered the motto "*Hessen vorn*" (at the forefront) to underscore its progressive educational reforms and common experiences to create awareness of the state and its heritage places. By celebrating together, the 10 days of festivities draws many people to one locale. Local music, plays, and concerts are accompanied by much drinking and dancing. Many Hessians assume this tradition goes back for generations.

CULTURAL ATTRIBUTES
_____ AND CONTRIBUTIONS _____

VISUAL ARTS

The main venue for contemporary art is documenta at Kassel. Unfortunately, they do not have any permanent collections, although some of the installations of Josepf Beuys can be viewed in the Darmstadt *Landesmuseum*. The museums in

Frankfurt (*Städel*, old and modern art) and Darmstadt *(Hessisches Landesmuseum)* have extensive medieval, Renaissance, and modern works. Wiesbaden's Hesse Museum has a fine collection of paintings by Alexej Jawlensky, who worked there for the last half of his life.

LITERATURE

In the early nineteenth century, the Brothers Grimm gathered information around Kassel for both their fairy tales and their dictionary of the German language. The *Goethehaus* in Frankfurt identifies the famous author's birthplace, while the Frankfurt School of philosophers and social scientists of the 1930s, most exiled during the Nazi era, has been honored with plaques. One of Germany's most prestigious literary prizes, the Georg-Büchner Prize, is awarded annually by the German Academy for Language and Literature *(Deutsche Akademie für Sprache und Literatur)* in Darmstadt. Sometimes the prizewinner has been controversial, but the award always aids the author's career.

MUSIC

Given the American postwar influence, it is not surprising to find many venues for jazz and contemporary music in Frankfurt and the larger cities. But the opera and classical symphony repertoire is also prevalent. Many cultural "factories" exist in the cities, which offer a great variety from rock to funk, from pop to rap music. Folk music remains a vibrant tradition in the countryside and at festivals. Darmstadt has an annual festival that features contemporary composers' works.

THEATER

Prosperity has left a rich legacy with major open-air festivals at Bad Hersfeld each summer, while at Giessen and other places the regional summer theater is strong.

CIVICS AND REMEMBRANCE

Hessen's state chancellory has published many *Landeskunde* (regional knowledge) studies since 1981. Those include a history focusing upon the democratic tradition of the region, especially of the 1848 revolution, and upon a special regional identity. The publications of the local office for political education have insisted that it is worthwhile to find what is common to all of the region and to strengthen the awareness of Hessen, since people need a steady reference point in a hectic and mobile world.

Only since the 1980s has that same office supported research on the Nazi era and then disseminated the results. Sites of persecution—the work camp at Frankfurt-Heddernheim, the women's camp at Preungesheim, as well as sites of resistance—have been identified. Sites relating to postwar crisis such as the airlift to Berlin (monument in Frankfurt) and to refugees from eastern Germany (at Philippsthal) existed by the 1980s. Some have been expanded to a series of museums (at Giessen, Rasdorf, Tann, and Wanfried).

In the 1990s an increased emphasis on the sites related to Nazi crimes saw a special focus on Hadamar, where from 1941 to 1945 some 15,000 mentally ill people were murdered. Similarly, the memorial site at Breitenau began to receive official support in 1987 after it had been created in 1984 by private initiatives.

Former synagogues at Assenheim, Auerbach, Erfelden, Gelnhausen, Grosskrotzenburg, Gudensberg, Hadamar, Klein Krotzenburg, Michelstadt, Pfungstadt, Roth, and Schlüchtern have been rebuilt, renovated, or acknowledged by markers. Stadtallendorf has an information and documentation center regarding armaments firms and the Nazis, especially the Nobel dynamite plant, which operated with forced labor. Camps, such as Trutzhain, where prisoners of war were mistreated, and Wiesbaden, where forced laborers worked under inhumane conditions, have been identified, and some serve as educational sites.

CUISINE

Locals claim to eat simply but copiously. A green sauce that might go with the green eggs and ham in the *Cat in the Hat* is a spring delicacy that comes from fresh herbs and has an appealing color and fragrance. Supposedly, only a person from Hesse can prepare real *Grüne Sosse* (green sauce), made with five or six different finely chopped greens, mayonnaise, and eggs. Smelly Limburger cheese and strong *fleischworscht* (meat sausage) supposedly fit with the harsh words *(Herbheit)* in the language and dialect. Locals acknowledge that even the apple wine has a slightly sour taste. Champagne is frequently drunk, though more is made in neighboring Rhineland-Palatinate. Rheingau wines, especially Rieslings, are the specialty of a stretch of villages and towns along the winding Rhine valley. To go with it a culinary elegance has developed in the larger cities.

KASSLER RIPPCHEN (THICK SMOKED PORK CUTLETS)

Serves 4

2 Kassler ribs per person	8 medium potatoes
20-ounce can or jar of sauerkraut	

The simplest way to make this meal is to find the marinated meat at a butcher's or German delicatessen. Buy 2 cutlets per person. If Kassler is not available, buy thick smoked pork ribs or loin and marinate overnight in 2 cups of white wine, 1 tablespoon of salt, 10 garlic cloves, 1/4 cup brown sugar, 1/4 cup melted butter, and 1/8 cup flour.

Sauté cutlets on low to medium heat in a large frying pan. Add sauerkraut and cook until steaming. Separately boil potatoes for about 20 minutes. Serve with butter for potatoes accompanied by Hessian beer or wine.

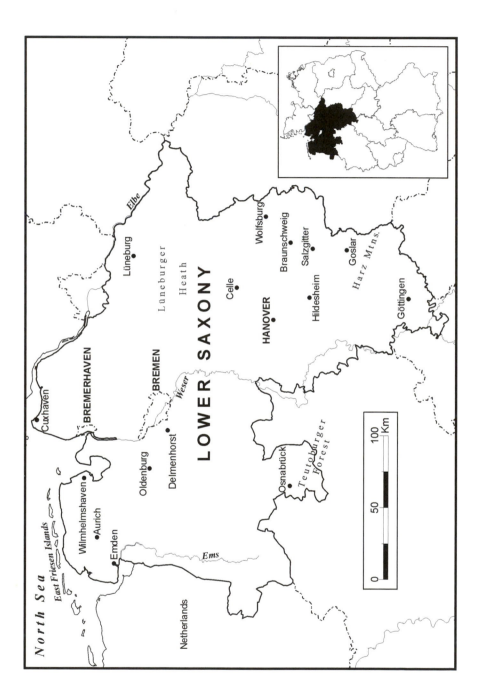

Chapter 8

𝕷𝖔𝖜𝖊𝖗 𝕾𝖆𝖝𝖔𝖓𝖞

SPECIAL ASPECTS

This lowland region, aside from the Harz Mountains in the southeast, contains many of the historical areas of premodern Germany in fairy-tale towns, along raw seacoasts, and within Imperial cities. At times, Swedes, French, English, and Prussians, among others, controlled parts or all of this territory. Combining quiet shores, remote heaths, and fine agricultural lands with industrial wharfs, automobile plants, camera and computer factories, Lower Saxony is a diverse entity. An artificial political unity imposed by the British after World War II melded East Frisians, Hanoverians, and other former Prussian provinces with smaller independent states, such as Brunswick and Oldenburg. The present state proclaims itself the land of the middle—in Germany and Europe—after being on the border with East Germany during the cold war. The former border areas, despite subsides, suffered isolation and economic underdevelopment, which has only slowly been altered since Reunification.

REGIONAL TRAITS

Lower Saxony is geographically the second-largest state with over 47,000 square kilometers and nearly 8 million inhabitants. Many speak *Plattdeutsch* (Low German) in which English and German words seem to be combined. For example, *pien* is pain; *bieten* is bite. North Rhine-Westphalia is to the south, Saxony-Anhalt to the east, Mecklenburg-Western Pomerania to the northeast, and Schleswig-Holstein and Hamburg to the north. Lower Saxony surrounds Bremen.

The coat of arms is a white horse on a red shield. Similar to Mecklenburg and Schleswig-Holstein, carved wooden horses' heads decorate the gables of many farmhouses and large barns to keep away evil spirits. The Harz Mountains are associated with witches, the night of the witches *(Walpurgisnacht)*, and the Faust drama (curiosity about the supernatural world).

GEOGRAPHIC FEATURES

The East Frisian islands in the North Sea provide sand beaches while the mainland coast between the Weser and Elbe rivers comprises tidal mudflats. The Ems River runs north near the western border with the Netherlands, where some of the land is swampy. The Weser River cuts through much of the region from south to northwest. Large heaths stretch around Lüneburg, while the Hildesheim Börde has rich soils in a flat area. In the south the Teutoburger Forest (mostly in North Rhine-Westphalia) is slightly higher than the Weser Hills in the center. Only the Harz area in the southeast contains mountains, which once produced silver and copper. Two-thirds of the region produces agricultural goods, such as smoked hams, honey, wheat, and animals.

Four major landscapes can be identified. A long coastline and major rivers tie the state to the sea. Mudflats and marshy coastal regions give way to sand and gravel as well as moor lowlands. The slightly higher middle areas have natural gas and petroleum, stone, and potash as well as clay and chalk. The southern highlands attain

Figure 8.1
Farmhouse, Lohe, Lower Saxony.

Source Courtesy of the author.

heights of 900 meters (just under 3,000 feet) and provide winter sport opportunities. The population is concentrated mostly in the middle and southern areas, except for Oldenburg (former administrative center) and Wilhelmshaven (military port).

HISTORY

The history of the region can be written as a patchwork, or one can use the version presented by the present state institutions. According to the state, Frisians and Saxons settled the area, with the latter creating an empire by the tenth century. Christianity spread and cloisters and churches were built from the fifth to the twelfth centuries. Reference is made to a multitude of fine medieval examples of Romanesque and Gothic style that still exist or have been restored. The Protestant Reformation, the emergence of absolutism, and the rise of Hanover as a dynastic state follow. Much of that story, for over 500 years (1200–1700), is developed to show a similarity to the general European pattern. This state perspective is in keeping with the emphasis on Lower Saxony as the land of the middle in Europe. After the beginning of the eighteenth century, a long period of territorial divisions begins. This is marked by constitutional conflicts out of which the Bismarckian Reich emerged in the 1870s. In that empire, the present region of Lower Saxony amounted to a series of small federal states and Prussian provinces without internal unity. After the empire's demise in 1918, during the Weimar Republic, Brunswick at first had left-leaning governments, while Oldenburg stayed among the most conservative. However, Brunswick soon became a Nazi stronghold and the crypt of the medieval cathedral was renovated in monumental style. The rural villages in Hanover also quickly turned to the Nazi party. After Nazism, the new political entity is presented as a quite natural unit.

If the patchwork approach is used, more subregional differences appear. The prehistory of parts of the region along the seacoast is quite different from the interior. Before the Frisians controlled the coastal region, small clan settlements had cleared land, built dikes, and drained swamps. Remains of their many graves have been excavated near Hekese, for example. Roads built of logs have been unearthed in the moors near Ossenbecker.

By the sixth century the Frisians from west of the Ems River moved eastward toward the Weser River. They made linen cloth, which traded widely in the Carolingian Empire. However, the Normans overran their main cities in the ninth century. The Frisians remained fairly independent within the Christian bishopric system as well as against the later Saxon expansion from the east. However, in the thirteenth century the bishop of Bremen and the count of Oldenburg began a lengthy and competitive struggle for dominance. Through all the shifts and changes the Frisian peasants retained many of their cooperative institutions and group traits. Frisian identity maintained itself through insistence on local freedom, which meant primarily the right to inherit land and pay taxes to none but the monarch. That meant two groups existed, those who had land and others—day laborers, domestic servants, and seafarers. Only the landowners participated in political and economic decisions. By the sixteenth century, the area fell under militarily stronger outside powers, though the winning of land from the sea and settling of moors continued. The rich built fortified churches and palaces, mostly in simple styles but of solid brick.

The wet climate, topography of windswept low coastal lands, and the proximity to the Netherlands have resulted in Frisians sharing many traits with the Dutch. A local motto says "God made the sea, but the Frisians the coast." Their bridges over canals and dikes could appear in Vincent van Gogh paintings. The local black dress trimmed with white or green (Trachten), the wooden shoes, their linguistic phrases, and peasant parsimony, even the windmills, appear similar. However, in 1945, when the Netherlands demanded part of East Friesland as compensation for German wartime destruction of dikes and loss of land, the Frisians protested and insisted on remaining German. Meanwhile the area, which in 1939 held less than 300,000 people, received nearly 100,000 refugees from eastern German territories. Perhaps to retain local identity, an East Frisian regional authority took responsibility for maintaining Heimat (heritage) knowledge. By contrast, in a reform of Lower Saxon administrative units in 1977, East Frisia became part of the Weser-Ems district centered at Osnabrück and, thus, the former administrative center Aurich lost most of its political influence. Social Democracy has been the strongest postwar political party. Even today, when East Frisians vacation in other parts of Germany, they are asked on their return what it was like to be in Deutschland. The area remains isolated due to lack of rail service except for those trains serving vacationers going through to the ferries for the islands.

Though the Frisians maintained semi-independence, at around 1000 the Saxons unified most of the territory of present Lower Saxony. Indeed, their empire extended north past Hamburg through Holstein, east along the Elbe River, to Magdeburg, down to Halle, south almost to Kassel, and included most of Westphalia past Dortmund. These Ottonian kings renewed the eastern Frankish Empire of Charlemagne. The bishops of Hildesheim complemented this political unity with cultural Christian enterprises, making illustrated books and golden reliquaries and building cloisters and churches. By 1024 the headship of the state went to the Salian clan from the Rhineland, and by 1073 the Saxons rebelled against that dynasty. In 1125 a Saxon again became king. Henry the Lion of this Brunswick line even controlled Bavaria for a time. But his son lost out to the Staufer, who created a new dynasty, Hohenstaufer, that ended Saxon rule. These rulers, preoccupied with crusades south of the Alps, rarely appeared in the northwest of their realm and the imperial residences, including the main one at Goslar, declined. Power became divided among some 40 princes, bishops, counts, and lesser-landed lords. However, one family, the Guelphs, began to consolidate territory, especially based on the dukedom of Brunswick-Lüneburg. Simultaneously, the ducal realms of Hanover and Oldenburg emerged.

The Protestant Reformation brought endless religious, dynastic, and territorial turmoil to the region. The East Frisian leaders proved relatively tolerant to various confessions. By contrast, Brunswick-Wolfenbüttel became the object of military struggles and repeated warfare. After many conflicts and legal disputes, a patchwork of religious holdings according to the ducal preferences emerged. In 1555 the princes finally agreed that their own religion would become the religion of the people of their territory. The choices made resulted in small Protestant areas (Brunswick for instance) surrounded by Catholic ones or Catholic cities surrounded by Protestant rural areas. Those decisions still influence the pattern of religious convictions at present. French, Swedish, and other armies despoiled much of the countryside during the Thirty Years' War (1618–1648). They especially ruined the towns and cities.

By the eighteenth century, fairly large territorial units emerged out of the small principalities, which encouraged a cultural renaissance at the courts of Hanover, Oldenburg, and Brunswick. Palaces, sculpted gardens, theaters, and court music thrived in both secular and religious territories. The rulers of Hanover became the reigning house in England with cultural and political influences moving back and forth, for example, in aristocratic manor house and garden styles. Meanwhile, the populace of farmers and day laborers survived in slowly improving farmlands and cottages, some in combined houses and barns. At the end of the century, through warfare, Napoleon politically reconstituted the region. He consolidated the large states and ended most of the small territories such as the bishoprics and dukedoms.

During the nineteenth century, the railway and industrialization increased the differentiation between larger cities such as Braunschweig or Hanover and the mostly rural areas of Oldenburg and Frisia. The Zollverein economically tied most small northern states to Prussia. Then the wars by Prussia against Denmark, Austria, and France (1864–1871) completely reordered the political boundaries, as Hanover became a Prussian province. Though the small states such as Oldenburg and Braunschweig theoretically remained independent within Imperial Germany, they served as Prussian hinterlands. During World War I they provided cannon fodder and foodstuffs.

Another significant nineteenth-century development was the emergence of the Hanoverian *Landeskirche* (regional church) as an autonomous Lutheran organization. In the late twentieth century, it would be among the first to have a female bishop. The movement emerged out of the revivalism *(Erweckungsbewegung)* of the early nineteenth century under the local leadership of Louis Harms. The intensity of religious faith has continued in the western areas of the state. Church attendance remains high and local village life is still strongly related to the church. Missionary work, both religious and social, within the country and abroad was and remains a significant element of church activity.

During the Weimar era, the various states went in many different ideological directions. Brunschweig, with a suffering industrial workforce, had a much more radical revolution in 1918 and 1919 than agricultural Oldenburg, where a peaceful transition from monarchy to republic took place. Cities such as Göttingen, with many students and retirees, also witnessed a calm shift from monarchy to republic. The northern seacoast cities, such as Wilhelmhaven and Cuxhaven, helped initiate the mutiny against the Imperial military, especially with the naval leaders bent on continuing a lost war in 1918. Afterward, those cities quickly shifted to conservative politics. However, the entire region experienced the economic downturn of 1929, which consolidated right radicalism, partly due to the lack of any resisting middle-of-the-road political strongholds by the Social Democratic or Center Party aside from Hanover. The farmers had already suffered market declines and welcomed any group that would help family units survive. The Nazis made promises to that effect. In addition to outside economic pressures, the Lower Saxon region, especially its peasant population, became attracted to Nazism. A well-known case study of the way the Nazis took over Nordheim shows the ideological transformation of a local elite.

The Nazi takeover and then "coordination," or destruction, of democratic institutions affected cities such as Hanover and Brunschweig by removing people from office and denying them a livelihood. Concentration camps, such as Bergen-Belsen, were quickly established to reeducate those who came from anywhere on the political left, especially Communists and Social Democrats. Later, Catholics would also discover that the regime, which they initially welcomed, sought to destroy their institutions. Persons of Jewish and *Roma* background lost all civil rights and, by 1938, their institutions and property. The farmers found that the "blood and soil" policies, which claimed to save the peasantry and its Germanic heritage, offered more façade than substance.

During and immediately after World War II, the region suffered drastically. Bombing destroyed the large cities because they were readily reachable by air from Britain. Hanover and Brunswick are usually, in the latter case perhaps wrongly, cited for the extreme extent of the damage. However, the coastal cities had their ports and wharf installations destroyed and rail connections disrupted. Postwar food and housing shortages (partly due to refugees from the east) convinced many that they were the victims as opposed to the victimizers of Europe, forgetting about the disappearance of Jewish neighbors or about the foreign slave laborers at industries such as the *Dora-Mittelbau* rocket installations carved into the Harz Mountains.

The British army occupied the northwest region of Germany in spring 1945 and could build on earlier connections between the British monarchy and Hanover. Mainly they wanted to restructure Prussia and end Nazi centralism. In 1946, the British government encouraged the creation of a new state, Lower Saxony, from the Prussian provinces and former small states of Hanover, Braunschweig, Oldenburg, and Schaumburg-Lippe. Hinrich Koch of the Social Democrats was appointed and then elected as leader of the new merged states. By 1951, a provisional constitution approved the merger.

Social Democrats (SPD) have mostly governed Lower Saxony. However, they were forced to govern in coalition, first with a regional party and then with Christian Democrats (CDU), who kept increasing their share of the vote. Except for a short period in the 1950s, the SPD provided the heads of the coalition governments until displaced by the CDU led by Ernst Albrecht in 1976. Gerhard Schroeder, a charismatic, middle-of-the-road pragmatist adept at using the media, returned the SPD to power in 1990 in a coalition with the Greens. In 1998, Schroeder used his Lower Saxon base to attain national power as chancellor. His successors, Gerhard Glogowski and Sigmar Gabriel, maintained Social Democracy with a majority in 2000. However, in 2003 the Christian Democrats under Christian Wulff were able to organize a coalition with the liberals. Splinter parties and interest groups have constantly challenged the norm in post-1945 Lower Saxony. At first a regional party, then a version of the Nazi party, then representatives of the eastern refugees, and finally the Greens have forced concessions—ranging from ideological statements and subsidies to refugees to environmental initiatives—from the government.

An important element in Lower Saxony's, as in Schleswig-Holstein's, post-World War II history related to refugees and exiles. A huge stream of people moved westward to escape the Soviet military. At first, 1944 to 1945, they left convinced by Nazi propaganda about the evils of Bolshevism. After mid-1945, many thousands were forced to leave according to Allied agreements to sort out the minority problems of central and eastern Europe. Mostly they moved knowing that the Soviets, Czechs, Poles, and others intended to exact revenge for the ravages of the Nazi security and military machinery, namely the horrors perpetrated by the killing units of the SS (*Einsatzgruppen;* killing squads) and German *Wehrmacht* (army) in eastern Europe between 1938 and 1945. No matter what the motivations, between 1944 and 1950 at least 2.3 million people streamed into Lower Saxony. Most had to bunk with farm families; many had to live in hutlike barracks at refugee camps.

These people brought immediate social problems, including diseases from displacement and malnourishment. In the short run, they brought radical politics. Seeing themselves as victims, they lobbied for the right to return to their homeland. But in the long run, they also brought skills and became integrated into Lower Saxon society.

The refugee presence, then the influx of so-called guest workers from southern Europe during the 1960s and 1970s to provide cheap labor in industries, changed the demographic makeup. So did the arrival during the 1980s and 1990s of more former Germans from eastern Europe and many asylum seekers from the war-torn Balkans. This raised the question of who could be considered a Lower Saxon. What identity did the mongrel have? This is an important question given the variety of smaller historical entities that merged in 1946. Much integration has been required in this region and more will be necessary if debt-ridden Bremen is melded with Lower Saxony, as is again being considered by a national commission on federalism.

Identity from history. In terms of people's attachment to land and place, the subregions of East Frisia, Harz, Lüneberger Heath, Ems lowlands, and specific cities such as Oldenburg, Hanover, and Brunswick, may mean more than the artificial construct of Lower Saxony. The stereotype of the slow but shrewd peasant Catholic in the west contrasts sharply with the quick-acting Protestant of the east. One delightfully un-modern Frisian, Otto Waalkes, known simply by his television and film name Otto, counters very well the stereotype of the East Frisians as the German hillbilly. He twists common linguistic phrases around, especially making fun of authority figures and of himself. For 30 years he has entertained with his special self-deprecating humor. Is he a Frisian or a Lower Saxon, or both? Though no measure exists for which German regions have more unity, Lower Saxony is not blessed with the historical identification that Bavarians can readily employ.

ECONOMY

Agriculture and forestry remain important, despite the state's desire to achieve high-technology status, especially with wind energy and electronics. In the 1990s automobiles, machine building, and food reprocessing led stable, if slow, economic growth. A few case studies may illustrate Lower Saxony's economic development.

Since 1862 Salzbergen, on the coast, has imported and refined petroleum. Oils for trains became a specialty. Destroyed by bombing, the plant has been rebuilt and has made the transition to supplying automobile lubricants and pharmaceutical products. By contrast, since 1835 the Hanomag in Hanover had produced steam engines, then locomotives and diesel motors. Also destroyed by bombing, the rebuilt firm concentrated on tracked vehicles and trucks. By 1960 it had 11,000 employees but shifted to construction machinery and eventually went bankrupt.

Another contrast is Volkswagen at Wolfsburg. The largest company in Lower Saxony dominates a company town almost exclusively devoted to automobile production. Founded in 1938 as part of the Nazi planned economy, the plant stood isolated in agricultural land. A town had to be created for workers. However, the choice of location included the Mittelland canal tying the Weser and the Elbe rivers with the railway line Ruhr-Magdeburg-Berlin. The Salzgitter steel complex nearby provided sheet metals. After the war the company was nationalized. Some profits go to the national and regional states and some to a large foundation supporting academic research. The success of the VW bug—the world's most produced car model—inside and outside Germany, resulted in a drastic expansion of the city and firm. The world's largest automobile factory had 65,000 workers by the mid-1980s and produced 4,000 vehicles a day. The automated production line is claimed to be the most modern in the world.

If the history of particular firms reveals one aspect of Lower Saxony's economy, the regional variety presents another. Steel, chemicals, and shipbuilding, especially luxury cruisers by the Meyer firm in Papenburg, contrast with specialty items such as pianos and cameras at Brunswick. At Salzgitter, MAN produces trucks. Natural gas and wind energy makes the state self-sufficient.

During the 1990s, the state's economy improved. Incomes still lagged behind the national average and unemployment, which had skyrocketed during the 1980s to near 12 percent, decreased. The most industrialized and successful part of Lower Saxony, Hanover-Braunschweig-Goslar in the southeast corner, remains the most export oriented. Crucial is the automobile industry, of which the motor is Volkswagen. Parts makers and suppliers to the industry have increased economic diversification by moving into smaller towns. Electrical production, steel, rubber, electronics, chemicals, and food processing are among the top industries.

However, industry remains very concentrated with Hanover dominating. Leaving aside the largest, Volkswagen, Hanover has four of the five largest firms. Salzgitter, Hildesheim, Stade, and Göttingen each have one of the top 10, while the port cities of Wilhelmshaven, Cuxhaven, and Emden have none among the top 15.

Hanover's trade fairs expanded immediately after World War II to replace Leipzig in the east and to restore a medieval pattern of commerce. The fairs increased in size until in 2000 the city hosted a world's fair, which may not have drawn the expected crowds but did give Hanover much publicity. Federal funds helped rebuild traffic infrastructure; high-speed train lines now connect Hanover to major cities in Europe.

Though only 4 percent of the workforce is in agriculture, it remains important. Raising cows, pigs, and chickens is big business as is processing food products. Orchard products provide seasonal employment. Recycling and creating pesticide-free foods are supported by the state.

Much emphasis recently has been placed on education and research as a support to the economy. Environmental issues and solutions are the specialty of the universities and colleges at Braunschweig, Clausthal, and Wilhelmshaven. Energy and transportation research *(Transrapid magnetic)* receives state support. The latter are the main high-technology areas as most of the manufacturing has remained in traditional industrial areas such as machine building and automobiles. The media landscape includes many private radio and television studios.

MAIN CITIES

CAPITAL

Hanover (population 525,000). Once the seat of the Guelph dynastic line, Hanover has become known for its trade fairs, which culminated in the world exposition, Expo 2000. The world's largest computer technology fair, Cebit, is held annually in March. By far the largest among the eight cities over 100,000, Hanover dominates the economic and political scene of Lower Saxony. An administrative and distribution center, the city once served as a courtly residence. The city has been and remains an important transportation crossroads for rail, road, and air traffic.

The imposing city hall sits on the edge of a large lake, but little of the old city remained after World War II bombing. The Allies especially wanted to destroy Hanover's machine building. As a result, by April 1945 the massive Imperial-style opera house stood like a Greek temple ruins surrounded by rubble. Today a red line in the central area of the city can be followed to find the main historical sites, some of which have been restored.

The city has had a strong industrial base since craftsmen built locomotives in the mid-nineteenth century. At present, machine building, metal reworking, electrical installations, rubber reworking, food processing, potash, and chemicals remain the major industries. VW builds buses and other vehicles in the suburbs. Hanover's universities, with 40,000 students, tend toward the practical subjects such as medicine and animal care. The technical colleges foster ties to industry, especially Volkswagen located in Wolfsburg. However, theater and music facilities as well as veterinarian studies remain strong in Hanover.

To prove that work and study do not make a complete person, Hanover claims the oldest sharpshooting festival, dating back to 1529. The festival includes ritualized

Figure 8.2
Half-timbered shops and housing, Hanover, Lower Saxony.

Source © Press and Information Office, Germany.

drinking in which four little glasses of *schnapps* are held between the fingers and poured into each other and down the throat.

The extensive eighteenth-century *Herrenhaus* gardens beside the palace are a reminder of the time when the Hanoverian and English royal houses were one. The gardens tend toward the formalistic, with hedges in symmetrical formations and flowers in perfect curves. The grounds are impressive for their immense size, and one large part contains over a thousand linden trees. A botanic garden adjoins the formal collection.

A regional museum offers art and objects from the medieval and early modern eras as well as archaeological artifacts. The Sprengel gallery is replete with modern art. Max Beckmann, Max Ernst, Paul Klee, and Pablo Picasso are represented, while the local contemporary Kurt Schwitters receives much space for his collages and painted ensembles.

Brunswick (population 256,000) is mostly an office-building and industrial complex; the old city is a surprising contrast. Built on an island and reachable from the sea by the Oker River, Brunswick served Henry the Lion as the base for his Guelph empire. Established by 1166, that empire disappeared but left a trading center with cargoes going to Flanders, England, and Russia. In the eighteenth century, the court served as a musical and theater center.

As with many smaller residence cities, today Brunswick offers a multitude of pleasant edifices, which once served the powerful. In Brunswick the city squares and their surrounding buildings usually constitute an aesthetic whole. The present scene is probably cleaner and prettier than when horses left their excrement, sewers flowed above ground, and few flowers adorned the windows. The post–Thirty Years' War prosperity of the city left marks everywhere, though nearly everything had to be rebuilt after World War II bombing. Today's castle square *(Burgplatz)* has a large statue of a lion in Henry's honor on the large cobblestoned area and is the site of the main cathedral *(Dom)*. The lion faces the elegant Romanesque *Dankwarderrode* castle from 1175. On one side is a half-timbered patrician masterpiece. On the other is the cathedral in a stone similar to the castle. On the "small castle" street, half-timbered houses date back to 1500 with the bends of their timbers hinting at their age. The crosspieces of the timbers all have designs and decorations carved into them. The old weighing station is quite different as it has red bricks set sideways between the brown timbering and each story moves farther out from the base. All the squares have fountains, some in very modern bronze form. Some craft guilds were rich enough to build in stone and left Renaissance structures decorated with symbols of their trades. The National Theater, built in the Italian Renaissance style in the 1860s, continues the court theater tradition going back 300 years. Goethe's *Faust* and Lessing's *Emilia Galotti* premiered in the pretty city.

The Duke of Brunswick's art collection includes mainly medieval works and artifacts. By contrast, the main state gallery (the Herzog Anton-Ulrich Museum) has many early modern masters (Vermeer, van Dyck, and Rembrandt). A regional museum contains local historical artifacts, especially from the Guelph era. Containing reliquaries, illustrated Bibles, crafts, and a very large collection of tools, the ethnographic museum complements the regional collection.

At present the main industries are packaging, microtechnology, and food processing. The universities' research strengths are in humanities and microelectronics. Nearby, at Wolfenbüttel, the ducal library *(Herzog August)* is in a town of endless half-timbered buildings. The library contains treasures such as medieval books of hours, illustrated maps, and rare prints and editions, many from the closed university of Helmstedt. A major treasure is Heinrich the Lion's beautifully illustrated *Evangeliar* (a twelfth-century religious handbook). The *Lessinghaus* in the same small city honors Gotthold Lessing, who spent his last sad 11 years writing serious theater pieces.

Osnabrück (population 168,000). Many Catholic churches and cloisters are a reminder of the medieval strength of the town on a major trade route. The market square of this agricultural distribution center with its large cathedral and representative city hall *(Rathaus)* also has square-gabled, stately commercial houses. By contrast, an old commercial building, the *Ladenhof*, has rounded gables with matching Romanesque windows. The wall of yellow, diagonally offset brick has stairs located on the outside in a side tower. The *Friedenssaal* (peace hall) still has the wood paneling from the time when one of the peace treaties ending the Thirty Years War was signed here. Osnabrück has many small industries, and the population to serve them mostly resides in a collection of monotone suburbs.

Oldenburg (population 150,000). This residence city, home to the duke of Oldenburg's court and administration, surrounds an elegant eighteenth-century palace with extensive parks. The castle *(Schloss)*, built on the site of a castle and reconstructed into a baroque form during the mid-eighteenth century, contains the regional art gallery. The gallery boasts the Grand Duke's collection, taken over in 1918, but modern works have been acquired, especially those of Franz Radziwill. Though bombed, Oldenburg's churches have been carefully restored. Many streets have large gable-front houses, especially on the *Lange Strasse*. The combinations of commercial and residential buildings have elaborate doors and large windows. Built in brick after the fire of 1677, many are five stories high. At present the city is mainly an agricultural distribution, administrative, and health center, though it seeks to become a high-tech one. The university is one of the supports for that aim.

Göttingen (population 130,000). This small university city on the Leine River is influenced by students and professors, as it has been since its founding in 1737. However, the middle-class merchants and infrastructure serve a fairly well off clientele, which expanded during the twentieth century. The university, once a place of critical thought and student radicalism, has shrunk. Recently, research institutes have been encouraged to seek to recover the prestige in subjects such as physics, which helped it garner more than 30 Nobel Prizes. Once it had among the most prestigious faculty in theology. The city center retains an air of being old, with its streets full of half-timbered houses running up and down the steep hills. A Handel Festival occurs annually and draws musicians and audiences from around the world. The *Altstadtfest* (old town Fest, actually a fairly new celebration of the city center) and the *Schützenfest* (very old shooting competition) are very popular with much sausage eating, drinking, and singing.

Wolfsburg (population 125,000). The novel *Die Autostadt* (1958) by Horst Mönnich is a biography of the automobile and this city. It summarizes the success story of the little people's car (VW) and the big company town. Started in the late 1930s, the Volkswagen factories have dominated this planned community. However, other industries have taken advantage of the infrastructure and high unemployment (17 percent in 2003). For example, the region's largest spicy sausage producer (Currywurst) is here. Some administrative buildings of glass and steel have been combined with reflective pools and grass in an effort to shift the image of the city from the grime and noise of conveyer belts. Dance festivals in the former energy-producing facilities of the VW factory hint at the attempts to create a diverse lifestyle, as well as to use empty and outdated facilities. The company is even exploring the creation of a university.

Salzgitter (population 115,000). This steel town's name reveals its earlier importance and continued relevance for the production of salt.

Hildesheim (population 100,000). Churches and museums hallmark this distribution city that suffered drastically in World War II. Yet the city with its cathedral, including the bronze statues, and St. Michael church has achieved recognition as a UNESCO world heritage site. Roman artifacts provide examples for modern elegant exhibitions in a special museum. The *Römer* and *Palizäus* Museum, rebuilt during the 1970s, has set a new standard for cultural exhibitions with its series on the Roman and medieval eras.

The marketplace has been almost totally reconstructed using traditional methods and materials, having been more than 80 percent destroyed by bombing. The cathedral is a noted example of simple, solid Romanesque style with sculpted bronze doors and many stone carvings. The St. Michael church, however, is the jewel with red and white offsetting stones for all its symmetric arches. Its ceiling is spectacularly decorated. It also offers a crypt and shrine. The city's legendary rosebush, which inspired the original building of the town and its churches, is still alive after a thousand years. A few kilometers outside the city is *Schloss Marienburg*, built in the 1860s in neo-Gothic, fairy-tale style.

Emden (population 50,000), **Aurich** (population 40,000), and **Wilhelmshaven** (population 40,000) remain small but significant cities for their immediate area as commercial and distribution centers. The former has a Volkswagen plant and the latter important naval facilities. Emden's art gallery features Henri Nannen and contains the East Frisian regional museum. The comic actor Otto established an *Otto-Haus* for his imaginary friends, the *Ottifanten*. Aurich's streets have many fountains and statues.

ATTRACTIONS

Numerous megaliths and mound graves remain, with some 500 in the heath at Pestruper, near Wildhausen. Dating from 800 to 600 B.C., some have huge stone coverings weighing as much as 50,000 pounds. The mystery of how the stones were moved and placed has not been solved.

Who has seen a bird whose beak is the size and shape of a shoe? The bird conservatory *(Vögelpark)* at Walsrode near Soltau offers a collection of exotic and local birds in aviaries and in open areas.

Aristocratic castles and palaces are well represented in the region. *Burg Bentheim, Clemenswerth*, and *Dankern* represent the rebuilt lodges, fortresses, and castles that became palatial residences. *Clemenswerth* began primarily as a hunting lodge for the bishop of Münster and Cologne. Between 1737 and 1746 he had a baroque hunting lodge two stories high built in circular form with rooms going off in four directions. Eight identical guesthouses are tied to the central square by walkways. They complete an octagon around the central palace. The Bavarian royal palaces served as models, hence the double staircase at the entrance to the main palace. A palace that is very opulent, full of angels, huge gold carvings, and endless decorations is at Bückeburg, a small city once known for the location of a school for the Nazi elite.

To see the half-timbered style of farm buildings in the setting of a closed farmyard and to experience the lifestyle of farmers and farmhands from the sixteenth to nineteenth centuries, no better place exists than *Freilichtmuseum* (open-air) *Cloppenburg*. More than 50 sets of buildings, including whole farmyards, windmills (three different styles), church, barns, and artisan workshops, have been brought together. They have been placed to replicate farmyards *(Höfe)* with ponds and fields. Some of the central hall house and barn combinations have as many as 18 horizontal beams crossing the uprights, so that a gable end of tiered small squares appears.

Raising horses was one of the important agricultural tasks, and Lower Saxony has many breeding farms that often display their studs at exhibitions in Celle.

If the combined half-timbered barns and hall houses that are scattered about the region show rural decoration and practicality, the carved fronts of town houses reflect urban opulence. The so-called fairy-tale route along the Weser River provides endless examples of half-timbered, well-maintained, and elaborately carved bourgeois houses. Special examples are in towns such as Hameln of Pied Piper fame. A main street of carved and colored half-timbered Weser Renaissance houses competes with the Pied Piper museum.

Holzminden and Münden can compete with any place for examples of half-timbered houses, especially the latter with some 700 examples. They tend to have short tightly crisscrossed beams making little rows like Xes beneath each set of windows. Indeed, Lower Saxony probably has central Europe's most extensive collection of such buildings. At Alfeld, the *Eicksches Haus* has carvings on all the crosspieces as well as on the supporting timbers. At the intersection of one street, two house sides are decorated and painted with large sculptures on the corners. The *Latinschule* (Latin school) there has depictions of the Reformation educators, such as Martin Luther and Philip Melanchthon, among its carvings. At Verden and at Rinteln, half-round and rectangular floral designs grace three-story houses with notable entrances.

Ironically, the rat catcher's house at Hameln is stone with decorations in stucco, mainly on the gables where the timbering is visible, as is the *Leibnizhaus*, home to the mathematician and scientist Gottfried Leibniz. Its fine façade is complemented by a modern neighbor but near an ugly parking garage on the other side. The list of half-timbered designs could continue with almost every town and village, such as Einbeck with three towers in front of its *Rathaus* and many decorated timbers, or Fallingsbostel, or Verden, or . . .

Goslar, with its *Kaiserpfalz* (Imperial castle), has a multitude of half-timbered houses, beautiful cobbled squares, and well-kept artisan buildings with wood decorations. The center offers a delightful unity to a city filled with historical sites and sculptures. Nearly every square has some reminder of an Imperial past. Cobblestones frequently are patterned to lead to a central point. Once home to the Salian monarchs who became emperors and unified much of the German-speaking realm, Goslar's main attraction is the Imperial castle overlooking the red-roofed city, which is a UNESCO world heritage site. A contrasting UNESCO site is the ironworks at Rammelsberg, representative of a special proto-industrial system of production.

Delmenhorst offers a different set of attractions. As a residential town it still has a palace, but in the nineteenth century it became an industrial city. It reworked staple goods such as tobacco, wool, and jute imported by Bremen shippers. Some of the factories and buildings offer insight into the history of technology and late-nineteenth century industrial architecture (water tower, market halls, and hospital).

More traditional fare is offered at Celle, where the dukes of Braunschweig-Lüneburg established a court residence *(Schloss)*. The small city served it, especially with luxury articles. One of the region's prettiest cities, it contains many well-preserved half-timbered houses, a fifteenth-century city hall *(Rathaus)* and eighteenth-century synagogue. The French-style garden is very manicured. Lüneburg, another pretty city, maintains its medieval center, which is mostly in Renaissance brick identifying Hanseatic connections. Exceptional decorated doorways (for example, Apothecary house) and gables trademark the once rich city. Lüneberg served as a transit area for salt. The salt museum there demonstrates the importance of this commodity for commerce and consumption. This city serves as a starting place for excursions to the heaths, which become pinkish-purple in late summer.

Figure 8.3
City Hall, Lüneburg, Lower Saxony.

Source © Press and Information Office, Germany.

The coast, with its weather, transportation possibilities, and its terrain, has influenced northwestern Lower Saxony. Its cities, such as Emden, Wilhelmshaven, and Cuxhaven, are marine centers with specialty shipbuilding and military installations. More important for tourism are the islands off the coast. They have fine, long sand dune beaches for nude and regular bathing, especially on Norderney and Borkum. Excursions to the red cliffs of Helgoland also permit escape from summer heat. Access is by frequent ferries. Though usually seen as backward, many coastal towns have modern art galleries, such as *studio a* at Otterndorf. Wilhelmshaven holds popular jazz festivals in a converted pump house. If one does not want to join the crowds, spas offer moor baths at Zwischenahn, among many places. At Jever, excellent beer is produced in an ultramodern brewery.

Lüneberg heath, Germany's oldest nature park, offers beautiful hiking territory. *Wattenmeer*, or tidal mudflats, in both directions from Cuxhaven, allow healthy seacoast romps with showers supplied for later cleansing. In contrast to the coast, many of Lower Saxony's forests have suffered pollution. More than a third of the forests have been damaged by acid rain and groundwater problems. To improve the situation, a dozen conservation areas were created across the state between 1959 and 1984, but danger to plants and animals remains. Small villages in various styles— round, half-round, stretched—have been preserved and placed under heritage protection, for example Schreyahn. Those villages often contain small Romanesque churches. The Harz Mountains remain a hiker's dream in terms of views and ease of access to accommodations.

Though the Herrenhaus gardens at Hanover are among the best known, the botanic garden *(Berggarten)* in Hanover began in the eighteenth century as a typical specimen collection. One corner, known as the *Paradiesgarten*, contains a variety of heaths, which contrasts with edging trees and plants.

CUSTOMS

The religiously mixed region celebrates many Christian festivals but some, such as lighting large Easter bonfires and giving decorated eggs, have pagan origins. In the summer months nearly every village and town has one or more *Schützenfeste* (shooting festivals), with processions, competitions, and balls. Herring festivals *(Matjesfest)* are very popular in East Frisia. In the fall, combined markets and fairs (*Jahrmarkt* and *Kirmes*) take place everywhere, while the larger centers have special events. Hanover offers *Maschseefest*, two weeks in August of lakeside cultural activities, and the *Altstadtfest* of modern music. Bad Harzburg has its salt festival, commemorated by fireworks. Seesen presents classical costumes of the area at a festival in early September. Similarly, in Bad Gandersheim each year theater festivals occur in front of the cathedral for thousands of spa guests.

Since the 1980s, Lower Saxon Days, annually fostered by the state to encourage an awareness of the region, rotates among cities. How the 6 percent of foreigners among the populace relate to the dancing and drinking festivities or to the attempts to emphasize a heritage of half-timbered houses and traditional dress

(Trachten) is not clear. However, the state seeks to integrate them into the politically created unity.

Sports are very popular, with 2.8 million members in sport clubs. The state has a program to modernize pools, fields, and halls. Handball is widely played by all sexes and generations, but the main loyalty is to professional soccer clubs.

CULTURAL ATTRIBUTES
AND CONTRIBUTIONS

VISUAL ARTS

Perhaps the most impressive visual arts are the half-timbered structures and the stone carvings of the many Romanesque and Gothic churches. Worpswede is among the many villages with half-timbered houses and barns. Usually associated with Bremen, the art colony village of Worpswede is on the moors in Lower Saxony. Though much changed, some of the places, such as Heinrich Vogeler's home, *Barkenhof,* favored by the original group (including Otto Modersohn, Heinrich Vogeler, Paula Modersohn Becker, Rainer Maria Rilke), continue to survive among the many private galleries and museums. Many generations of artists have been inspired by the windswept, isolated moor landscapes cut by peat canals.

Can a combination of surrealist paintings represent a region? Franz Radziwill probably intended to portray an era more than a place, but his surrealist self-portraits, starkly mechanized landscapes, and reflective seascapes may be representative of the diversity of Lower Saxony. Many of his paintings are in the *Oldenburg Landesmuseum.* Other local painters such as Adolf Hoelzel, Jan Voss, and Emil Nolde are among the twentieth-century painters whose works appear. One of the main medieval maps, the *Ebersdorfer Weltkarte* (showing an imaginary highly illustrated world in six parts), is from the Benedictine cloister south of Lüneburg. Kurt Schwitters Dadaistlike collages are a contemporary contrast.

To encourage visitors to view some of the earlier landscape paintings of the Jewish artist Felix Nussbaum and other regional artists in a different fashion, the Osnabrück cultural-history museum combines them with items from the area.

Sculpture by locals such as Karl Prantl accompanies a mile of sculpture near Bad Bentheim. Also known as the bowling alley of the monks, the modern installations contrast with the art of cloister *Frenswegen* nearby. Similarly, in Lingen, local sculptors and international colleagues have re-created landscapes by adding angular objects that provide a strong contrast to the rural landscape.

LITERATURE

Gotthold Lessing wrote his classic work advocating religious tolerance, *Natan der Weise* (1779), among other plays, during his last years in Wolfenbüttel. His outlook underscored cosmopolitanism. By contrast, Wilhelm Raabe's (1831–1910) stories employed specific settings in Lower Saxony. Though some consider his writings anti-Semitic, his fiction can also be read as the rise (and fall) of little people. Some critics assert that Wilhelm Busch's (1832–1908) moralistic, even brutal, children's stories can be seen as representations of the populace's special regional traits. Do his Max and Moritz tales of children transgressing rules—such as trying to get more or too much to eat by choking a neighbor's chickens to death with strings with corks on the ends—illustrate more than peasant ways of instilling honesty and moderation? Still popular are the similar late-medieval stories of the wise fool, Till Eulenspiegel, whose numerous escapades provide insight into the peasant mentality. Certainly, the Brothers Grimm worked here, though many of their "German" fairy tales were collected in Hesse (and some came from Alsace). The Grimms also collected materials for their 20-volume German dictionary. Some claim the story of the hare and the tortoise illustrates the style of the people of the region: quick and different thinkers. The Brothers Grimm were among those who lost their posts at Göttingen University because of their liberal views. Also among those dissenting professors in 1837 was the constitutional theorist Friedrich Dahlmann, who protested state censorship. During the 1920s, Richarda Huch penned many critical essays and became the first woman in the Prussian Academy.

Foremost among the writers concerned with the region was Hermann Löns. He popularized the heath area by creating a mythical people defending Saxony against outsiders. His novel *Wehrwolf* (1910) idealized these heath people as stubborn, independent warrior peasants. Focusing attention on the people and their practices, the Lower Saxon *Heimbund* (homeland society) seeks to maintain regional traditions by publishing books on customs and costumes. Simultaneously, the Institute for Lower Saxon Language serves Bremen and Lower Saxony by studying and supporting the regional dialect.

CIVICS AND REMEMBRANCE

The state office for political education seeks to create a unified history for the region. Its ethnographic *(Landeskunde)* studies and historical accounts press much together that once operated separately. For instance, Brunswick and East Frisia had little in common until joined together by the British military occupation. However, the state has published many books trying to demonstrate the existence of a clan, state, and inhabitant awareness of Lower Saxony. While presenting a continuous historical unity, it also seeks to identify a regional identity. Therefore, it constructs a history for the whole region, though whether the people living there have a unified identity beyond taxes and roads is questionable.

In addition, for educational purposes, this office acknowledges the strong Nazi past of the region and tries to foster understanding of parliamentary democracy, including tolerance of ethnic diversity to overcome negative attitudes toward foreigners. Concentration camps, which started mostly as labor camps draining marshes or digging clay, include Bergen-Belsen (north of Hanover near Celle) and Pappenburg (south of Emden). They are now educational and memorial sites. Foreign slave laborers predominated in Bergen-Belsen, where the majority died of hunger and overwork as did Anne Frank.

The presence of the past has been well represented in Hanover, where the market church has bronze doors embossed with a scene created by Gerhard Marcks. The left portal depicts someone misleading the populace and all the drastic consequences for common people. The right portal offers scenes of hope and reconciliation. Another monument seeks to remember those driven out of their east European homelands. Nearly a million people passed through the refugee camp at Friedland, where large broken walls of remembrance have been erected.

CUISINE

Some of the world's best beers come from the northwest of this area. *Jever Pils* is increasingly popular and selling far beyond its East Frisian source. For bock beer, Einbeck, where it originated, is the place. Serving raisins preserved in rum *(bohntjes)* at baptisms is common in northern areas, especially East Frisia.

Fish is normal fare all along the coast and rivers. Hams, sausages, and bread varieties are myriad, especially from Ammerland. Blueberries from the heath near Lüneberg and kale *(Braunkohl)* provide seasonal fare. Perhaps, though, the best-known culinary activity relates to asparagus, sometimes referred to as *Spargelfressen* (asparagus gobbling) in the springtime.

SPARGEL (WHITE ASPARAGUS WITH CREAM SAUCE)

Begin with 8 to 10 pieces of asparagus per person. Wash carefully in cold water and break off ends by holding between hands and bending gently. Peel with very sharp knife to remove tough skin.

While boiling the asparagus for about 10 minutes, make a béarnaise sauce, or after boiling simply sprinkle a hard cheese over the spears. Serve with thinly sliced ham and boiled new potatoes. Strawberries and cream are the classic dessert with asparagus; sometimes rhubarb sauces with quark and shortcake or cheesecake are offered.

CHEESECAKE

Crust:

2/3 cup butter	1 teaspoon vanilla
2 1/3 cups flour	1 beaten egg
1 teaspoon baking powder	1 tablespoon milk
1/3 cup sugar	

Cut butter into flour, baking powder, and sugar as for pastry. Mix next three ingredients into flour mixture and press into a 9″-by-13″ pan.

Cake batter:

4 eggs

1 cup sugar

1 tablespoon lemon juice

1 cup sour cream

1 1/2 pounds dry cottage cheese

1 package Dr. Oeteker vanilla pudding
 (or 2 tablespoons cornstarch and
 1 teaspoon vanilla)

Beat eggs until light and foamy. Gradually beat in sugar. Beat in lemon juice, sour cream, cottage cheese, and pudding mix (can be blended in a food processor). Pour over crust and bake at 350°F for 1 hour or until firm. Turn off heat, open oven door, and let stand for 1 hour before removing from oven.

Chapter 9

Mecklenburg–Western Pomerania

SPECIAL ASPECTS

The region comprises a long coast beyond which rolling plains and lake districts mark a rural world with small cities. Many little villages lie scattered over a country-side, which often has straight, tree-lined roads *(Alleen)*. Extensive forests, especially in the east, reflect the unspoiled nature and perhaps underdeveloped economy of the whole region. *Plattdeutsch* (Low German) is no longer common in everyday parlance. Despite the progressive elements in their new constitution, the people are still stereotyped as slow and backward. At present, the area's Slavic origins and heritage are emphasized in the regional identity.

Nature and climate remain significant to a rural and coastal region: Little rain but high humidity and much wind, as well as slowly changing moderate temperatures, predominate.

REGIONAL TRAITS

The second-smallest state in terms of population (1.8 million), and the least densely populated, Mecklenburg–Western Pomerania borders Poland and the Baltic Sea in the northeast and is 23,200 square kilometers. Lower Saxony and Schleswig-Holstein are to the west and Brandenburg to the south. The coat of arms and flag have four fields representing historic units: two black bulls' heads represent the two Mecklenburgs—Schwerin and Strelitz—on yellow backgrounds, opposite a Pomerian griffin and a Prussian eagle on silver.

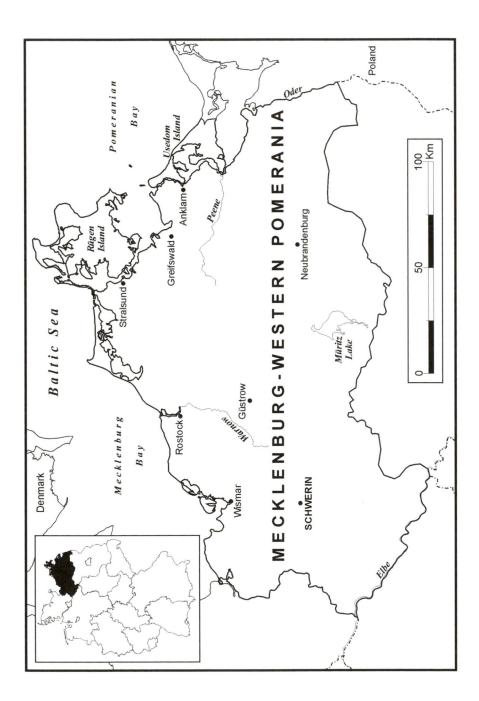

GEOGRAPHIC FEATURES

Chalk cliffs on the Baltic seacoast and on outlying islands such as Rügen, memorialized in the patriotic Romantic paintings of Caspar David Friedrich, break the monotone of the coastal plains. The coastline itself is varied with steep cliffs, sand, and numerous inlets *(Bodden)* with reeds. Many lakes of varying sizes, including Germany's second largest (Müritz See), dot the landscape, especially in the center. Only small rivers, such as the Warnow and Peene, run north, while the Müritz-Elde east-west waterway connects with canals to make a 200-kilometer transportation system. The southwest has much sand-based heath, while the northeast contains better clay soils. Nearly the whole area is agrarian with many waterways in the generally flat, glaciated landscape, though the coastline can be rugged. Storks, cranes, and swans complement the usual songbirds.

HISTORY

Outside influence has been persistent for this borderland. Raiding Vikings, Christian monks, Danish and Swedish expansionists, Russian conquerors and liberators (from the Swedes and French)—many have passed through or tried to take over the area. As dukedoms, the two Mecklenburg grand duchies of Schwerin and Strelitz had quite different and separate developments than Pomerania did as a province controlled by Prussia. Other duchies, such as Ratzeburg and Staargard, operated independently for a time. All of the region, though, has repeatedly been subject to warfare and dynastic strife. In the twentieth century, relations with Poland, occupation and dominance by the Soviets, and a "quiet" revolution have repeatedly threatened the survival and shape of the region.

Prehistoric megaliths and grave sites comprised of huge boulders attest to some 8,000 to 10,000 years of settlement. Archaeological finds for later periods indicate villages, for instance at Vineta, tied to Danish seafarers. Still later, Wends and Slavic tribes shared the area but left limited evidence. An archaeological museum near Gross Raden tries to re-create the living conditions of a Slavic group, the Obotrite. It shows housing, baking, large defense works, and horse keeping.

The Obotrite leader, Niklot, who founded a dynasty in 1131, may have lost the major battle with the eastward-expanding Saxons under Henry the Lion, but Niklot's Christian son received most of the realm as a fiefdom and the dynasty survived. By the thirteenth century, Christian cloisters with Romanesque or Gothic brick churches covered the countryside. Thousands of colonists from lower Saxony and Westphalia settled in the area and mixed with the local population. They developed villages and brought the three-field crop-rotation system of agriculture.

Feudalism and warfare shifted social relations drastically. A feudal regime of aristocratic rule from manor houses had begun to transform peasants into serfs by the time of the Reformation. That religious struggle posed the question of which version of Protestantism, Lutheran or Calvinist, would predominate. By the late sixteenth century, Mecklenburg's rulers opted for Lutheran, Pomerania mainly for Calvinist convictions. The religious and dynastic conflicts devastated the region. A folksong reflects the destruction, especially of the Thirty Years' War (1618–1648): "May bug fly; your father is off to war; your mother is in Pomerania; Pomerania has been burned away; fly May bug fly." Swedish and Habsburg armies passed through, living off the land, which meant mainly living off the peasants and serfs. Poland also had designs on the territories to its west. Estimates of Mecklenburg's population in 1600 run to 300,000. After the war, some 50,000 remained. The peasants increasingly became serfs with heavy obligations. In the early eighteenth century, the financial burden of wars against Sweden with Mecklenburg on the side of Russia reinforced the aristocrats' position against the ducal rulers. The feudal lords had their feudal rights extended and confirmed in 1755. They had total control over their serfs, and many more independent peasant lands were converted to serfdom. The special characteristic in Mecklenburg was the power of the feudal lords *(Ritterschaft)*, whose manors dominated the region and the economy.

Most of the coastal cities, such as Wismar, Rostock, Stralsund, and Greiswald, operated independently for much of the late medieval and early modern era. They participated in the Hanseatic League of north German trading cities, moving salt, fish, furs, and grains. They prospered and their market squares, with well-built and finely decorated commercial houses, still attest to those riches. Swedish occupation of many coastal cities destroyed the league by the late seventeenth century. The Swedes kept much of western Pomerania and parts of northern Mecklenburg (Wismar, Poel Island, and the area around Neukloster) as war booty until the Napoleonic era.

Mecklenburg, politically an independent part of the Holy Roman Empire, split into two in 1701: Mecklenburg-Schwerin and Mecklenburg-Strelitz. The ducal rulers, in combination with their aristocratic aides, ran a repressive regime while building fine manor houses and palaces for themselves. For example, in 1733 the opulent *Neustrelitz* palace became a ducal residence. Another converted hunting lodge became the showcase of *Ludwigslust* palace and ducal residence from 1772 to 1776. In 1753 the duke founded the first German acting academy in Schwerin. Such high culture set the tone for aristocratic society. Meanwhile, restrictive inheritance laws regarding the division of land became enshrined in the constitution of 1755, which lasted until 1918. Decreed by the ducal rulers, it gave extensive rights to the aristocrats while restricting the peasants.

Between 1803 and 1813 France occupied the lands and began to reform the laws, though torture had been outlawed in 1763 and flogging forbidden in 1802. Only in 1820 did serfdom, which included the lord's right to decide who married whom and when, end in the Mecklenburgs; in Pomerania it had ceased earlier. In 1815 both Grand Duchies of Mecklenburg became part of the German federation and Pomerania a Prussian province (purchased from Sweden). The ties to Prussia were consolidated by the marriage of Luise (1776–1810), of Mecklenburg-Strelitz, to Friedrich Wilhelm III. As queen of Prussia she became very popular as an intelligent representative of patriotic women aiding charity organizations. Meanwhile, most peasants owned little land. Even the manor houses of many lords and aristocrats were modest, so that fine palaces and gardens were less common and less opulent than their western equivalents. Nevertheless, the present state has a registry of over 1,000 castles, palaces, and manor houses.

During the Imperial era the two Mecklenburg duchies, with Mecklenburg-Schwerin four times the size of Mecklenburg-Strelitz, remained the economically least developed and politically most backward of German states. Representation operated by estates *(Stand)*. Pomerania's situation amounted to the same within the Prussian three-class voting system and authoritarian state administration.

Mechanization began to affect agriculture during the nineteenth century, but horse and human power prevailed in many regions. In some areas technologically progressive lords introduced mechanical reapers and threshers. Sugar beets, potatoes (for foodstuffs and alcohol), and grains were the staple items of production and consumption. Cattle, and especially sheep, provided meat and materials for clothing. Fish from the seacoast and inland waters supplemented a sparse diet, but many villages remained self-sufficient through their own weaving, carpentry, and leather working. In the nineteenth century, many migrated to Poland and Russia but especially westward, including beyond the Atlantic.

The revolutionary changes at the end of World War I ended the lords' control over domestic servants and day laborers as well as deposing the dukes and monarchs. Agricultural workers could, and did, strike to obtain better working conditions. Both Mecklenburg states and the Prussian province of Pomerania became republican and Social Democrats governed, sometimes in coalition with liberals. By the end of the Weimar Republic, voters had shifted to the right, mostly voting conservative before supporting the Nazis. By 1932, a Nazi-conservative coalition governed in Mecklenburg. More slowly, Pomerania moved in a similar direction. During the Weimar Republic large estate owners and small farmers experienced increased indebtedness, which helped turn them toward radical politics.

In 1934 the two Mecklenburgs were reunited. During the Nazi reorganization of districts, Pomerania remained in Prussia. Being rural and militarily as well as economically not very significant, the Third Reich had less impact on this region than many others. However, by the late 1930s, armaments production increased. For example, the Ernst Heinkel aircraft works, founded during 1920 in Warnemünde, served as a base for making military planes. Peenemünde became a site for experimental rocketry and would eventually produce the V-rockets with slave labor. In 1937, coastal spas became vacation spots for those loyal to the regime through the "strength through joy" movement.

Simultaneously, repression against leftist individuals and Jews removed both from public life and in most instances deported them to concentration camps. Leftist labor groups and members of the confessing church offered some resistance.

War and its aftermath transformed the region. Cities such as Rostock experienced very heavy bombing. From 1944 to 1945, the region suffered drastically from food shortages, due to the influx of refugees and expellees as well as from military battles and occupation. In 1945 Mecklenburg and Western Pomerania came under the occupying Soviet military administration. The new state of Mecklenburg–Western

Pomerania was a combination of a previous state and a Prussian province. But in 1947 the Soviets, by decree, abolished the title of Western Pomerania. At that time nearly 40 percent of the population comprised refugees and expellees from the former eastern territories. De-Nazification meant that leading Nazis, war criminals, and industrial and large landowners lost their properties. The land reform, approved by plebiscite in 1946, divided and distributed the large estates. In 1949 Mecklenburg became the sole designation for the region as a state within the German Democratic Republic. In 1952, that state disappeared into administrative districts; after Reunification a new state was created in 1990 restoring the name Pomerania. Under the GDR the farmers and craftsmen of the region had done fairly well. Further, state planning fostered shipbuilding and transportation improvements. The GDR increased industrialization and began to modernize the region, including rights for and participation by women. At present, nostalgia for the past regime remains high, especially in an area of about 20 percent unemployment; some places, such as Anklam, have 50 percent unemployed.

Since the mid-1990s, extensive rebuilding and renovation of the cities and attempts to market the region for tourists has been partially successful. For instance, the Pomerania Bodden Landscape Nature Park drew over 2 million visitors in 2002. Politically since Reunification, Social Democrats (SPD) and the Christian Democratic Union (CDU) have been outpacing the Party of Democratic Socialism (PDS), the reformed Communist party. At first the CDU had the most support and governed with the Free Democrats. However, the decline in employment and crises in agriculture and on the wharfs led to extensive strikes. In 1994 the CDU and SPD joined in a coalition. Since then, Social Democracy has received the most electoral support (approximately twice the CDU and PDS), especially in the cities, and has led the governments. The first coalition of SPD and PDS was formed in 1998 and continues. The units in the local administration have been decreased and streamlined, and the constitution includes direct citizen participation to maintain the heritage of the "quiet" revolution of 1989.

Mecklenburg–Western Pomerania's dual coastal and agricultural past has left the populace identifying with the countryside. Presently that identity is fostered by an emphasis upon tourism in unspoiled nature. However, two other elements from that past and the lay of the land have an impact on regional identity—the centuries-long struggles against aristocratic rule is reflected in dissenting politics and a desire for peaceful solutions to world disputes. Some observers suggest that living in harmony with the seasons and in direct contact with nature results in a populace that knows one has to accept what cannot be changed. The peasants' strength in knowing that political regimes pass, the land and the sea remain, is much in evidence.

ECONOMY

Next to Thuringia, this is economically the weakest region of Germany with high unemployment and structural difficulties since Reunification. Agriculture and some industrial strongpoints, such as Rostock, have dominated the economy. Recently, rebuilding infrastructure has fostered tourism and high technology though population decline continues.

Small pockets of industrial production, such as shipbuilding at Rostock, which grew during the 1950s and 1960s with new port facilities, have not fared well internationally during the 1990s. Two major crises hit the wharves during the 1990s, which before 1989 had served protected eastern markets. Recently, however building cruise ships has become a successful niche. Fishing and fish processing, as well as processing agricultural products, continue to be important industries.

During GDR times the farmers' and small craftsmen's skills were required for the collective farming system and for maintenance of machinery, so both groups did fairly well. However, technology in agricultural machinery lagged behind the West. After Reunification, the large collective entities were broken up. That took a heavy toll on established patterns of working, especially for women, and left high unemployment. Some industries, such as fertilizer plants at Rostock, have survived and commerce with the Baltic countries extended. The area remains Germany's main region for rye, wheat, and sugar beets.

State-subsidized initiatives in telecommunications, expansion of the autobahns, and building dams for cheap energy have not solved the unemployment problem. No self-supported growth has been achieved, though some developments in building aircraft and rapid transit may provide workplaces for skilled laborers. Tourism is the hope of the future, especially exploiting the seacoast, though large hotel complexes have also appeared on the inland lakes. One of the most sophisticated fish processing plants of the world is being built on Rügen. The forests are seen as a potential economic resource. Transshipping of goods to Scandinavia and Russia aids the larger ports such as Rostock and Sassnitz.

MAIN CITIES

CAPITAL

Schwerin (population 98,000). This beautiful administrative city is built around many lakes, palaces, and parks. The Grand Dukes had their original castle and main residence on an island in the large Schwerin Lake. The palace *(Schloss)* is one of the most significant buildings in the historical style *(Historismus)* and was expanded after 1848 with materials matching the original stone. The railway came late enough (1847) to have the imposing terminal placed at the edge of the old city. Museums, a gallery, and many of the state offices are in fine minipalaces rebuilt for their present purpose. The theater, reflecting the strength of dramatic arts, is in an imposing nineteenth-century building.

Rostock (population 198,000). This Hanseatic city has been rebuilt, since World War II bombing and artillery destroyed its central core. During the 1960s its Hanseatic Quarter served as a model of reconstruction in the GDR, but its suburbs offered prefabricated, dull edifices. Recently, more areas have been renovated and modernized; for example, a long double tunnel under the Warnow River has eased traffic circulation. The city has a new art gallery as well as museums about shipping, Hanseatic commerce, and transportation. Most impressive is the Hanseatic Quarter with carved and half-timbered fronts to restored seventeenth-century artisan and traders' houses. The city hall is a brick Gothic marvel with towers and colorful baroque façade. To aid employment, the *Marineamt* (naval office) of the national military has relocated here. Beer brewing continues a Hanseatic tradition. The university, founded in 1419 as the first north European university, is reviving an earlier respect for its research capabilities, especially in medicine, humanities, and marine-related subjects.

Stralsund (population 58,000). With a university of applied sciences and a tradition in beer brewery, this port city also boasts an imposing central square. Renovated commercial houses from Hanseatic days surround it. At present, the most important cultural offering is the Marine museum.

Neubrandenburg (population 79,000). Founded in 1248, its walls remain intact and enclose a pretty, unified old city. Four large decorative gates and many watchtowers, built in brick during the fifteenth to seventeenth centuries, remain. The half-timbered houses, especially on the Neutor street and the Wiekhäuser, are among the most attractive examples of post-Reunification restoration. The Maria church has been renovated into a concert hall. Fritz Reuter (1810–1874) lived in and wrote appreciatively about the city, and Theodor Fontane (1819–1898) included it in his novels. Sport is strong: The city boasts Olympic medallists in canoeing, swimming, and light athletics. Located on the beautiful Tollensee, many venerable oaks grow on the city's outskirts.

Greifswald (population 53,000). This pretty city with many brick baroque buildings has a bright red *Rathaus* with high gable façade. The *Giebelhäuser* (or gable houses), also on the market square, seem to have one arch piled upon the other. The museum in the classical Quistorp building contains the Gallery of the Pomeranian state. It has masterworks from the late Renaissance and nineteenth-century greats, including Philip Otto Runge, Caspar David Friedrich, Vincent van Gogh, and Max Liebermann. The university, founded in 1456, is among the oldest in Europe. Its fine baroque administrative building dates from the eighteenth century.

Many coastal cities such as Rostock, Wismar, Stralsund, and Greifswald had been Hanseatic cities, and much of their architecture reflects the redbrick Gothic style of the Northern Renaissance. Wismar is especially well endowed with half-timbered houses dating back to the Hanseatic era.

ATTRACTIONS

Seacoast villages with cottages covered in reed (straw) roofs and gardens full of flowers are plentiful. Manor lords controlled most of the plainer inland villages, though most have solid stone churches and some half-timbered buildings as at Kyritz. The countryside offers numerous bike paths. The coast has a multitude of spas, including some huge resorts at towns such as Warnemünde or Binz on Rügen and Henningsdorf on Usedom. A refurbished luxury spa is at Heiligendamm. There the White Town on the Sea—a series of white villas facing the beach—goes back to 1793 when aristocrats began to take the cure, though mud baths only became fashionable later. Each of the islands or peninsulas, as at Darss or Zingst, has its own special characteristics, for instance, the many old fishermen's cottages at Zingst. But all have long, sandy beaches on which much sand castle building has been undertaken since before World War I. On some beaches the tradition of nude bathing, especially popular during GDR times, continues with a flagpole dividing the nude from the covered or, one could joke, those without clothes and those with binoculars. The beaches sport high-backed chairs or beach baskets *(Strandkörbe)* that are almost cozy little houses. The front of the basket has a cover, which can be opened to the sun or closed to protect against the frequent winds.

The multitude of towns and small cities, some like Wismar, Barth, or Anklam, with historic Hanseatic buildings are all near water and open country. Anklam, the hometown of Otto Lilienthal, boasts a modern, hands-on museum, which challenges the claim that the American Wright brothers first achieved heavier-than-air flight. Hikers and wanderers through such towns experience a heritage slowly built over centuries being used as well-preserved attractions in the present. The variety of carvings on doors and windows, painted in stark blue or green, fill tours through the fishing villages with repeated aesthetic surprises.

The Mecklenburg coastal region is surprisingly rich in heritage buildings. One author writing on German gardens wondered how a region so poor in resources had managed to create so many artistic monuments. He simply forgot the extent to which serfs and peasants were exploited in early modern times. Some of the noteworthy buildings are monumental churches, some are straw-roofed farmhouses in a central-hall style where animals and people shared space. Some are spa buildings, and many are palaces with gardens. Many were kept up, restored, and renovated during GDR times, even if they lacked the paint and polish of what postwar western Germans did in their areas. Remarkable is the extent to which the GDR maintained the basic structure of edifices as well as how much less this rural area suffered war damage than others. Though the date of rebuilding is not always clear, what is evident and fortunate for succeeding generations is that so much has been maintained. Perhaps not every church and every old farmhouse is worthy of sightseeing, as hinted by one detailed inventory in a series of heritage books published as the GDR was disappearing. But the extent of the remains belies the idea that everything in the GDR decayed or was not maintained.

Here only a few examples from each type of the thousand edifices identified in the inventory will be noted. The *Rathaus* at Schönberg illustrates the use of bricks, which were set up in square or rectangular form, between timbers. The open-air museum there presents a straw-roofed farmhouse with main timbers supported by smaller ones and one timber set diagonally at each side of a rounded entry. The entry, or *Diehl*, similar to other northern areas, is set back in order to have a covered protected space during the wet, cold, and windy winters. The crossed horses' heads at each gable end helped keep away evil spirits, similar to practices in Lower Saxony and Schleswig-Holstein. The traders' houses in Wismar provide one of the most comprehensive collections of Hanseatic residences combined with shops. Exceptionally well maintained with strikingly diverse gable designs, the city could serve as a location for movies set in the seventeenth century. Among the many Romanesque and Gothic churches built in brick, with hundreds of examples ranging from tiny village chapels to cathedrals in the cities, again the case of Wismar illustrates some of

Figure 9.1
Romanesque village church, Vehlow, Mecklenburg–Western Pomerania.

Source Courtesy of the author.

the special elements of the region. Its cathedral has a solid tower, flying buttresses, a rose window in a side gable, and many brick patterns placed in individualized ways.

The stone village church at Wuticke reveals many changes and additions and contains a curious hanging angel. Another church at Heiligenhagen has a wood tower with octagonal roof. Heiligendamm contains numerous imposing spas and a health retreat—buildings ranging from the early nineteenth to twentieth centuries. It was the first German sea spa. Most religious buildings exude solidity with lowness and clarity of design, though some churches contain extensive decorations, especially carved altarpieces, for instance, at Rethwisch. The landscape is dotted with manor houses, though some of the most interesting sites are the hand-carved and lavishly painted doors on simple cottages.

Two national parks in Mecklenburg–Western Pomerania were established to help protect the environment of the Baltic coast. A small one takes in the chalk cliffs of Rügen, while a very large one covers Darss, Zingst, Hiddensee, and Westrügen. The coast has suffered extensive pollution, including from warfare (the Allies dumped poison gas and sank ships in 1945), from industrial waste (especially GDR chemical refuse), and from city sewage.

In contrast to nature's attractions, the aristocracy left many architectural creations that reflected its European tastes and interactions. *Ludwigslust* is one of the most attractive palaces of northern Europe. This "Mecklenburg Versailles" served as the court residence beginning in the late eighteenth century. The "golden hall" is two

Figure 9.2
Manor house, Krumbeck, Mecklenburg–Western Pomerania.

Source Courtesy of George Buse.

stories high with crystal chandeliers, mirrors, and large windows. Much of the decoration was done with papier-mâché. Some of the ducal collection of curiosities remains on display. Concerts continue the tradition of court music. The gardens, Mecklenburg's largest, partly designed by Peter Josef Lenné, include waterfalls and English-style shrubbery. A special canal had to be built to obtain sufficient water for the ponds and pools. Lenné also designed the park and gardens for the manor at the village of Krumbeck. Güstrow castle is another baroque pearl, built in 1556, allowed to decay, then reconstructed in the 1960s and 1970s.

The aristocracy's passions, especially during the eighteenth and ninteenth centuries, included collecting specimens and constructing gardens. Many emulated Western prototypes. Regional variants include *Ludwigslust's, Schwerin's,* and *Neustrelitz'* palace gardens. These sculpted works are partly overgrown, though the original outlines and central walkways remain. By contrast, a twentieth-century (1934) botanic garden at Greifswald is more informal with emphasis upon trees and shrubs, as opposed to classical sculptures and hedges.

A different type of attraction is a windmill museum at Woldegk. Four types have been restored, with one that demonstrates grinding. The Alt-Schwerin open-air museum in the Lake Müritz district near Malchow has a working "Dutch" windmill and demonstrates the development of agriculture and life on the land, mostly before the twentieth century. A hall-style farmhouse dates from the seventeenth century. Complementing these is the open-air ethnographic museum *(Mecklenburger Volkskundemuseum)* at Muess near Schwerin.

CUSTOMS

As the seasonal celebrations of Easter and Christmas predominate in most rural societies, escaping to the seashore on weekends, sometimes to spas, has become possible with the automobile culture, which has grown since Reunification. GDR rites of passage, such as the secular version of church confirmation *(Jugendweihe)*, continue. In some fishing villages, as on the peninsula Mönchgut, local dress *(Trachten)* can be seen on festive days. Schwerin offers music, especially chamber and orchestral, at annual music festivals. A film festival offering artistic and aesthetic films has a high reputation.

CULTURAL ATTRIBUTES
——————— AND CONTRIBUTIONS ———————

VISUAL ARTS

Caspar David Friedrich, together with Philip Otto Runge, provided impetus to Romantic painting. Friedrich's pensive self-portraits (1810), his symbolic landscapes aimed against the French, but also reflecting the isolation of the north and the overpowering resilience of nature, influenced many artists. The wide openness of the seacoast, the power of ice, and the reliance on self—such are Friedrich's themes. They are brilliantly executed using the Mecklenburg landscape. After Greifswald he taught at Dresden and captured that area on canvas. His paintings are to be found in all major German galleries. A special Friedrich section of the state museum in Greifswald shows many of his works, as well as the family's soap and candle shop, which provides context to his simple background.

Ernst Barlach sought to re-create Russian peasants' simplicity and piety in his sculptures. Some, like the *Avenger*, evince fire and brimstone; others, like the *Floating Angel* hanging in Güstrow's main cathedral, evoke eternity. Güstrow has a large collection in his former atelier and in the castle. The collection includes his plays, graphics, and sculptures in media from stone to wood and ceramics.

Contemporary, more abstract, and critically intended paintings and cultural works were not tolerated during the GDR era. Painters such as Fritz Brockmann, who created political collages, had difficulties but persisted in his work, which is now recognized.

LITERATURE

Fritz Reuter (1810–1874) is considered the national writer of Mecklenburg for two reasons: He wrote mostly in Low German, and his stories focused on the common people of the region. His success came from *Ut mine Festungstid (Of My Time in Jail)* and *Ut de Franzosentid (During the French Occupation)*. In his early life, Reuter participated in the 1848 revolution and had to serve a long jail sentence. However, by 1911 his local literary reputation had attained such stature that even the ducal couple came to an unveiling in his honor. His birthplace calls itself *Reuterstad Stavenhagen*. Hans Fallada, author of *Little Man, What Now?* spent time in prison in his hometown of Greifswald. His own experiences about common people facing harsh times during the 1930s reappeared in his novels. His house at Carwitz, where he composed many of his works while in internal exile, is a museum.

Contemporary writers, especially in GDR times, sought refuge on the quiet coast. By the 1970s a small literary colony existed near Schwerin Lake. Christa Wolf and Sarah Kirsch had country houses, though only Wolf wrote about the disappearance of rural solitude. The novelist Günter Grass, winner of the Nobel Prize for Literature, has recently written a much-debated historical novel *(Krebsgang)*, which explores the theme of post–World War II refugees as victims.

CIVICS AND REMEMBRANCE

In Rostock, historical stones "to trip over" are reminders of a difficult past. For example, one points out the case of a Jewish dentist forced to leave the university in 1933. He chose suicide. Another recalls a Jewish judge who died in *Auschwitz* in 1942. Such acts of remembrance complement public demonstrations against the war in Iraq and readings by Günther Grass from his novel about the drowning of German refugees at war's end. The state office for political education seeks to present the

Figure 9.3
Half-timbered housing, Kyritz, Mecklenburg–Western Pomerania.

Source Courtesy of the author.

history and geography of the region as well as fostering understanding of parliamentary democracy. Concentration camps, such as the one at Wöbbelin, created under the Nazis and some reused by the Soviets, have become museums and memorial sites. That office also seeks to present a positive identity by thorough accounts of the Mecklenburg and Pomeranian past, including courageous efforts by individuals to maintain dignity in the face of social and political hardship. Much emphasis is placed on employing that past to create a regional identity through a common historical experience. More than nostalgia for GDR stability is being found and offered to youth who have only experienced transitions.

Greifswald, among numerous cities and towns, has many monuments to the GDR dictatorship. Those include plaques identifying Stasi offices, places where persons were arrested arbitrarily, and a strike by medical students in 1955.

CUISINE

Some of the culinary delights, such as solid bread and sausage, are similar to other areas of Germany. Marinated herring accompanied by *schnapps* is a favorite, as in most of the northern regions. A local specialty is roast ribs *(Rippenbraten)*. Ribs with much meat left on them are stuffed with prunes and roasted for about half an hour. One specialty is shared more with Sweden and western Poland than other parts of Germany: *Perogen*. These should not be confused with the related Polish pierogies.

Perogen (Filled Potato Dumplings)

Cook 3 medium potatoes, drain and mash. Separately grate 8 medium potatoes very finely. Put uncooked grated potatoes in a sieve or bag and squeeze out water. Drain the water. Save the starch, which collected under the water. Add half of the starch to a mix of the mashed and grated potatoes. Knead to form dough.

Filling:

1/2 pound dry cottage cheese, quark, or ricotta cheese	1 tablespoon sugar
1 egg	

Prepare filling by mixing cheese, which has been blended in a food processor, with egg and sugar.

Shape potato dough into open balls (about 2″ diameter) with 1 tablespoon of filling in each ball. Seal the balls carefully. Boil in big pot of boiling water, gently putting in 1 ball at a time. The balls will descend and in about 10 to 15 minutes rise to the surface, meaning the submarines are ready for action. Remove with slotted spoon. The Perogen balls can be eaten as they are with a bit of sour cream as sauce. Usually the Perogen are fried in bacon fat and served with bacon. Sour cream is optional.

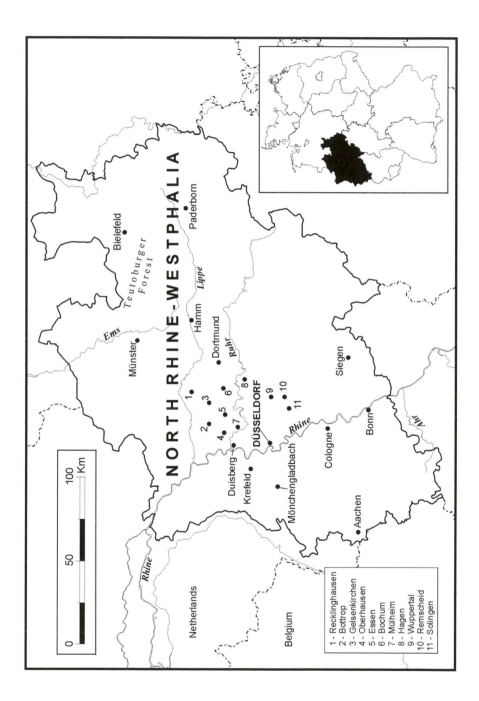

NORTH RHINE-WESTPHALIA

Bielefeld

Teutoburger Forest

Paderborn

Ems

Lippe

Hamm

Münster

Dortmund

Ruhr

Siegen

1
3
5 6
2 7 8
4

DÜSSELDORF

9
10
11

Rhine

Bonn

Ahr

Duisberg

Krefeld

Cologne

Mönchengladbach

Aachen

Rhine

Netherlands

Belgium

0   50   100   Km

1 - Recklinghausen
2 - Bottrop
3 - Gelsenkirchen
4 - Oberhausen
5 - Essen
6 - Bochum
7 - Mülheim
8 - Hagen
9 - Wuppertal
10 - Remscheid
11 - Solingen

Chapter 10

𝕹𝖔𝖗𝖙𝖍 𝕽𝖍𝖎𝖓𝖊-𝖂𝖊𝖘𝖙𝖕𝖍𝖆𝖑𝖎𝖆

SPECIAL ASPECTS

With 18 million inhabitants, this is the most populous state. It has as many people as all the new states added during Reunification in 1990. More than 10 percent of the populace is foreigners; in some large cities the percentage reaches nearly 20 percent. Fourth largest in terms of size, the state covers 34,080 square kilometers. The region surrounds the Rhine/Ruhr coal and steel basin, once the mining and industrial heartland of Germany. As a post–World War II political merger of three separate entities, North Rhine-Westphalia (NRW) amounted to an attempt by the British occupiers in 1946 to overcome the Prussian past. The military values identified with Prussia, which controlled much of the region after 1815, and the armaments factories, associated with Alfred Krupp firm at Essen, have disappeared. The state is fostering a new regional identity as a "core area of Europe." Much emphasis is placed on culture, high technology, and ecological industries with ties to Europe. However, older stereotypes remain: Westphalians are considered to be especially stubborn, those from the Rhineland as especially lively.

REGIONAL TRAITS

Created out of former Prussian provinces (Rhineland, Westphalia), small states such as Lippe, and pieces of other territories, North Rhine-Westphalia combines large cities along the Rhine and Ruhr rivers with much wooded terrain and extensive farmland. Urban centers predominate, with more than 30 cities with populations of over 100,000, far more than elsewhere in the country.

Names of some cities such as Charlemagne's capital, Aachen (Aix-la-Chapelle), underscore that the medieval state boundaries of France and Germany were very different from the present ones. The Eifel subregion once marked the much fought-over boundary between France/Belgium and Germany. Friendly relations and open borders, including with the Netherlands, have replaced the enmity.

There are five distinct dialectic groups in Westphalia and four in the Rhineland; if a person speaks quickly using the local dialect in Cologne, someone from Bielefeld can have difficulty understanding. The coat of arms and flag display the historical territories joined to make the state: the silver Rhine against a green background, the horse of Westphalia against red, and the rose of tiny Lippe on silver.

GEOGRAPHIC FEATURES

The swift-flowing, broad Rhine River pushes through the west, but it does not divide the region as it serves as a commercial lifeline from Switzerland to the Netherlands. The Ruhr, which moves through a valley covering coal beds, flows west-erly into the Rhine at Duisburg. An arch of territory in the north half of the region comprises the agricultural lowlands of Münsterland. In the southwest corner, the Eifel highlands dominate the area west of the Rhine and north of the Ahr River. To the east of the Rhine, in the south-central part of the region, are the Bergisch highlands. Farther east lie the Rothaar (red hair) hills, which divide the region from Hessen. The slightly higher region of neighboring Rhineland-Palatinate borders the southwest. In the west, present political boundaries have little meaning as a similar landscape continues into Belgium and the Netherlands. Lower Saxony borders the northeast, where the Teutoberger Forest provides some highlands.

A great variety of landscapes can be found between Aachen on the edge of the Eifel highlands in the northwest and Bielefeld and Paderborn on the flatlands of the east. Similarly, much diversity divides Münster on the plains in the north from Bonn and Siegen in the hills of the south. In between, especially in the north, lie very productive agricultural lands, comprising one-fourth of the territory. One-fifth remains forest, prominent in the Bergisch highlands.

At the southern edge of the region, near where the Rhine emerges from its narrow gorges, Bonn and Cologne are the beginning of the conglomeration of cities that stretch along the Rhine and then link almost like a cross. Mönchengladbach, Krefeld, Moers-Duisburg, Oberhausen, Bottrop, Mühlheim, Essen, Bochum, Dormund, and Hamm are on the Ruhr axis. Another axis runs from Düsseldorf through Wuppertal and Remscheid to Hagen. Yet another goes from Cologne to Solingen and Remscheid. During the nineteenth century, mining and smelting changed the small agricultural distribution centers and medieval trading towns into industrial complexes, but much open territory and parkland remains. Canals link the Ems, Lippe, Ruhr, and Rhine rivers in the northern plain area.

HISTORY

Given the size of the region, most of its subregions have distinct histories that only recently have been melded into the semblance of a whole. The displays in the *Rheinisches Landesmuseum* in Bonn hint at the layers of civilization, which have left their marks on the landscape. The museum presents models of prehistoric communal existence by the Celts who lost out to Germanic tribes by 100 B.C. The museum is especially rich in the technology and lifestyle of the conquering Roman legions. Though prevented from expanding to the east by the tribal chief Varius (or Hermann the German) during 9 A.D. in the Teutoberger Forest, the Romans retained control of the Rhine until approximately 500 A.D.

In the western part of the region along the Rhine, Roman remains are frequently encountered. Bonn, Cologne, and Xanten were important Roman garrison and trading towns. At Xanten the extensive Roman ruins have been turned into an archaeological park, with amphitheater and reconstructed temple. Some of the remains of bridge pillars, cranes, and fortifications, including the long defensive *Limes* (stone and earthworks), have been restored and are on display. At Cologne, one can take an elevator and descend to the excavated Roman ruins of houses and streets below the present city. Beside the cathedral, the Roman-German Museum has been built around a Roman dining room floor mosaic. That rich museum contains lamps (some with erotic artwork), statuary (especially honoring the dead), glass, jewelry, and military hardware. Most impressive are the remains of aqueducts, which snaked through the Eifel hills for miles bringing springwater to Cologne. The Romans were able to dominate the region for hundreds of years by mixing with as well as exploiting the population.

The area west of the Rhine is a microcosm of the way layers of civilization affected this region. After the Celts, the Romans built sophisticated towns based upon enslaving the populace. Once that empire collapsed by the fifth century, the Catholic Church's missionaries populated valleys with monasteries and churches. Indeed, the missionary churches and cloisters were, along with the multitude of small principalities, the main bearers of civilization until the Renaissance. Many of the cities became independent trading entities. Dortmund, for instance, obtained the right to brew beer in 1296 and became one of the most important commercial centers of the Hanseatic League. By the sixteenth century, coal mining had already become an organized activity.

In the south and east of the region, many castles remain. The castles illustrate the struggles to develop territorial control and impose tolls along the rivers. Simultaneously, in the early medieval era a network of monasteries and church administrative units developed church holdings. Nearly every cloister contained a Romanesque church, many later rebuilt in the Gothic style. From that era the patchwork of bishoprics, princedoms, and small political units, such as Berg or Kleve, led to a dense collection of churches at Cologne, at Bonn, and at each small trading center. But the patchwork also made the area one of constant warfare. Each lord sought to control larger realms with more peasants to exploit and tolls to extract. The bishops and archbishops of the Catholic Church participated actively in those very secular struggles, eventually holding large territories, for example, south of Cologne and around Münster. By the seventeenth century they built themselves fabulous hunting lodges and palaces, such as *Augustusburg* at Brühl, between Bonn and Cologne.

However, the Reformation challenged the Catholic Church's preeminence well before that. At first only some cities accepted the new faith after many debates. However, in 1555, the imposition of the rule that the princes', or ruler's, religion would be the religion of the territory meant that this region became a religious patchwork to match its political one. The Thirty Years' War re-posed the question of religious attachment in brutal form. For three decades (1618–48) the rampages of French, Swedish, and Imperial Habsburg troops destroyed the commerce and the prosperity of the countryside. The petty principalities, including leagues of cities, proved incapable of defending their realms. In the fine wood-paneled city hall at Münster, a peace underscoring religious toleration finally emerged. By then population decline, looted cities, and destroyed culture marked the area.

Over the next century rebuilding took place. By the mid-eighteenth century, canals, coal mining, and iron smelting hinted at the future. However, the bishops and small princedoms reestablished their authority and exacted enough taxes from the peasants and towns to build fine courts. Palaces imitating France's Louis XIV's, Versailles, courts with highly ritualized levées, and cultural refinement in terms of music and theater allowed the upper classes an illusionary world. The peasants slowly gained some rights and Prussia expanded into the region (mostly by marriage and inheritance), but only the French revolutionary and Napoleonic era decisively transformed the petty state structure of the region.

After 1800, Napoleon secularized the areas along the Rhine, created new political entities, and gave a large territory east of the Rhine to his brother as the Kingdom of Westphalia. This rearrangement of the political boundaries continued as he annexed parts of the Rhineland to France and exploited most of western Germany economically. In this region as elsewhere, the response to French imperialism included resentment of outside control and desire for national strength to prevent further domination. In 1815, Prussia obtained extensive territory in the Rhineland as a bulwark against France. Only a few of the small pre-1789 states and none of the religious territories were restored. Much of the future North Rhine-Westphalia existed within the Prussian Rhineland and Westphalian provinces, though few of the present inhabitants acknowledge that Prussian heritage.

Industrialization proved crucial to the area and marked its identity. In 1801, the first steam engine pumped water from mines in the Ruhr. Those at Franz Haniel's Essen shaft reached over 100 meters in depth by the 1840s. Railways from Cologne reached into the Ruhr during the same decade. Though the customs union (*Zollverein*) slowly increased Prussian influence after 1834, coal, iron, and textiles from this region proved decisive for its status as a great power. The Rhine and Ruhr commercial cities, the metalworking of Solingen, and the textiles of Elberfeld and Barmen (today's Wuppertal) expanded on the backs of peasants, who became miners and mill workers. Mining and metalworking, textiles, and transportation machinery set in place physical edifices that still mark this region. High mine towers with huge wheels to move people and goods up and down the shafts, immense factories and rolling mills, brick towers to direct the ever-bellowing smoke, and railways carved through the hillsides served as the cathedrals of the nineteenth century.

People moved and moved again to follow jobs and to improve their circumstances. A town of 3,000 redistributing agricultural goods, such as Bochum in 1800, could become a belching city of 250,000 by 1900. Duisburg, a small trading center of 5,000 in 1800 could become a fabricating center of 300,000 by 1900. The expansion of the Rhine/Ruhr cities and the influx of migrants from eastern Germany and from eastern Europe transformed place and people. Entrepreneurial and innovative families such as the Thyssens, Mannesmanns, and Krupps garnered immense wealth in a few generations. That allowed them to purchase or build villas and to adopt the lifestyle of the aristocracy. By 1900, German industrial and military strength was increasingly based on this huge industrial machine, forging armaments and consumer goods.

Simultaneously, labor organized in trade unions, in Social Democracy, in Catholic lay associations, and in many leisure organizations, including neighborhood pigeon-raising clubs. Some strikes, in 1891 and 1905, stopped production but hardly altered the lifestyle of *Siedlungen* (colonies) around industrial plants, of proletarian awareness, and of patriarchal families. However, those urban patterns did not touch the lifestyle of peasants in the Eifel or other rural areas, except to supply migrant laborers.

World War I witnessed an expansion of the region's industrial might but also demonstrated its limits. Workers, who had never received their share of the wealth they helped to create, demonstrated, protested, struck, and finally rebelled. They were repressed in 1917 but helped overthrow the Imperial state and create a republic in late 1918. They were again repressed in 1920 when they sought to assure that the reactionary generals did not regain power. They failed, yet in keeping with their belief in national dignity, many sought to help the country against French occupation during the Ruhr crisis over reparations in 1923. Their passive resistance helped undermine the French attempt at dominance in the Rhine-Ruhr area, as France sought to separate parts of the Rhineland from Germany. The world's worst inflation ruined many livelihoods, and society split into many factions. Social Democrats vied with Communists, Catholics with Social Democrats, and Nazis with conservatives for party members and parliamentary voters. The Nazis made few inroads in the region until the Depression in 1929, and even then they remained a minority.

Generations of workers became tied to industry. Some authors think they became a special Ruhr populace. By the 1890s the idea of social rights, inspired by a very strong labor movement, emerged. The struggle for an 8-hour day (48-hour work week), for decent working conditions in narrow mine shafts or next to raging furnaces, for fresh air in dust-filled textile factories employing women and children, and for subsistence wages provided impetus to large organizations, ideological debates about social justice, and Socialism. In 1911, even the state factory inspectors acknowledged that over a million industrial accidents maimed and killed workers each year. Social Democracy and trade unionism became a way of life in company towns as a defense system against employer exploitation. Most employers still operated with assumptions about having total control of their factories and feudal rights over workers' lives. The struggle for emancipation from harsh existence with few rights—Prussia had a three-class voting system restricted to males until 1918—continued through the 1920s.

Once the Nazis attained power, they sought to break both the laborers' and the churches' organizations. Communist organizations were immediately forbidden, their members beaten and imprisoned. For a short time, an organized underground actively resisted the regime. Most Social Democrats had to go into internal exile or try to work from across the border in Belgium and the Netherlands. Catholic youth organizations were threatened and some of their leaders protested but with little impact. The trade unions were dissolved and members melded into the Nazi party labor front. By the late 1930s, the Ruhr had been integrated and homogenized into the Nazi system through a district reorganization of state boundaries. Concentration camps such as at Niederhagen served to control and to punish. Local Gestapo headquarters in Dortmund and Düsseldorf worked with informers to expose those who did not follow the racial laws and continued to have contact with Jews. By 1939, many Jews had emigrated, and after 1941 most of the remaining ones were shipped east to be executed.

During World War II this area took the brunt of Allied bombing. The Allies wanted to totally destroy the Ruhr armaments production complex. In the course of the carpet bombing, the cities—built without planning so that industrial and living quarters were intermingled—received blow after blow. Electrical dams and waterworks as well as industrial plants and rail lines received the main barrages, though in the end a surprising amount of the underground and rolling mill infrastructure remained in place.

To prevent the Ruhr from again becoming an armaments base, the occupying Allies blew up many industrial plants and made the industries part of an integrated European network of steel and coal production. The region quickly recovered economically, especially since Britain needed coal and the Korean War opened markets, which the United States was not servicing. By the late 1950s, once the Allies insisted on Germany's membership in NATO and having a military, armaments production followed.

Automobiles, eventually tanks, and trucks rolled from the assembly lines until in 1966 the first coal crisis and then the oil energy crisis of 1973 followed. Only with subsidies could the industries that required rationalization and mechanization continue. Mine owners pooled their resources and markets. By the mid-1970s, international competition from the Far East meant that the production of Ruhr coal and steel would continue to decline. By 1980 only subsidies, promised until 1995, kept some plants functioning but did not stop the decline of employment. The shift to cleaner industries, to higher technologies such as nuclear energy and electronics, had begun. However, two decades of difficult transition kept re-posing the question what would all the workers do in all those industrial plants in the future. By then publishing, media, and many newer approaches to textiles and a return to some handicraft specialty production had found niche markets. Culture became the code word as research centers and new universities supported novel approaches to economic development.

After World War II the region, which began as an artificial British construct, became a mixed area in terms of politics and ideology. Socialization and nationalization with worker codetermination, meaning workers sitting on plant boards, set the immediate postwar tone. Unionism attained record levels of membership and influence. Though the still-ideological radical Social Democrats (SPD) and the conservative Christian Democrats (CDU) gained similar percentages of parliamentary votes in 1947 and 1950, the CDU at first led the government with an all-party coalition. In 1950, Karl Arnold started a CDU dominance in coalition with smaller parties, which lasted until 1966. Similar to the shift at the federal level, in 1966, Heinz Kühn organized a SPD/liberal coalition that lasted until 1978. After 1980, the Social Democrats reigned on their own, but by 1995 they had to return to coalition government, with the Greens. At present a SPD/Green coalition is in power, but the situation is very tenuous as economic and financial difficulties plague the large deindustrializing cities of the region. The ex-federal president, Johannes Rau, headed the SPD government of the state from 1978 to 1998, and was replaced by Wolfgang Clement, who moved to Berlin in 2002 as federal finance minister. Peter Steinbrück (SPD) presently serves as prime minister.

Identity from history. Overcoming pollution and reinventing themselves are common themes in publications about the region. The move away from nineteenth-century dirty industries and the cleanup of the landscape are sometimes equated with remaking the people. Certainly the slogan, "We from NRW," frequently appears as an identifier. It seems to mean that the populace is not going anywhere even if industry is disappearing. The concept exudes pride in what has been created or rebuilt in a place threatened in turn by pollution, war, and changing markets. The idea of having made a cultural landscape signifies identification with a region that politically did not exist as a unified entity before 1947.

In 1961, the state began to foster an understanding of regional history through exhibitions documenting the region's diverse roots. That year the exhibition, entitled "Electoral Prince Clemens August," held at his Brühl palace, tried to illustrate how much of the present state's territory this religious prince had controlled. In 1972, a large state-supported history of the region by Peter Hüttenberger commemorated the 25th anniversary of the state. Simultaneously, the state archives presented a very large documentary exhibit on the region's history, emphasizing its similarities in diverse areas. A book series, published with state support and that has grown to over 50 volumes, presents aspects of the region's historical developments.

Some advocates of a regional identity insist that the state colors, flag, and coat of arms are "beloved" signifiers of regional attachment, though attempts to create a state anthem failed. Cultural prizes and medals honoring those who have contributed to the region seek to increase regional awareness, but perhaps awareness simply exists due to the size of the region and its importance within the country.

ECONOMY

Until the nineteenth century the cities—many of which once belonged to the Hanseatic League because ships and commerce used the Rhine and Ruhr far upstream—mainly distributed agricultural and craft products. Rye and wheat for bread, barley for beer, flax for cloth, salt, and potatoes were transported and sold, especially to north-ern port cities. Knives, fancy silver, and linens were exported. In the nineteenth cen-tury, mining for coal close to the surface expanded; soon pumps allowed underground mining and the whole Ruhr valley became a system of shafts and tunnels. The earth's surface constantly shifted as underground water courses found new paths in aban-doned tunnels or as old workings collapsed due to rotting timbers. Workers migrated between the cities, which grew at tremendous rates. By the end of the nineteenth century, the Rhine-Ruhr area became an industrial complex leading the world in coal and steel production.

Transforming that nearly monolithic economy into a diversified and adaptable economy has been the main regional task since the 1970s. In 1970, industrial production (energy, water, mining, reprocessing, and construction) accounted for over 50 percent of the region's output. By the mid-1990s it had dropped to about 30 percent. Meanwhile, service industries increased from about 15 percent to 35 percent. Trade, transport, and public services each have remained at around 15 percent.

At present, the region produces around one-fifth of the country's total produc-tion. Media, food processing, chemicals, automobiles, electronics, and machine building are the main industries. In the Ruhr, coal and steel remain significant, but the growth industries are automotive, electronics, and environmental science. Along the Rhine, chemicals at Leverkusen, automobiles and media at Cologne, and insurance at Düsseldorf illustrate the region's increasing diversity. The Lower Rhine produces textiles and clothing as well as processing foods. The Bergisch and Siegerland areas have many small high-quality steel (knives, razors, and utensils) factories. Westphalia and Lippe specialize in clothing and furniture.

One politician has pointed out that research has become the main raw resource of the region. Supporting that perspective is the development of higher education. At the end of the war the new state had three universities, located at Bonn, Cologne, and Münster, plus the technical college at Aachen, which has been elevated to full university status. Most important was the founding of new institutions, resulting in easier access to higher education in the industrial centers of the Ruhr. Between 1961 and 1972 universities were created in Bochum; Dortmund; Düsseldorf; Bielefeld; Duisburg; Essen; Paderborn; Siegen; Wuppertal; and, in 1974 at Hagen, a university for distant learning. The opportunity to attain higher education encompassed the whole region, especially for working-class children. Over half a million students per year populate the universities and colleges. Knowledge-based industries have spread accordingly, and the cities that are home to the institutions appreciate their local eco-nomic importance.

Another economic indicator is the spread of trade fairs. They were already important during the 1920s. In the post–World War II era, Cologne's became the most significant. Düsseldorf is not far behind Cologne, while Essen and other cities organize specialty fairs.

Media and media production, especially radio and newspapers, were a concern of the British occupiers. They insisted on a decentralized system, so they located West German Rundfunk (WDR) in Cologne. It has become the media center of the region, including radio, television, and video production as well as music. The head-quarters of the giant publishing firm Bertelsmann is in the smaller city of Gütersloh.

Though not a traditional tourist area, the region has many hotel bookings due to business and weekend excursions. Such tourism fits well with the rich cultural collections. A UNESCO study, which is much cited by state officials, claimed that NRW is one of the world's top five most significant cultural regions. The cathedrals at Cologne and Aachen, the *Rathaus* at Münster, *Augustusburg* palace at Brühl, the Wallraf-Richartz and Ludwig art collections at Cologne, the Wilhelm Lehmbruck sculpture collection at Duisburg, the Folkwang gallery at Essen, the state art collection at Düsseldorf, and the innovative theatres of Bochum and Recklinghausen with their festivals, are among the reasons.

MAIN CITIES

This region has many more large cities (30 over 100,000) than any region of Germany, but many are in difficult financial straits. Unemployment is above the national average and increasing. Oberhausen and Bielefeld are on the edge of bankruptcy. So many cities are so close together that geographers speak of an urban conglomeration of 10 million people where one city melds into the other; over 5 million people live along 50 kilometers of the Ruhr River. Urbanization and industrialization in the nineteenth century linked the transportation and traffic infrastructures and perhaps created a hardworking Ruhr people *(Ruhrvolk)*. At that time, the subregions provided the main *Heimat* (homeland) with which to identify. In the following, not all the large cities will be given the description they deserve since they have been rebuilt and all contain special attributes in particular corners. However, since so many share industrial landscapes and since many suburbs reflect the similar styles of late nineteenth- and early twentieth-century mass building of workers' colonies *(Siedlungen)*, they do not offer as many attractions as other areas.

CAPITAL

Düsseldorf (population 570,000). The city has repeatedly been rated as Germany's most expensive in terms of hotel accommodations and cost of living. Center of the fashion industry, a rebuilt and modern city, it has sometimes been plagued by right-radical extremism against foreigners. On its perimeter the city has many old industries, but the center is high tech. Unemployment has stabilized at around 10 percent, while for more than a decade the number of foreigners has remained at around 16 percent. Parks along the Rhine and palaces such as *Benrath* provide pleasant areas for strolling.

As an administrative city, capital of the most populous state and one that had to plan state economic diversification since the 1970s, Düsseldorf has many offices and bureaucrats. The *Stadttor* is a huge glass and steel "gate" that contains the office of the prime minister. The building symbolizes the strong role that the prime minister's office has in the government as well as the importance of state leadership in seeking new direction. Unknown to many is that until Berlin took the limelight with its extensive building program in the 1990s, Düsseldorf probably led the country with interesting and imaginative public and private buildings. Among them is the stylized series of overlapping half circles in which the regional parliament meets.

Düsseldorf is a leading trade fair city. Its 15 fairs attract over a million visitors annually. Frankfurt and Hanover attract more, but in fashion, the city has trumped all others, though Berlin seeks to challenge it.

The city has the theater, museums, and galleries expected of a large capital city, namely the state theater, the largest regional museum, and the very extensive state art gallery. Since the region is so large and earlier had such financial strength, the city has had the benefit of being home to a well-endowed, special collection of contemporary artworks. The local art gallery is especially strong in modern art, partly due to the art school, which had already trained many leading painters and sculptors by the 1890s. The extensive collection begins with postimpressionism. In the post-World War II era the city attracted many artists, such as the photographers Bernd and Hilla Becher, Georg Ebers, and Joseph Beuys.

Cologne (population 970,000) is the largest city with more than 15 percent foreigners. Like Berlin, Hamburg, and Munich, Cologne and the immediate hinterland is inhabited by a million-plus people. Almost exclusively Catholic until after World War II, an influx of German and foreign migrants started to make the city multicultural. Yet the city continues many Catholic traditions, especially processions on religious holidays. Its Roman ruins and Romanesque churches, especially the imposing Gothic cathedral *(Dom)*, plus the glass and steel trade fair buildings, are a reminder of the thousand years of its commercial and Catholic past. The Greek merchants, Spanish restaurants, Turkish street vendors, and Italian workers at the Ford plant illustrate what the 1960s brought.

The inhabitants at the time of the Roman advance up the Rhine decided to cooperate rather than fight. They mixed with the Roman legions, which built a military colony—hence, the city's name—on a checkerboard pattern. The Romans built aqueducts, which brought water from far in the Eifel hills to the south. Remains of the brickwork exist. Indeed, one Cologne author wrote a bestseller entitled *Into the Roman Empire by Elevator,* because some ruins are directly under the *Rathaus* and can be accessed by an elevator. More Roman civilization and technology can be seen in the German-Roman museum next to the cathedral. The museum includes models of bridge building as well as refined glass and jewelry. The collection of small erotic oil lamps usually draws crowds of students.

Some of the medieval circular city walls and gates remain, especially in the pattern of streets in the old city. Most impressive are the Romanesque churches in each parish. Most were destroyed down to the walls by World War II bombing but were rebuilt by the 1960s. Nearly every parish in the older sections of the city has one: St. Apostle on the New Market, St. Maria, St. Pantaleon, St. Gereon. They probably comprise the world's most compact collection of Romanesque buildings, with decorated pillars and arches of alternating colored stone. The church towers helped define the city skyline until post-World War II office and apartment blocks were built. However, the massive cathedral *(Dom)* remains the city's trademark.

Commerce, including important trade fairs, has determined the city's fortunes for centuries. Railways and *autobahns* have aided the transport of goods, some of which move on the Rhine. Since World War II the media, especially radio and television, have been important because of regional and international broadcasting. Daily and regional newspapers, as well as book publishing, continue to be strong elements in the local economy. Concrete and ceramic industries have been important, but Ford's main automotive plant has been an industrial mainstay since the 1920s.

In Cologne the *Rosenmontag* (Monday before Lent) parade culminates three days of *Karnival* (carnival) fun. Bright red and white uniforms with an excess of un-military-like medals and fool's hats, plus miniskirts for the girls below tight-fitting fake military jackets, predominate. Clever costumes and innovative masks combined with much drinking and simple fun mark this Rhineland event for which everything stops except the flow of beer *(Kölsch)* and wine. Carnival is celebrated in all Rhineland towns and villages, but Cologne's is one of the best. Each year well-prepared processions combine satirical and politically incorrect floats, endless uniformed groups mocking authority, as well as loads of free candies tossed from the floats. Everyone's participation adds to the spectacle.

The city is a shopping center for the surrounding area as well as the cultural mecca of the southern part of the region. Its art collections, especially the medieval masters in the Wallraf-Richartz Museum and the contemporary ones in the Ludwig collection, are among the most comprehensive in the world. The city museum, the carnival museum, the archdiocese museum, the East Asian museum, and the ethnographic museum *(Rautenstruch-Joest Museum)* complement the art collections with objects. Given the diversity of religions, the high percentage of foreigners, the number of private galleries and trade in paintings and objects, cosmopolitanism has evidently trumped Catholic provincialism.

In addition to cultural strength, Cologne is an industrial, media, and energy producer. Ceramics, automobiles, electrical instruments, and brown coal plants contrast with the "clean" office industries of radio, television, and printing. Cologne is one of Germany's media centers for sending as well as producing television and radio, which have made the city more vibrant. The size of Cologne's medieval Romanesque churches and Gothic cathedral hint at the richness and influence of the Catholic Church in this area's past and present. All had to be rebuilt after roofs and some walls were destroyed by bombs. Since the 1960s, Greeks, Spaniards, Italians, and Serbs, as so-called guest workers, supplied skilled labor. They stayed and made the city more colorful and drastically improved the restaurant scene.

In Cologne many traditions coexist: Some relate to Catholic rituals, others to a long season of carnival celebrations with lavish processions and parties. Some traditions relate to enjoying the special local beer *(Kölsch)* in thin glasses at long tables where people sit with strangers. Other local customs, such as music and singing clubs, find expression in choirs or jazz clubs on the *Heumarkt*. The city has many attractions, including a ceramics museum, large zoo, many church choirs, and orchestras. Its cultural offerings, including concerts at the bishop's palace in Brühl south of the city and theater tradition, are strong. An aerial cable car takes one over the Rhine.

Essen (population 590,000). The second-largest city of the Ruhr area originally was built around the Krupp armaments factory. The city exemplified the skilled labor of its workers but also the feudal outlook of the owners. In the nineteenth century, social housing with libraries came at the expense of being a loyal, deference-paying subject of the firm in a tightly controlled company town. By the 1880s, 70,000 men worked for the metal-processing firm. The family firm is gone and Krupp has become a publicly traded stock company, which has merged with its competitors, such as Thyssen. The family's *Villa Hügel*, shielded from the sight of the factories by carefully shaped gardens, is open to the public and symbolizes the changed relations of city and industry.

As elsewhere in the Ruhr, coal and gas remain important industries, but the dominant employer is the Rheinisch-Westphalian-Electricity (RWE) works. Trade fairs have become important to the local economy.

By 1912 public outcries pointed to the pollution problem. However, since the 1960s the cleanup has been thorough, partly due to the decline of steel production, though rolling mills continue to operate. It also reflects the awareness that dumping waste into rivers or allowing smoke to fill the air is a health as well as an aesthetic issue.

Once the home of big steel and coal, Essen has carefully recultivated its image as a cultural center. Its theater and museums have achieved international acclaim. The theater, founded by an industrial philanthropist in 1892, the collections of twentieth-century impressionists at Folkwang gallery, the gardens designed in 1929, and the central artificial lake constructed from 1931 to 1933, seem incongruous with the legendary industrial image. The transformation from smoky black past culminates in the white and curved walls and light marble stairs of the hip Aalto Opera house. Almost as a concession to the industrial past, the mine shaft and head frame, at the *Zollverein* mine, built in art nouveau style, has been preserved.

Dortmund (population over 590,000). With a large port, major university, and many breweries, the largest city of the Ruhr area more readily made the shift from industrial mover of coal and steel to mover of paper and ideas than many Ruhr cities. Once part of the Hanseatic League of trading towns, the iron and steel firm Hoechst transformed Dortmund during the nineteenth century. Day laborers from the farms worked in industry during the week and returned to their agriculture chores according to season and need. In the late twentieth century, trade fairs, insurance companies, sports events (especially soccer), and casinos have supported the shift away from a mono-industrial economy.

Duisburg (population 525,000) was a main steel-producing center by the late nineteenth century. Thyssen's huge works have been reduced to empty structures. The port remains significant for coal transport. Duisburg is becoming a computer, especially software, center and reflects the shift from industrial production to service and knowledge industries. Helping that shift is the university. The Wilhelm Lehmbruck Museum has many works by one of the twentieth century's major sculptors.

Bochum (population 380,000). In 1965 the Ruhr University opened and helped move an industrial giant toward a service city. Steel produced by Bochum Association started in 1844 using cheap coal. The last coal mine closed in 1973. Since then Opel is among the largest employers, but many smaller auto parts companies supplement it. Shopping at the *Kaufhaus Kortum* remains a traditional experience with its arcades and special displays, coffee and cake corners. One of the industrial cathedrals, a pavilion hall with a partial glass roof built for a trade fair in 1902, serves as a hall for music and special events. Among the first museums dedicated to mining and visited by about 400,000 people per year is the Deutsches Bergbau Museum founded in 1930. From its shaft towers one can see over the city, but most impressive are the models of mining through the ages and the underground tours illustrating the stages of development from pickaxes to automated extraction. A research center focused on the history of mining—the technology and the labor conditions—supports the educational mission of the museum.

Theater is especially strong; the city has a reputation for dramatic innovations in the *Bochumer Festspiele*. The huge *Ruhrhalle* can be used for symphonic as well as youth concerts. Sports, especially soccer, are strongly encouraged with swimming pools and fields.

Wuppertal (population 370,000). Known for its hanging train, this textile center has had to adjust its economy. Higher-educational institutions and research centers are among the attempts at economic diversification. Tourists are offered historical train rides and much green space in the Neander valley. The city sees itself as the economic and cultural center of the Bergisch hill area. It has a dance theater company, a historic city hall, a research institute for climate and energy studies in relation to the environment, plus proximity to the airports serving Cologne and Düsseldorf.

Bielefeld (population 323,000) is just outside the Ruhr metropolis area. A small agricultural distribution and trading center in the early nineteenth century, linen fed its economic growth. Textiles and clothing now combine with food (Oetker), paper (Graphia), and luxury goods. Over 30 percent of the labor force is in processing, and nearly 45 percent are in service industries. Medical and health research are strong sectors of the local economy. A large technology center has investments in biotechnology, and the research institutes work closely with the university.

Bonn (population 290,000). The small university and retirement city became the temporary capital of the country after 1949. Slowly the ministries took on permanency with large office buildings and thousands of bureaucrats. The university expanded simultaneously. Embassies multiplied, and the towns and villages around Bonn with their green spaces and conservation areas, especially in the *Siebengebirge* (Seven Hills), became home to bureaucrats. Bonn village became Bonn province as a very livable place; restaurants and boutiques expanded and Cologne, with its theater, music, and museums, was only 30 kilometers to the north. Slowly Bonn's local gallery expanded from its base with many August Macke works. The Beethoven Hall did not match the acoustic requirements of the modern world but brought many fine artists from Mstislav Rostopovich to Ludwig Güttler. The Museum for the History of the Federal

Figure 10.1
University at Bonn in former eighteenth-century palace, North Rhine-Westphalia.

Source Courtesy of Inter Nationes, Bonn, Germany.

Republic demonstrated that an *Erlebnis* (daily existence) museum was possible. After Reunification, eastern Germans, who insisted that their GDR experience needed to be recorded as well, mimicked the approach at Eisenhüttenstadt and Leipzig.

Bonn's recent history fits well with the North Rhine-Westphalia post-World War II experience. Having lost its role as capital, it too has experienced retrenchment, loss of its economic role, and financial support, as have the Ruhr cities.

Gelsenkirchen (population 300,000). From 624 inhabitants in 1839 to 340,000 in 1926, the city's growth demonstrates what mining and industry did to rural Ruhr areas. Since the 1960s, population has declined in proportion to the problems of coal mining. The city is closely associated with its soccer club, FC Schalke 04, which won seven national titles and plays in a huge stadium.

Mönchengladbach (population 260,000). A Catholic city until well after World War II, it was home to the propaganda arm of the church against Social Democracy. Its textiles made it the Manchester of the Rhine, even if working conditions were not as drastic. As regional headquarters of NATO as well as many employers' organizations, the city has become an administrative center. The Romanesque basilica dates from the thirteenth century.

Münster (population 260,000). The medieval walled city traded in all directions. The ring, which enclosed the old center, is still visible in street patterns. At its center is the great cathedral with astronomical clock, market square, and city hall. Many federal administrative offices, a large university, and colleges helped to make a formerly commercial and distribution center into a large middle-class city. Research institutes, especially in ethnology, pharmaceuticals, and chemicals, provide the economic base. Its diverse cultural offerings include a city theater, botanical garden, and zoo. The historic struggles of the city include the sixteenth- and seventeenth-century religious wars in which divergent sects were brutally repressed by the local bishop. At the end of the Thirty Years' War, the treaty introducing religious toleration to Europe was signed in the wooden-paneled city hall, which is open to the public.

Aachen (population 240,000). As capital of Charlemagne's empire in 800, the city received its trademark: the octagonal Romanesque cathedral with offsetting black and white stones. Currently a spa and casino center, it previously depended on textiles and trade in them. Many products from rubber and plastic to machinery and umbrellas are produced here.

Krefeld (population 240,000). Though once an important textile center, only a few silk mills and a textile museum attest to the past. Linens and silks were complemented by machinery, carriage, and chemical industries. The latter and food processing remain. A palace in the suburb of Linn holds a local museum.

Oberhausen (population 225,000). Oberhausen was founded in 1862, though the first ironworks already existed nearby in 1758. The main one, *Gute Hoffnung*, opened in 1782. In seeking to make the transition away from mining and smelting, the city financed or supported huge malls, entertainment and leisure centers during the 1970s and 1980s. But employment slowly declined and population slowly aged. Seeking to renovate its image, the city fostered an international short film festival. A new central city "CentrO" seeks to draw youth, while a new theater supports the move to cultural activities. A renovated palace is home to the new Ludwig Gallerie, which has art from many cultures and forms, including comic books.

Hagen (population 210,000). University-level education via video, mail, and internet is the key to economic diversification. Art nouveau buildings, such as the train station, reflect the era of industrial prosperity and the art movement funded by the philanthropist, Carl Ernst Osthaus. The museum named after him contains postimpressionist collections. He purchased from the art colony "New Style." The city also has a local museum, but more important is the open-air museum illustrating Westphalian building styles and especially agricultural work methods from the sixteenth to twentieth centuries.

In the half-timbered buildings, guides explain artisanry such as smelting, tanning, and dyeing. A nearby castle, *Hohenlimburg*, dates back to the thirteenth century but contains a museum showing modern rolling mill methods of handling steel. A stately manor house at Werdringen, is part of the city's attempt to emphasize its closeness to nature. A special project of the Osthaus-Museum is a research guide listing all the concentration, labor, and reeducation camps that existed during the Nazi era. This Project Deutschland has created a large databank with over 3,000 entries.

Hamm (population 180,000). Since the stoppage of nuclear energy, ecological industries have opened in previous mining sites. Once a Hanseatic commercial center and the residence of Markisch counts, a moated Renaissance palace and churches with carved altars hint at a preindustrial past. The area around the city is surprisingly green, and among the tourist offerings is the world's largest mountable building in the shape of an elephant with rooftop garden.

Figure 10.2

City Hall where the Treaty of Westphalia was signed in 1648, Münster, North Rhine-Westphalia.

Source © Press and Information Office, Germany.

Mülheim an der Ruhr (population 175,000). The industrialist and financier Mathias Stinnes helped make this the largest Ruhr port. Stinnes, Thyssen, and Mannesmann all had major steel and rolling mills here. One of the largest coffee-roasting firms still exploits the transport and energy possibilities of the city's location. A medieval castle at Broich and a cloister at Saarn point to earlier functions and present excursion possibilities. The city advertises its parks and "fountain" festival as the time when the inner city becomes a "theater and a buffet." The main theater events in summer are accompanied by jazz and trumpet concerts.

Herne (population 175,000) offers the Emser Valley museum and the largest regional fair; Solingen (population 160,000) still produces quality knives; Leverkusen (population 160,000) is dominated by Bayer chemicals of aspirin fame; at Neuss (population 150,000), the machine factory goes back to Nikolaus Otto and his invention of the internal combustion engine in 1876.

Paderborn (population 130,000). Identified with Catholicism since it attained an archbishop, Paderborn has a theological school at the university. The Gothic cathedral dates from the twelfth century. The city is a trading, machine-building, electronics, and plastics center.

Recklinghausen (population 125,000). Presently known for the Ruhr Festival, which provides weeks of dramatic novelties and traditional offerings, this was once a small trading and religious center. In the nineteenth century mining and administration expanded the population. An icon museum and turn-of-the-twentieth-century city hall plus a miner's cooperative hospital are the major items to view.

Remscheid (population 120,000). Many houses have shale-shingle roofs as in Solingen and in the Bergisch area. Once an important commercial center, machine building has provided the main livelihood since industrialization. Testing machinery and tools is a specialty. Many tools have been developed and built here. The Wilhelm Röntgen museum honors the inventor of X-rays.

Though perhaps unfair in not delineating their special aspects, the following cities also pass the 100,000-inhabitant mark: Bottrop, Siegen, Bergisch Gladbach, Moers, and Witten. While all cities have interesting aspects, and those in North Rhine-Westphalia are no exception, not all of their traits and attractions can be noted. In addition, these cities mostly resulted from unplanned nineteenth-century industrial expansion. Similar urban constructs appeared around factories. Hence, they offer limited architectural novelty. Often they buried heritage below brick and concrete. The cities in this area are mostly special for their magnitude and their survival—their shift to different economic functions and the greening of the whole region since the 1970s.

ATTRACTIONS

Düsseldorf is known for its discos, where the supermodel, Claudia Schiffer, was discovered. Perhaps for youth the attraction is the mass entertainment in the many large halls or the thronged annual fun fairs *(Kirmes)* with breathtaking rides. Or is it the variety of beers from Warstein, DAB, Krombach, Hannen, and Veltins to a multitude of small local brews?

To stay with the monumental: The Zollverein Coal Mine industrial complex in Essen is a local heritage site. Old industrial buildings, including gas storage tanks, have been converted into cultural uses such as art galleries, dance halls, and trade-show venues. Some Bauhaus buildings have been saved and made into museums. International Emscher Construction Park was a 10-year (1989–1999) attempt to illustrate what had been built along this river. Old industrial workplaces, with machinery, huge wheels, dynamos, mine shafts, and towers, as well as the new knowledge-oriented parks, as at Gelsenkirchen, and the rebuilt Duisburg grain storage sheds have been turned into museums. Citizens have been involved in the design of new living blocks, which until recently were the company colonies of a previous era. Bochum's Deutscher Bergbau Museum was among the first of the successful attempts to save the industrial heritage and to put it to cultural and educational use.

If industrial and technological masterpieces are to become attractions, there is a special one in Wuppertal. In 1900, Kaiser Wilhelm II opened an engineering feat. To solve the problem of urban transport in a densely populated river valley, a train track was hung from suspension girders over the river. With a J-shaped support coming down from the girders, the trains were hung below by an upside-down J-shaped system. The "hanging" railway has run successfully with no accidents for over a hundred years, and on Sundays one can ride in the emperor's plush coach.

The era just before the major industrial upswing of the mid-nineteenth century can be experienced at the Westphalian open-air museum outside Hagen. Water-driven hammer mills and handicraft production with ingenious pulleys and cogs can be seen in a series of half-timbered buildings.

In contrast to the industrial heritage, the area is especially rich in Romanesque churches and cathedrals, including the famed octagonal chapel of Charlemagne at Aachen. Though perhaps not as ornamented with carved capitals as the Romanesque architecture of southern France, the Rhineland contains many fine examples of churches and chapels. This is especially so in Cologne, where nearly every parish had a monumental church. Many lost their roofs and some their walls to World War II bombing, but nearly all have been carefully restored. Some smaller parish churches outside major cities have survived a multitude of reigns. For example, the two-tiered Romanesque church, connected by an octagonal opening between the levels, at Schwarzrheindorf outside Beuel (across the river from Bonn) still has its intact frescoes telling the story of the Creation. Similarly, near Hattingen, a village church has eleventh-century wall paintings of St. George fighting the dragon. Many of the region's castles and palaces in the north are surrounded by water, some from diked rivers, others from artificially created lakes. At Herten, such a "water palace" (*Wasserschloss*) is surrounded by a huge park, and one part of the city has 81 half-timbered houses. Similar half-timbered structures were not destroyed in many villages, such as Holzwickede with its manor house, or Königswinter across the Rhine from Bonn.

If medieval churches have survived or been restored, some castles, such as at Burg or Burggrafenberg, have been frequently rebuilt as museums and contain armor and swords. More typical along the Rhine, as at Bad Godesberg, are mainly medieval ruins, though the gate at Kleve, in massive brick, has stood since 1393.

Figure 10.3
Half-timbered sixteenth-century house, Königswinter, North Rhine-Westphalia.

Source Courtesy of the author.

However, not much is left of the medieval stone castles west of the Rhine because the French King Louis XIV tried to have them systematically destroyed. To show the many styles of half-timbered buildings in the region, the open-air museum *(Freilichtmuseum)* at Kommern-Mechernich has a collection of houses, barns, and work sheds. If that reveals how peasants lived in two rooms and slept in five-foot beds, the palaces of the next period reveal much about the bishops, princes, dukes, and counts. They had beautiful edifices in which to listen to music, to parade their finery such as wigs and chamois gloves, or to show off their hunting skills.

At Brühl, an archbishop demonstrated his taste for the secular world with a baroque palace. In addition to the main palace, *Augustusburg*, with its formal garden, a hunting lodge is set among the woods while the palace faces formal rococo gardens. This palace complex is a UNESCO world heritage site. Many other palaces have not attained the fame of Brühl but are still worth a stop, including *Hugenpoet an der Ruhr*, the water palace *Dyck* near Reydt, *Borbeck* in Essen, *Laer* of the count of Westphalia, and *Wewelsburg* in Paderborn.

One set of UNESCO heritage sites is more traditional: Aachen's octagonal Romanesque cathedral created during Charlemagne's reign. The alternating black and white stone in symmetrical fashion is difficult to discern because the building is crowded nearly hidden among a complex of urban buildings. Inside its majesty is evident, however. Another UNESCO site is the Gothic cathedral at Cologne. One of the biggest cathedrals north of the Alps, it contains relics holy to the Catholic Church.

The double spires, which can be climbed for views over the city and Rhine River, date from the mid-nineteenth century. The size of each individual stone pillar, which helps support the high arched roof, amazes most visitors until disturbed by a priest in robes dangling a money box and demanding coins to maintain the structure. Pigeons have been eroding the building with their droppings for a thousand years. In the last century, pollution from brown coal and automobile emissions have further added to the erosion.

Do zoos (in Cologne and many of the larger cities) and many companion animals, including pigeons, reflect the need for contact with animals by people only a century away from a rural environment? Perhaps the many dogs substitute for the standard family in the increasing single population. Dog walking has become a sport. The hilly countryside above the main rivers provides many opportunities for walking and hiking (also mountain biking). Hiking in the Siegerland or Bergisch hills and especially in the Eifel is a vacation and weekend activity. Special *Volks-Wanderung* (people's walks) with medals to acknowledge participation are common. Since many people from neighboring Belgium and the Netherlands participate, they become a 40-kilometer chat and European intermingling. On the route, pubs are among the places where one has cards stamped marking the five-kilometer intervals. The amazing aspect of the Rhine/Ruhr area is the extent of green spaces between the large cities and around them.

Half-timbered buildings survive in many places. Freudenberg burned almost totally in the mid-seventeenth century, so the rebuilt town has an unbelievable uniformity. Its black and white half-timbered houses seem to march up the hills. They provide a unified picture with slightly varying patterns under shale roofs. In the Eifel, many have been preserved, including in the *Kommern* open-air museum on the border with Rhineland-Palatinate.

CUSTOMS

Shooting competitions with processions and balls organized by 1,700 clubs; pigeon breeding in the Ruhr; wine blossom festivals along the Rhine; carnival, especially in Cologne and Düsseldorf—the area has many traditional and new celebrations. The Christian rites of passage—confirmation and funerals as well as pilgrimages—remain strong among Catholics, while Easter and Christmas are used as excuses for festivities by all. The latter usually include egg coloring and hunts or markets with mulled wine. St. Martin's Day is celebrated with paper lanterns and evening processions.

May Day trees are specially celebrated in parts of the Rhineland. An unattached female over 16 and supposedly a virgin is identified by a group of male youths. She is auctioned as a May bride for walks and dances; the tacit agreement of the female has been attained through nods and winks. The person who pays the most for such a "bride" becomes the May King and his partner the Queen. During the night of the auction, a decorated birch tree is attached to the house of the maiden. This former way of declaring love has become a widespread ritual.

Figure 10.4
Carnival dance, North Rhine-Westphalia.

Source Courtesy of the author.

Sports are especially strong in the region and were included as a state responsibility in the constitution of 1992. They are considered as important as art, culture, and education and are fostered for health as well as sociability. Professional soccer dominates men's public interest with major clubs at Cologne, Mönchengladbach, Leverkusen, Bochum, Gelsenkirchen, and Dortmund. However, some 20,000 small clubs with 4 million members demonstrate the strength of amateur and participatory sports, including running, hiking, mountain climbing (in unused industrial complexes), biking, sailing, handball, and tennis clubs. *Volkswanderungen,* or people's walks, are common. Efforts to foster elite athletes, especially with an eye toward Olympic competition, include a sports university at Cologne and special support programs.

CULTURAL ATTRIBUTES
AND CONTRIBUTIONS

VISUAL ARTS

Perhaps stronger in collecting than creating visual arts, unless the cathedrals in stone and steel are counted, this area's galleries house among the richest collections in the world (note specifics under **Cities** and under **Attractions**). Individuals such as the sculptor Wilhelm Lehmbruck (1881–1919) carved and crafted in Duisburg, and the painter August Macke (1887–1914) worked in Bonn while the painter/installer Josef Beuys (1921–1986) operated in Düsseldorf.

LITERATURE

A relatively new area with an industrial base often produces talented individuals who leave their homeland and contribute elsewhere. Until the 1980s, that maxim may have applied to the Rhine/Ruhr area. Since then, universities, cultural diversification, and research development have provided opportunities for a new class to stay. However, local pride had always been strong. Erik Regen wrote novels about industrial work and living spaces, including its political difficulties, in the 1930s. Others wrote works reflecting on the love-hate relationship with a homeland with which they identified but one in which a social situation and pollution undermined body and soul.

So-called workers' literature by Heinrich Hauser and Georg Schwarz tried to combine modern technology with self-conscious, even individualistic workers. These authors were forbidden under the Nazis or driven into exile. After World War II, the Group 61 founded in Dortmund sought to write about work conditions. Perhaps Max von der Grün, as a former miner, captured coal mining best in *Irrlicht und Feuer* (*Misleading Light and Fire*). Certainly Günter Wallraf, an experienced factory worker, captured attention with his methods. Hiding his identity and his intent to publish his experiences, he worked in, and exposed the dangers of, industrial work and the dubious practices of the *Bild* (news-picture) boulevard press.

Among the most famous authors from this region is Heinrich Böll, who made World War II and its aftermath, especially soldiers' experiences, known to a wide public. His *The Train was on Time, Billiards at 7:30*, and other novels that showed the difficulties of soldier homecomings, lonely women, fatherless children, and restored political hypocrisy won him the Nobel Prize in 1972. By then he had affronted the federal political authorities. He had turned to exposing the meaninglessness of military service (*Ende einer Dienstfahrt* [*End of a Service Trip*]; also a movie) and the state's involvement in the process of destroying the ideals of a naïve person (*Die verlorne Ehre der Katharina Blum* [*The Lost Honor of Katharina Blum*] also a movie). Böll lived in and identified with the increasingly cosmopolitan Cologne.

Perhaps not strictly literature, the result of the historical method of oral history has provided much insight into daily life, protests, the daily experience of Nazism, and self-awareness of the average person in this region. *Werkstattgeschichte* (workshop history), *Alltagesgeschichte* (daily life history), and feminist groups have recovered much of the Ruhr workers' culture, women's experiences, and neighborhood activities during the first half of the twentieth century.

MUSIC

The cities and districts provide most of the funds to support choirs, orchestras, and musical theaters. Miners' choirs and instrumental groups have a long tradition. Most large cities have a symphony and/or chamber orchestra; many have special ensembles. Even smaller centers such as Herford and Hagen have orchestras, due to their status as administrative centers. Music festivals may honor prominent composers associated with a city, such as Bonn, which celebrates Beethoven each year. Contemporary music is fostered at Witten, and major competitions such as the piano festival of the Ruhr are spread over 60 cities. All forms of music, from jazz to pop, from church to Latin American, have strong followings and receive wide recognition via radio.

CIVICS AND REMEMBRANCE

The task of historical studies has been very complex here, given the diversity of states and events that occurred in this region. Recently, the state has placed much emphasis upon finding a regional identity, though some of that effort goes back to the 1980s. The local office for political education fostered a constructed historical understanding of a unified region (which it was not). Since then, people in the Ruhr have made special efforts to acknowledge a polluted industrial past but also focus on the potential for a different future.

One author suggests that local memorials are especially strong in this region. He points to the many local monuments, for example the statue of Hattingia in Hattingen. She represents the fallen of the 1870–1871 war with France. Of course, many statues of the 1890s honored Bismarck and the Kaisers in this Prussian area. Some industrialists, whose firms had dominated Ruhr cities such as Krupp or Thyssen, also had busts and statues honoring their entrepreneurial talents, though sometimes it simply demonstrated their ability to influence local councils. After World War I, as in France, nearly every town and city square needed an acknowledgement of the war dead in stone.

As a region that once had a very large labor movement, only limited acknowledgement of the efforts to emancipate workers and women has attained notice in public spaces. The Ruhr, along with Saxony and Berlin, was a major part of a million-member, then-still-radical, Social Democratic movement before 1914. Part of that movement fought the employers and the state. But only a few monuments reflect their challenge to 70-hour work weeks, rooming houses with 10 persons to a room, and subsistence wages. Those who demanded suffrage and opposed state repression were honored with monuments in Essen, Duisburg, and Hagen during the 1920s, but the Nazis destroyed these efforts to highlight social justice. In the late 1950s, the work of miners, steelworkers, and metal makers found recognition in many cities, including a bronze work in Essen showing the steep mine shaft being worked. That has a place of honor in front of the train station, but its emphasis is on work, not on the ideological struggles to improve it. Since the economic decline of industry, some of the idle and outdated machinery placed on display has been termed "monuments to unemployment."

Among the largest attempts to make a positive image out of all the plant closings has been the 10-year project to create an industrial park out of the Ems, the International *Bauausstellung Emser Park* (international construction park, meaning buildings). A green industrial area is to combine living, working, and leisure. Some of the old industrial edifices are to remain and the traditional workers' colonies to be renovated. The project has generally succeeded.

Some monuments are reminders not of wars and destruction but simply of earlier local situations. At Bochum, a cow herder and his dog received a place of honor. At Münster, the *Kiekemann*, or man with a basket on his back bringing rabbits and produce to market, has been memorialized in front of a pub.

Among the interesting sculptures in the landscape of NRW are two dedicated to the division of the country. At Münster, since 1960, and at Recklinghausen, since 1959, split wall-like angular columns tied by chains or wires represented the division but continuing ties of the country. In Bonn, the House of the History of the Federal Republic shows post-1945 objects and events that frequently touched people's lives, including fashions, toys, gardens, and automobiles.

Since the 1980s, much focus has been on the sites of Nazi repression and resistance. The era is acknowledged with plaques identifying places of repression, including those from which Jews were shipped to their death and synagogues burned. At Bonn, Essen, Issum, Wuppertal, among other centers, destroyed Jewish houses of prayer have been identified. The villa of the *Gau* (district) Nazi leader Josef Terboven has become an educational and memorial site at Münster. A series of documentation centers, many of which have educational programs attached to them, have been created. Some of these expose conditions in Soviet prisoner of war camps (Senne, Stukenbrock, Hermer, Soest). Cologne has a research center that displays documentation about all aspects of the Nazi regime. An early acknowledgement of this troubled past is the Oberhausen remembrance hall, established in 1962.

CUISINE

The region is home to many classic beers, such as Bitburg, Warstein, and Dortmund (DAB), but also of specialty ones such as *Kölsch*, brewed and served in thin glasses in Cologne, and *Alt* (special dark) at Düsseldorf. Beer, as the working man's drink, accompanied the second breakfast, the sandwich break in the morning, also lunch, and then at supper. The southwest, especially below Bonn and in the Ahr valley, has been more wine oriented. With the middle class and state bureaucrats coming to dominate among the populace, wine consumption has increased, especially on festive occasions.

This large region is home to diverse breads such as pumpernickel and ryes. Westphalian ham and diverse Mett-sausages (with and without onions, fine, coarse, spiced . . .) go well with such strong breads. The usual variety of sausages, especially salamis, can be found in every butcher shop.

No one can go to Bonn or Cologne and not have *Reibekuchen* (potato pancakes with hardly any onions or egg). Nearly deep-fried in fat, they tend to be eaten hot out of the pan in the marketplace in batches of three. One other food item has to be made according to the taste and ability of the consumer. These are *Brötchen* (little buns, crusty on the outside and soft inside), cut in half, covered in quark (type of soft fresh cheese), and then ladled with sugar beet syrup. The latter is sticky, very runny, and much more delectable than molasses. The syrup tends to run over the edge of the quark.

Though the ritual of having afternoon coffee and cake is not restricted to this region, it is very widespread, especially at restaurants overlooking the Rhine and along paths or premonitory. In fancy places the ritual can cost as much as a meal.

By contrast to that leisurely ritual, *frites* (french fries) and *currywurst* (curry sausage) are the preferred daily fare and fast food of the region. Sports events and street snacks usually involve *frites* and sauce on cut-up soft sausage, both served on paper plates.

Turning to the more filling but still economical: Sauerbraten was a traditional Sunday dish of the poorer people. It involves marinating a less choice cut of meat. Presently, it is served in more refined ways with noodles as opposed to potatoes.

RHINELAND SAUERBRATEN

3 pounds beef round or blade steak	1/4 cup butter
1/4 cup whole peppercorns	5 or 6 strips of bacon
1 tablespoon mustard seeds	2 cans or packets of beef broth
1 tablespoon whole cloves	2 tablespoons flour
2 bay leaves	1/4 cup water
3 onions, diced	2 tablespoons whipping cream
2 cups white vinegar	

Cut meat into 8 or 9 thin slices and place in large glass pan. Mix peppercorns, mustard seeds, cloves, bay leaves, onion, and vinegar and pour over meat. Refrigerate for 2 to 3 days.

Drain and save marinade. Add butter and 1/2 of marinade to meat and bake at 350°F for 1 hour. Turn over meat and place bacon over it and cook another hour.

Strain off the marinade, leaving meat warming in oven. Put sauce in large pot, add beef broth and heat. Mix flour and water in a jar and add to broth at low heat, then bring to a boil and reduce heat. Just before serving stir in cream and pour over meat. Serve with noodles. Meat can also be rolled and held together with toothpicks to make a nicer presentation.

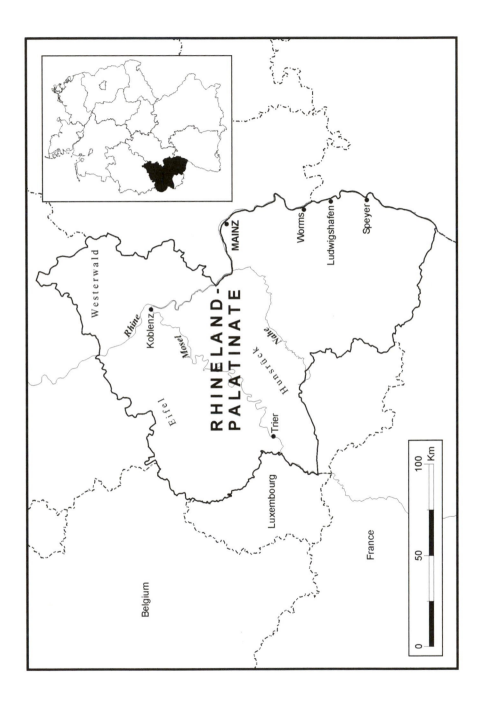

Chapter 11

Rhineland-Palatinate

SPECIAL ASPECTS

Identified with the wine and song of traditionally agricultural and tourist areas along the Rhine and Mosel rivers, the Rhineland-Palatinate is the German region visitors want to package and take home. The whole area is an attraction, with every layer of civilization—Roman ruins, medieval castles, Romanesque and Gothic cathedrals, baroque palaces—present in profusion. The so-called German Wine Road runs from the French border at Schweigen-Rechtenbach, north past Neustadt, to Grünstadt west of the Rhine. Old fortifications as well as half-timbered houses are all well preserved, painted, and perhaps much more refined than when they were built.

REGIONAL TRAITS

Geographically, this is a small and new state of 20,000 square kilometers with 4 million people. In 1946 the French occupiers combined Bavarian Palatinate, parts of Hesse-Darmstadt, as well as parts of the former Prussian Rhine provinces to make the new state. Those main political entities have some similarities on the surface. For instance, many of the historical events, such as Roman occupation and medieval migrations, affected all the area. Yet subregions remain significant for local identity, often reinforced by competition between the neighboring towns and cities. Eifel, Hunsrück, Rheinhessen-Palatinate, and Westerwald have geographic and historical connotations with which locals associate. Local dialects remain much in evidence in the rural areas. The people have been stereotyped as charming and known for carnival fun.

The coat of arms has a griffin below a cross on a white background with a wheel on the right.

GEOGRAPHIC FEATURES

River erosion of shale deposits formed much of the land. The hilly, rocky terrain is fairly similar throughout the state. The Rhine River runs north-northeast through the north and serves as boundary to the east with Hesse and Baden-Württemberg. France and Saarland are to the south, Luxembourg to the southwest, Belgium to the west, and North Rhine-Westphalia to the north. The Mosel River winds through steep shale cliffs in the northwest toward the Rhine in a northeasterly direction. The Nahe River more directly traverses the central area toward the Rhine at Bingen. The small Ahr River is mostly within Rhineland-Palatinate but sometimes serves as border with North Rhine-Westphalia. All the large cities and much of the population are located on the major rivers.

HISTORY

Aside from the Celtic tribes, much of the prehistorical record relates to the Neanderthal skeletons found near Ochtendung. In 1997, a skull and bones were unearthed in the volcanic rock of the region. These confirmed the famed Neanderthal finds of the nineteenth century. Other excavations near Andernach confirm habitation going back 13,000 years. Depictions of women, scratched in shale and carved from bones, have been found in the cult site at Gönnersdorf. However, the main finds relate to the Roman era, and these are well displayed in the Roman museum at Trier. Mosaics, statuary, jewelry, and glass illustrate the life of the military and administrative caste.

During the medieval era, much of the region was dominated by small feudal holdings with the Catholic Church providing the main civilizing and administrative unity. Out of this era emerged the large number of Romanesque cathedrals and churches that now dot the land. Some had been rebuilt in Gothic style by the time the Reformation challenged Catholic preeminence. During the late medieval and early Renaissance, this region's prosperity culminated in the founding of universities (1473 in Trier, 1477 in Mainz). The urban patricians prospered from handicrafts and trade.

The Reformation caused religious and social turmoil. At the decisive Imperial meeting at Worms in 1521, Martin Luther refused to recant his protests against Catholic Church abuses. His religious beliefs found quick acceptance. Protestants established themselves in many cities such as Worms and Mainz, though eventually the Catholics regained most of the area during the religious wars. By the end of the destruction of the Thirty Years' War (1618–1648), Catholicism had been reestablished in most of the region. Henceforth, this remained the core region of the Holy Roman Empire.

In 1793 at Mainz, a number of liberals, influenced by the ideals of the French Revolution, founded a republic. The monarchs and aristocrats who had generally supported the reactionary émigrés from France immediately sought to repress it and succeeded. Napoleon soon ended the petty principalities by incorporating much of the territory into France in 1802 and secularizing many properties in 1803. Later he introduced the French version of indirect Imperial control by setting up a Rhineland Confederation. After Napoleon's ultimate defeat, in 1815, some of the small states were restored. However, Mainz fell to Hessen and most became Prussian provinces, while the Palatinate fell under the control of Bavaria. In 1832 the latter state had no qualms about repressing the next attempt by the liberals to demand a more free and unified country. At Hambach, some 30,000 students celebrated liberty and advocated national unity. Similarly, in 1848, revolts over food shortages and lack of suffrage overthrew some monarchs, or at least displaced them for a short time. By 1849, these attempts at reform had been repressed by Austria, Prussia, and Russia, though legal norms relating to individual rights had been improved.

During the late-nineteenth century industrialization began to affect the region's cities. Simultaneously, living conditions deteriorated for peasants and laborers, some of whom emigrated. Three ideologies were available as means of redress. Karl Marx's socialism sought to convince the workers that only through organization and revolution could the capitalists be forced to share wealth. The Catholic bishop Wilhelm von Ketteler, by contrast, offered a social Catholicism, which advocated Christian philanthropy in conjunction with lay organizations. Simultaneously, Friedrich Reiffeisen began a cooperative movement through which workers and peasants invested savings and, as consumers, bought in their own stores. None of these ideologies won a decisive battle by the mid-twentieth century, though the Catholics and cooperatives had the most influence outside the larger cities.

During World War I and World War II, the region suffered heavily. Troop movements and bombing physically destroyed the land and cities. Loss of life among the peasants, recruited as soldiers, was especially high. In between, during the Weimar era, the Prussian provinces and Bavarian Palatinate tended to be conservative. The economic depression of 1929 undercut many livelihoods and radicalized the population, mostly toward the racist right but also to the far left. Once in power the National Socialists reorganized the region by party districts. In addition to jailing leftists, the Nazi regime eradicated the large and prosperous Jewish communities, especially at Mainz and Speyer. When American troops occupied the region in 1945, war weariness prevailed.

The French replaced the Americans in July 1945. By August 1946 they decided on a territorial configuration that became the present state. To establish parliamentary democracy, local elections preceded regional ones. Within a year in Koblenz an advisory council agreed to a temporary coalition government that prepared a constitution. In a plebiscite only 53 percent agreed to the new constitution. The state government had to work from this low base of confidence. In 1950, Mainz became the capital, also without overwhelming enthusiasm. Yet, during 1975, in a plebiscite regarding reattachment of areas around Koblenz, Trier, and Montabaur to neighboring states, the populace supported the existing political unity. Some see the results as proof that the postwar creation had finally become a solid entity.

The region's main political parties have traditionally been the Christian Democratic Union (CDU) and Social Democracy (SPD). Smaller parties, especially the Free Democrats (FDP; liberal), and after 1987 the Greens, have had influential roles. After a short period of all-party rule (including nationalists and Communists), Peter Altmeier created a coalition of CDU and SPD in 1951, then of CDU and FDP in 1955. That coalition remained under his leadership until 1969, when Helmut Kohl took over. After 1971, Kohl led a majority CDU government and made the state his longtime fief. When he moved to federal politics in 1976, Kohl bequeathed the realm to Bernard Vogel, who remained in office until 1988. In 1991, for the first time, the SPD won more votes than the CDU. In coalition with the FDP, Rudolf Sharping led the SPD government until 1994. Kurt Beck, who continued the SPD coalition with the FDP, replaced him. Elections in 1996 confirmed that coalition. An SPD-liberal coalition remained in office in 2000.

ECONOMY

During the 1950s the state ministries included justice, culture, health and welfare, agriculture, foodstuffs and forests, internal, finances, work, economics and transport, and reconstruction. By the 1980s the list was comprised of internal affairs and sport, justice, finance, culture, agriculture, vine-culture and forests, economics and transport, social-health, and environment. State planning played an important role in the revival of the postwar economy around the agriculture base, and the ministries of vine-culture, forestry, and agriculture remain important.

Only chemicals, with the huge BASF firm at Ludwigshafen, and petrochemicals, at Wörth on the Rhine, hint at the state's modest industrial strength. Chemicals and related industries account for one-fifth of employment. Just over 100 firms have over 500 employees each, with many related to auto parts. Most are small companies that build machinery, reprocess foods, and rework stone or earth (concrete, ceramics, and gravel). Electronics is a latecomer.

In the mid-1970s as many people worked in administration as in industrial production and commercial enterprises. Over 100,000 people worked in forestry and agriculture (vineyards), with only twice as many in trade. By the late 1990s the pattern had not changed very much, except for the increasing dominance of service industries and increasing unemployment, which remains at 10 percent. Rhineland-Palatinate has continuously been among the receiving states in the federal system of equalization payments.

At present, chemicals, forest products, wines, and auto parts continue to provide employment. Tourism is strong because of the pleasing vineyards, the castles, and palaces of the region. The major firms are BASF (chemicals) tapes and cassettes at Ludwigshafen, Boehringer machinery in Ingelheim, Schott glass and IBM computers at Mainz, Pfaff clothing and Opel cars in Kaiserslautern, and Mercedes-Benz vehicles at Wörth. About 40 percent of production is exported, though the region's white wines have had difficulties because of the increasing world preference for red wines.

Some 16 universities (Mainz, Kaiserslautern, Trier, and Koblenz) and colleges are seeking to maintain international academic standards. Some, such as Speyer's public administration or Trier's theological college, serve special interests. Koblenz has a private business college. The main research centers focus on artificial intelligence, chemicals and polymers, and literature. Mainz is a media center with the ZDF (Central German Television), Europe's largest. Many small private broadcasters operate here or in other parts of the state.

The Rhine and Mosel rivers remain important transport routes, and the region is well served by major *autobahns*.

MAIN CITIES

CAPITAL (SINCE 1950)

Mainz (population 202,000). Celts and Romans left evidence that they liked it on the Rhine, and both had capitals here. The administrative tradition dates from that time as well as from the Christian era. By 1100 the Mainz archbishops became among the most important in central Europe. The large cathedral *(Dom)* is testimony to the city's and the church's wealth. In the 1440s Gutenberg created the printing press, which would spread the ideas of the Reformation that challenged the Mainz archbishops. Gutenberg's invention, combining elements from the local wine-press, tough paper, and moveable type, is among the attractions of a city that has developed a world-class museum related to printing. Visitors can try their hand at using the high tech of the sixteenth century.

After the devastations of the Thirty Years War, with French and Swedish occupation, the city culturally blossomed again during the Enlightenment era, especially in painting and architecture. During the French and Napoleonic era, after an experiment with republicanism, the city became part of France; in the nineteenth century it came under Prussian, Hessen, and Austrian control.

World War II bombing destroyed much of the old city. The old center and the university have been rebuilt, and parks along the Rhine provide green space.

Known for its well-prepared and elaborate annual carnival festivities, the city also has fine theaters, museums, and restaurants. Especially noteworthy is the Roman-German Central Museum, with one of the best collections of Roman objects.

Ludwigshafen (population 190,000). Dominated by the chemical giant BASF, this industrial city has many administrative as well as industrial towers. The palace and gardens are a reminder of the city's origins as a princely residence.

Koblenz (population 130,000). As a former residence, then a military city, Koblenz still has many army barracks. For a long time it represented Prussia's influence in the southwest, having been obtained as an anti-French buffer on the Rhine after 1815. However, the huge fortress of *Ehrenbreitscheid* above the city has had little military significance since the seventeenth century and now serves as a large film archive for the country. A railway crossroads, transportation has always been important since the Mosel flows into the Rhine here. The point at the confluence of the two rivers has a demonstrative name, *Deutsche Eck* (German corner), to underscore that the Rhine is German (not French). Presently an administrative and tourist city, it offers nearby castles such as *Stolzenfels* (rebuilt by the crown prince in the nineteenth century).

Trier (population 110,000). Once one of the four capitals of the Roman empire, it had extensive baths, a large amphitheater, and a walled town with gates. Remains of the Porta Nigra, the three-story, black stone gate, the nearly complete amphitheater and baths can be explored. The ruins at the baths include the remains of an intricate water system to heat floors as well as to provide hygiene. The baths, made of long bricks, allow insight into the level of comfort at Roman military and trading complexes. Grave statuary at Trier goes back to the Celts, while the medieval era left a Romanesque cathedral as well as cloister churches with symbolic carvings. Pilgrimages to see the Catholic relics continue though the height of that mass movement was reached in the nineteenth century. The baroque era in turn left a highly decorated church and palace. The large market square has a mix of half-timbered and more recent buildings. Museums have displays illustrating each of the historical phases. The state regional archaeological museum includes Roman floor mosaics, the church diocese museum contains many relics, and the *Karl-Marx-Haus* offers documents for secular pilgrims.

ATTRACTIONS

One could go from Adenau, with its half-timbered houses accompanied by fairy-tale sculptures near the large castle ruins of Nürburg, to Zweibrücken, with its baroque palace and rose gardens. Alsenz, with only 1,500 people, has a half-timbered *Rathaus* on arched supports, while Alzey has 16,000 half-timbered treasures. The latter buildings go out from a marketplace with fountains, sculptures, and iron lacework, plus a castle. At the other end of the alphabet of places, Zell on the Mosel reveals another large palace and Romanesque church with carved altar. There the castle, similar to the ones at Nürburg and Alzey, had its walls breached by the French under Louis XIV.

Even the history of little places reveals the region's rich heritage of buildings, the intermingling with neighbors (mostly through war and dynastic linkages), and the common European styles employed with local distinctions. Here only major places will be presented with a few smaller ones included to show the regional identification with the land, its creative history, and the care given to maintain it.

The major remains of Roman civilization can be encountered at Trier. However, throughout the Eifel remains of wells, manor houses, and aqueducts provide evidence of the control the Romans exercised from their military encampments. Only Trier, though, has achieved UNESCO world heritage designation because it has a complex of city gate, Roman palace, two sets of baths, Roman bridge, as well as extensive complementary medieval edifices. The *Rheinische Landesmuseum* at Trier displays mosaics and many artistic as well as practical objects.

The medieval era left numerous fortifications and religious edifices. The Eifel and the Rhine valley especially show the medieval castles, though they were mostly rebuilt during the nineteenth century. The cloisters, such as *Maria Laach,* are accompanied by superb examples of Romanesque churches. Worms (known as *Nibelungenstadt*) and Speyer cathedrals are among the height of achievements in that style. Speyer's Imperial *Dom* has been included on the UNESCO world heritage list. Its symmetrical four towers, its huge apse, and straight lines, accompanied by the Roman arch, exemplify the best of the Romanesque style.

The many restored and renovated varieties of castles and palaces make this a tourist destination. In the 1970s, sheep were still run across major roadways in the Westerwald. The Eifel remained a quiet backwater, though people increasingly commuted to work in the cities. The forests and lakes of the high Eifel still provide a tranquility no longer found along the Rhine. Regardless of whether the wind still blows cold in the Westerwald—according to the local folk song—the area contains castle ruins and historic monuments at Neuwied and Alternkirchen. Its nature park, Rhine/Westerwald, and the nature park Nassau, to the south leading into the Taunus uplands, provide ideal forested hiking areas. By contrast, the nature park of Palatinate forest contains many castles *(Landau, Neustadt)* and spas *(Bad Bergzabern, Bad Dürkheim)* on its edge.

The locals take pride in the many castles and palaces of their homeland *(Heimat).* At Montabaur, a fine illustration of rebuilt baroque exists, while at Pirmasens and Zweibrücken quite different styles are in evidence. At Nassau, the castle has five corners of a fortress hung out over high walls. At Wessel, the fortified church tower is known as the *Ochsenturm* (ox tower). Even Ludwigshafen has half-timbered hatch work on top of a Roman fortress base. Burresheim in the Eifel is perhaps the castle that feels the most medieval; one has to enter a gate almost sideways.

The Eifel and Palatinate are castle country, though nearly all the castles were breached by the French during Louis XIV's attempt to control and to gain the Rhine. Many restored examples hint at the territorially cut-up world of the medieval era. Burg Eltz escaped French destruction, and its charming, isolated setting makes it attractive to tourists. The combination of castle and chateau sits on a craggy rise. The same family has owned the partly stone, partly half-timbered and multitowered work for centuries. In the Palatinate Landau, by contrast, is made from stones symmetrically set up the side of a hill. The castle at Ida-Oberstein, once a ruins, has been rebuilt.

The Eifel and Palatinate area are also rich in medieval remains, such as the monastery of *Marie Laach.* Next to a circular volcanic lake, the monastery contains a courtyard with a Spanish-inspired set of lions supporting a fountain. The church is superb in its simplicity and is considered one of the best examples of Romanesque architecture in the entire Rhineland area. Onslaughts of tourist buses have ruined its tranquility, however.

Along the Mosel River some castles stand out from the shale heights with the castle/palace at Cochem among the most prominent. It has, like Bernkastel-Kues, been much rebuilt, but both offer tremendous views over the meandering river with its steep banks. Many of the rustic towns have been so covered with paint and the roads so filled with tourists that the charm is left only in the fine Riesling wines. But many fine hiking trails lie beyond the river heights between Mosel and Ahr, where one can see the twisted church at Mayen, the baths at Daun, and many smaller castle ruins. Nature reserves have been established on the borders with Belgium and Luxembourg.

The stretch of Rhine River, known as the Rhine Gorge *(Mittelrhein)*, south of Koblenz to Mainz, is best seen from a boat cruise. This was the world's second river valley to be placed under the protection of UNESCO as a declared world heritage. The castles—*Stolzenfels, Rheinfels, Mäuseturm*—and the vineyards with fine cities such as Boppard, St. Goar, Bacharach, and Bingen can be viewed glass in hand. This is the region of knights and maidens that has inspired poets and painters.

To see how the peasants lived, the *Rheinisches Freilichtmuseum* (open-air) at Kommern near Mechernich has brought together houses, barns, and sheds from the whole northern section of the region. All date from the fifteenth to the nineteenth centuries and some contain period furnishings. Peasants slept in five-foot beds and the children in pullout drawers beside them. Half-timbered houses from the sub-regions of Westerwald and Eifel are well represented. Ironically, the museum is just over the unmarked border in North Rhine-Westphalia.

A very different attraction is from the twentieth century. The Nürburg Ring is a car racetrack in the Eifel, which for many years, but especially since the 1950s, has been used to test vehicles. Private vehicles can access the track on some days.

CUSTOMS

Which does more to maintain tradition and develop regional identity: Carnival at Mainz, Rhine Palatinate Days, or *Kaiserslautern* soccer club? The Mainz carnival is a week of fun-filled activities. These are well-prepared and well-orchestrated events, though the joking is always at the expense of authorities whether in politics, entertainment, or business. The Rhine Palatinate Days, initiated in the 1980s as a way to foster regional identity, rotate among cities and towns. They seek to present local heritage, including dancing, singing, and dress *(Trachten)*.

Sports are strong with many amateur gymnastic and sport organizations. Nearly a million people are members of some association, encouraged by the state as a way to improve health. Among professional teams, *Kaiserslautern* soccer has become the main team for the region with thousands of fans, identifying colors, and much common experience (including wins, losses, and drinking in honor of both).

Shooting competitions and celebrations are as common as carnival clubs. Some places continue older local festivals. For instance, "fish spearing" means eating baked fish combined with jousting at Worms in early September. As expected in a strongly

Catholic area, the Christian traditions of Easter and Christmas, church processions, and pilgrimages remain strong, as does church membership, which is well above the national average.

CULTURAL ATTRIBUTES
AND CONTRIBUTIONS

VISUAL ARTS

The Heylshof gallery at Worms contains medieval and Renaissance masters (Rubens), while the Hans-Arp foundation at Rolandseck (in a converted train station) offers changing exhibits that mostly present recent works. Koblenz also has a modern art gallery, the Ludwig museum, which features French works. Its regional museum *(Landesmuseum)* contains many objects including art of the region from Roman times to the twentieth century.

LITERATURE

Perhaps Carl Zuckmayer's *Der fröhliche Weinberg (The Happy Vineyard)* embodies the region, especially the Romantic fashion in which the 1952 movie presented the visual images. The strength of women, as presented in the original play staged in 1925 in Berlin, is lost in the popularized version. That a fistfight occurs at a wine festival probably reflects an earlier era. Today's youth tend to express themselves in graffiti. The more urban and radical perspective of Anna Seghers (1900–1983) appeared in her *The Seventh Cross*. Popular in the 1920s, she lived in east Germany after Mexican exile during the Nazi era. Later, the critical outlook of Alfred Andersch (1914–1980) appeared in his prize-winning stories, such as *Winterspelt*. Very popular are the crime and detective novels, many set in the Eifel hills, by Jacques Berdorff.

MUSIC

Village festivals, especially wine festivals, are accompanied by much singing of folk songs, and church choirs are a strong tradition. The larger cities such as Mainz and Worms have symphony orchestras, with the major opera company at Mainz. Music and theater festivals are held all over the state, especially during the summer at castles and palaces. Specialties include international organ music and choir festivals, mostly held in the early fall in former cloisters. Italian and church operas are being highlighted at present.

CIVICS AND REMEMBRANCE

Dealing with the Nazi past came late to the region. Helmut Kohl, as previous head of the region and as chancellor, tended to avoid responsibility for the Nazi past. Sometimes unfortunate phrases emerged from his impatience with other countries and their focus on the Nazi era. Instead, he wanted to illustrate postwar German achievements and contributions, including that his favorite region had achieved good relations with France. The state of Rhineland-Palatinate organized a partnership with the nearby French Bourgogne region before the federal state acted to cement friendship. Did Kohl represent those whose perception was that other countries were holding Germany to higher standards than they themselves practiced? Certainly, one of Kohl's attempts to deal with the past proved particularly unsuccessful. In 1986 he helped organize the visit of U.S. President Ronald Reagan to a war cemetery at Bitburg. Members of the Waffen SS, the military arm of the worst Nazi organization, were buried there; what was to have been reconciliation turned into scandal. Yet, it raised awareness of the Nazi past.

What does the office for political education in Kohl's region promote? Older publications on the homeland *(Heimatkunde)* offered information on parliamentary democracy mixed with strong boosterism. More recently the claim is of an identity brought about through sports, festivals, and having remained together for over a half century. The perspective offered is that diverse parts have grown together and "found their unmistakable uniqueness" *(unverwechselbare Eigenstandigkeit)*. But the latter remains vague. Certainly, support for heritage in terms of churches and castles is strong, but coming to terms with the Nazi past seems to have been slower and less thorough than in other regions. But by 1987, the state office also published works pointing out the memorial sites for victims of Nazism, and the former large, special concentration camp at Hinzert had become an educational and memorial site.

CUISINE

The wines from the Mosel and Rhein-Hessen areas have been the major white wines of Germany. Indeed, the region is Germany's most important producer, with about 60 percent of the country's output. The Riesling varieties are known in the wine world as among the best whites. The Ahr Valley offers subtle reds. Bitburg is known for its beer, though the brewery operates in many other places as well as its hometown.

Though Chancellor Kohl loved to show his home region to guests from abroad, not many were enthralled by his favorite tripe dish and would rather have eaten better parts of the pig. Pork is a common ingredient of local specialties, but *döner kebab*, pizza, and pasta have taken over city fast foods. Potato soup remains a local favorite nearly everywhere. Recently, gourmet fare has turned to local products in dishes such as *Eifeler Wildragout*. It is a combination of wild boar and deer with wild mushrooms served with dumplings.

POTATO SOUP

2 pounds potatoes	pinch of salt
2 medium onions, diced	pinch of marjoram
1/3 pound of smoked Speck	1/4 cup cream
1 tablespoon butter	2 egg yolks
2 cups meat stock	2 pinches of black pepper

Cut raw potatoes, onions and Speck into small cubes. Sauté onions and Speck in butter until golden. Add to potatoes and meat stock and bring to boil. Reduce to simmer for 20 minutes. Add salt and marjoram.

Separately mix cream and egg yolks and slowly add to hot soup without bringing to a boil. Add pepper to taste.

Poorer people added Bockwurst (cheaper type of sausage); the richer version is served with little bits of smoked trout scattered on top.

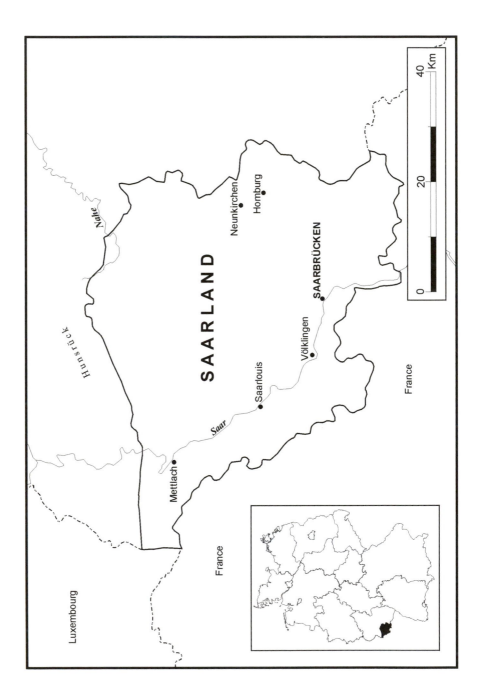

Chapter 12

Saarland

SPECIAL ASPECTS

Being tiny (the smallest state aside from the three city-states) and having survived, Saarland has shifted back and forth between French and German control, mostly because of its coal resources and steel industries in the nineteenth and twentieth centuries. Heavily wooded and cut by its meandering major river, the Saar, the small region now seeks to be the bridge for German-French cultural encounters, including their cuisines. It also offers visitors bridges to the past at one of Europe's geographic and conflict crossroads. Roman villas, medieval churches, coal and steel museums, and contemporary sculptures. Surviving against greedy outsiders has been replaced by welcoming visitors, who can view, eat, and travel well but are asked to leave the rolling countryside undisturbed.

REGIONAL TRAITS

Saarland contains just over a million people in its 992 square miles. Economically depressed since the 1960s due to reliance on the coal and steel industries, which lost out to oil and other energy sources as well as to Asian producers in the 1960s and 1970s, Saarland is slowly recovering. It is shifting to information technology and tourism. Its coat of arms has four fields referring to the multitude of historical rulers of the region: two of lions, one of a red cross on white background, and one of three eagles. The flag bears the coat of arms superimposed on the federal flag. Rhineland-Palatinate surrounds the state to the north and east, with France to the south and west, while Luxembourg just touches on the northwest.

Figure 12.1
City Hall, Saarbrücken, Saarland.

Source © Press and Information Office, Germany.

GEOGRAPHIC FEATURES

Three rivers cut through the hilly uplands that dominate the landscape: the Nahe in the northeast, the Prims running southwest toward the largest, the Saar. The latter traverses the western part of the region from south to north and mouths in the Mosel in next-door Rhineland-Palatinate. Where the Saar River cuts through the Hunsrück massif (or rock cliffs), it winds back and forth between steep cliffs. The Hunsrück runs along the northern edge, but nearly all Saarland terrain is rugged and hilly with peaks between 500 and 600 meters (1,500 to 2,000 feet).

HISTORY

The ups and downs of the landscape are mirrored in Saarland's turbulent history. The Celts tried to defend their bronze and gold ornamented civilization against the Romans before the time of Christ. Remains of a huge ring wall (misnamed *Hunnenring*) two miles long surround one of the heights of land at Nonnweiler-Otzenhausen. Thirty feet high and 100 feet wide at places, it is mostly made of quartz stone. By 100 A.D., the Roman legions imposed stability and left some fancy villas with mosaic floors, for example, at Perl-Nennig. But, as in the future, the area was ruled from outside: the Roman administrative and military centers at Trier and Metz.

The Franks next conquered the area by the eighth century, though the accompanying Christian missionary activities continued the administrative domination from distant cities. In the late medieval era the influence of the outside continued as Trier, Metz, Lorraine, and Palatinate rulers fought over and fractured the region politically. The Reformation added a layer of religious division, though the majority remained Catholic. The multitude of earldoms, princedoms, and duchies, which fought over or inherited parts of the area, left many fine palaces and developed some court culture. It provided little prosperity for the populace, and the Thirty Years' War (1618–1648) destroyed the cultural blossoming. The wars of Louis XIV of France, lasting into the early eighteenth century, decreased the population and destroyed most military strong-holds but left a huge French earthwork fortification at Saarlouis. The era of the Enlightenment, especially under the dukes of Nassau-Saarbrücken, improved the legal codes, administrative structures, and educational level of the elite. But the petty princely divisions continued and the population remained rural, uneducated, and poor.

The attempt to attach the region to some religious or political outside interest continued during the French Revolution and Napoleonic era. In 1793, some of the Saarbrückner declared themselves part of republican France, and many of the aris-tocracy fled east. French administrative rule under the military occupation of Napoleon modernized the government but also integrated it with France's depart-ments, run from Metz and Mainz. In 1814, some cantons remained part of France, but the peace of 1815 gave most of the territory to Prussia as a province and a small area to Bavaria. The region became, according to some, an industrial colony of Prussia run from Berlin and Koblenz. During the nineteenth century, France repeatedly demanded the restoration of the earlier, more eastern, boundary, especially once the extent of coal resources became known.

In the mid- to late-nineteenth century, both Germany and France wanted con-trol over the Saarland and its coal and the Lorraine iron ores. Germany gained the latter in 1871 after winning the Franco-Prussian War. Huge steelworks, such as those of Baron von Stumm and the Völklingen works, dominated the booming economy due to cheap rural labor. Workers trekked to the mines and mills, living in barracks or brick row houses, but went home to work their small farms on the weekend. The Catholic Church and the Prussian state fought for the loyalty of the population as evidenced in the conflicts over who could authorize and control the visions of the Virgin Mary at Marpingen, a rural backwater of shepherds and day laborers, in 1876. The late Imperial era proved to be the most prosperous for the mining and smelting industries, and organized labor struck, mostly unsuccessfully, for higher wages and improved working conditions.

As a result of Germany's defeat in World War I, the Saarland ended under French economic control while under the political jurisdiction of the League of Nations. The attempt to integrate the area culturally and economically with France failed. Both the French administrators and the steel bosses were seen as foreigners. In 1935 a very large majority voted to be reunited with Germany. Whether leftist (Communist or Social Democratic) or Catholic, a majority voted for reunification, despite or because of the Nazi regime. The Hitler regime played up the idea of the Saarland as a German defense bulwark against France, with its supposed Bolshevism and Jewishness, and all political parties except the Nazis were dissolved. Some 6,000 people went into exile, mostly to

France. Concentration camps, for example *Neue Bremm*, and the other centralized repressive measures of the Third Reich destroyed Saarland's political independence though not its identity. Resistance to Nazi rule reemerged during the war. In 1944 the U.S. military conquered, but in 1945 France occupied and again dominated the region. A French high commissioner had decree rights, and in 1948 Saarland became part of a customs union with France. A socially concerned and clerically run state under Johannes Hoffmann tried to maintain some degree of Saar independence.

In 1955, some 90 percent of the population voted to end its semi-independent status and to rejoin Germany, which occurred in stages between 1957 and 1959. With all the shifts in sovereignty, a person living in the Saarland during the twentieth century could experience seven different currencies in one lifetime. The oddities of the region's history include that in the World Cup soccer matches of 1954, which the German national team would win, the German team first played against the Saar "national" team.

From the late 1950s through the 1970s, with only tiny breaks, the conservative Christian Democratic Union (CDU) under Franz Röder led the Saarland. The liberals declined from 25 percent to 5 percent of the vote, while the Social Democrats slowly gained from15 percent to 40 percent between 1955 and 1980. As the economic crisis of an undiversified economy based in mining and steel drastically increased unemployment, from 6 percent in 1980 to 13 percent by 1984, voters lost confidence in the CDU. In 1985 the Social Democrats, with strong support from organized labor, won a majority under Oskar Lafontaine. He successfully reorganized the steel industry and bargained for federal financial support. Later he would use his widespread popularity and Saarland organizational base to enter national politics. During the 1990s the CDU and SPD split the vote, though the CDU held a one-seat majority in 1999 and thus formed the government. Regardless of political party, all emphasize Saarland as a European bridge as opposed to a borderland or bulwark. A recent survey found that some 32 percent of Saarlanders considered Europe their *Heimat*, or homeland, compared to 6 percent in Germany as a whole.

Local history and identity began to be emphasized during the 1950s by homeland celebrations *(Heimatfeste)* that underscored medieval costumes and closeness to nature. By the 1970s, it included a revival of dialects and claims about special joy in life and local savoir faire. Though few knew how to make the local delicacy (pancakes), traditional food, drink, and folk music received public and state support.

MAIN CITIES

CAPITAL

Saarbrücken (population 190,000), as capital, is the only city with over 50,000 inhabitants. Most working people have middle-class service-sector and educational posts. The residential palace of the Graf of Nassau-Saarbrücken and parks honoring

French-German reconciliation complement the theater, gallery, and museums of an administrative city. The ducal palace, originally built to emulate Versailles, has been restored and houses the large Saarland History Museum. The state theater is powered by wind and seeks to present innovative works. Music and film festivals occur each year. The state orchestra, like the theater, moves around the region giving performances. The university, founded by France in 1948, has an international orientation with special ties to France. Computer scientists and economists have tried to develop practical research applications for regional industry and to foster economic growth.

ECONOMY

What was once almost a mono-industry based on mining and smelting has become somewhat diversified since the 1970s. At Mettlach, the ceramics company, Villeroy & Boch, operates a highly productive and innovative enterprise that exports a large part of its stone- and glassware. Despite their slow decline since the 1960s, the coal and steel industries continue to provide employment due to state subsidies. Automobile and steel production, as at Dillinger and Saarlouis, rely on the older resources. Many small research centers related to computers and electrical information technology also benefit from state support. The Saarland, Lorraine, and Luxembourg, or Saar-Lor-Lux, have developed an integrated transportation and economic system. State-sponsored and university-related centers for computers, for nondestructive testing, for medical technology, and for development of new materials hint at a different future.

Though much of the population lives in small towns or rural areas, aside from garden farming and small orchards, agriculture is limited. Vineyards in the Nahe and lower Saar valleys provide fine white wines.

ATTRACTIONS

The first industrial museum to be given a UNESCO heritage designation is the Völkingen steel complex, which stopped production in 1986. Artists' studios and cultural events use the former work space in new ways. Völklingen also boasts an impressive art nouveau city hall. Another industrial museum, featuring mining, is at Bexbach. Roman villa mosaic floors and reconstructions of floor plans and walls exist at the outdoor Roman Museum on the outskirts of Homburg. The fortress, which the military engineer Sebastien de Vauban built for his warlord Louis XIV of France, is a massive earthworks in the shape of a star at Saarlouis. In and near it are bistros and cafés with Michelin-rated restaurants.

South at Merzig is a fine example of Romanesque church architecture. At Mettlach a ceramics museum explains the eighteenth-century development of porcelain, known as white gold, and illustrates ceramics from all eras. A 12-kilometer (eight-mile) drive from Tholey to St. Wendel offers the Saarland Sculpture Street of nearly 40 contemporary works. The Saarland Pre- and Early History Museum at Saarbrücken has an extensive collection of armlets, rings, clasps, and other jewelry from the prehistoric era. Bronze armbands from Rubenheim and Merowingian jewelry from Altheim illustrate recent finds. The Saarland History Museum in the capital mostly offers twentieth-century themes, including life in the Third Reich and relations to France. At Gollenstein a huge megalith—some 20 feet high—provides a puzzle regarding its origins and probable cult meaning. The European Culture Park at Gersheim allows visitors to experience Gallo-Roman times.

The wooded countryside with its varied terrain is ideal for biking, hiking, and skiing with stops in small villages for good food. Windsurfing, waterskiing, and kayaking are popular in the Saar-Hunsrück Nature Park. Seeing the huge bend in the meandering Saar River *(Saarschleiffe)* is a must for visitors.

CUSTOMS

In the past, men dressed with blackened faces and horned hats pulled decorated wagons and collected eggs for the poor before Easter. They sang in local dialect "quack, quack, three eggs please, six in the pan and we want a dozen with a half pound of bacon or we will not leave your house door." At present, carnival is the main annual dress-up event with special masks and costumes. However, mine workers' organizations, historical associations, and sharpshooting clubs also provide colorful processions and festivals, and in Saarbrücken, Oktoberfest runs for two weeks. Village and "old" city festivals have been revived or invented to become annual affairs and occasions for consumers to support local crafts and foods.

Sports are strong at the local level, with over 400,000 enrolled in clubs. Associations are especially strong, including those devoted to ecology and culture.

CIVICS AND REMEMBRANCE

The office for political education provides information to schools and to the public about democracy and how parliamentary government functions. It also seeks to educate the region on its history and especially to provide an understanding and foster remembrance about the Third Reich. It has installed plaques at sites of Nazi repression and created museums at concentration camps, such as *Neue Bremm*, which used slave labor.

CULTURAL ATTRIBUTES AND CONTRIBUTIONS

Limited leisure and state-controlled industry with no university but strong clerical direction meant that provincialism long prevailed. However, in the struggle to win the mind of the populace, *Heimat* museums, an art college, and a gallery were created in the 1920s by the French-influenced administration. The Nazis responded in the late 1930s by supporting a district theater and radio expansion. After World War II, a renewed French cultural offensive began with support for theater and the arts. Part of that effort involved founding a university with four faculties and professors from France, Switzerland, and Germany. Miners' children and lower-class individuals no longer needed to leave the region to attain higher education. In the refounded art college of 1946, Otto Steinert, one of the creators of "subjective photography," taught along with other masters. In addition to the Saarland Historical Museum, which contains archaeological and regional artifacts, the Museum of Modern Art in Saarbrücken has a fine collection of classic German artists: Käthe Kollwitz, Wassily Kandinsky, Paul Klee, Emil Nolde, Max Pechstein, Karl Schmidt-Rottluff, Ernst Barlach, and Paula Modersohn-Becker, among others. Sculpture is also well represented with Auguste Rodin, Wilhelm Lehmbruck, and especially Alexander Archipenko.

Among authors who used local events and landscapes as background, Arthur Binz (1893–1958) and Johannes Kirschweng (1900–1951) stand out. Kirschweng, a Romantic, used his home village to spin a web of historical stories. Gustav Regler (1898–1963) moved from Catholicism to Communism in his emigration and return to his homeland after World War II. His novel, *Das grosse Beispiel (The Large Example)*, is set in the Spanish Civil War in which he fought. In contrast to Kirschweng's preoccupation with peasants and traditional rural life, Alfred Petto (1902–1962) wrote about the fate of industrial workers. Among contemporary authors, Ludwig Harig has attained widespread acknowledgement.

During the nineteenth century, music in the Saarland followed European patterns of house, church, and court concerts but also of wandering musicians such as the Buchta family. Folk music received much state support but also had political overtones during the Nazi era.

In painting, court portraits and imitations of European styles also predominated until the late-nineteenth century. Karl Röchling, a Berlin court painter originally from Saarland, worked with Adolf Menzel to promote historical scenes and Carl Becker-Gundahl offered monumental equivalents. Albert Weisgerber experienced some of the usual life pattern of expressionists—Munich and Paris—before death in the trenches, like his compatriots Franc Marc and August Macke. During the 1920s a local association of artists provided the basis for regional variants of international trends and a base for training succeeding generations. Similarly, in architecture, styles from predominant European trends and from Prussia made their mark, for example, the Prussian Karl Schinkel and later Peter Behrens. In the twentieth century, using art nouveau and art deco styles, Saarland builders left wonderful edifices, including factory, house, and office façades. After World War II, the Catholic Church again became an important patron with churches such as *Maria Königen* at Rotenbühl, in wraparound brick. The restored palace in Saarbrücken has a central glassed-in addition designed by the architect Gottfried Böhm.

CUISINE

Local beers or homemade apple and pear wines and brandies still quench the thirst of a populace that has remained close to its rural roots.

Since the eighteenth century the potato has served as the basis for most common and daily fare, but now French-influenced varieties of culinary arts are marketed under the motto "living like a king in France." For instance, the Hostellerie Bacher at Neunkirchen and the Hostellerie Hubertus south of Borostal Lake are among the

13 restaurants with star ratings in the best guides. At home, in pubs or at festivities, locals eat cakes with a plum or peach topping. A simple ring sausage with boiled potatoes is among the traditional miner's fare. Miners also often took a one-pot meal, *Eintopf*, to work; the dish is still popular as a hearty soup as well as a way to use leftovers.

EINTOPF

1 tablespoon butter

1 large onion, diced

1/2 cup soup greens (parsley, celery tops, small carrot, and green onions, finely diced)

1 1/2 pounds chicken, beef, or lamb, cut in small pieces

2 cups of water or meat broth

2 large potatoes, cut in small pieces

the same quantity of vegetables (any combination of carrots, cabbage, green beans) as meat and also cut in small pieces

1 teaspoon salt

1/2 teaspoon pepper

In large pot melt butter, sauté onions and soup greens until onion is transluscent. Add meat and brown lightly, about 10 minutes. Add half the water or broth and cover pan and cook over medium heat for about 10 minutes. Add potatoes and vegetables, the rest of the water or broth, and, salt and pepper, and cook for about 30 to 40 minutes. Sometimes a boiled Frankfurter-style sausage is served in the *Eintopf*.

Chapter 13

𝕾𝖆𝖝𝖔𝖓𝖞

SPECIAL ASPECTS

Sometimes the Free State of Saxony is seen as the country's heartland, because in the medieval era Saxon kings ruled most German-speaking lands. In historical reality, those Saxon monarchs ruled the area of present-day Lower Saxony and not the eastern territories. Certainly, Saxony became the industrial heartland of eastern Germany in the nineteenth century within the triangle Dresden, Leipzig, and Chemnitz. It retained that designation for the first half of the twentieth century. The state presents itself as having been progressive and culturally creative. At present it fosters the claim to being "Motherland of the Reformation." Previously, in the early industrial era, "Red" Saxony provided a home to workers' movements for social and political rights. In 1989, Saxons led the protests that resulted in the fall of the Communist regime in eastern Germany.

REGIONAL TRAITS

The population of 4.5 million covers 18,413 square kilometers, making this area one of the more densely populated of the eastern states. Four-fifths of the population is urban, with the rest mostly in large industrial towns. In the northeast, overlapping with Brandenburg, the 60,000 Sorbs, a Slavic minority, have so far maintained their identity and their language. The regional Saxon dialect is sometimes difficult for people from other German areas to understand as letters are slurred and some simply disappear off the ends of words. Saxony borders on Poland in the east and the Czech Republic on the southeast, touches Bavaria in the southwest, while Thuringia is to the west, Saxony-Anhalt to the northwest, and Brandenburg to the north.

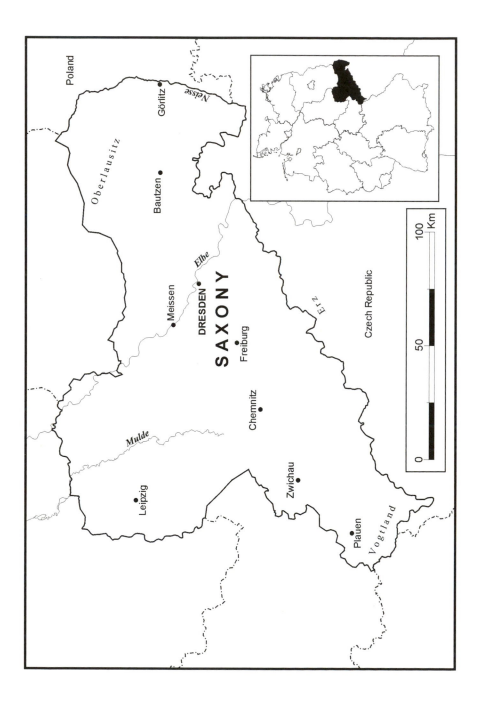

The coat of arms and flag show black and yellow horizontal stripes with a diagonal green band from which four flower emblems emerge, each part representing one of the ducal houses of the territory.

GEOGRAPHIC FEATURES

The region today is shaped like a left-leaning triangle. The Elbe River runs through the middle in a northwesterly direction. The western side is hilly countryside, which in the north contains soft coal near the surface. Since the 1920s, but especially during the GDR era, open-pit mining caused serious pollution and destroyed villages. Uranium mining has left craters and radiation in the southeast. The northern part of the state is more flat and agricultural. The Mulde River runs north through the western part—the flatlands surrounding Leipzig. Most of the south rises in quite high hills in the Erz and Lausitzer uplands.

The subregions, with which some locals identify, are the Vogtland hills in the southwest, Oberlausitz lowlands in the northeast, Leipzig lowlands, and Erz Mountains, which merge into the Saxon Swiss sandstone cliffs above the Elbe River. In the Erz, the *Fichtelberg* is the highest point at 1,200 meters (3,500 feet).

Figure 13.1
Lookout at Königstein over the Elbe River, Saxony.

Source © Press and Information Office, Germany.

HISTORY

The long version of the region's history mythologizes the medieval era when Saxon kings imposed political unity on a very large territory around 1000 A.D. In actuality, the Saxon-Meissen line only controlled the present-day territory just before the Reformation. The short version focuses on the late nineteenth and early twentieth centuries for a possible different outcome to the regional and German past, especially during the Weimar era. The labor movement's reform alternatives to authoritarianism and racism have been highlighted. Historians have underscored the strength of the Socialist and Communist movements during the industrial era and, recently, the successful revolt against dictatorship. In sum, the region has had a tumultuous past.

The region's early history is similar to that of much of the European post-ice age eras. Prehistoric artifacts go back to the Stone Age. South of Leipzig at Markkleeberg, numerous artifacts have been excavated, though permanent settlements seem to have emerged only about 5000 B.C. Archaeological finds, such as the wooden well shafts at Eythra, include decorated ceramics and leather wares. Various Germanic and Slavic tribes fought over and moved through the very thinly populated region for the next thousand years. Some of the Germanic tribes from Holstein, the Sahs or swordsmen, were among the Anglo-Saxons who migrated to England while others took over much of what became northwestern Germany. Around 800, Charlemagne militarily subjugated them and forced Christianity upon them. But by 880, the Saxons had reconquered much of the territory north of the Erz Mountains.

Under Heinrich I (873–936), the region between the Elbe and Mulde rivers became a unified entity and he stopped the Slavic incursions. Fortifications, as at Meissen, served as defense posts, from which Otto I declared himself as monarch. The dukedom of Saxony and earldom of East Saxony provided supporting units. Meissen became a powerful Catholic bishopric with religious and cultural responsibilities for much of the political realm as well as a missionary outreach toward the east.

During the next centuries many challenges to the dukedom and earldoms emerged, and various aristocratic groups fought for control. Simultaneously, the missionary work and expansion toward the east continued with the founding of cloisters and churches. By the late fifteenth century, two sons of Prince Friedrich II, Ernest and Albert, ruled present-day Thuringia, Saxony-Anhalt, and Saxony from Dresden. The Meissen-Saxon state again became the strongest within the German-speaking lands until divided in 1485 at Leipzig. Albert continued to rule from Meissen; Ernst and his followers moved to Weimar and built residential palaces at Wittenberg and Hartenfels (Torgau). He founded the university at Wittenberg where Martin Luther studied and taught. The division of the realm undercut the Wettin dynasty and resulted in a series of smaller states, such as Saxon-Meissen, Saxon-Weimar, and later Saxon-Meiningen and Saxon-Gotha. Historians postulate a very different outcome to German history had the division of 1485 not occurred.

Saxony at present terms itself the motherland of the Reformation, though Wittenberg, or Lutherstadt Wittenberg as it is now called, is in Saxony-Anhalt. Since the various Saxon territories previously overlapped and were geographically intermingled, both states can and do claim Luther as, quite legitimately, does Thuringia. The Saxon prince Friedrich the Wise certainly aided Luther in his struggle with the Catholic Church and the German emperor. Both Saxon dynasties eventually converted to Protestantism and supported the Protestant movement. Luther wrote most of the Augsburg doctrinal guidelines in Torgau.

Among the contexts within which the Reformation operated were the humanistic training in the universities and the economic growth of the fifteenth century. Artisan crafts, mining, and trade had helped develop cities such as Leipzig. The dukes expanded schools and sought to develop small industries, such as smelting, and to make agriculture more efficient. Libraries and art collections expanded until the Thirty Years War retarded developments. Indeed, the whole seventeenth century of religious, dynastic, and social conflict undercut culture, though many half-timbered houses date from this era.

By the mid-eighteenth century, economic and political conditions improved. In terms of political influence and military capability, the Saxon region had become the equivalent of the Austrian, Prussian, and Bavarian realms. Under August the Strong (1694–1763), the possibility of an enlarged Saxon state emerged as he sought to gain Poland. He exploited his role as an elector of the Holy Roman Empire in dynastic disputes. Like other absolutist monarchs with Enlightenment values, he developed large artistic and cultural collections. Architects were hired to design new palaces, gardens, galleries, and libraries. The state engaged in manufacturing weapons and porcelain. Dresden became a treasure chest of palaces and courtly pleasures. August also sought to control Poland, converted to Catholicism, and paid huge bribes to expand state power. But he infringed on Prussian interests, and Frederick II of Prussia took the important geopolitical region of Silesia from Austria, with which August had allied. Frederick not only won a series of wars, he took over Saxon troops and enforced huge payments to his war chest. Yet he allowed the Saxon state to survive. That state developed academies for mining and arts, expanded manufactures, and improved agricultural methods. However, most of those cultural and economic improvements only helped the well-to-do. When the peasants had the opportunity during the French Revolution to revolt against feudal burdens, they did it with vehemence. But they were quickly repressed.

During the Napoleonic era, Saxony joined Prussia in its challenge to the French emperor. In 1806 they were soundly defeated. Napoleon elevated the Saxon dukes to the status of a king, but only within the Rhineland confederation, which Napoleon controlled. After 1807 the new King of Saxony even held sovereignty over Poland as a grand duke, yet again, under Napoleon's direction. Despite being hemmed in politically, Saxony profited from the blockade of British industrial goods. The good fortunes were reversed with Napoleon's next adventures. Some 20,000 Saxon soldiers participated in the French-Russian wars after 1812; less than a thousand returned. In the struggle to remove Napoleon, Saxony's territories became a major battleground. Napoleon's troops, as well as the Russians and Prussians, lived off Saxon lands. At the Battle of Nations near Leipzig in 1813, Napoleon and Saxony lost. The price for being Napoleon's ally included nearly 100,000 dead and wounded. For being on the losing French side, the Saxon people paid and starved, while the king sat in a Prussian prison and a Russian governor ran the state. Some of the populace and independent Saxon troops joined the other side and participated in the remaining battles of liberation against Napoleon as well as in the occupation of France. Though Prussia demanded all of Saxony to compensate for war costs, the European diplomats, concerned about a balance of power, restored Saxony, though half its northern territory went to Prussia.

The King of Saxony-Weimar decreed a very limited constitution in 1816, but Saxony itself only obtained a limited constitutional monarchy in 1831, after the unrest of 1830. The advisory parliament *(Landtag)* represented only the elite. More important than the political developments were the economic ones. Many textile factories were founded in imitation of England. Thus, administrative unity and bureaucratic forms substituted for wide political representation, though peasant rights slowly improved. Railways aided internal communications and helped develop markets for more industries. Steamboats on the Elbe River joined steam locomotives, tying the state together. These transportation improvements included reaching out to neighboring areas via the Prussian-dominated customs union, which Saxony joined in 1834.

As in other states, the Revolution of 1848 in Saxony witnessed similar demands for expanded political representation by the liberal middle class. After the initial revolts and establishment of a provisional government, debate centered on a new constitution. In the factional infighting, the democrats won a majority in the state elections and they favored universal suffrage. In Dresden, radicals advocated a republic and major social changes. In mid-1849, Prussian and Russian troops aided the brutal repression of the attempt to modernize Saxony. The restored monarchical state reestablished estate society, though some legal improvements occurred.

In 1866, the Saxons again chose the losing side as the Prussians defeated the Austrians in the war over spoils from the conflict with Denmark. Saxony was forced to become part of the North German Confederation and then the Bismarckian Reich in 1871. At this time, Saxony seemed to be a major center of reactionary politics and social control. Yet, within a generation it became known as "Red Saxony," due to the growth of a radical labor movement. Growth of commerce and industries made the difference, since by the 1860s more than half the populace earned their incomes from trade, commerce, and industry. Textiles, beer brewing, machine building, and chemical industries expanded. By the 1890s, Leipzig trade fairs presented the region's wares to an international market. One-third of the world's hides traded here. Educational and research facilities expanded with new technical schools.

Industrialization fostered urbanization. Leipzig increased from 170,000 in 1871 to nearly 500,000 by 1914; Chemnitz more than doubled from 70,000 to 180,000. Strikes to improve working conditions, especially the length of the workweek, repeatedly stopped the textile industries, notably in 1903. However, the living standard of the workers in industrial firms remained abominable. Housing, safety, pay rates, as well as lack of political and social rights fostered a response from laborers. Often led by disgruntled artisans, they sought emancipation as well as social decency.

Ferdinand Lassalle saw that workers could not rely on liberals or conservatives for reform. He, and then August Bebel and Wilhelm Liebknecht, laid the basis in Leipzig for German Social Democracy. By 1914, Social Democrats held all the *Reichstag* constituencies in Saxony thanks to universal male suffrage. In the regional Saxon system, however, voting restrictions prevented real participation. In 1905, even more restrictions to limit the suffrage hindered any start at fair representation.

During the nineteenth century, Saxony had an authoritarian political culture. Its belated and limited constitutionalism, its almost paranoid anti-Socialism and increasing anti-Semitism marked public life. Despite that already in 1903, the Social Democrats won 22 of 23 *Reichstag* seats, the other being held by an anti-Semite.

The Saxon state remained conservative, while some of the populace became progressive and emancipatory. Among the progressive elements were modernist art movements. They rebelled against the academy's official restrictions and created their own galleries or simply seceded from the academies. By 1900, Gotthardt Kuehl tried to promote impressionist art and, just as in Hamburg, Berlin, Weimar, and Bremen, encountered stiff opposition in Dresden. By 1914, his modest challenge to official art gave way to the assertiveness of the Brücke expressionists (Ernst Kirchner, Max Pechstein, Emil Nolde, Karl Schmidt-Rottluff, and Erich Heckel).

In 1914, the Saxons still independently declared war, though the German Kaiser in effect preempted command rights over the Saxon military. The state provided some 750,000 troops, of whom 230,000 died. Some strikes in 1917 and early 1918 hinted at the problems that the war had brought, namely a further division of society. Inflation and starvation as well as political ideals led to the overthrow of the Saxon monarch along with all the others in November 1918.

At first, Social Democracy operated a coalition government, which had difficulties with social unrest in the spring of 1919. The national government sent troops in response. Elections returned a coalition led by Social Democrats, which wrote a state constitution by 1920 for the Free State of Saxony. Seeking to fundamentally alter state and society, the ruling coalition set out a strong reform agenda. A coalition of Social Democrats and Communists in 1922 and 1923 tried to implement it, but the national government deposed the coalition by military intervention. Through emergency decrees and a state of siege, the national president and the *Reichswehr* ended the Saxon experiment in modest social democracy. Those actions drastically weakened labor and aided the right wing during the Weimar Republic.

The Saxon liberals and conservatives who ruled after 1923 as commissars, and then as coalition governments, ended the eight-hour day and undercut social support systems. But they had few answers to the economic depression of 1929. In Saxony, the industrial downturn brought desperation as unemployment exceeded 30 percent, higher than much of the country. Already before 1933, the Nazis attained 45 percent of the vote, whereas before the Depression they had hardly any adherents.

Saxony quickly melded into the Nazi dictatorship after 1933. The state was administered as a Nazi district *(Gau)*, the labor movement's institutions were destroyed, and the modern art and cultural contributions of Dresden were repressed or held up to ridicule. Concentration camps to reeducate opponents opened in

Bautzen and Waldheim. Euthanasia murders were carried out at Sonnenstein and Bernburg. The first major deportations of Jews (who were not German citizens) to Poland occurred from Leipzig during the mid-1930s. However, the labor movement, especially the Communists, opposed the regime and some conservatives shifted to opposition, especially during the war. Thousands of opponents, and even minor protesters, received the death penalty in the Dresden-Leipzig area.

Bombing drastically affected Leipzig in late 1943, Chemnitz and Plauen in 1944. The senseless firebombing of undefended and strategically unimportant Dresden in February 1945 resulted in at least 35,000 civilian deaths. By that time, most Saxon factories operated with forced labor from Poland and the Soviet Union. At the end of the war, those workers wanted to return to their homelands, just as Germans from the east streamed west to avoid revenge for the atrocities committed by Nazi organizations, such as the killing squads and SS and the German military.

Torgau, where American and Soviet troops met at the Elbe River, symbolized Allied unity in 1945. When the Americans withdrew and left the area, the Soviets established a harsh military occupation, which included special camps for alleged as well as real Nazis. The Nazi elite were tried, punished, and dispossessed. De-Nazification included confiscation of industrial plants. Land reform, approved by plebiscite, broke up large estates. After the spontaneous anti-Fascist committees were shunted aside, the Communist and Social Democratic parties merged under pressure from the Soviet Union into the Socialist Unity Party (SED). By 1949, when the GDR emerged in response to the creation of the western federal republic, a domestic surveillance system kept track of real and imagined opponents. That would eventually become the extensive spy system of the Ministry of Security, or Stasi. Bautzen, the most infamous GDR jail for dissidents, became a code word to invoke fear.

Simultaneously, the reorganized state of Saxony received hundreds of thousands of refugees expelled from Poland and Czechoslovakia with Allied agreement. Euphemistically termed population transfers, this amounted to a harsh ethnic cleansing. Many refugees would move farther west, while some received farms and homes in Saxony from those dispossessed by land reform and from others who had fled the Soviet-occupied areas due to their Nazi involvement. Some fled in fear that the Soviets would take revenge on them for the Nazi and military brutality in Russia between 1941 to 1945. The refugees, mostly women accompanied by children or the elderly with few possessions, proved to be a difficult social problem because of lack of housing and limited foodstuffs.

In 1949, the reconstituted Saxony provided many leaders for the new GDR, and its industrial base provided much of the potential for the economy. However, in 1952, the state itself disappeared into three administrative districts based on Leipzig, Dresden, and Chemnitz (named Karl Marx Stadt, a GDR title that would be reversed after Reunification).

During the 1950s and 1960s, Saxon industries slowly revived, mostly serving the eastern block of countries, although through the West German fiction of a still-unified Germany, the GDR also made free deliveries to western Germany.

During the 1980s, Saxons led the way in the push for internal reform and to remake the GDR into a real social democracy. Long before they were noticed in the West, the demonstrators, in the churches, and especially on the main squares, demanded new elections. Then they demanded changes of personnel, and finally they demanded freedom to travel. Since the mid-1980s, two overlapping processes undercut the stability of the GDR. Many young people demanded the right to move westward, since most knew that economically the GDR was falling behind the West. Second, the reform course of the Soviet Union and then of Hungary undercut the ability to restrict the population and limit its demands for reforms. The peace and prayer movement in the Leipzig and Dresden churches fostered peaceful and non-violent protests, which led to the candlelight vigils and silent marches that undercut the regime. The revolts of November 1989 transformed the GDR as the crowds occupied the Stasi headquarters in Leipzig and Dresden, as populist democratic groups formed, and as western parties campaigned with western monies in the eastern election.

However, unification has not only a positive but also a questionable history. At Hoyerswerda in northwestern Saxony, the difficulties of coming to terms with unemployment and freedom resulted in skinhead neo-Nazis attacking and killing foreigners. The process of integrating East Germans into western patterns and values after two dictatorships ironically posed the question of the meaning of many similar attacks in western German states. Saxons soon shifted politically to the moderate right, but economically the process of adjustment is still under way. Women, having had access to abortion, to support for children while at work, and to high levels of employment in well-paying positions, suffered much during the adjustment period, which some think is still continuing. Modernization meant more than closing uncompetitive factories and mergers with western firms. It also meant high rates of unemployment, discrimination (middle-class jobs were being taken by managers from the West), and eventually nostalgia for a cozy way of subsidized, slower life despite the dictatorship of spies, arbitrary rule, and the narrow cultural world of the GDR.

The Christian Democratic Union (CDU) has ruled Saxony continuously since Reunification, achieving majorities in 1990 (54 percent), 1994 (58 percent), and 1999 (57 percent) under Kurt Biedenkopf, who has retired. Georg Milbradt (CDU) has been the head of the ministry since 2002. Social Democracy has repeatedly declined in its share of the vote; in 1999 it attained only 10 percent, well behind the Party of Democratic Socialism (PDS, with nearly 23 percent). The red kingdom (color and slogan identified with the left) seems to have become the black castle (color identified with conservatives). The government advocates entrepreneurship and self-reliance but accepts large federal subsidies for building projects such as trade centers, stadiums, and railways.

Identity from history. What is the self-image that is fostered by the state and the office for political education about this region? The emphasis is upon the long history of the *Kulturland* Saxony and the democratic impulses in overthrowing the GDR. "Saxon Days" seek to foster a regional identity tied to a traditional past.

ECONOMY

At present 60 percent of the workforce is in the service sector with many small firms driving the economy. Food production, machine and metalworking, and automobiles are the main industries, as they were during the Imperial era. During the GDR era, the Dresden-Leipzig-Chemnitz triangle continued to produce machines, beer, automobiles, chemicals, and created 40 percent of the total output of the country. In 1997, within the unified country, Saxony only produced 3 percent of total German industrial output, and even with large subsidies, economic growth had declined to about 2 percent. An old saying maintains that what Chemnitz produces, Leipzig trades and Dresden consumes.

After the breakdown of the GDR, unemployment soared due to the collapse of industries, some of which could not compete in western markets, some of which were bought by western firms and closed to terminate competition. Introduction of western currency undercut well-established eastern markets. The sale of large state-owned concerns mostly resulted in closures or extensive reduction in the workforce or replacement by machinery from the West. Some of the sales were cause for financial scandal, such as questionable deals involving former chancellor Helmut Kohl. He had promised that the eastern states would be blossoming economic landscapes, but he seemed to have been better at hiding illegal party funding and feathering friends' nests. Unemployment, when Kohl was defeated in 1998, officially stood at over 17 percent (early retirees were not included in the count, nor were the women who had been shunted out of the workforce).

The potential of the region is great. The base for it includes numerous specialty colleges (mining at Freiberg), some for arts and dance that complement the important traditional research university in Leipzig, and the newer ones at Dresden and Chemnitz. The university at Leipzig had been especially strong in humanities. Solid education and highly skilled labor have been a tradition and fostered by state investment. Following Baden-Württemberg, internship arrangements with employers have been introduced. Further, autobahns enter Saxony from all German sides of its triangular shape and converge near Dresden, so that vehicular traffic is facilitated. Trade fairs at Leipzig go back hundreds of years, and renovated rail and air transportation links to the city have renewed their importance. Europe's largest railway station, at Leipzig, is a glass and steel complex built to support the commercial and book fairs. The fairs draw clients and promote new products. Housed in a glassed dome with accompanying display halls, Leipzig's fairs challenge the western competitors in Cologne, Hanover, and Frankfurt. Chemnitz has a Volkswagen plant. At Görlitz, Siemens continues to build turbines. Dresden has become the computer chip capital of Europe. Mostly, though, smaller firms with less than 20 employees predominate and are hoped to be the dynamic element for the future.

Some examples of success already exist. The firm A. Lange & Söhne in Glashütte has revived the family specialty watch factory abandoned during GDR times. It has captured international markets with the highest-quality, mostly handcrafted luxury timepieces. By contrast, Meissen pottery continuously maintained a

Figure 13.2
Dresden at night, Saxony.

Source © Press and Information Office, Germany.

tradition of high-quality chinaware, dinner services as well as figurines, which is sold around the world. Since 1710, two years after a Dresden researcher (Johann Böttger) discovered the formula for this "white gold," Meissen ceramics have set standards for the highest-quality porcelain. Hand-painted, with an insignia of crossed swords, Meissen remained a major export item during the GDR era and after.

Saxony has been the most successful of the new states with much investment in computer chips and fiber optics. Packaging created from wastepaper, auto parts, robotics, food processing—especially potatoes—pianos, compressors, glassware, computer software, steel girders, micromeasurement instruments, bicycle wheels, air conditioners, diet foods, and even rust removal from old locks are among the specialties that have succeeded mostly in export markets. But unemployment remains stubbornly well above 15 percent.

MAIN CITIES

CAPITAL

Dresden (population 520,000) suffered drastically from firebombing in February 1945. But the city, which previously had been strongly bombarded by Prussian artillery in 1760 and slightly by French artillery in 1813, again recovered. It was rebuilt mostly during the 1950s and 1960s. In the 1990s another drastic renovation took place. At present it is trying to become the computer chip capital of Europe and has benefited from being the state capital as well as designated the European cultural capital in 1999 (with many special subsidies).

The administrative and light industry city contains many cultural treasures. Its Green Vault *(Grünes Gewölbe)* contains Europe's finest royal jewelry collection. Its bridges and churches on the edge of the Elbe helped designate it the Florence of the north. Among the notable churches is the city church where Luther preached; Lucas Cranach painted the altar, J. S. Bach served as organist, and Gottfried Herder was pastor. Dresden's *Zwinger*, the eighteenth-century baroque palace with a formal park, mostly destroyed by bombing and rebuilt during the 1960s, contains one of the fore-most galleries of Renaissance art in the world. An unusual museum is dedicated to hygiene, everything related to health and the body. An older version, which opened for the international hygiene exhibition in 1911, drew a million visitors and empha-sized race and purity. The newly reopened museum demonstrates the way in which the human body works. Some 30,000 items are in the collection. Specific rooms relate to living, dying, eating, drinking, and sexuality.

Leipzig (population 500,000, declining) is perhaps the most modern-appearing city in Saxony. Bombing destroyed much of the central core, but much has been rebuilt in its previous style, especially around the expanded railway station, one of Europe's largest. The marketplace by the old city hall and the nineteenth-century shopping arcades are a reminder of an earlier city not so dominated by concrete and steel. In the 1990s, Leipzig competed with Dresden for the number of cranes rebuild-ing the city. Most spectacular is the glass-roofed and gold-steel-beamed trade center at the edge of the city near the airport. It is surrounded by halls and entertainment ven-ues with 100,000 square meters of display space. At 250 meters long, 80 meters wide, and 30 meters high, the main arched hall dominates its area of the city.

Famous for its trade fairs that continued during Communist rule, investment in the fairgrounds has restored them to new vigor. As the German entry for the Olympic Games in 2012, Leipzig has begun constructing new sports facilities in a city already endowed with Olympic-size swimming pools and sports venues from GDR times. Some of the World Cup soccer matches of 2006 will take place in a new stadium (tinged by bribery scandals). Visitors to the trade fairs and sports events can arrive at a reconstructed main railway station with convenient ties to the Leipzig-Halle international airport.

The city looks back on a tradition of 800 years of trade with major fairs since the medieval era. Toward the end of the Imperial era, 100,000 visited the stands. The Saxon state had long helped the city by forbidding competition in the neighboring cities. By the Weimar era, many other fairs challenged Leipzig's attempt to monop-olize trade fairs, and at present many cities, such as Berlin, Düsseldorf, Cologne, and especially Hanover, assert their rights in certain markets created while Leipzig repre-sented the GDR.

The other trademark is as a book city. Leipzig has been a publishing but also library city for hundreds of years. Lutheran writings, especially pamphlets, were published here in the 1520s. Later, cheap book editions for students made Leipzig the rival of Frankfurt in the publishing business. The university library built over hundreds of years became one of the foremost in Europe. Encyclopedias and lexicons came off the various presses. In the Imperial era, specialty publishers, such as Insel, produced books of poetry as works of art. From the Imperial era through World War II and the GDR era, Leipzig was home to the national library and sought to preserve at least one copy of every German publication. The tradition of rare books and artistic publishing remains strong and again is being fostered. The high-rise on the main square, built during GDR days and formerly housing the university, symbolizes the shape of an open book (some 30 stories tall). Though a contrast to its surroundings, it is not out of place with the cityscape that has a huge arched railway station near large department stores *(Specks Hof)*, an old-style exchange on the snack market *(Naschmarkt)*, and arcades with columns and statues under glass.

The city has many literary and historic sites. *Auerbach's Keller*, built in the sixteenth century, became famous for a scene in *Faust* by Johann von Goethe after he had spent student days drinking there. It can be accessed directly from the refurbished arcades, though its ceilings now have nineteenth-century decorations. Goethe thought of Leipzig as a miniature Paris. The restaurant itself serves local cuisine, as does *Barthels Hof.* Another favorite Goethe haunt still exists and is one of Europe's oldest coffeehouses, *Zum Arabischen Coffe Baum.* The *Thomaskirche* (St. Thomas Church), where Johann Sebastian Bach composed and conducted, houses the well-known boys choir Bach directed. The Gothic edifice has been restored and repainted. A museum across the street features Bach artifacts. The New Opera House fits well into the cultural scene of a city known for music. The new *Gewandhaus*, built in GDR times, supports the city's strong music traditions by providing an acoustic masterpiece for its symphony orchestra directed by Kurt Masur.

The *Nikolaikirche*, where for eight years prayer meetings and candlelight vigils took place, remains the symbol of the peaceful overthrow of the GDR. From it, protestors marched around the ring of the old city. Inside, a black and white diamond floor is in contrast to a set of palmlike pillars, with leaves providing the ceiling.

The city's name means place under the linden trees. The *Auewald* still makes a long strip of green through the city, partly because Daniel Schreber, a physician, insisted that children should have places to play. From a playground dedicated to him in 1864 emerged another movement, to have sandboxes, flowers, and vegetables. This eventually led to creating small garden plots, *Schrebegärten*, on which little sheds developed into weekend houses and a few plants developed into gardens for workers with little space in crowded apartments. Eventually, 4,600 such tiny plots existed in Leipzig, and most large cities followed suit.

Near Leipzig, 1.2 million tons of iron and concrete are a reminder of German nationalism. In 1913, that amount was piled together to commemorate Napoleon's defeat at the Battle of Nations in 1813. Inside, huge sandstone figures 30 feet high honor those who fought for their fatherland. The huge monument is impressive for its size and took 15 years to erect. Five hundred steps to the lookout permit time to reflect on the meaning of wars. During GDR times, the writer Erich Loest used the monument in his novel, *Völkerschlachtdenkmal* (Peoples' War Monument), to argue sarcastically that the Saxons always sided with the losers.

Chemnitz (population 315,000). A steel and glass congress center with reflecting pool symbolizes the move toward service industries in the eastern rust belt. In the 1820s, with machine tools and textile looms, a small trading center began the move to industrialization. Cloth and machinery such as locomotives and bicycles preceded chemical and electrical industries. Brown coal, as the main energy source, created much pollution that attacked the medieval buildings, such as the Benedictine cloister churches. World War II bombing left little of the old city, though the old *Rathaus* and the art nouveau new *Rathaus* survived. The central city, when still called Karl-Marx-Stadt during the GDR, was graced with a nearly 40-foot statue of Marx in 1971.

Zwickau (population 120,000). Three million Trabants *(Trabis)* came off the assembly line before Volkswagen took over the plant after Reunification. This small commercial center gained prosperity before the Reformation from nearby silver mines and trading in cloth. That wealth can be seen in the numerous buildings of the rich trading patricians, the *Rathaus* from 1403, and the five-story gables of the half-timbered *Gewandhaus*. In the nineteenth century, machine building and textiles expanded the population. In the twentieth century, armaments, machinery, and automobiles helped maintain employment until the collapse of the GDR.

Görlitz (population 80,000, declining). On the border with Poland, it suffers 25 percent unemployment, which will probably become worse since its neighbor across the Neisse River has joined the European Union. Already, a black market of Polish low-wage workers exists. A large subsidized media park depends on state finances. The city is pretty with many historic buildings, but behind the façade rests a difficult social scene.

ATTRACTIONS

Hiking has always been common in the heights of land between the Elbe River in the east of the region and the Mulde's two branches in the center and west. Many castles dot the landscape, but the region is more known for palaces such as the Dresden *Zwinger* and the water-surrounded, five-towered *Moritzburg*. The former holds one of the major collections of sixteenth- to eighteenth-century European art, while the latter is set in a charming lakelike landscape (it was once a hunting palace on an island). Also carefully designed to fit a resculptured landscape is the garden palace near Dresden, a summer pleasure palace based on French baroque models. Torgau also has a large palace near the Elbe River.

Among the notable Romanesque and Gothic churches, the Freiberg cathedral stands out. Its lean pillars support a finely arched roof without too much interior decoration. A series of apostle sculptures grace the walls and pillars. Most important is the entrance with its Golden Gate from 1230. The Romanesque pillars with triumphal arches and carved capitals are reminiscent of southern France.

Rich Renaissance town halls with decorated gables and clock towers can be found in numerous towns and cities. For example, the old city hall in Chemnitz is constructed in late-Gothic style, and the one in Plauen has an elegant steplike gable with *glockenspiel* and clock. Freiberg's *Rathaus* is fairly simple, as is the one at nearby Oederan with its round-corner tower.

Many smaller towns and villages still show neglect from the GDR era, but in some the half-timbering has been restored and repainted. Others suffered the modernizing disease, so evident in North American cities, where concrete and blocklike buildings with plain façades replaced intricate old handiwork.

A different type of museum is Lichtenstein's Daetz-Centrum which exhibits wood sculpture. A number of industry museums exist, including one at Chemnitz.

Dresden, known as the Florence of the north, has many notable collections and attractive street scenes. The court church *(Hofkirche)* with high open spire and simple interior lines, is near the *Semperoper*. The latter appears almost like a large Greek temple atop a hill due to its staggered stages and rectangular external form. Dresden's Green Vault displays royal jewelry, its porcelain collection contains many Meissen pieces, and its art gallery has an extensive collection of old masters (Rembrandt, Rubens, Cranach, Canaletto, Raffael). A roof that looks like a mosque is actually the delicate ironwork on a cigarette factory, while a former finely decorated milk shop has become a museum. In the villa suburb of Loschwitz in Dresden, the *Leonhardimuseum* offers exhibitions of local artists' works. The building itself is a work of art: half-timbering with yellow insets on which is inscribed much of the family history of the eighteenth and nineteenth centuries. The prehistory and ethnology of the region is housed in a large former villa (Japanese palace).

Many cultural sites include the Erich Kästner Museum, emphasizing his detective and children's books; the Konrad Zuse Museum in Hoyerswerda, in honor of the inventor of the computer; and the Carl-Maria-von-Weber Museum in Dresden.

In Leipzig, some older and newer buildings compete for sight-seers' attention. The famed *Auerbach's Keller* is below shopping arcades reconstructed in nineteenth-century style. The city bath appears to have been brought from Turkey, as its entry walls have the symmetrical patterns of an Asian palace. The *Zeitgeschichtliches Forum* in Leipzig depicts daily life in the GDR, containing everything from automobiles to kitchens.

Near Leipzig, the huge monument to the so-called Battle of Nations, inaugurated in 1913, 100 years after liberation from Napoleonic occupation, illustrates the Imperial era's elite's lack of taste in self-promotion.

CUSTOMS

Dresden's classical music festival is the largest in eastern Germany but is threatened to close due to financial difficulties. By contrast, the Dresden *Stollen* market (dating back to 1443) goes for weeks before Christmas with much *Glühwein* and consumerism. The biggest folk festival, the *Annaberger Kät* processions, derive from former pilgrimages to see holy earth from Rome. The secularized present version is mostly concerned about seeing sausages and beer. In Lausitz, another religious ritual is a religious ride at Easter. Wearing a tuxedo and cylinder hat, the rider on a decorated horse takes a myrtle wreath and cross while a flag bearer receives a church flag for a tour around the parish. A newer tradition is witches fires on *Walpurgisnacht* (30 April–1 May) to get rid of the bad and make room for the good.

Karl May Days, celebrating American native culture as perceived by a writer who never crossed the Atlantic, are celebrated annually at Radebeul. A large museum there presents the author's life and writings.

In order to foster identity with the region and the restored state, political leaders initiated the Day of Saxons festival in 1992. It seeks to advance awareness of the traditions, customs, and traditional dress *(Trachten)*. Larger towns or cities compete for the honor and the monies to host the celebrations, mostly organized by local associations of *Heimat* advocates.

CULTURAL ATTRIBUTES
AND CONTRIBUTIONS

VISUAL ARTS

The anonymous creators of Romanesque treasures, such as the Golden Gate entrance to the Freiberg cathedral, are insufficiently acknowledged. Such works should receive as much publicity as the baroque creations of Matthäus Pöppelmann, the architect of the Dresden *Zwinger*. However, the high level of wood carvings in the form of church altars and choir chairs do receive some acknowledgement.

In painting, Max Klinger (1857–1920) and Max Pechstein (1881–1955) sometimes employed local themes and landscapes, while Otto Dix (1891–1969) ended attacking the bourgeois world from which he came. Dix's experience of World War I trench warfare destroyed his illusions about the utility of aesthetics.

LITERATURE

Georgius Agricola (1494–1555) is foremost among the region's many humanists who examined religious texts and began to codify the world. His explanations and depictions of minerals, mining, and metalworking remained the standard works for centuries. Gottfhold Lessing composed some of his tracts and plays supporting religious tolerance as part of the Enlightenment. By contrast, after 1813 Johann Fichte penned diatribes against Napoleonic occupation. In the 1870s, August Bebel's *Die Frau (Women in The Past, Present and Future)* exposed the double standards for women and called for their emancipation. Some may not consider his feminist tract literature, but it was among the nineteenth century's best sellers and still inspires women. Simultaneously, Karl May wrote his imaginative and escapist novels about North American natives. Before the Nazis censored his work, Erich Kästner wrote some of his children's books here, though mostly he is associated with Berlin. During and after the GDR era, Erich Loest penned many insightful texts. His work, *Die Nikolaikirche*, captured the protest movements that ended the other German state.

THEATER

Cabarets in Dresden and Leipzig, Sorb folk theater, plus state theater companies in Dresden and Leipzig are among the variety offered. The state theater has a long tradition with classical works. Special is the Leipzig workers' theater, a part of the *Arbeiterbildungs Institut*, or workers' educational committees. Already strong before World War I, during the Weimar era it premiered works such as Bertolt Brecht's play *Baal*. Secondly, in 1918 and 1919, they initiated what became a regional, then a national, tradition: playing Beethoven's 9th Symphony on New Year's Eve.

MUSIC

Heinrich Schütz (1585–1672), sometimes termed father of German music for his Protestant psalms, headed the Dresden court orchestra for 55 years. Carl Maria von Weber's supposedly "national" opera, *Der Freischütz* (1821), had its inspiration in the Saxon Swiss area in response to Napoleonic occupation. Nineteenth-century notables include the architect Gottfried Semper (1803–1879; after whom the Dresden opera house is named); the Schuberts, with their romantic compositions; and Kurt Masur, who reestablished the international reputation of the *Neue Gewandshaus* Symphony in Leipzig after 1981 and conducted there and in New York. During the 1980s, Ludwig Güttler made his international reputation as a classical trumpet player in Dresden, where he still conducts. All the large cities, but especially Dresden and Leipzig with boy and adult choirs, have chamber and symphony orchestras as well as many small ensembles. An international dance week, a Dresden jazz festival, and the Vogtland folk music festival hint at the variety of music offered.

CIVICS AND REMEMBRANCE

In 2004 the Leipzig or Saxon model of having one organization to deal with memorializing all victims of dictatorship failed, because some lobbying groups thought that one set of victims might get more attention and funding than another. Much has been achieved, though, through monuments and memorial sites regarding both the Nazi and Communist dictatorships. The main GDR prison in Bautzen has become a place to view and to learn about a site of repression. The Stasi investigative prison in Chemnitz has a commemorative plaque, as do the many sites where uprisings occurred in June 1953, as in Dresden. In some places the victims of Fascism and Stalinism are remembered, especially where internment camps served both regimes.

An institute for contemporary history (Forum) opened at Leipzig precisely 10 years after the huge demonstrations on 9 October 1989. It seeks to research and disseminate the ramifications of the GDR dictatorship. The Nicholai Church and square, where most of the candlelight vigils took place, has a pillar honoring the church and the participants.

The Nazi era is also well remembered. Many sites of concentration camps, slave labor camps, and sites of deportation of Jews are identified. The office for political education seeks to encourage an understanding of the evils of the past as well as the need for informed citizens in the present.

CUISINE

Known for coffee and potato consumption, beer drinking is on the increase. Some Saxon beers such as *Radeberger* and *Wernesgrüner* have attained wide recognition, and their breweries have done well since Reunification.

As in Mecklenburg–Western Pomerania and in Thuringia, potato dumplings are Sunday fare. Called *greigeniffte*, they are made with pressed raw potatoes. Another version is *quarkkäulchen* (potato cakes), in which potatoes are cooked with the peel, peeled while hot, pushed through a sieve or press, and allowed to cool. Quark is also put through a sieve and mixed with the potatoes to which sugar, lemon peel, nutmeg, cinnamon, eggs, and flour are added. Cookielike heaps are pressed together and fried in oil. They are served with a sprinkle of sugar while hot.

Claimed to be authentically local are *Pfefferkuchen* (pepper cakes), but they have little to do with pepper, since they are a combination of honey, egg, and paprika in dough that rises for 10 days (similar to Nuremberger *Lebkuchen*, but do *not* try to tell that to a Saxon from Pulsnitzer). Another regional specialty is Leipziger *Lerche*—originally a pie made using skylarks, but after a disaster decimated the skylarks and their killing was forbidden in 1876, a baker made pastries filled with marzipan.

Dresden Stollen (Christmas Cake, or The "Calorie Bomb" from Dresden)

2 pounds flour	6 ounces mixed peel
4 ounces yeast	1/2 pound slivered almonds
1 cup (or somewhat more) lukewarm milk	1 pound raisins
pinch of salt	1/4 pound dried currants
1 pound butter	1 shot glass of rum
1/3 pound sugar	powdered sugar for dusting
1 ounce grated lemon peel	

Make primary yeast dough and let it rise. Add the lukewarm milk, salt, butter, and sugar. Knead thoroughly. Add the other ingredients. Knead again and let the dough rise again. When the dough has risen enough, form 2 long pieces, roll them flat, and fold one half over the other. Put on a greased baking sheet. Let the dough rise again, bake 1 to 1 1/2 hours at 350°F. Take Stollen out of the oven and brush with melted butter and dust with powdered sugar.

Chapter 14

𝕾𝖆𝖝𝖔𝖓𝖞-𝕬𝖓𝖍𝖆𝖑𝖙

SPECIAL ASPECTS

If Saxony claims to be the motherland of the Reformation, Saxony-Anhalt calls itself the cradle. Wittenberg has been renamed Lutherstadt Wittenberg (Luther-City). Medieval castles and churches abound. Some model villages and institutions representing Enlightenment-era attempts at agricultural and educational improvement are also cause for local pride. The past thus plays a part in the identity ascribed to the present. Saxony-Anhalt emerged as a state in 1945 when the Soviets combined the former Prussian province of Saxony with the small duchy of Anhalt. The state disappeared in 1952 in an administrative reorganization of the German Democratic Republic (GDR) and reappeared with Reunification in 1990. Frequently, the claim made is about the state being a young land, yet with a long historical background due to the Reformation as well as the kingdoms, duchies, and princedoms that once held sway. A major concern is to overcome the image and the smell of industrial pollution produced by chemical factories based in brown coal, without increasing unemployment.

REGIONAL TRAITS

The population of 2.7 million is mostly in a triangle near the center of the state's 20,444 square kilometers. Like Hessen and Thuringia, this is a landlocked state surrounded by other German regions. Lower Saxony is to the west, Brandenburg is to the northeast, Saxony to the southeast, and Thuringia to the south. The coat of arms has many symbols representing previous political entities that ruled parts of the territory. At the bottom is a bear, referring to Saxon monarchs. It is set against a white background and moves across a red gate below black and gold stripes across which a

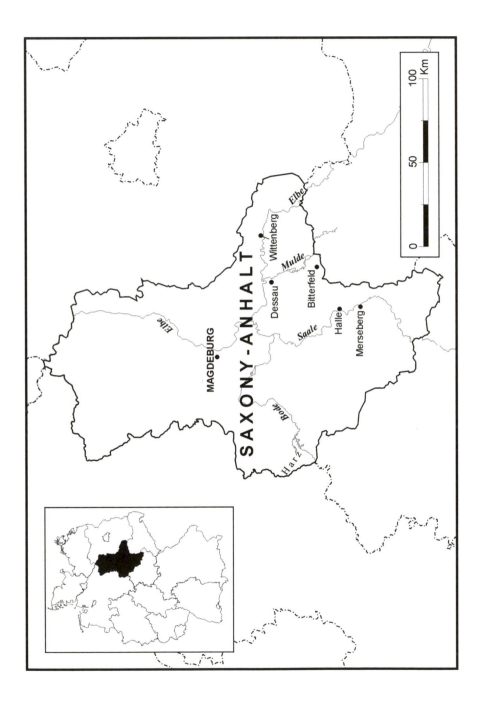

diagonal green ribbon with floral pattern runs. In the top right corner is a small black Prussian eagle on white.

GEOGRAPHIC FEATURES

The Elbe and Saale rivers, with their smaller tributaries, the Bode and Mulde, run northward through the center and drain most of the region. The *Mittellandkanal* (central canal) ties east and west across the northern lowlands. The south is rolling hills edging up to the Harz Mountains in the southwest with the *Brocken* at 1,200 meters (nearly 4,000 feet) as the highest point. That part is more forested than the northern plains. Some salt and copper remain, but the main resource in the east of the region is brown soft coal. The latter, emitting much pollution in its use, supported the chemical industries, and its digging and reworking ruined parts of the landscape.

HISTORY

In the medieval era, princes and dukes ruled small areas of the region. Under Albert the Bear, the far north served as the basis for his creation of the Mark Brandenburg in the twelfth century, of which it remained a part until 1815. Prussia obtained more of the area through war and purchase so that by the beginning of the eighteenth century, it controlled the west down to the Harz Mountains. After the Napoleonic wars, the Prussian province was consolidated and became the administrative districts of Magdeburg and Merseburg. The Prussian province of Saxony thus controlled nearly all of present Saxony-Anhalt except the southeast corner. There, Anhalt comprised five duchies that in the Revolution of 1918 became a free state. In 1933, that small area was combined with Brunswick by the Nazi reorganization of states. In 1944, the Prussian districts again became provinces, which the Soviet occupying administration combined with Anhalt in 1945. A democratically elected parliament created a constitution in 1946 with the capital at Halle. Small border changes have occurred since then, but the greatest change occurred in 1952 when the state was dissolved into two districts centered on Magdeburg and Halle. In 1990, after Reunification, the state was restored with the capital at Magdeburg.

A political history of the region misses important religious, social, and economic components. The prehistorical era left evidence of Neolithic inhabitants. Later, Celtic tribes made bronze bars for trade and employed fine ceramics. From the Roman era, grave sites as at Leuna contain fine gold ornaments and vessels. Copper and salt were mined and used well before Carolingian times. Many fortresses and defense works served local lords and later Saxon kings. The building of Romanesque and Gothic cathedrals and cloisters proceeded during the eastward expansion of Christianity after the ninth century in this region. One can almost follow the push eastward against the Slavs, as well as the missionary activities of the Catholic Church, by noting the eastward march of fortifications and churches.

The area became the basis for Saxon power in the early medieval era. Large cloisters, such as at Hersfeld and Fulda, ran an extensive economic system while consolidating Catholic influence. Bishoprics such as Halberstadt took over the task of Christian missionary work toward the east. Simultaneously, the peasants were tied to the land as serfs with many feudal obligations. Revolts against the combined Carolingian kings and their Saxon lords in 841–842 failed and feudalism prevailed. The clan of Liudolfinger gained territory through war and marriage to eventually emerge as kings ruling most of present Saxony, Saxon-Anhalt, and Thuringia. Under Heinrich I (919–936), the area between Harz and central Elbe came under unified rule, exercised from the strongholds *(Pfalz)* capable of supporting the large court. Hence, huge castle complexes emerged at Allstedt, Madgeburg, Merseburg, Memleben, Tilleda (known as Kyffhaüser), and Wallhausen, plus a series of lesser ones. Such places also served as defense works against incursions, especially by the Hungarians during the tenth century, and as a base for conquering the Slavs. During this era the many Romanesque (Gernrode) and Gothic (Merseburg, Magdeburg, Naumburg) churches with their fine carvings were built and rebuilt. In some towns and cities, traders and artisans sought independence and created separate administrations evident in the building of city halls (half-timbered at Wernigrode), churches (in brick at Stendal), and walls or towers (at Halle, Quedlingburg, Salzwedel, Stolberg). Statutes of Roland, the symbol of city independence and trading rights, appeared on market squares (Haldensleben, Stendal).

Crucial for the outlook of the populace was the Reformation. Economic development of the mining region Mansfeld-Eisleben in the hills near the Harz accelerated the growth of cities and of a wealthy middle class of merchants and lawyers. Salt, iron, and silver provided commercial resources. Martin Luther came from such a socially rising, commercial-legal family. Many of the middle-class disliked the onerous church burdens and relic selling of the archbishop of Magdeburg. Luther not only nailed his thesis to the church door at Wittenberg, but his ideas were debated in the towns and cities of this region, which quickly became a stronghold for Protestantism.

The Thirty Years' War devastated the area; Magdeburg supposedly ended up with 450 people from a prewar population of 35,000. By then, through war and marriage alliances, the Prussian state had expanded into and controlled the northern and western parts of the region. When the Prussians took over Magdeburg in 1680, they made it into a military fortress and thus further hindered its long-term economic development. However, in alliance with the Saxon monarchs, they developed much of the realm.

Religion played another major role during the late seventeenth and eighteenth centuries. The Saxon monarchs advocated educational and agricultural improvements. In their absolutist efforts they received support through the Pietists' movement, which advocated personal development. The university at Halle, founded in 1694, became the center of Enlightenment advancement in central Europe through the work of the philosopher and legal scholar Christian Thomasius. He ended the persecution of witches. Together with Christian Wolff in philosophy and Gottfried Leibniz in mathematics, their work encouraged rationalist reforms. Among the most influential were the Francke charitable institutions and book publishing. The Francke foundations became educational centers that fostered intellectual revival and influenced academic developments. Halle became one of the foremost Enlightenment-era universities, its students such as Gerhard Müller and Georg Steller helping to understand Siberian people and plants while in the service of the Russian Academy of Science. Johann Reinhold Forster, who helped James Cook to understand the botany of the Pacific during his second voyage (1772–1775), gained knowledge at Halle that he passed on to his son, Georg, who would recount the voyage in a best-selling philosophical travelogue.

The dukes of Anhalt built a special pavilion to display the large ethnographic collection, which the Forsters brought from the South Seas. By then the dukes of Anhalt-Dessau had become involved in reforms. Leopold I developed Dessau as residence city and undercut the aristocracy. He encouraged the development of Rousseau-style educational principles in his realm. Some claim that the origins of modern education lie in Dessau with the work of Johann Basedow. The duke certainly introduced religious tolerance and encouraged the end of harsh military discipline. Leopold knew and was influenced by Enlightenment authors such as Rousseau, the philosopher Johann Lavater, and Forster. Even Goethe applauded his achievements. At Worlitz-Dessau, a special garden complex containing the South Seas pavilion began an association of the beautiful with the utilitarian. That complex altered garden and palace styles toward the classical, looking more to England neo-Gothic country houses than French baroque palaces for inspiration.

The 1830s custom union ended internal tolls and aided the growth of industry in the region. Shipping on the Elbe River increased, especially with steam-driven boats of the Magdeburg steam line. Railways tied Magdeburg to Halle and Leipzig. By the 1870s a dense set of railway lines covered the region. The main roads were straightened and hard surfaced. As a result, local products could reach new markets. Those products included sugar (from cane and beets), brown coal, potash, wood, machines, and chemicals. Brown coal and chemicals eventually became most the important, but machinery signaled the shift to industrial production.

Nineteenth century industrialization brought horrid living and working conditions. Partly out of those emerged a strong labor movement, which also sought civil and political rights. Magdeburg and Dessau mostly became Social Democratic strongholds by World War I; later, Halle and Merseburg shifted to the Communists. These were the bases on which post–World War II political unity was imposed by the Soviets in creating the Socialist Unity Party.

The 1920s had already seen a shift in industrial production to more technologically based goods such as airplanes. Hugo Junkers had patented his metal airplane before 1914. During the 1920s he continued to experiment, and by 1932 he had fashioned his three-motor passenger type. This would be the most built passenger plane until World War II. Such industries would provide the basis for armaments once the Nazis attained power in 1933. They fostered the production of zinc, oil, energy, and especially chemical materials (Buna and Wolfen). Synthetic fibers and other products helped create the world's largest color film plant and the emergence of artificial rubbers, methanol, and nylons.

The 1920s also saw the founding with state support of the Bauhaus at Weimar under Walter Gropius. Prominent artists from the modern movement such as Lyonel Feininger, Gerhard Marcks, Wassily Kandinsky, Paul Klee, and Oskar Schlemmer taught there. When Weimar refused to continue to support it, the innovative design and learning project moved to Dessau. However, a right-wing government closed it in 1932. It was revived during GDR times as an architectural and educational research institute.

The town of Torgau became the symbolic meeting place of Soviet-U.S. troops in the "heart of Germany" on the Elbe River. Anti-Fascist committees made up of three Communists, three Social Democrats, and three liberals pushed the Allies to remove tainted Nazis from public life. In July 1945, the Soviets combined the Prussian province of Saxony with Anhalt. They also insisted on land reforms by breaking up big estates and nationalizing large industries. In 1952, the state disappeared into a series of administrative units. In 1990, after Reunification, the region regained statehood.

The conservative CDU ruled in coalition with the liberals until 1994. Then the SPD led a minority government with the Greens and Bündnis 90. None were able to prevent the destruction of industries nor to arrest unemployment. After 1998, the SPD led a minority government, but in 2002 the CDU took over.

ECONOMY

Though only employing few people, agriculture remains important, especially for potatoes, grains, sugar beets, and vegetables. Forest resources combine with brown coal, potash, stone, shale, and gas. Many of those resources relate to the main industry: chemicals. Highly engineered products and machine building are other traditional industrial areas. After Reunification the region received much investment money from the West as well as subsides to help rebuild infrastructure. Transport routes tend to lead through the north to Berlin and through the south to Leipzig. Revamping the cities and reorganizing industrial production reduced the workforce, but administrative positions and some high-tech electronics have been introduced.

Chemical industries remain the most important, especially with a large Bayer plant at Bitterfeld. The American glass company Guardian, at Wolfner, produces specialty products, seeking to gain from the architectural trend to employ special glass and plastics. Many smaller electronics firms have had difficulties surviving. Typical of continuing economic difficulties, in 2004, Bombardier closed a large rail vehicle plant at Halle and thus terminated 4,000 jobs. Much hope is placed in tourism, especially in relation to hiking, kayaking, and cultural possibilities. The latter include special gardens (Dessau-Worlitz), the Romanesque Road of cathedrals and churches, galleries and Reformation sites.

—————————— MAIN CITIES ——————————

CAPITAL

Magdeburg (population 227,000). This medieval trading center has been destroyed and rebuilt more than once. In the late Middle Ages it attained archbishopric status and in 1188 city rights within the empire. The Protestant Reformation succeeded by 1524. The Thirty Years' War depopulated it due to inflation, looting, and killing. After the devastation, the city lost its independence and came under Prussian jurisdiction (until 1934). The bombing during World War II destroyed much of the inner city. After 1945, the huge Gothic *Dom* (cathedral) and the Romanesque cloister *(Unser Lieben Frauen)* had to be completely rebuilt. However, during the nineteenth century, planned parks had sought to provide green space for citizens and workers, and those continue to shape the city.

The present administrative and industrial city has a restored *Rathaus* near the old market square. In 1989, protest vigils, which helped lead to the overthrow of the GDR, occurred at the cathedral. A major problem has been the slow decline of population.

The city has tried to remake its image as it shifted from heavy machine building to becoming a regional capital. The port and autobahn connections provide good transportation systems. The university and the technical college have been expanded, while trade fair and industrial park infrastructure are being built. As the administrative functions of the new regional capital expanded in the 1990s, office building has not kept up with demand. A renewed emphasis on culture includes acknowledging local notables such as the musician, Georg Telemann.

Halle (population 238,000). Once important for the salt trade, this remains a significant industrial city. Some success stories reveal the economic potential of a skilled workforce that saw Reunification undercut most industries. Kathie baking products has a large distribution system for its ready-mix cakes developed in GDR times. Already by 1970, its products sold in West Germany, and since Reunification the company has expanded abroad. Transportation connections have improved, especially the autobahn link to Magdeburg.

During the Renaissance, Cardinal Albrecht von Brandenburg had *Moritzburg* built as a pleasure palace and sought to develop Halle as a residence city. As with other cities where the Reformation quickly triumphed, the Thirty Years War brought drastic reversals. However, by the mid-eighteenth century, the university produced humanist and Enlightenment scholars who served at academies everywhere in the world. The philosopher Christian Wolff and theologian August Francke were among the prominent minds. At present, science and technology receives more support than the humanities.

The *Altstadt* has a well-preserved area and the cathedral is a very large Romanesque structure. But more special is the *Händelhaus*, where the composer, Georg Friedrich Händel (1685–1759), was born. The large hall named after him is the venue for concerts as well as one of the main places for the international children's choir festivals. An informative salt museum illustrates the original basis of the city's wealth.

Merseburg (population 35,000) and **Bitterfeld** (population 16,000) lie in a line with Halle, identified with the "dirty" chemical and coal industries during the GDR push for industrial production. Both cities suffered drastic reductions of population due to almost complete termination of brown coal mining. Merseburg, though, has a large cathedral and is proud of its fables, especially about ravens. The German Chemical Museum explains the creation of artificial synthesis, especially of fibers, which are crucial for the creation of film, clothing, and industrial goods. A technology museum emphasizes flight and transportation from bicycles, to GDR automobiles such as the Trabi, and Focke airplanes.

Dessau (population 79,000). Though associated with the artistic innovations and political struggles of the Bauhaus during the Weimar Republic, during the same era the Junkers airplane factory did much more for the local economy. By the 1930s, Stuka fighter planes joined the mail and passenger planes with which the company had started. The city hopes to benefit from tourism, since the Bauhaus has been designated a UNESCO heritage site.

Lutherstadt Wittenberg (population 45,000). Wittenberg remained a poor city until the founding of its university in 1502. Its dean aided Martin Luther, who taught with the teacher Philip Melachthon during the time Luther developed his challenge to the Catholic Church. The city has renovated Luther's house, the former university, and the convent where Luther lectured. The church where Luther preached contains a three-piece altar painting by Lucas Cranach, another humanist friend of the reformer. Everywhere in this city, which seeks to base its tourism on the Reformation-era heroes, the Protestant reformers appear as statues or are mentioned on plaques. A new museum focusing on Lucas Cranach's times includes a book by Martin Luther that he helped illustrate. The artist and the religious reformer were close friends. A replica of a Gutenberg printing press shows how their ideas were disseminated. The other Lutherstadt, Eisleben, has tried to hitch itself to the Reformation wagon by highlighting where Luther lived and his family worked.

ATTRACTIONS

A great variety of heritage sites exist. Besides natural ones, most relate to the medieval era, the Reformation, the half-timbered towns, and the creations of the princely courts. The Garden Kingdom of Dessau-Wörlitz emerged in the eighteenth century, modeled on English landscape design. Both the nobility and the general public (gentile bourgeois) were delighted by the fountains, flowers, and hedges. They were also educated about nature. That purpose continues to be met by this UNESCO heritage site. The 18th century archaeologist and art historian Johann Winckelmann suggested designs that the duke, after a visit to Italy, had made into temples, pavilions, grottoes, and bridges over canals and lakes between carefully sculpted tree scapes.

The Harz Mountains, parts of which were security zone reserves in GDR times, have pristine hiking areas. Resort towns such as Schierke offer posthiking liqueurs made of local herbs. Others, such as Thale, publicize the local legends related to witches and giants. One trail leads to the witches' dancing place *(Hexentanzplatz)*, where *Walpurgisnacht* or, Witches' Sabbath, is still celebrated on April 30. More popular hiking trails converge at Stolberg. From one trail at the Luther-Oak, one can try to find the outline form of a bird that Luther saw in the landscape of the Stolberg Valley. Well-known and replete with local legends about witches is the *Brocken*, a huge outcropping with various trails to the top from which the sunset or sunrise is traditionally watched by hikers.

Quedlinburg is the city with perhaps the most half-timbered houses in Europe and has been designated a UNESCO heritage site. Its cobblestoned streets are filled with carved fronts illustrating sculpting and painting skills. Each façade varies, and each corner has a novelty of forms and patterns in wood, brick, and stone. The early Saxon kings had their main fortress and family crypts here (Schlossburg Romanesque church) when they dominated and unified northwestern Germany after 900. Outside the seventeenth-century city hall, as in Bremen, stands a statute of Roland symbolizing the freedom of the city. The city also has one of the finest collections of Lionel Feininger's (1871–1956) delicate paintings in a museum devoted to him after the artwork was returned from Soviet Russia. The church treasures dating back to the medieval era were not so lucky. Stolen in 1945 by an American officer, only a few were returned and then for huge sums. Just outside the city to the south at Gernrode is St. Cyriacus Church, dating from 959, which is one of the best examples of German Romanesque architecture.

Wernigerode is known for beer, cobbled squares, and mingled Renaissance half-timbered houses. The *Altstadt* meanders in medieval style among the many notable buildings, though the *Rathaus* is the most spectacular. It is known as the *Buntestadt am Harz*, or colorful city by the Harz.

A sharp and angular contrast to half-timbered houses is at Dessau. Though also surrounded by much concrete and gray suburbs, the city has sought to improve its central area. The Bauhaus school of architecture, founded during the 1920s, is another UNESCO heritage site, because that architecture inspired so much twentieth-century building and decoration (Chicago, New York, and Toronto, as well as Berlin, have examples of the work of Walter Gropius and Mies van der Rohe). The Bauhaus transformed the way architecture was taught by combining an understanding of color with a feeling for a material's appearance plus relating the capability of materials with the purpose of the design. The Dessau Institute presently combines a museum with a teaching and research institute.

Salzwedel in the far north once belonged to the Hanseatic League and became quite prosperous as a trading center. Its association with the old province (Altmark, as part of Brandenburg) can be followed in a museum. The building is a three story half-timbered edifice with a round tower in front, which serves as entry and staircase.

Recently, the so-called Romanesque Road has been rediscovered. The region has a large collection of cathedrals, castles, and chapels built in this style. The *Naumburger Dom*, a fine example of Romanesque architecture, is worth a trip from Halle. Its life-size statutes of 12 founding donors have simple flowing robes combined with medieval symbols of their status. But most impressive are the lines of the idealized visages of Ekkehard and Uta. Quedlinburg castle as well as St. Servatius church are solid examples. Grönigen's cloister church is a refined one with decorated ceiling and octagonal tower. Merseburg's cathedral *(Dom)* tends toward the solid, while the Burg Falkenstein with its half-timbered ramparts and huge tower is almost like a rock upon a rock. Many village churches have their own patterns with little additions protruding in various directions. Examples are at Pretzien, Stegelitz, and Engersen. Jerichow and Halberstadt, like Magdeburg and Merseburg, have larger examples with crypts and huge central halls. Some show their dual purpose as fortress and church, as at Havelberg. Many of these Romanesque churches have carvings on the capitals, which can compete with the French equivalents.

A special type of attraction is the Wittenberg *Haus* of History (house), which shows everyday life in the GDR. Typical crowded conditions of refugee families in the 1940s are in one display. Plastic furniture from the 1960s is in another room, while bathroom eccentricities appear in some. Oral history projects and photographic exhibitions are also on display.

At Blankenburg the state music academy is near the *Michaelstein* (Romanesque) monastery, which has housed the Telemann Chamber Orchestra since 1968. The area seeks to increase tourism by advertising its castle. Similarly, Wernigerode publicizes its half-timbered houses and late-Gothic city hall.

CUSTOMS

Walpurgisnacht, or the night of the witches on April 30, involves the burning of huge stacks of wood on hilltops. Some locals reenact the rituals supposedly related to the times of the witches with their sabbats, or nocturnal meetings. In the past, many were executed for supposedly having participated in such rituals; today, many create illusions about the old beliefs. Special gatherings are held at the *Brocken* mountaintop and at the *Hexentanzplatz* (witches' dancing place) near Quedlinburg, where the Bode River emerges from a narrow gorge in the Harz Mountain National Park.

Some local customs, such the *Hüttenröder Grasedanz* (grass dance), go back a hundred or so years, when women went to the fields to fetch grass for goats and cows. At the weekend celebration to mark the end of hard work, the women are honored. They choose their dance partners as well as elect a queen. On Sunday, grass is auctioned and the winner gets to dance with the queen.

CULTURAL ATTRIBUTES
———————— AND CONTRIBUTIONS ————————

VISUAL ARTS

The number and quality of Romanesque buildings have led to the creation of a Romanesque Road that roughly encircles Madgeburg. At Dessau, the Bauhaus offers modern architecture and art (Johannes Itten, Kandinsky, Klee, and Schlemmer) while the state *Galerie Moritzburg* at Halle has an extensive collection of late-nineteenth and early twentieth-century works. Only some of those artists worked or spent long times in Saxony-Anhalt. By contrast, Lucas Cranach (1472–1553) is identified with the region, and many of his works are in the Anhalt gallery in the palace *Georgium* in Dessau. In Madgeburg, a large sculpture collection in the cloister *Unser Lieben Frauen* emphasizes works from eastern Germany during GDR times.

LITERATURE

Enlightenment authors associated with or from the region include the scholar of antiquity, Johann Winckelmann, and the philosopher Christian von Wolff. The poets Friedrich Klopstock, Heinrich Heine, and Novalis spent time in the region. Heine wrote emotionally about the *Brocken*. Goethe and Schiller organized a court theater at *Bad Laustädt*, one of Europe's oldest spas for the elite. Christa Wolf, in *Der geteilte Himmel (The Divided Heaven)*, uses post–World War II Halle as backdrop, aptly comparing it to layers of an onion, for a young woman's first experience of big-city life and political awareness.

MUSIC

Among the many composers and conductors who worked in the church music world, one of the fathers of German classical music, Heinrich Schütz, worked here, as did Johann Sebastian Bach, Georg Händel, and Georg Telemann.

CIVICS AND REMEMBRANCE

The regional office for political education encourages the understanding of parliamentary democracy as well as of local history. Themes from the 2003 program include sessions for students and the public on "schools without racism," democracy and tolerance, and Europe and globalization. In addition, the presentation of regional history seeks to further cement identification with the heritage of the area. Hence, the historical studies published by the office include many about Saxony-Anhalt as a free state. However, they also focus on sites of Nazi persecutions and East German dictatorship. The Nazi concentration camp system, especially the subcamps near Magdeburg, is publicized. A dialogue forum at Marienborn discusses ways to overcome the east/west division in Germany. It includes memorials about eastern Germany's dictatorship from the Soviet occupation until Reunification in 1990. For instance, Bitterfeld, Magdeburg, and Eisleben, among many places, have plaques to remember those arrested and victimized after the revolts of 1953. The prisons at Halle and the Stasi offices have become memorial and educational sites. The sites of the liberating demonstrations in Magdeburg emphasize the positive results of civic involvement.

CUISINE

Wernigerode beer is popular outside the region as well. Information about traditional food is lacking, perhaps because the region is such a new creation. Certainly all the usual sausages, sauerkraut, and dark breads are available, but so are pommes frites (french fries), pizza, and *döner kebab*. Potatoes are the main staple. At Quedlinburg, the *Kartoffelhaus* (potato house) serves them in various ways (fried with Speck, as pancakes, baked).

Potato Pancakes

1 pound onions, diced	2 eggs
2 pounds grated potatoes, with excess water drained	pinch of salt
1/4 cup butter	two pinches of pepper

Sauté the onions separately in a bit of the butter until translucent. Once the onions have cooled, thoroughly mix with the grated potatoes as well as the eggs, salt, and pepper. Shape thin patties (about 1/4″ thick by about 3″ round) by hand and fry in butter at medium heat until golden on each side.

Chapter 15

Schleswig-Holstein

SPECIAL ASPECTS

Water and the coast with ebb and flow define the region, as sea and lowland combine on this windy peninsula. The cuisine is heavily influenced by the sea, as are the brick houses built low to the ground. Some of the land has been recovered from water with dikes and drainage. The climate is cool and wet, with much rain in July and August. Quiet reflective people, cautiously embracing each change that comes mostly from outside, is the stereotype, an image that overlaps with assumptions about their Scandinavian neighbors. "*Moin, moin,*" which sounds like "mon, mon," is the good-day greeting.

REGIONAL TRAITS

A population of 2.7 million lives in a sparsely settled, 15,729 square kilometers. *Plattdeutsch*, (Low German), is widespread and in daily use, so that a cow *(Kuh)* becomes *kow*, similar to English, and ditch *(Graben)* is *grof*. Few large cities but many hamlets reflect a heavily agricultural and craft-oriented region. Hamburg and Lower Saxony lie to the south, Denmark to the north. After centuries of conflict, the border with Denmark is no longer a dividing line. People on both sides learn each other's languages and foster student exchanges.

The flag and coat of arms have two vertical halves. On the left are two black lions with long fishlike tails representing the two former provinces on a yellow background. On the right is a white design representing the leaf of a nettle, the Holstein flower, on a red background.

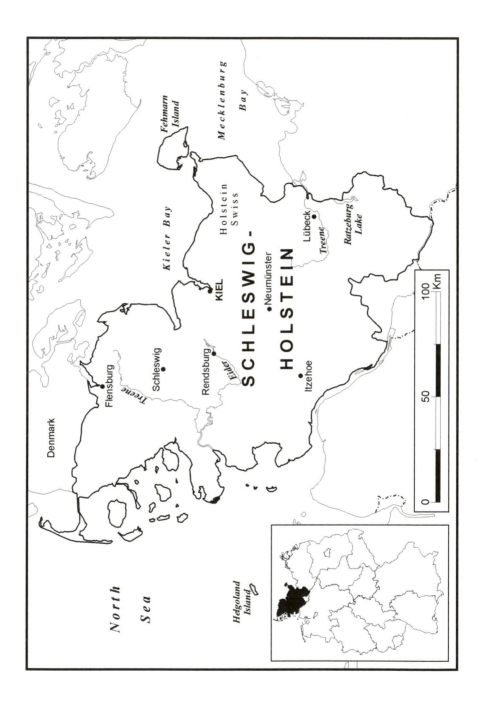

Figure 15.1
Tidal mudflats (Wattenmeer), Schleswig-Holstein.

Source © Press and Information Office, Germany.

GEOGRAPHIC FEATURES

Numerous small lakes interrupt windswept lowlands with good soils, little short streams (Eider, Trave, Treene), and hills that the locals term *berge* (mountains). The highest is 168 meters in the southeastern Holstein Swiss area. All of the area shows signs of heavy glaciation, which left moraines and boulders. The North Frisian islands dot the northwest seacoast, and some land is accessible only at low tide. Helgoland is a large red sandstone island far off the west coast. One large island, Fehmarn, off the east coast provides a stepping-stone to Denmark's Lolland. Mud tidal flats on the west coast are rich in nutrients and support seafood. Ecological concerns about protection of a pretty countryside have led to planning and land use regulation. Some of the lake areas have become nature parks (Westensee, Holsteinische Schweiz or Holstein Swiss). Though the 100-kilometer canal tying the North Sea with the Baltic Sea is the most important change to the geography, many smaller ones, such as the Lübeck-Elbe canal, are significant for local commerce.

HISTORY

Torn between Denmark and Germany from the fifteenth to the twentieth centuries, historical focus has been on that tense relationship. Sometimes that emphasis has neglected the important early history and post–World War II developments. The prehistory of the region left many rune stones, grave sites, villages, and human remains.

Some evidence exists from the hunting and gathering, but also seafaring, tribes. Some is from the habitations before the most recent ice age, but most dates after that. By 500 B.C., many mound graves and rune stones left evidence of a society working in bronze metals, making clay pottery, and engaging in distant trade. Sunken wooden ships have been excavated, restored, and displayed at the Husum Shipping Museum. Idols in wood from this era have been preserved, and some are in the regional museum of Schloss Gottorf.

The great migration of peoples during the fourth to sixth centuries saw many groups moving into or through the region. The Wends entered Holstein from the east by the seventh century and some stayed, whereas the Angles and Saxons pushed on toward England. A watery defense works divided Saxons to the southwest from Wends to the northeast, while Danes tried to push southward. Simultaneously, the Christianization of the region began, especially once Charlemagne integrated much of the region into his empire around 800. The Danish king had a defense works built, known as the *Danewerk*, parts of which remain. He also established the port of Haitabu with a half-circle of wooden defense works. By the tenth century, it became one of the most important trading centers between the east and west Baltic areas, a forerunner of the Hanseatic towns. At present it has one of the best archaeological museums.

Despite the Danish-Saxon division, Christianization continued, especially in the south. The Cistercians built many cloisters and churches, as at Cismar. Romanesque and Gothic churches in brick and stone began to cover the peninsula.

Through the whole late medieval era, Danes, Swedes, and Saxons fought over control of the area. Despite the conflicts, trade continued and decisively affected the development of towns in which artisan crafts emerged. The Hanseatic League, to which Lübeck belonged and partly led, illustrates the importance of the Baltic trade in furs, salt, fish, and grains.

A union of the dukedom of Schleswig and the earldom of Holstein took place in 1440. That union tied the future fate of the principalities as many succeeding rulers sought to replicate it. During the Reformation, the diplomatic maneuvering of the European great powers complicated the dynastic situation, but Protestantism readily won by the 1540s. The religious conflicts, however, continued as Swedes, Hapsburgs, and others sought to dominate and impose their Calvinist or Catholic convictions. During the Thirty Years' War, parts of the area were devastated, but mostly the disruption of trade impacted the region. Most important for the populace was the expansion of serfdom as the peasants' economic situation declined.

As the Danish state lost resources, it had difficulties maintaining control over Schleswig-Holstein. By the mid-nineteenth century, Prussia saw possibilities for northern expansion. That was achieved by warfare in 1864 and 1866. After that, the north Schleswig issue of a population of mixed Germans and Danes festered until the plebiscite of 1920 partly ended the minority issue and regulated the boundary. The large border city of Flensburg remained German but declined in economic importance.

During the Imperial era, Kiel far outstripped the other similar-size cities of Altona and Flensburg. Two main developments supported expansion from 51,000 inhabitants in 1885 to 107,000 in 1900 and 211,000 in 1910: shipping and especially shipbuilding, which brought an accompanying industrialization. Trade remained significant, but previously important industries, such as brewing and milling, mainly served local markets, while the wharves expanded greatly. Once an Imperial marine station was established, the population increased again, but the 30,000 marines and sailors were never integrated into Kiel society. In response to the industrial working conditions and lack of political rights within Prussia, workers organized unions and the German Social Democratic Party. By World War I, in Kiel especially, the latter party had strong representation. The mutiny of marines and sailors at the end of the war reflected the radicalization of the labor movement, but the revolution remained peaceful.

One of the earliest and most Nazified areas during the early 1930s, Schlewsig-Holstein had suffered economically and turned to right-wing parties by the early 1920s. The Depression of 1929 drove the populace to more radical voting. In 1928, the Nazi party had 4 percent support; in 1930, 27 percent; but by July 1932, 51 percent. After the Nazis attained power, they adjusted the district boundaries. In 1937, border changes included placing Altona and Wandsbeck with Hamburg, while Lübeck went from Oldenburg to Schleswig-Holstein. These changes remained after World War II, when the area came under British occupation. During the Nazi era, the rural population generally supported the repressive regime.

The slow route to post–World War II democracy led through constitutional struggles in the late 1940s. The reconstituted state became part of the Federal Republic, though some efforts were made to regain the territory lost during the Nazi era. After a period of competition between the Christian Democratic Union (CDU) and Social Democracy (SPD), with the refugee parties playing the spoiler, the CDU ruled from 1958 to 1983. At first, Uwe von Hassel worked in coalition with a refugee party and the liberals until 1963. Then Helmut Lemke led a coalition with the liberals until 1971. Gerhard Stoltenberg, in turn, led a majority CDU government until he moved to federal politics. Uwe Barschel replaced him during 1982. Barschel caused a major scandal during his reelection campaign. He misused the press and his office in a dirty tricks electoral campaign, one that his SPD opponent, Björn Engholm, sought to exploit. Engholm won the 1988 election with over 54 percent of the vote. After Barschel committed suicide, Engholm eventually had to resign in disgrace for his own part in seeking to manipulate the press.

Since 1988, Social Democracy has mostly ruled a conservative populace in coalition with smaller parties. The first woman head of a regional state, Heide Simonis, who took over in 1993, acknowledged that due to the scandals, a new political beginning was in order. In 2000, the SPD gained 43 percent of the vote and the Christian Democratic Union 35 percent so the coalition of SPD and Greens continues to rule under Simonis.

Identity from history. At present, some state representatives assert that the region is a bridge between the Continent and Scandinavia. Certainly much trade moves in that direction and cultural exchanges reinforce relations. One premier initiated an Ars-Baltica Project that tries to document the common cultural attributes of seaside lands.

The state hymn from 1844 emphasizes a land surrounded by sea. Supposedly, a regional awareness of the state created after 1945 has slowly grown. Its goal is to include tolerance as expressed in the new constitution of 1990. That document acknowledged the need to foster and protect minorities, namely the Frisians and the Danes.

ECONOMY

Due to the number of refugees and expellees, the state had grave difficulties immediately after the war. Integrating outsiders and providing employment proved difficult for a state with few resources. In 1939, the territory had approximately 1.6 million people. Due to the influx from the east, by 1946 it contained 2.7 million. Since most were peasants and artisans, their skills were useful, and they were successfully integrated over the next decades.

Schleswig-Holstein hardly participated in the economic boom of the 1950s. But it did undergo the shift of the economy toward industrial and then service industries from the 1960s and 1970s through the 1990s. At present, only 2 percent of the production value comes from agriculture and forestry, while the service sector accounts for over 35 percent, industrial production approximately 20 percent, while trade and transport have remained stable at around 20 percent. A high proportion of personnel is in administrative positions.

The region has remained a relatively poor cousin to its southern neighbors, who moved ahead with high technology, especially in automobile exports. Since the federal system of equalization payments began in the 1960s, the region has been on the receiving end of financial transfers. Though handicrafts and agriculture remain strong, shipbuilding and armaments production has proven an unreliable support for the northern economy. Food processing, many small industries, and shipping have been the mainstay, with some tourism. In the last 20 years, university and research centers have provided a small entry to the electronics world. Marine and medical centers have helped the larger cities, especially Kiel.

Until the 1980s, public media, especially radio and television from North German Radio in Hamburg, dominated. Then private broadcasting emerged. However, the same company (Springer) that ran the private broadcasting system tended to control print media. During the 1990s, some competition had been reestablished through mergers of the main small competitors.

—————————— MAIN CITIES ——————————

CAPITAL

Kiel (population 230,000) is on a large firth, which cuts deeply into the city. Physically, the harbor still dominates with its cranes, yearly Kiel Week regatta, and marine activities, though fishing is a minor industry. Mostly Protestant, the population is heavily involved in service industries and administration with over 11 percent unemployed. The wharf and harbor continue to employ over 5,000 people. Industry, including processing agricultural products and commerce, provides employment for about 30 percent of the workforce.

As with administrative cities, it has a major theater and gallery of nineteenth- and twentieth-century works. But the city, heavily bombed during World War II, has much concrete. The medieval city was not reconstructed, and few historical points of interest draw the visitor. Some 30,000 students attend the state's main university.

A large monument to German naval sacrifices in both world wars juts into the sea 20 kilometers north at Laboe.

Lübeck (population 217,000). The *Holstentor* slowly sinking beneath the weight of its large round brick towers is one identifying trait for this Hanseatic trading city. Its unspoiled, brick and half-timbered *Altstadt* (central old city) has been designated a UNESCO world heritage site. Another trademark is the *Rathaus*, with its special façade of glazed brick and series of towers with coats of arms.

The *Untertrave*, the lower opening to the Trave River on the Baltic Sea, determined the fortunes of the city by offering a well-protected harbor. The gabled patrician houses in stacked brick flow from one street to another and have left examples from earlier prosperity, for example, the *Haus der Schiffergesellschaft*, now a pub. Salt granaries, one of the staples of the city's commerce and important to the fish trade,

Figure 15.2
Holsten gate in front of baroque (seventeenth-century) brick church and commercial buildings, Lübeck, Schleswig-Holstein.

Source © Press and Information Office, Germany.

are also solid brick. The *Burgtor* is part of the medieval wall. Due to bombing, many of the churches had to be rebuilt, including the huge cathedral with its stark interior. Similarly, the Heiligen-Geist Hospital was rebuilt and its wall paintings restored. Beer brewing in the *Wahmstrasse* continues a Hanseatic tradition. Lübeck's combination of massive gates, baroque brick city hall, its rebuilt churches, but especially its streets with patrician houses, makes it one of Germany's prettiest cities.

Thomas Mann immortalized the city in his epic of the rise and decline of a commercial family. His novel, *Buddenbrooks*, was supposedly based on his own family. He captured the mental attitude of Hanseatic patricians who were more concerned about material rather than spiritual growth and stability.

A number of smaller cities have not quite become important commercial centers. **Neumünster** (population 82,000), like **Itzehoe**, has a central location. **Rendsburg** is an artisan and trading city noted for its canal crossing. **Flensburg** (population 88,000) is the northernmost German city.

ATTRACTIONS

Special enough to become a national park in 1985 are a multitude of western beaches with mudflats for *Wattlaufen* (mudflat walking or running). At low tide the flats are exposed for romping, sliding, and bathing in the oozing rich black soils. Much of the seacoast on the eastern shore is rougher but good for windy strolls.

The Vikings, Angles, and Saxons fought over this terrain and left many signs of early habitations. Well-reconstructed and highly educational are the *Haitabu* ruins. This Danish settlement shows fishing and boatbuilding. The life of the early inhabitants is explained in a superb museum, which includes the ringed village itself. The defensive ring wall of stone and wood can be followed.

The next stage of life in this rural region is well demonstrated at Molfsee, where an open-air museum near Kiel re-creates farm life since the medieval era, though mostly with emphasis on the nineteenth century. Most buildings, including the long "hall houses," which combined barn and living quarters under one roof, are of brick with reed roofs. Some 70 buildings have been brought together, including mills and smithies spread over meadows and forests. Begun in 1961, the museum has become Kiel's major attraction. Another open-air museum is at Husum, where the North Frisian lifestyle is preserved. The Ostenfelder farmhouse with special gardens exemplifies a local building style with half-timbering and a brick long hall under a high reed roof. On the peninsula of Eiderstedt, supposedly the largest farm buildings in the world have hayloft and living quarters all under three-story-high reed roofs.

Far in the south (below Lübeck), half-timbered houses at Mölln meld into another nature preserve. They become more interesting as the setting for some jovial stories about Till Eulenspiegel whose name equates with a mirror of dummies held by the wise owl. He supposedly died here in 1350. A statue with an intricate fountain honors the wanderer with the fool's cap. In folklore, he is a trickster who held a mirror in front of the respectable bourgeoisie, exposing their hypocrisy and sometimes their stupidity. During the 1930s, a local satirist, A. Paul Weber, used Eulenspiegel in his graphics to re-create his pranks. The city hall, a fourteenth-century Gothic building with a fine brick gable, is on the same square as the fountain.

Also south of Lübeck is the *Luftkurort* (fresh-air spa) of Ratzeburg. The old city sits on an island in Ratzeburg Lake. Its solid brick Romanesque cathedral dates from the 1160s. The choir chairs have coats of arms carved on them. To honor the heritage of many postwar refugees, a Mecklenburg museum is in a half-timbered house from 1690. An A. Paul Weber museum shows many of his lithographs, etchings, and woodcuts. In 1937, the Nazis arrested him because of his art. Another museum shows the sculptures and sketches of fellow artist, Ernst Barlach, who lived here from 1878 to 1884.

Some buildings illustrate the diverse cultural heritage of the region. At Meldorf, a large Gothic cathedral is built over the remains of a Frankish-era Romanesque one. Similarly, the south side of St. Petri cathedral in Schleswig is massive brick layered over earlier foundations. The purest example of Gothic architecture may be Lübeck's large *Marienkirche*. A detailed bronze baptismal and an astronomical clock complement the fine ceiling lines. The influence of the Netherland style of Renaissance can be seen in a toll entrance gate at Seedorf.

Quite different is a late-nineteenth-century technological achievement, the canal connecting the Baltic and North Seas. Opened in 1895, it sought to improve trade but also make possible the deployment of Wilhelm II's navy against the British. Halfway across the peninsula, at Rendsburg, a hanging ferry *(Schwebefähre)* conveys people over the canal and under the long sweeping railway bridge, high enough for oceangoing vessels to pass beneath. Rendsburg has a notable central square with many half-timbered houses and carvings, especially on the city hall.

The countryside has many palaces and manor houses from the era of aristocratic dominance before the nineteenth century. Examples include *Glücksburg* near Flensburg, which is built out onto the water of a fjord. A white-walled, three-story structure with gray-roofed towers on the corners of a rectangular building, the *Wasserschloss* (water palace) is considered the jewel of northern palaces. It is built over a Cistercian cloister. The small town beside it reveals its planned street design as a residence city. An impressive manor house, but dating mainly from the nineteenth century, is *Schloss Rantzau* near Lübeck. Another courtly residence, again three stories, dressed in white with gray roof and tower and facing a lake, is the *Plön* palace. In the nineteenth century the Danish royal family used it as a summer residence. Though also near water on a peninsula, the *Eutin* palace is an eighteenth-century rebuilt and less elegant edifice.

Schleswig celebrates its Viking heritage on a long weekend of festivities, but its main attraction is *Schloss Gottorf*, which contains the large state museum. Religious objects including altars, daily utensils, and furnishings are part of the extensive collection. The palace is large enough to have galleries devoted to the era of Dürer and to art nouveau. However, the special gallery offers German Expressionism (Emil Nolde,

Ernst Barlach, Alexej Jawlensky, Christian Rohlfs, Oskar Kokoschka). Another floor holds the main state archaeological museum. Perhaps the mummified corpse, found preserved in the moors with noose around the neck, provides partial insight into the punishment systems of the prehistoric Wends, but the 1,500-year-old Anglo-Saxon ship recovered from the sea bottom certainly illustrates their fine craftsmanship. The oak boat, which held 36 rowers inside its sweeping sides, has had a special home built for it, the *Nydamhalle*.

Nearby is the reconstructed remains of the Viking (Swedish, Danish, Norwegian) trading center, Haithabu. The half-circle defense works have been identified and many trade goods found. Walking the circumference can help to rediscover the size of the completely destroyed town, in which some 1,500 people lived. Life of the era can be experienced in the museum, which has excellent displays and explanations. It includes an 18-meter Viking trading ship recovered off the coast.

Nearly every town in this region (Ahrensburg, Amrun, Aukrug, Bad Oldesloe, Bargteheide, Bonstrup, Brunsbuttel, Eckernforde, Heiligenhafen, Reinfeld, Schonwalde, Tonning) has its *Heimat* (homeland) museum. These are a strong tradition throughout the state and seek to keep a formerly vibrant agricultural and village world in the populace's consciousness. A related aspect is the windmill museum at Fehmarn, the dike museum at Oldenburg, and the island museum at Pellworm. All depict the struggle to deal with wind and sea.

The Otto von Bismarck Museum at Aumuhle-Friedrichsruhe at the main manor house of this aristocratic leader of Prussia is combined with the family mausoleum. Recently, a Bismarck research center opened as a foundation funded by the federal state. Also focusing on the life of an aristocratic family is the Count Rantzau Museum at the family manor in Barmstedt.

Most attractive in the region are the unspoiled coasts and countryside, which allow bathing and bicycling in tranquility. Hiking is also popular. One can still find small fishing villages with reed roofs, whitewashed walls, and gardens full of flowers, as at Leck. Spas along the coasts include some huge resorts such as *Heiligenhafen*, but it is easy to escape to isolated areas. Some of the coastal islands (Halligen) that are cut off from the mainland at high tide are excellent for bird-watching. On the west coast of the island Fehmarn, a waterfowl reserve is home to 180 species.

CUSTOMS

Nearly every local area has some special festivity. Kiel has its annual regatta, which in June takes over the city for over a week. In February, the so-called *Umschlag* (ice breakup in the harbor) is an annual excuse for a festival with formal-dress processions and strong drinks (against the cold). In May, Kappeln celebrates herring days, when these fish are served in diverse ways. In June, Karl May Days at Bad Segeberg celebrate the imagined version of the Wild West according to a writer who never visited the United States. Viking Days occur every second year at Schleswig with boat rides and historical dress. Dittmarschen and Rendsburg have annual olden days with the former focusing on its cabbage heritage.

CULTURAL ATTRIBUTES
AND CONTRIBUTIONS

VISUAL ARTS

The Ernst-Ludwig-Kirchner center at Fehmarn/Burg offers more information about Kirchner's life than just his paintings. He had been forbidden to paint by the Nazis and his style condemned. Emil Nolde's experience was much the same, and his retreat has been turned into a museum at Seebull.

LITERATURE

Brothers Thomas and Heinrich Mann hailed from Lübeck, about which the former wrote in *Buddenbrooks*. In later life, they mostly associated with or challenged national values in Berlin. Ernst Barlach sold some of his sculptures to local churches, and his memory and works are celebrated with a museum at Wedel (though the museum is associated with Hamburg). Friedrich Hebbel, the idealistic dramatist, is honored with a museum at Wesselburren (Dittmarschen). In recent times, a number of authors have used the Schleswig-Holstein countryside as a quiet place to write. These include Siegfried Lenz, the Nobel Prize winner Günter Grass, and Sarah Kirsch.

More specifically tied to the region are authors such as Klaus Groth (1819–1899) and Theodor Storm (1817–1888). Groth offered his emotional poetry and novels in a regional version of Low German. His novel *Quickborn* (1853) used local characters to epitomize the strength of individuals living in tune with a harsh land. Perhaps the most representative author is Storm, whose *Schimmelreiter* (1888) novel captured some of the melancholy and isolation of the seashore.

MUSIC

Much in the way of music is offered, for example, at the manor house Salzau. This state cultural center offers a festival of jazz emphasizing ties to the Baltic cities. Carl Maria Weber (1786–1826), born in Eutin, wrote what was supposedly a national opera, *Der Freischütz*. The annual Schleswig-Holstein state-supported music festival is at present the most promoted event and takes place in various parts of the region. In addition, many cities offer a variety of music events during the summer.

CIVICS AND REMEMBRANCE

Even smaller cities such as Rendsburg have museum displays of Jewish life and its destruction during the Nazi era. At Ladelund, a former concentration camp (an extension of the main camp at Neuengamme) has been converted into a memorial and educational site. It provides an example of the history of repression under the Nazis as well as the use of slave labor in 1944. Over 300 people, out of some 2,000 inmates from a dozen countries, died.

The state office for political education in Kiel fosters understanding of parliamentary democracy and regional history. Part of that history is devoted to exposing the Nazi past, its concentration camps, and persecutions. Another part seeks to present Schleswig-Holstein history, including fostering an identity for the whole region. The refugees and exiles from the east have received attention since they made up a large part of the experience of the region. Recent publications of the office for political education include the Jewish history in Schleswig-Holstein, traits of the region, women, and democracy. Conferences about having to leave eastern German territories after World War II address the refugee question.

CUISINE

As in Hamburg, eel soup remains a traditional dish, but in Schleswig-Holstein it is cooked with a variety of meats. As in Bremen, *Kohl und Pinkel* (kale with grit sausage), is common in winter. Since Dittmarschen is the cabbage capital of the country, many dishes include various types of cabbage. Another local dish is buttermilk soup, which contains smoked sausage. Fish such as flounder and plaice are served plainly grilled but sometimes with *Speck* (bacon) and served with *Stachelbeerkompot* (gooseberry jelly). Smoked fish, or sprats, is readily found in markets. A truly hearty breakfast is a *Schnitzel Holstein*, named after the duke who loved a big veal cutlet topped by a fried egg, anchovies, sliced beets and pickles, and a large side dish of fried potatoes. Specialty sweets exist in many German places, but gourmands claim that Lübeck marzipan—a mix of almond paste with rose water covered in chocolate—is in a class of its own.

A traditional dish in central Schleswig-Holstein is *Birnen, Bohnen, und Speck* (pears, beans, and bacon). This version of a one-pot meal is eaten when beans ripen, using smoked *Speck*.

Pears, Beans, and Speck

2 pounds of bush beans	14-ounce can of pears
1/4 pound Speck, diced	

Lightly steam beans for 3 to 4 minutes. Sauté Speck and beans together for a couple of minutes, then add pears and cook briefly until heated through.

Chapter 16

Thuringia

SPECIAL ASPECTS

Forests and centrality, or "Germany's green heart," are frequently used to describe the region. One of the smaller, less-populated eastern states, Thuringia was reconstituted after Reunification in 1990. Geographically at the center of the reunified country, Thuringia seeks to provide major transportation contacts by widened *autobahns* and high-speed trains. This would restore its ancient role as central trading axis in Europe. Advertising itself as Germany's strong center, it emphasizes its universities and research and high level of culture. In seeking to attract new companies, end the outflow of residents, and bring in tourists, state representatives claim Thuringia provides a calm lifestyle. Advertising focuses on "Classical Weimar," the sites where the literary giants Johann von Goethe and Friedrich Schiller worked and wandered. Proximity to unspoiled nature in spas and primeval forests is a repeated theme for visitors. Though this region helped establish High German as the national language, many local dialects remain in use.

REGIONAL TRAITS

Some 2.5 million people live in 16,000 square kilometers. The majority of the populace resides in midsized cities that stretch in a line across the north: Eisenach, Gotha, Erfurt, Weimar, Jena, Gera, Altenburg. Though medieval remains such as castles and cloisters abound, two eras, the Reformation and the Enlightenment, decisively impacted the region. That is evident in a few names from the many whose influence went far beyond the region: Martin Luther, Lucas Cranach, Thomas Müntzer, Johann von Goethe, Johann Herder, and Friedrich Schiller. The cultural

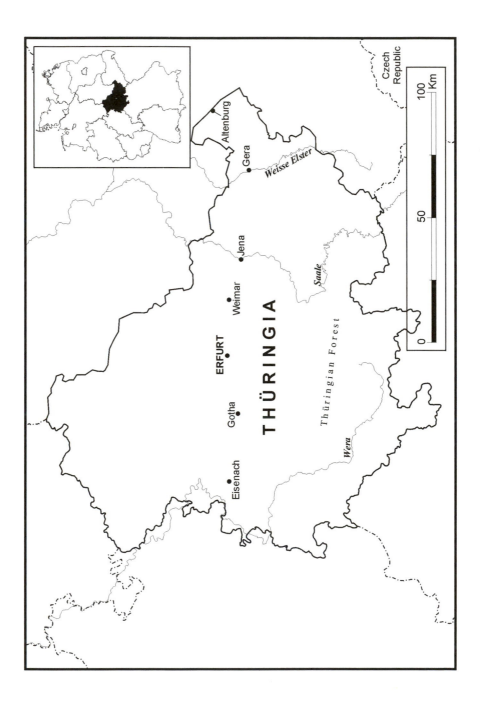

contributions associated with those names frequently legitimized the claim to being Germany's heart. The flag and coat of arms is a lion with red and white stripes surrounded by eight white stars representing historical units.

GEOGRAPHIC FEATURES

The hilly, partly mountainous countryside has many forested uplands, small farms, and tiny villages. The latter contain many specialty crafts, such as glassblowing and wood carving, because of the availability of wood and water. The Saale River, sometimes widened by electrical dams, runs south to north providing a link from Saalfeld to Rudolstadt and Jena. West of the region is Hesse starting at the Werra River, to the south Bavaria, and to the southeast, past the Weisse Elster River, lies Saxony. The northwest just touches Lower Saxony and Saxony-Anhalt. The large Thuringian Basin with its good soils makes specialty agriculture an important economic activity. The Thuringia Forest, stretching along the south of the whole region, and Saale River valley provide escape for leisure. The Rennsteig hiking trail along the major height of land runs the length of the Thuringia Forest. The *Grosse Beerberg* is the highest point at 982 meters (3,000 feet).

HISTORY

The present state comprises numerous historical entities, some of which have overlapping and some quite separate histories. Just as Germany's central location in Europe led to many boundary changes, so too has Thuringia's, due to dynastic marriage or inheritance arrangements and especially due to wars.

Long before those medieval and early modern patterns emerged, prehistoric hunters ranged the woodlands. Remains of skulls at Ehringsdorf near Weimar document *Homo sapiens* going back perhaps 100,000 years. By 10,000 B.C., clans making pottery had shifted to a more sedentary lifestyle. Metal, especially bronze, and woven cloth have been found in the *Hügelgräber*, or burial mounds, some with large stone markers. Fine jewelry demonstrated artistic skill, and stone walls around major hills reflected military capability in defensive settlements, for instance, at Gross Gleichberg. The Celts who entered this area from the south enlarged the fortifications. They have left many grave sites from which weapons, tools, and jewelry have been excavated as at Eischleben, Körner, and Römhild. When the Romans began to impinge on the region by 100 A.D., they found a fairly unified, tough group whom they termed Thuringi. Later, those people proved able to defend themselves against Saxons and Franks from the west. They allied with the invading Huns during the fourth century. When the Huns were defeated farther west, the Thuringia drew back and developed their own region.

From this era an identity of regional unity developed, despite all the later divisions. But by 531, the Saxons and Franks defeated the Thuringians, and the Franks began a lengthy dominance. However, Saxons and Slavs, who respectively occupied western and eastern parts of the territory, kept challenging that dominance. Simultaneously, Christianity brought a new dimension to the outside influences. Erfurt attained the status of a Catholic bishopric with obligations west as far as Mainz and endless missionary efforts to the east. To defend the Frank's Carolingian realm, fortresses appeared on nearly every hilltop. From the eighth to the fifteenth centuries, hundreds emerged, many of which still exist.

The fortresses served to defend the trade routes that ran in both directions through the region. That trade in fish, furs, salt, and metals (iron from the Thuringia hills) gave it the material basis upon which cultural riches of universities and Romanesque and Gothic churches were built during the medieval and Renaissance eras. From Spain and France through the Thuringian cities toward Russia, the route ran along a course, which the nineteenth-century railway would follow. North-south, another trade route tied coastal cities to Nuremberg and southern trade goods.

Two periods proved especially crucial to the history of the area and to the identity of the region. The Lutheran Reformation, in its widest cultural and social sense, and the Enlightenment's intellectual fervor provided Thuringia with the ammunition to claim itself "Germany's strong heart." During the Weimar Republic and again recently, both the political left and right claimed that national heritage for themselves, with widely different meanings attributed to German identity.

The Reformation amounted to a religious and social upheaval. Debates about religious belief and rituals occurred in every village and city. The Protestants won though they remained dependent upon the princes, such as Frederick the Wise of Saxony who helped Martin Luther after his banishment. Luther hid at the Wartburg castle near Eisenach in 1521 and translated the Bible. However, the Reformation challenged authority in many forms. Some Protestants thought social reforms as necessary as religious ones. The preacher Thomas Müntzer organized peasants to revolt against the endless controls and taxes of the lords. In towns such as Mühlhausen, merchants and artisans had demanded participatory rights in the city council. Thus, they identified with Müntzer's cause. The lords and princes brutally repressed the social uprising, though Protestantism triumphed. In the GDR the rebelling peasants and artisans, but especially Müntzer, attained heroic status. A huge panorama (over 1,700 square meters) from the 1980s by Werner Tübke, in the style of Pieter Brueghel's canvases, depicts the epic struggle of the last major battle in the Peasant's War at Frankenhausen. This is still a tourist attraction. But after Reunification in 1990, Luther has far outdistanced the radicals in historical memory. Sites associated with Luther have been refurbished and events relating to his life identified for tourists.

The third element of the Renaissance/Reformation era often is given too little attention. The Renaissance humanistic studies that led to the Reformation had emerged from strong universities such as at Erfurt, where Luther studied, and Jena. In addition, that Renaissance included the development of visual arts, especially painting and sculpting (for instance, altars carved from lime wood). Those activities, like choral music, were church related and often supported by the *Stadtbürgertum*, the better-off urban commercial and artisan leaders. One member of that group, the portrait painter Lucas Cranach (1472–1553), left strong traces in Weimar: his decorated house and his grave with a sculpture of him. Most of the buildings of his contemporaries were damaged in wars and some were simply replaced in the next stage of economic growth. Sometimes they lost out to the preferences for a different style. Another artisan craftsman, Tilman Riemenschneider (1460–1531), learned the craft of carving by wandering the region and left evidence of his skills at the church in Bebra.

The religious wars in the wake of the Reformation followed endless dynastic conflicts for control over the Thuringian Basin. The Holy Roman emperor repeatedly sought to regain the area for Catholicism, even sending the murderous Spanish Duke of Alba against the Thuringian Protestants united in the Schmalkalden League. Though the Protestant states lost the territorial war, they won religiously in Thuringia, except for a northern area around Eichsfeld (and for a time, Erfurt), which remained Catholic. Four major dukedoms emerged: Saxony-Weimar, Saxony-Gotha (later Saxony-Coburg-Gotha), Saxony-Eisenach, and Saxony-Altenburg. After the devastation of the Thirty Years' War, Duke Ernst (the Pious) of Gotha developed an absolutist state that fostered academic improvements at higher-level schools and the university of Jena. He rebuilt the Renaissance palace in Gotha as a residence and administrative center. His court supported serious church music. Hence, another name became intimately tied to Weimar, Johann Sebastian Bach. Born in Eisenach, Bach served in various churches before becoming court music director in 1714 for seven years. The duke granted small territories to each of his own 18 children, and in each fiefdom palaces appeared including some with theaters and support for musical entertainment. Under Ernst August I (1707–1748)—a brutal ruler—the building of baroque palaces greatly expanded, among other places at Weimar, Rudolstadt, and Gera.

Thuringia's great cultural spree came in 1775 with August I's successor, Carl August. Weimar, as a court, influenced many other dynastic centers. Its version of the Enlightenment era demonstrated the dominance of the aristocracy as well as the cultural revival of the area after the devastation of the Thirty Years War. Usually identified with the intellectual giants Goethe and Schiller, the court-supported cultural endeavors moved in much broader currents. Among many, the poet Christoph Martin Wieland and the preacher and philosopher Johann Gottfried Herder worked at the court. The duke's mother, Anna Amalia, had hired Wieland as a tutor. In many ways, she initiated the court's new flowering as she introduced Carl August to Goethe.

Later (1826), Joseph Meyer published his *Conversations-Lexikon* in Gotha, one of the leading and popular encyclopedias. It became a standard German reference work for the next century.

The history of Thuringia has been tied to the interests of its neighbors and the princes who ruled it. For instance, during the Reformation, Frederick the Wise of Saxony defended and hid Martin Luther, while during the Enlightenment, Duke Carl August of Saxony-Weimar-Eisenach tried to compete with larger courts in cultural opulence. Like his predecessors, Carl August dallied in the usual aristocratic pastimes of constructing palaces and gardens. However, politically and socially, all the Thuringian states remained backward if one looks beyond the court and high culture.

The Napoleonic reorganization of German states impacted strongly on the region. Thuringia became part of the French-dominated Rhineland Federation and had to pay high occupation costs. However, administrative reforms gave the cities greater self-government and a rudimentary constitution, decreed by the duke of Saxony-Weimar in 1809. The name Thuringia reappeared as a designation for the region; however, the Congress of Vienna recognized at least eight dukedoms in 1815, so that small-state political divisions remained.

During the nineteenth century, partial industrialization increased labor migration to the cities, though small-scale agriculture and handicrafts remained significant for employment. Special metalworks (guns were made at Suhl) hinted at the economic potential in the small handicrafts. Making toys, textiles, and porcelain dominated the village-based economy functioning on a putting-out system. Glassblowing proved especially important for scientific instruments. An economic boost came from the rail lines punched through the landscape in both directions. Eventually, a large repair depot at Meiningen became the basis for restoring and renovating locomotives.

After midcentury, Carl Zeiss developed optical instruments with the help of a Jena professor adept in the physics of optical refraction, Ernst Abbe. Simultaneously, Otto Schott developed novel ways to reconstitute glass, making it impervious to high temperature fluctuations. Despite spectacular successes by the Zeiss and Schott optics and glass factories, Thuringia remained relatively undeveloped compared to neighboring Saxony. However, a strong urban labor movement emerged from among journeymen artisans. The state, which proved more liberal than Prussia, allowed Social Democratic congresses to be held on its territory during the Imperial era when the party was still outlawed or suffered repression for its radical challenge to an authoritarian society with horrible working and living conditions. The list of places at which the Social Democratic Party held congresses reads like the names on the axis of cities in Thuringia: Gotha, Eisenach, Erfurt, Jena. Social Democracy did well in the region despite the electoral restrictions, which excluded women and those with little property. Suffrage for all, including women, would only be achieved when the Social Democrats came to power in 1918, overthrowing the Thuringian and Saxon rulers.

By 1920, because of adjustments of boundaries with Prussia and the dissolution of small states in 1917, the present configuration of Thuringia emerged. By 1921 it had a democratic constitution. During the Weimar Republic, Thuringia demonstrated extreme diversity in politics, economics, and culture. For example, ultramodern architecture and art developed at Weimar in the Bauhaus led by Walter Gropius. But it did not last past the mid-1920s, as the middle classes did not wish to fund such experiments. Economically, metal and machine building expanded to meet railway needs, especially since Erfurt became the crossroads of the national rail system. The Depression of 1929 forced drastic employment and salary reductions. Similarly, in politics after the revolution in 1918, a left-wing SPD coalition government emerged that in 1920 helped defeat a right-wing attempt to restore the military and aristocratic prewar system. By 1923, the Thuringian government moved further left in coalition with the Communists. The national government dissolved it, after which the political right gained strength. Thanks to the Great Depression, by 1930 National Socialism had made sufficient membership and voting gains to be in the government. Their minister responsible for culture quickly outlawed alleged or so-called *Negerkultur* (Negro culture). The state became a comfortable spot for the Nazis and those who thought in terms of "race and *Volkstum* [pure people], blood, and soil." Hence, Thuringia melded quickly into the Nazi system when they achieved power nationally in 1933. Initially, some worker groups offered resistance to the repression of the regime. But Thuringia quickly became homogenized within the Third Reich, under the direction of a Nazi district leader. Industries such as optics and metals increasingly shifted to armaments or military-support production. The repressive side of the regime appeared in 1933 with Buchenwald concentration camp, near Weimar. At first it mainly held Communists and Social Democrats for supposed reeducation; by 1938, Jews and "asocials" were confined; later it became a place of death for thousands. The Gustloff small armaments firm established itself next to the camp to exploit inmates as cheap labor.

The cultural festivals associated with Luther, Schiller, and Goethe continued throughout the Nazi era. Increasingly, the emphasis shifted to German purity, national unity, and assertions that those intellectuals would have welcomed the Nazi renewal of German "idealism." Weimar, as district *(Gau)* city, welcomed Hitler on the Adolf Hitler Platz and built the first "hall of the people's community." Another hall honored philosopher Friedrich Nietzsche and yet another William Shakespeare. The role of Jews as seen by composer Richard Wagner in supposedly ruining German music received approval. In 1940 the local elite had no difficulty, in the presence of Hitler's representative, to claim unity with the top of the party, the state, and the military, as well as being grateful to the "green heart of Germany, the beautiful Thuringia."

During World War II, thousands of slave laborers from eastern Europe worked in the armament industries. To avoid bombs, the Nazi regime had slave laborers tunnel new industrial installations into the rock walls of hillsides and mountains. Less war damage by bombing meant that Thuringia served as a refuge for Germans from Poland and eastern areas, as well as having better living conditions in the immediate postwar era.

Though American troops liberated most of Thuringia in April 1945, by Allied agreement the area came under Soviet control in July. The Soviet military occupation after 1945 introduced a new set of controls in politics and society. They immediately replaced the anti-Fascist Social Democrat, Hermann Brill. De-Nazification dispossessed many industrialists, and land reform redistributed large estates. Industrial plants were taken as reparations. The cultural icons Goethe and Schiller were honored by the Soviet military as bearers of tolerance and freedom for all humanity. In 1949, Goethe's 200th birthday, or the Goethe Year, the Socialist Unity Party used him for legitimizing their emphasis on the cultural appreciation of Goethe by the German working class. Novelist Thomas Mann attended but spoke in measured words about not being Communist as well as not being anti-Communist.

By 1949, thorough border controls to the West tried to limit population movement. By then the GDR included Thuringia as one of its regional states. That state disappeared into three administrative districts centered on Erfurt, Gera, and Suhl in 1952.

During the GDR era, the region had the geographic disadvantage of being adjacent to the closed border. Economically small industries, including toys and glass, plus automobile production as at Eisenach, continued pre–World War II traditions. But huge energy installations at Gera and the expansion of Jena's optics and glass-works brought workers to the main cities. Few industries achieved high-technological capabilities, but the influx of workers meant building prefabricated and unsightly apartment blocks. Among the industrial centers and industries that received large investments and attained high standards in the GDR were microchips at Erfurt and the Zeiss optical works at Jena.

A social transformation took place in rural towns. Diverse occupational and educational opportunities opened for women. The state provided support for children and families so that society became more equal. Though some places found themselves "at the end of the world" geographically, they developed assumptions about social rights. Frequently, strong communal ties maintained an older sense of local identity. In this "niche society," little farms and crafts maintained continuity with German folk traditions, including Catholic rituals in the Eichsfeld area.

After Reunification, Thuringia reappeared as a federal state in 1990. Many industrial firms disappeared due to competition with the West. Large collective farms were divided. Even the more modern firms had difficulties. The optical industry, for instance, lost more than a third of its workforce in five years through reorganization. Since then, high unemployment has plagued development, but the beginning of an economic shift to high-tech industries has been made. The Eisenach Wartburg auto-mobile plant has been converted into a modern production system. BMW once operated at Eisenach and has returned. Opel, the German subsidiary of General Motors, also has a new and highly productive plant. A core of specialized labor exists in industrial cities such as Gera and Jena where Jenaoptik and Schott have plants. Newer universities at Ilmenau, Schmalkalden, and a recent addition at Nordhausen have joined the famous ones at Jena and Erfurt. All give priority to working with industrial and financial partners, with most of the latter being western German firms.

Politically, Thuringia, since Reunification, has been a place of party competi-tion. At first, until 1994, the Christian Democratic Union (CDU) led a coalition with the liberals. In 1994, once the economic difficulties had reached serious levels, a Great Coalition of CDU and Social Democracy (SPD) sought to stabilize the sit-uation. In 1999, the CDU gained a majority and ruled on its own. The prime min-ister was Bernhard Vogel, who had been head of Rhineland-Palatinate, but he has been replaced by Dieter Althaus (CDU). In the 2004 *Landtag* elections, the CDU obtained a majority under Althaus but with reduced votes (down 5 percent). The SPD declined to 14.5 percent (down 4 percent), while the Party of Democratic Socialism (PDS, or liberalized Communists) increased to 26 percent.

Does being repeatedly squeezed by outside influences in nearly every era create a populace with a defensive air and reserve toward foreigners? Has the double cultural blossoming of the Reformation and Enlightenment eras and the continued access to unspoiled nature provided the base for a local pride that will sustain the region into a new technological era? Thuringia seems underdeveloped, but its present political leaders think a positive answer to such questions is possible as they reemphasize the cultural heritage of the region.

ECONOMY

In Germany, Thuringia is in last place in terms of economic productivity and output. The large firms of Zeiss and Schott at Jena have moved to western management styles, which mean drastically reduced employment. Jenaoptik and the construction materials firm Mühl have become publicly traded companies. The latter has declared bankruptcy. Presently, tourism is being touted. For example, state funds have been spent to expand winter sport facilities at Oberhof and to develop the cultural sites associated with Luther and the Reformation. Small industries such as toys, glass, and guns continue to produce, but growth is limited. The Gera electricity and energy sector have been downsized since Reunification, so fewer jobs exist in more competitive plants. However, at Kölleda near Sömmerda, a modern motor factory is being erected.

Agriculture has shifted to agrarian-business from the collective farms by keeping large holdings. They seem to have survived the transition. Growing specialty barley for beer brewing continues a long tradition.

The research potential of the universities, especially with direct contacts to industrial firms, is one of the hopes for the future. The technical university at Ilmenau is supposed to supply in microelectronics and machine building what Jena has done in optics. Glass-related industries continue a regional strength.

———————— MAIN CITIES ————————

CAPITAL

Erfurt (population 203,000). The "city of flowers" contains many fine patrician houses, churches, and monasteries. Its cathedral, numerous churches, and cloisters once gave it the name of German Rome. Crossroads of travel routes, especially of trains and *autobahns*, make it the center of the state politically and economically as well as administratively. For over a century under Prussian control, the early nineteenth-century city had to recover from being burned by Napoleon.

Located on the Gera River, its *Krämer* (peddlar's) bridge still supports commercial houses (like Ponte Vecchio in Florence). A few half-timbered houses survived along the Anger, a street that also contains neo-Gothic and art nouveau examples from the late nineteenth and early twentieth centuries. City rebuilding during the 1950s broke open some of the medieval street pattern.

Large gardens, including an eighteenth-century botanical and church or cloister grounds, provide green space. Numerous regional museums (about the city, natural history, garden history, and area history) are typical of an administrative city. With a large Siemens plant, major university, and unspoiled surroundings, the city presents itself as modern yet tied to its regional past.

Gera (population 115,000). This industrial city produces machine and gas tur-bine parts and has ties to the energy industries. Huge industrial chimneys (600 feet) and prefabricated housing complexes attest to the GDR attempt to foster industrial growth. Its old city core is still fairly extant, dominated by the high steeple of its Renaissance *Rathaus*.

Jena (population 100,000). The city is known for the Zeiss optical and glassworks founded in 1854. Famous people, such as Karl Marx, attended Jena's university. That institution developed high-level research labs and worked with local companies, especially during the Communist era, so that optical instruments, ceramics, and glass technology continued to be developed. Parts of the old city contain half-timbered houses and traditional student pubs. The battlefield where Napoleon defeated the Prussians in 1806 is close to the city and underscores the external influences acting on this region.

Weimar (population 62,000). This beautiful small city, which was spared World War II bombing, is famous for its identification with the humanistic spirit associated with Friedrich Schiller and Johann von Goethe. In 1919, Weimar hosted the National Assembly in the National Theater, where the first democratic constitution of Germany was written. The square in front of the theater has a statue of the two literary giants. Goethe's house is preserved, and visitors can see original furnishings as well as manuscripts. His country house and Schiller's residence have also been pre-served, as well as those of many contemporaries such as Charlotte von Stein. Many rich traders' and artists' half-timbered houses, such as that of Lucas Cranach, the por-trait painter, illustrate the decorative style and earlier prosperity of the urban artisans.

Selected as the Cultural City of Europe in 1999, Weimar's economy received a large tourist boost by the many subsidized concerts, readings, and presentations, most of which centered on Goethe, Schiller, and Bach.

Gotha (population 49,000). Some of the medieval city core remains. In the late nineteenth century, the labor movement held congresses here. Perched above the city is the largest castle in Thuringia, *Friedenstein*, built in the mid-seventeenth century. Now it contains the city's main theater and museums (natural history and artifacts). The city boasts easy access to nature, especially hiking trails and parks.

Eisenach (population 44,000). Before Reunification, the Wartburg automobile rolled off outdated assembly lines. Now Opel and BMW have major plants as the city seeks to revitalize industries and gain western markets. The Wartburg castle, a UNESCO heritage site, sits above the city and remains its main tourist attraction, though the city has sought to emphasize other sites in the region related to Luther.

ATTRACTIONS

Martin Luther led the Protestant Reformation, and many of the places related to his life are scattered throughout Thuringia. Foremost is his study in the *Wartburg* at Eisenach, where he translated the Bible and supposedly threw an inkwell at the devil.

Figure 16.1
Wartburg, Thuringia, showing old city wall fortification. The Wartburg was
Martin Luther's hideaway in 1521.

Source Courtesy of the author.

Over the centuries, crafts such as glassblowing and making Christmas decorations have provided employment in small villages and towns. In the village of
Lauscha, glassblowing has existed for centuries. Since the mid-nineteenth century,
the artisans have employed centralized gas blowers and thus could create wonderful
decorations en masse but with individualized shapes. The shops and furnaces can be
visited. Though now also mass-produced in other countries, garden dwarfs originated in the village of Graftenröder, where they are still made of clay and wood.

Due to deep valleys and difficult terrain for laying railway track, bridges are plentiful. One marvel is the Göltzschtal Bridge, built in the arch fashion of Roman aqueducts. It is 78 meters (200 feet) high and 574 meters (16,000 feet) long and was completed out of red sandstone in 1851.

Castles and palaces in the countryside match museums and galleries in the large cities. For example, the castles *Friedenstein* in Gotha or *Heidecksburg* in Rudolstadt have been well restored. The *Wartburg*, a UNESCO World Heritage Site, is the most famous, and tourists seeking traces of Luther and what inspired his beliefs come from all over the world to see it. Some visitors ride donkeys up the fairly steep hill on which the large castle complex with restaurants and boutiques sits.

The forests and valleys provide extensive areas to hike, ski, and relax in spas. Winter sports opportunities abound in the highlands, especially at Oberhof. Known for one of Europe's main ski jumps, it also offers cross-country and some downhill skiing. Many spas can be identified with the word *Bad* (bath) in front of the name, and some have become resort centers with extensive amenities for well-to-do urban-ites. A very extensive system of hiking trails crisscrosses the region, with the *Rennsteig* being among Germany's longest. It goes along the crest of mountains, like the Appalachian Trail in the eastern United States.

A favorite activity of the aristocracy was to modify nature to attain a particular harmony or variety. This desire, plus attempts to collect specimens for educational and medicinal purposes, led to creating gardens. Botanic ones can be found at Jena, started in 1586 for medical studies. Its collection of mountain plants is extensive, but other species are well represented. Another special alpine collection is worthwhile for its location as well as its worldwide scope at the *Oberhof Rennsteig* gardens high in the hills above Gotha. It started in GDR days. For examples of the more classical, aristocratic, sculpted variety, Weimar offers a palace garden at the *Belvedere* and at Tiefurt. A small but charming one is Goethe's rose garden on the Ilm River. These gardens adjoin summer residences. Some, by having been overgrown, have attained a greater naturalness.

The cities and towns left a different heritage, often in the form of half-timbered buildings. A fine example of the stylized wood patterns by which towns or individuals made their decorative mark is the *Rathaus* at Heinrichs, a village that is now a suburb of Suhl. Above the stone foundations, the *Wartburg* also illustrates the use of partly rounded timbers. In Wasungen, the main street has many buildings with rectangles and elongated crisscross patterns between the main timbers.

Weimar's long list of attractions has already been noted, but its National Theater, and the many sites relating to Goethe and Schiller, are set in a fine urban landscape. Shopping streets with tiny boutiques were developed in the 1990s.

Mühlhausen retains a compact old central district, including much of its medieval wall and gates. Some of the medieval public buildings, such as the *Rathaus*, churches, and cloisters, remain. Tiny streets run in all directions. Altenburg also has a medieval core, and its palace with park is a huge reminder that this more industrialized city once was a prince's court residence, but it has had little attention since 1918.

CUSTOMS

Though Bach *Wochen* (Weeks) are held in all major cities, popular are the annual *Fassnachte*, or night carnivals. For example, the Wasungen *Fassnacht*, started in 1322, is a festival with dress-up processions, sausage stands, and dancing. Fairs are frequent in towns and villages during the autumn. Eisenach's *Sommergewinn* is very popular and traditional: The symbolic burning of a man of straw who represents winter follows processions and activities on what are called celebration meadows. The Catholic Eichsfeld area has its own church processions and festivities. Theater, one of the strengths of the eighteenth-century ducal courts, has continued in Weimar and Erfurt, but the lack of financial support has made its future questionable.

CULTURAL ATTRIBUTES
AND CONTRIBUTIONS

VISUAL ARTS

Wooden and metal toys are as much an art as a craft, as are the altars, choir chairs, and other church embellishments common in the region. Porcelain decorating employed many artists in an area once rich in factories where "white gold" was invented in the eighteenth century.

LITERATURE

The cultural giants who enlivened the Weimar court, Johann Wolfgang von Goethe and Friedrich Schiller, figure large in the standard courses on German literature. Goethe's poetry ("Über allen Gipfeln ist Ruh' . . . " [above all summits is peace . . .]) and plays such as *Faust* are classics not only in Germany but in most languages of the world. Schiller's historical plays, such as *Maria Stuart* or *Wallenstein*, have attained similar stature. These thinkers, like Shakespeare, addressed basic human motivations and couched their findings in refined but accessible and beautiful language.

Wieland's poetry is more emotive and Herder's theoretical writings more known for having helped define the concept of the nation. Not to be forgotten were the important roles women played in this society, as mistresses, as inspiration, and as salon leaders. For example, Charlotte von Stein, in addition to a long liaison with Goethe, had literary ambitions that were partly fulfilled. All these intellectuals provided an atmosphere for the Weimar court, which made it the envy of Europe.

Cultural contributions in Thuringia did not end with eighteenth-century Weimar. The nineteenth and twentieth centuries saw many regional variants. A precursor of television's soap operas can be found in the stories of Eugenie John Marlitt. Many of these romances appeared in installments in the entertainment weeklies during the 1870s. Friedrich Nietzsche is also identified with the area since his sister deposited his archive in Weimar.

GDR authors continued the literary tradition by establishing a national research center in 1954 for classical German literature.

MUSIC

Orchestras and choirs continue a music tradition partly based on church origins. The Weimar cultural festival, the Thuringian Bach Weeks, and summer organ presentations complement the Rudolstadt dance and folk festival.

CIVICS AND REMEMBRANCE

The central office for political education offers publications about the history of the region. A dual track is followed: first, fostering democracy by offering materials, presentations, and seminars especially for school-age students on parliament, political parties, and on being an informed, involved citizen. A second effort involves upholding the memory and acknowledging the negative past of the Nazi era. The latter includes placing plaques where Jews, *Roma,* or homosexuals were attacked or made to disappear. A sample program of lectures during 2003 included "Child Euthanasia in Thuringia," "Concentration Camps as Sites of Remembrance," and "Terror against Homosexuals." Since Reunification, much emphasis has been placed on the sites where persecution took place and resistance existed during the GDR era. For example, the Stasi office in Bad Langensalza has become a memorial site for anti-Fascist victims, at Bettenhausen a plaque honors those exiled from the GDR, and at Erfurt a documentation center presents the Stasi working methods. Others, as at Jena, honor those who revolted against the regime in June 1953. A whole museum dedicated to the division of the country is at Eichsfeld.

Buchenwald, just outside Weimar, remains the most important regional site of Nazi atrocities. The very large concentration camp has been preserved and partly restored. A statue by Fritz Cremer memorializes the inmates and a museum provides educational information. At *Dora-Nordhausen,* where slave laborers worked to place German rocket installations underground in the Harz Mountains, a memorial site commemorates the 16,000 who lost their lives there.

CUISINE

Thuringia *bratwurst* is perhaps the most famous culinary item that has spread to many parts of Germany. The sausage contains a mix of roughly ground pork with some fat, lightly stuffed into the pork covering so that it cracks when grilled. Cardamom seed goes inside, mustard is outside. It is served with ends overlapping a tiny round bun. Wild boar, from the forests where they feed on oak acorns, serves gourmet tastes, while geese from small farms are common on festive occasions. *Klösse* (potato dumplings) must be light, according to one regional expert. They are made similar to Perogen in Mecklenburg in that the moisture is squeezed from raw grated potatoes. Some of the starch, which collects under the squeezed-out moisture, is then used to combine the raw grated potatoes with the cooked mashed potatoes to make a dumpling. They are placed in boiling water until they rise. Filled with roasted breadcrumbs, they make a meal in themselves.

Another local specialty is cakes, whether onion or fruit on pastry. Supposedly, at real farmers' weddings at least 20 varieties appear. Beer remains the customary drink, and special dark beers (*Köstritzer*, for example) compete with other local brews.

CHRISTMAS GOOSE

A 7- to 8-pound goose serves 8.

Filling:

2 large onions, diced	1 cup white bread crumbs
butter	2 eggs
4 cloves garlic, crushed	2 tablespoons (or more) sherry
goose liver, finely chopped	salt, pepper, and marjoram to taste
1 pound ground lean beef	

Preheat oven to 400°F. Sauté onion in butter until translucent. Add garlic, goose liver, ground beef, bread crumbs, eggs, and sherry. Add salt, pepper, and marjoram to taste. Stuff into washed goose, which has been lightly rubbed with salt. Sew shut or pin. Oil bottom of roasting pan lightly (put goose on rack in pan). Once goose is in the oven, baste every 30 minutes, adding a bit of water if necessary. Roast for 25 minutes per pound. For a crispy skin, brush goose with saltwater during last basting. Let stand for 10 minutes in open oven (heat off). To make gravy, pour drippings into fat remover, then into saucepan, add more sherry, and reduce while goose rests. Serve with roasted potatoes and cauliflower.

Glossary

Altstadt: old city

Autobahn: freeway

Bad: spa or bath

Bayern: Bavaria

Burg: castle or fortress

Bürger: citizen

CDU: Christian Democratic Union

CSU: Christian Social Union

Dom: cathedral

Döner Kebab: Turkish sliced meats served in a pita

Eisbein: smoked pig's hocks

Fachwerk: half-timbering

Fasnet/Fasching/Fassnacht: carnival

FC: football club

FDP: Free Democratic Party

Freikorps: volunteer troops after World War I

Freilichtmuseum: open-air museum

Gau: district

GDR: German Democratic Republic—former East Germany

Gemütlich: convivial

Glühwein: mulled wine

Heimat: homeland

Hessen: Hesse

KPD: Communist Party of Germany

Land: state

Länder: regions

Landtag: state parliament

Lebkuchen: honey cakes

Mecklenburg-Vorpommern: Mecklenburg-Western Pomerania

NSDAP: National Socialist German Worker's Party-Nazis

Niedersachsen: Lower Saxony

Nordrhein-Westfalen: North Rhine-Westphalia (NRW)

Ossies: term for former East Germans

PDS: Party of Democratic Socialism

Pfalz: Palatinate

Rathaus: city hall

Reichstage: Imperial diets

Rheinland-Pfalz: Rhineland-Palatinate

Sachsen: Saxony

Sachsen-Anhalt: Saxony-Anhalt

Schloss: castle or palace

SED: Socialist Unity Party

SPD: Social Democratic Party

Spaetzle: pasta

Stasi: state security or secret police of East Germany

Thüringen: Thuringia

Trachten: local costumes

Volksfest: people's holiday

Weindorf: wine village

Wessies: term for former West Germans

Westfalen: Westphalia

Zwiebelkuchen: onion cake

Chronology

9 A.D.	German tribes under Arminius defeated Roman legions at Teutoburger Forest, hindering Roman advance eastward.
200–400	Germanic tribes (Goths, Lombards, Visgoths, Angle-Saxons) conquered parts of the Roman Empire and established themselves in present-day Spain, Italy, France, and Britain while Franks, Allemannes, Saxons, Frisians, among others, established territorial realms in what would become German-speaking lands.
800	Karl, king of the Franks (Charlemagne of the Carolingian line) based at Aachen, was crowned in Rome to legitimize his empire, though it would be divided among his sons with the eastern section forming the basis of the later Germanic territories.
919	Henry of the Saxons was elected monarch and established the Ottoian central European empire.
Ninth–thirteenth centuries	Towns such as Bremen, Cologne, Hamburg, Berlin, Frankfurt, Nuremburg, and Augsburg established and eventually became cities with trading rights.
962	Otto II controlled most of present-day German territory and sought to re-create Charlemagne's realm though various linguistic and ethnic groups such as the Thuringians, Bavarians, Alemannes, and Saxons continued to operate as independent counts and dukes.

1024	Salian monarchs struggled for supremacy against the papacy using the term the Holy Roman Empire after 1157, but regional and linguistic differences predominated among Franks, Saxons, Frisians, Thuringians, Bavarians, Guelphs, and Swabians within the realm.
Twelfth and thirteenth centuries	Concept of a two-part Reich, comprising a monarch and regional territories, established the legal basis for regionalism. The monarch was seen as the equivalent to the head while the territories, led by various counts, were seen as parts of the body.
Thirteenth–sixteenth centuries	League of Hanseatic cities, which included Bremen, Cologne, Hamburg, Lübeck (among others from Novgorod to Paris), controlled most trade in northern Europe.
1517	Martin Luther challenged the papacy, which marked the beginning of the Protestant Reformation. He received support from the central and northern regionally-based princes. Protestants appealed to the aristocracy of the German nation, underscoring the importance of independent territories within the empire.
1500s	Spread of the Reformation by debates, warfare, and conversion reinforced princely control of various regions as religious beliefs related to princes' territories by 1555. The main dates of the acceptance of Protestantism include Saxon states, 1522–1539; Hesse, 1527; Württemberg, 1536; Pomerania, 1534; Brandenburg, 1539; Holstein, 1542; Mecklenburg, 1549; and Palatinate, 1556.
1618–1648	Thirty Years' War devastated most of central Europe as Swedish and French troops pillaged the country and inflation destroyed the economy, bringing drastic population decline. The German states and cities such as Magdeburg were especially hard-hit. The Holy Roman Empire of the German Nation under the Austrian Hapsburg dynasty only nominally controlled the realm compared to the territorial states, which consolidated their local power bases in Saxony, Bavaria, and Brandenburg.
Seventeenth–eighteenth centuries	Territorial growth and the rise to great power status of the Prussian-Brandenburg state, which challenged Hapsburg Austrians, Saxon Polish monarchs, and Bavarian Wittelbachs for preeminence in the German-speaking realm.
1803	Holy Roman Empire of the German Nation was dissolved by Napoleon Bonaparte who ended sovereignty of many petty states, princedoms, city-states, and bishoprics. He annexed large parts of western German-speaking states to France. German national liberation movements

grew in response to French taxes, occupation, and the divide-and-rule approach to the German states.

1815	Confederation created of 39 German states, including Austria, which was preeminent. This organization confirmed the diversity and the independence of regional states in Germany.
1834	Prussian-dominated customs union *(Zollverein)* tied together the northern German states.
1848	Revolutions, advocating social reform and national unity, occurred in most German states and cities. The leaders attempted to establish a national constitution but failed after intense debates about the form of the state and states, including criteria for inclusion of non-Germans.
1866	North German Confederation dominated by Prussia was forced on most northern German states (Baden, Württemberg, Bavaria not included) and explicitly excluded Austria. Hanover was taken over by Prussia.
1871	German national state *(Reich)* was founded with a federal state system but remained politically dominated by Prussia. The monarchies such as Bavaria, the princedoms such as Baden or Mecklenburg, and the city-states such as Bremen and Hamburg remained independent states within the empire.
1873	Federal regulations standardized weights, measures, and coinage, but some regional postal and railway systems remained independent.
1875	German Social Democratic Party (SPD) was formed at the Gotha congress and by the twentieth century was the largest political party with representation in all states.
1876	The Bayreuth (Bavaria) Wagner festival was inaugurated.
1878	The Semper Opera House was completed in Dresden (Saxony).
1880s–1890s	Series of radical, and sometimes racist, nationalist leagues such as the Pan Germans, the Navy League, and the Colonial Society were founded, emphasizing homogeneity within the national empire.
1882	Munich Secession art movement was established with its challenge to court norms.
1886	King Ludwig II of Bavaria, builder of castles such as *Neuschwanstein*, drowned.
1898	Berlin Secession art movement was established.

1900	New civil code set out the legal norms for the whole country.
1901	Pergamon Museum displaying a Greek altar was opened in Berlin.
1903	German Museum for Science and Technology was opened in Munich.
1905	Expressionist art group *Die Brücke* was founded in Dresden.
1911	*Der blaue Reiter*, almanac of expressionist and abstract art, was published.
1914	World War I began. Kaiser Wilhelm II declared that he knew only Germans (no parties, no separate states). Conscription and military demands led to central state direction of manpower and the economy.
1917	Anti-Berlin resentment, due to the centralization of the economy and immense loss of life, reinforced regional attachments.
1918	Mutinies in Kiel and among marines began a revolution to end the world war and to transform society. The revolutionary events spread from the seacoast to Bavaria and to Berlin.
1919	Communist Party of Germany (KPD) was established with regional strongholds in industrial cities such as Berlin and Stuttgart and the Ruhr region.
	Treaty of Versailles was signed with extensive loss of territory by Germany, especially in the east.
	First democratic constitution, adopted by the Weimar National Assembly, confirmed a federal state structure of independent regional states, though the railways were nationalized and the military centralized.
	German Workers Party (later National Socialist German Workers Party; NSDAP, or Nazis) was founded. Adolf Hitler became a member of this right-wing, racist, and radical group in Munich.
	Bauhaus school of modern architecture was established at Weimar.
1920s	Berlin became identified with modernist culture (cabarets, interactive theater, films, and music associated with individuals such as Max Reinhardt, Bertolt Brecht, Kurt Weill, and Marlene Dietrich).

1920	Eupen and Malmedy were turned over to Belgium; Danzig was proclaimed a free city.
1921	Plebiscite was held in Upper Silesia, but despite results favoring Germany, most of the territory was given to Poland.
1923	Ruhr occupation and hyperinflation fostered separatist movements in Rhineland.
1929	Economic depression devastated Germany. It resulted in a sharp increase of radical leftist (KPD) and rightist parties (Nazis) with a simultaneous decline of the political middle (liberals, SPD, Catholics), though many regional variants underscored urban/rural and social differences.
1933–1934	Establishment of the Nazi dictatorship; termination of any independence of the federal states.
1938–1939	Austria annexed; Czechoslovakia dismembered after occupation of Sudetenland.
1939	Start of World War II, occupation and annexation of Poland, creating new regions such as Warthegau.
1940	German forces invaded and occupied Denmark, Norway, Belgium, the Netherlands, and France, followed by air war against Britain.
1941	Hitler declared war of annihilation against the Soviet Union, followed by massacres of Communists and establishment of killing camps, mostly in Poland, aimed at eradication of the mentally ill, Jews, and homosexuals. War was declared on the United States.
1942–1944	Wannsee conference on Final Solution to the Jewish Question led to height of the Holocaust.
1943–1945	Height of Allied bombing, which destroyed German cities, including firebombing of Hamburg and Dresden.
1945	Defeat and unconditional surrender ended World War II, creating a massive influx of German refugees from eastern Europe into western German areas. All of Germany occupied by the victorious Allies, and eastern German regions handed over to Poland and the Soviet Union.
1945–1947	Regional states were re-created as the Allied victors redrew the map of Germany by creating new political entities such as Lower Saxony, North Rhine-Westphalia, Rhineland-Palatinate, Hesse, Mecklenburg, Saxony-Anhalt, though also confirming Bremen, Hamburg, Schleswig-Holstein,

	Bavaria, Thuringia, and Saxony. Berlin was placed under four-power Allied control and Saarland under French jurisdiction. The cities began to rebuild by removing rubble, while land reform in the east undercut the former elites.
1946	Local elections in the western zones of occupation resulted in Christian Democratic Union (CDU) majorities; in the eastern zone of occupation, a forced merger of SPD and KPD created the Socialist Unity Party (SED).
1947	Allies decreed the dissolution of the state of Prussia.
1948–1949	Land and water access routes to Berlin were blockaded by the Soviets, so the city was supplied with food and coal by British and U.S. "raisin" bombers.
1949	Federal Republic of Germany was created with the Basic Law as its temporary constitution. Federalism, based on a federation of regional states, was enshrined in the constitution in the West. The German Democratic Republic was created in the East with confirmation of five main states—Mecklenburg, Brandenburg, Saxony, Saxony-Anhalt, Thuringia—and East Berlin, though the economy was centralized.
	Konrad Adenauer headed the CDU coalition government with its "temporary" capital at Bonn.
1950s	Cities were rebuilt, much faster in the West than the East. In Bavaria, the Christian Social Union (CSU) began its long reign, while in North Rhine-Westphalia, a slow shift to SPD from CDU began. In all regional states except Bavaria, the CDU and the SPD competed for leadership in coalition governments mostly in combination with support from a shifting small party of liberals, the Free Democratic Party (FPD). The *Bundesrat*, or upper house, representing the regional states supported federalism and acted as a brake on the centralism of the Bonn government.
1952	GDR was restructured so that its regional states disappeared.
	Baden and Württemberg were combined into one regional state.
1957	Saarland rejoined the Federal Republic of Germany as the 11th federal state after a plebiscite. An agreement was reached between the regions and the central state about financial equalization between richer and economically weaker areas.
1960s	Youth counterculture and New Left politics challenged the established political elite with hippie styles,

	university disruptions, and anti-Vietnam protests. Later, terrorist cells and the feminist movement caused further reconsideration of societal values and the nature of democracy.
1961	Construction of the Berlin Wall finalized the separation of eastern and western German states and regions. The Frankfurt trials of Nazi perpetrators raised questions of public knowledge and complicity in the murder of Jews during war.
1968	East and West German states sent separate teams to the Olympic Games in Mexico.
1969	Willy Brandt headed a SPD coalition government and introduced an extensive social reform program. Externally, his *Ostpolitik* sought to normalize relations with eastern European states as well as the GDR.
1970s	But especially during 1980s and 1990s, acknowledgement of German responsibility for Holocaust and barbaric acts against Slavs, Soviet prisoners of war, and reprisals during German occupation of European states in World War II. An extensive public discussion of genocide and brutalities led to the building of monuments to acknowledge the victims as well as the need to remember a difficult past so as to prevent its repetition. Regional offices for political education introduced programs to inform the public and to disseminate knowledge about the Nazi past as well as to memorialize victims.
1971	Four Power Agreement on Berlin began to normalize relations between the two German states.
1972–1973	Basic Treaty between eastern and western Germany acknowledged the existence of two states and both became members of the United Nations.
1982	Helmut Kohl established a CDU coalition government.
1983	Greens were elected to the federal parliament having had representation in various states such as Hesse, where they joined the government in 1985.
1987	Uwe Barschel, CDU minister-president of Schleswig-Holstein, committed suicide after the exposure of his government's dirty tricks politics.
	More than 4 million foreigners lived in the Federal Republic, mostly in industrial cities.
1988	Franz Joseph Strauss, longtime CSU leader of Bavaria, died.

1989

Numerous demonstrations in the German Democratic Republic for liberty and against managed elections.

Berlin Wall was opened, leading to collapse of the GDR.

1990

East and West Germany unified under terms of the West German constitution, within its federal structure. In the east, the states of Mecklenburg–Western Pomerania, Brandenburg, Saxony, Saxony-Anhalt, and Thuringia were reestablished and East Berlin was joined to West Berlin.

1990s

During the first years after Reunification, antiforeigner violence arose in both east and west. Simultaneously, large transfers of monies and managers (Wessies) aimed to rebuild eastern Germany on a western model, which resulted in much resentment by former easterners (Ossies). Unemployment rates remained very high in the east (sometimes 30 percent), and economic development moved very slowly, mostly directed from the west.

1990s to present

Offices for political education in each new state sought to acknowledge the difficult past of the Nazi and the GDR eras but also to develop positive identities for the new regions. The long-existing offices in the western states continued this dual educational work: exposing and memorializing the past while pointing to a positive regional identity based on having rebuilt the country physically and spiritually since World War II.

Selected Bibliography

The materials available to learn about German regions keep increasing at a fast pace. The Internet has made mountains of haphazardly organized information accessible.

Among the best overviews that summarize the German states at present is Wehling, Hans-Georg, ed., *Die deutschen Länder. Geschichte, Politik, Wirtschaft* (Opladen: Leske + Budrich, 2002). This book and the individual studies on each state published by the offices for political education are among the most informative on present-day regional situations. For an older, but very informed geographic approach, see Dickinson, Robert E., *Germany: A General and Regional Geography* (London: Methuen, 1953).

The role of federalism is tersely presented in

Sturm, Roland, *Föderalismus in Deutschland* (Opladen: Leske, 2001). A solid analysis in English is Umbach, Maiken, ed., *German Federalism: Past, Present, Future* (Basingstoke: Palgrave, 2000), especially the introduction.

Each state has produced regional studies and they will be listed below.

Among the recent English overviews that give consideration to regional aspects are:

Lewis, Derek, *Contemporary Germany: Handbook* (London: Arnold, 2001). Contains a section on the *Länder* and emphasis on cultural differences.

Lord, Richard, *Contemporary Germany: Handbook* (Portland: Graphic Arts, 1996).

Phipps, Alison, ed., *Contemporary German Cultural Studies* (London: Arnold, 2002), notes regional elements in languages, food, media, and identities.

Turner, Barry, *Germany Profiled* (London: Macmillan, 2000). This is mainly a statistical guide but does summarize information on each state.

—————————— HISTORICAL SERIES ——————————

An old collection on the federal states is *Deutschland. Porträt einer Nation* (Gütersloh: Bertelsmann, 1986), 10 volumes. Though outdated with regard to political developments, the geological and geographic overviews are especially well presented with maps and pictures.

In the early 1990s, after the demise of the German Democratic Republic (GDR), the *Länder* were to some extent rediscovered. Travel became easier, but during 30 years of division the two Germanies had become different societies. People wanted to visit and to see the areas and the people that previously had been difficult to access. Many series of edited essays and larger studies sought to introduce the eastern areas to the Wessies, as the Germans from the older states were called. They also tried to explain the western states to the Ossies. One example is Hartmann, Jürgen, ed., *Handbuch der deutschen Bundesländer* (Frankfurt: 1997).

A pictorial series, with one volume for each state, is among the best portrayals of the landscape and heritage buildings. It is published by Bucher of Munich (1994ff), with the series entitled *Edition-Die Deutschen Länder*, some of which have appeared in English. They contain vignettes, maps, documents, overviews, and a list of major attractions in each town. Some include cuisine and folklore, but all present the countryside through spectacular photographs.

——— JOURNALS AND POPULAR MAGAZINES ———

German Life (since 1994)

This popular magazine has existed only for a decade, but it has succeeded in bringing short articles to a wide North American public. It covers the major cities, towns and villages, foods and drink, music festivals, and nearly every aspect of German society. The image is sometimes one of a country of endless half-timbered villages, castles, and parks. The magazine's advertisements reinforce the stereotypes of sausage, beer, and dirndls. But on the whole, the materials are delightfully varied and offer special insights on the extent to which traditional Germany survives in its many regions.

Deutschland (available in English, French, and German, published by the national government)

This colorful magazine presents primarily the positive economic and cultural aspects of contemporary Germany. However, its stories emphasize the newest developments and the writers are very knowledgeable. It has run special articles on each of the *Länder*, starting in 2003 with Baden-Württemberg and Bavaria. The other states follow alphabetically. The magazine can be accessed, including back issues, at www.magazine-deutschland.de.

—— GOVERNMENT INFORMATION OFFICES ——

An overview of Germany, *Facts about Germany*, is the Federal Republic's view of what is important to know about Germany. Also available in English on the Internet at http://www.tatsachen-ueber-deutschland.de/389.0.html, this little handbook emphasizes economics and society, but the beginning section of the annually updated volumes provides a concise account of the German federal states (population, makeup of government, history, main products, some of the culture). This offers a basic beginning; similar to what is in handbooks such as Buse, Dieter K., and Juergen C. Doerr, eds., *Modern Germany: An Encyclopedia of History, People and Culture* (New York: Garland, 1998), 2 volumes, which has an entry for each state. Regional differences have to be dug out of Sandford, John, *Encyclopedia of Contemporary German Culture* (New York: Routledge, 1999), and Pommerin, Reiner, *Culture in the Federal Republic of Germany, 1945–1995* (London: Berg, 1996), though both acknowledge federalism's impact on education and support for the arts.

Federalism is very strong in Germany. Each state has an important office for political education, though they coordinate some of their efforts through a national office. These offices are well represented on the Internet, either through the central office or through the office for each state. Some sites have translations or are partially in English. They are a gold mine for understanding regional identity and what in Germany is termed *Landeskunde*, or the knowledge about a place: its geography, demography, ethnography, and history. Most important, these offices have and continue to foster a particular version of civic self-understanding, including the history of their own region. They present comprehensive historical accounts, which include problems such as the experiences and roles of each region during the Hitler regime. Publicizing Holocaust sites and other places of repression or resistance are among the memory work they undertake. For those who read German, the *Landeskunde* volumes published by these offices provide among the best aids to understanding German regions, since regional experts have usually written them. It is instructive to compare their older publications with ones written after Reunification. The latter present a more thoroughly researched history acknowledging the problems of the past compared to the limited focus on constitutions and cultural contributions in the earlier popularizations that seem almost like weak propaganda.

That each state has such an office is perhaps an example of the homogenization within the German federal system despite the emphasis on regions. The official sites of each state, of their tourist offices, and of the offices for political education are:

—————— BADEN-WÜRTTEMBERG ——————

Official site: http://www.baden-wuerttemberg.de/
Tourist site: http://www.tourismus-baden-wuerttemberg.de/
Landeszentrale für politische Bildung: http://www.lpb.bwue.de/

BAVARIA

Official site: http://www.bayern.de/
Tourist site: http://www.bayern.by/
Landeszentrale für politische Bildung: http://www.stmuk.bayern.de/blz

BERLIN

Official site: http://www.berlin.de/
Tourist site: http://www.btm.de/
Landeszentrale für politische Bildung: http://www.landeszentrale-politische-bildung-berlin.de/

BRANDENBURG

Official site: http://www.brandenburg.de/
Tourist site: http://www.reiseland-brandenburg.de/
Landeszentrale für politische Bildung: http://www.politische-bildung-brandenburg.de/

BREMEN

Official site: http://www.bremen.de/
Tourist site: http://www.bremen-tourism.de/
Landeszentrale für politische Bildung: http://www.lzpb-bremen.de/

HAMBURG

Official site: http://www.hamburg.de/
Tourist site: http://www.hamburg-tourism.de/
Landeszentrale für politische Bildung: http://www.politische-bildung.hamburg.de/

HESSE

Official site: http://www.hessen.de/stk/
Tourist site: http://www.hessen-tourismus.de/
Landeszentrale für politische Bildung: http://www.hlz.hessen.de/

─────────────── LOWER SAXONY ───────────────

Official site: http://www.niedersachsen.de/
Tourist site: http://www.niedersachsen-tourism.de/
Landeszentrale für politische Bildung: http://www.nlpb.de/

─────────────── MECKLENBURG ───────────────

Official site: http://www.mecklenburg-vorpommern.de/ & http://www.mvnet.de/
Tourist site: http://www.auf-nach-mv.de/
Landeszentrale für politische Bildung: http://www.mv-regierung.de/lpb/

─────────── NORTH RHINE-WESTPHALIA ───────────

Official site: http://www.nrw.de/
Tourist site: http://www.nrw-tourismus.de/
Landeszentrale für politische Bildung: http://www.lzpb.nrw.de/

─────────── RHINELAND-PALATINATE ───────────

Official site: http://www.rlp.de/
Tourist site: http://www.rlp-info.de/
Landeszentrale für politische Bildung: http://www.politische-bildung-rlp.de/

─────────────── SAARLAND ───────────────

Official site: http://www.saarland.de/
Tourist site: http://www.tourismus.saarland.de/
Landeszentrale für politische Bildung: http://www.lpm.uni-sb.de/lpb/

─────────────── SAXONY ───────────────

Official site: http://www.sachsen.de/
Tourist site: http://www.sachsen-tour.de/
Landeszentrale für politische Bildung: http://www.slpb.de/

───────────── SAXONY-ANHALT ─────────────

Official site: http://www.sachsen-anhalt.de/
Tourist site: http://www.sachsen-anhalt-tourismus.de/
Landeszentrale für politische Bildung: http://www.lpb.sachsen-anhalt.de/

───────────── SCHLESWIG-HOLSTEIN ─────────────

Official site: http://www.schleswig-holstein.de/
Tourist site: http://www.sh-tourismus.de/
Landeszentrale für politische Bildung: http://www.politische-bildung.schleswig-holstein.de

───────────── THURINGIA ─────────────

Official site: http://www.thueringen.de/
Tourist site: http://www.thueringen-tourismus.de/
Landeszentrale für politische Bildung: http://www.thueringen.de/de/lzt/

RELATED SITES ───────── FOR THE WHOLE COUNTRY ─────────

http://www.politische-bildung.de/lpbs.htm (Portal on Politischen Bildung)
http://www.germany-tourism.de/

As mentioned, Wehling, Georg-Hans, ed., *Die deutschen Länder. Geschichte, Politik, Wirtschaft* (Opladen: Leske, 2000), is a summary volume presenting the 16 states. The references at the end of each chapter list some of the regional studies published by the individual states. The volume also addresses the issues being debated at present in regard to federalism.

The main studies by the offices for political education offering a combination of geography, history, economics, and special traits of the German states include the following:

───────────── BADEN-WÜRTTEMBERG ─────────────

Bausinger, Hermann, *Baden-Württemberg: eine politische Landeskunde* (Stuttgart: W. Kohlhammer, 1975).
Borcherdt, Christoph, *Geographische Landeskunde von Baden-Württemberg* (Stuttgart: W. Kohlhammer, 1983).

Wehling, Hans-Georg, ed., *Baden-Württemberg. Vielfalt und Stärke der Regionen* (Stuttgart: Landeszentrale für politische Bildung, 2002), celebrates 50 years of the combined state by an exemplary illustrated volume emphasizing the subregions.

BAVARIA

Roth, Raier A., *Freistaat Bayern. Politische Landeskunde* (Munich: Landeszentrale fuer politsche Bildungsarbeit, 2000).
Ruppert, Karl, *Bayern: eine Landeskunde aus sozialgeographischer Sicht* (Munich: Wissenschaftliche Buchgesellschaft, 1987).

BERLIN

Berlin: Eine kleine Landeskunde (Berlin: Landeszentrale für politische Bildung, 2002).
Biedenkopf, Kurt, et al., eds., *Berlin-Was ist uns die Hauptstadt wert?* (Opladen: Leske and Budrich, 2003).
Ribbe, Wolfgang, and Jürgen Schmädeke, *Kleine Berlin Geschichte* (Berlin: Stapp, 1994).

BRANDENBURG

Büchner, Christiane, and Jochen Franzke, *Das land Brandenburg. Kleine politische Landeskunde* (Potsdam: Landeszentrale für politische Bildung, 2002).

BREMEN

Gerstenberger, Heide, ed., *Bremer Freiheiten. Zur Geschichte und Gegenwart des Stadt-Staates Bremen* (Bremen: Temmen, 1987).

HAMBURG

Bilstein, H., ed., *Staat und Parteien im Stadtstaat Hamburg* (Hamburg: Landeszentrale für politische Bildung, 1997).

HESSE

Heidenreich, Bernd, and Konrad Schacht, eds., *Hessen. Eine politische Landeskunde* (Stuttgart: Kohlhammer, 1993).

LOWER SAXONY

Seedorf, Hans-H., and Hans-H. Meyer, *Landeskunde Niedersachsen* (Neumünster: Landeszentrale für politische Bildung, 1992, 1996), 2 volumes.

MECKLENBURG–WESTERN POMERANIA

Historischer und geographischer Atlas von Mecklenburg und Pommern (Schwerin: Landeszentrale für politische Bildung, 1995, 1996), 2 volumes.
Schwabe, Klaus, *Mecklenburgische und vorpommerische Identität* (Schwerin: Landeszentrale für politische Bildung, 1996).

NORTH RHINE-WESTPHALIA

Alemann, Ulrich von, and Patrick Brandenburg, eds., *Nordrhein-Westfalen. Ein Land entdeckt sich neu* (Cologne: Kohlhammer, 2000).
Fehling, Walter, ed., *Nordrhein-Westfalen* (Köln: Kohlhammer, 1984).
NRW Lexikon. Politik, Gesellschaft, Wirtschaft, Recht, Kultur (Opladen: Leske + Budrich, 2000).
Rohe, Karl, ed., *Nordrhein-Westfalen. Eine politische Landeskunde* (Düsseldorf: Landeszentrale für politische Bildung, 1985).

RHINELAND-PALATINATE

Rheinland-Pfalz-Unser Land. Eine kleine politische Landeskunde (Mainz: Landeszentrale für politische Bildung, 1999).

SAARLAND

Das Saarland. Politische, wirtschaftliche und kulturelle Entwicklung (Saarbrücken: Landeszentrale für politische Bildung, 1991).

SAXONY

Gerlach, Siegfried, ed., *Sachsen. Eine politische Landeskunde* (Stuttgart: Landeszentrale für politische Bildung, 1993).

—————————— SAXONY-ANHALT ——————————

Holtmann, Everhard, and Bernhard Boll, *Sachsen-Anhalt. Eine politische Landeskunde* (Magdeburg: Landeszentrale für politische Bildung, 1997).

—————————— SCHLESWIG-HOLSTEIN ——————————

Wenzel, Rüdiger, ed., *Schleswig-Holstein. Eine politische Landeskunde* (Kiel: Landeszentrale für politische Bildung, 1992).

—————————— THURINGIA ——————————

Rassloff, Steffan, *Thüringen. Blätter zur Landeskunde* (Jena: Landeszentrale für politische Bildung, 2003). This can be accessed at www.thueringen.de/lzt/

A small selection of more academic regional studies in English (if historical and geographic, ethnographic, and linguistic studies were included, this could be expanded almost endlessly, especially for the late-nineteenth and twentieth centuries, due to the numerous studies focusing on the regional aspects of Imperial Germany and the regional origins and impact of Nazism):

James, Peter, *The Politics of Bavaria—An Exception to the Rule: The Special Position of the Free State of Bavaria in the New Germany* (Avebury: Aldershot, 1995).
Jorg, Mathias, *Regional Interests in Europe: Wales and Saxony as Modern Regions* (London: Frank Cass, 2004).
Ladd, Brian, *The Ghosts of Berlin* (Chicago: University of Chicago Press, 1997), which is especially strong on memorial sites.
Padgett, Stephen, William Paterson, and Gordon Smith, eds., *Developments in German Politics 3* (Durham, NC: Duke University Press, 2003).
Read, Anthony, and David Fisher, *Berlin: The Biography of a City* (London: Hutchinson, 1994).
Regional Policies in Germany (Washington: Organisation for Economic Co-operation and Development, 1989).

—————————— TRAVEL GUIDES ——————————

Just as children's books are an easy way to enter foreign cultures, travel guides provide an easy start to knowing what is available about foreign lands. Germany is well served by very informative and detailed (sometimes too detailed) travel guides. Unlike foreign guides (such as Fodor) that try to squeeze a whole country into one huge volume, the German ones frequently appear as a series. They often provide the highlights regarding the attractions of each region. However, some also give much historical and geographic information coupled with appropriate illustrations. For instance: the *DuMont Kunst-Reiseführer* presents Germany's regions, sometimes by political criteria (Schleswig-Holstein, Hessen), by cities (Munich, Cologne), and frequently by geographic or historical units (Eifel, Rhine, Ruhr). However, only a few of these are available in English.

The ones on the new states re-created after 1990 are especially to be recommended, for example, Würlitzer, Bernd, *Mecklenburg-Vorpommern* (Cologne: DuMont, 1993), and Müller, Hans, *Thüringen* (Cologne: DuMont, 1996), though the latter too readily blames the GDR for all problems without looking further into the region's mixed history.

Similarly available only in German are the superb *Merian* guides, published approximately 10 times per year as a picture series with informed commentary. They usually include large pullout maps and pictures showing local attractions. The contents emphasize diversity but rarely equate the present states with regions.

In English: *Germany: A Phaidon Cultural Guide* (Engelwood Cliffs: Prentice-Hall, 1985). This can be recommended for its breadth of coverage and its illustrations, while the Michelin guide *Germany* is highly reliable as a slim one-volume concise presentation.

Quest-Ritson, Charles, *The Garden Lover's Guide to Germany* (New York: Princeton Architectural Press, 1998), is well informed with limited text and good pictures but biased (pro-Britain with Cold War-era feel).

Archaeological research is very strong and receives support from each state as part of the regional heritage efforts. An excellent exhibit has had its extensive catalogue turned into a demonstration of artistic photography while showing regional patterns: *Menschen. Zeiten. Räume. Archäologie in Deutschland* (Stuttgart: Thiess, 2002). A similar work for one important aspect of the arts is Kaiser, Wolfgang, "Romanesque Architecture in Germany" in *Romanesque*, ed., Rolf Toman (Cologne: Könemann, 1997): 32–73, in which the spatial extent of this style in Germany is underlined.

Index

ABOUT THE AUTHOR

Dieter K. Buse is Professor of History at Laurentian University, Sudbury, Ontario, Canada, and the author (with Juergen C. Doerr) of *Modern Germany: An Encyclopedia of History, People and Culture, 1871–1990* (1998), among other works.